SOLOVYOVO

SOLOVYOVO

The Story of Memory in a Russian Village

Margaret Paxson

WOODROW WILSON CENTER PRESS
WASHINGTON, D.C.

INDIANA UNIVERSITY PRESS
BLOOMINGTON & INDIANAPOLIS

EDITORIAL OFFICES
Woodrow Wilson Center Press
One Woodrow Wilson Plaza
1300 Pennsylvania Avenue, N.W.
Washington, D.C. 20004-3027
Telephone 202-691-4029
www.wilsoncenter.org

ORDER FROM
Indiana University Press
601 North Morton Street
Bloomington, Indiana 47404-3797
Telephone 800-842-6796
Fax 812-855-7931
iuporder@indiana.edu
http://iupress.indiana.edu

Printed in the United States
of America on acid-free paper
2 4 6 8 9 7 5 3 1

Library of Congress Cataloging-in-Publication Data

Paxson, Margaret.
    Solovyovo : the story of memory in a Russian village / Margaret Paxson.
        p.   cm.
    Solovyovo is the fictitious name of a small village in the Belozerskii Raion
of Vologodskaia oblast' used to protect the name of the real villagers.
    ISBN 0-253-34654-1 (IUP : cloth : alk. paper) — ISBN 0-253-21801-2
(IUP : pbk. : alk. paper)
    1. Ethnography—Russia (Federation)—Belozerskii Raion (Vologodskaia
oblast')   2. Belozerskii Raion (Vologodskaia oblast', Russia)—Social life and
customs.   3. Memory—Social aspects—Russia (Federation)—Belozerskii
Raion (Vologodskaia oblast')   4. Belozerskii Raion (Vologodskaia oblast',
Russia)—Rural conditions.   5. Paxson, Margaret.   I. Title.
DK511.B3853P39   2005
947'.19—dc22
                                                                2005008551

Woodrow Wilson International Center for Scholars

The Woodrow Wilson International Center for Scholars, established by Congress in 1968 and headquartered in Washington, D.C., is a living national memorial to President Wilson. The Center's mission is to commemorate the ideals and concerns of Woodrow Wilson by providing a link between the worlds of ideas and policy, while fostering research, study, discussion and collaboration among a broad spectrum of individuals concerned with policy and scholarship in national and international affairs. Supported by public and private funds, the Center is a nonpartisan institution engaged in the study of national and world affairs. It establishes and maintains a neutral forum for free, open, and informed dialogue. Conclusions or opinions expressed in Center publications and programs are those of the authors and speakers and do not necessarily reflect the views of the Center staff, fellows, trustees, advisory groups, or any individuals or organizations that provide financial support to the Center.

The Center is the publisher of *The Wilson Quarterly* and home of Woodrow Wilson Center Press, *dialogue* radio and television, and the monthly newsletter "Centerpoint." For more information about the Center's activities and publications, please visit us on the Web at www.wilsoncenter.org.

Notes on Transcription and Proper Names

In this book, I use the Library of Congress style for transcription, with a few exceptions for mostly proper names that have entered the common lexicon with a different spelling (e.g., Chechnya, rather than Chechnia, and Yeltsin, not El'tsin). For the sake of readers unaccustomed to Russian pronunciations, I have used the nonstandard transcription Solovyovo for Solov'evo.

Except for the names of important cities and geographical features, place names and names of villages and villagers have been changed. In rare cases, people have been split in two (i.e., they are referred to by two separate names) in order to further protect their identities.

Алексею и Людмиле
с благодарностью
за всю их красоту и доброту,
за их исцеляющие руки и сердца.

Contents

Introduction
IULIIA'S HANDS[1]

* * *

The story of memory in Solovyovo starts with a pair of hands—hands that have grown numb over time, wooden. She has to strike those hands against a chair or a leg or another hand just to beat some feeling into them.

Iuliia[2] has been beating her hands this way in the eight years that I have known her. Her small hands with their smooth, thick fingers have been her livelihood, wielding scythes and shovels and plows and rakes, pulling roots and carrying pails of water, and rinsing clothes in the icy waters of Lake Tikhonskoe. But last year, something changed. "It's no use," Iuliia told me last summer. "I can't milk the cow anymore. We'll slaughter Lushka once there is a solid frost."

Iuliia has been living in the tiny village of Solovyovo, about 300 miles north of Moscow, for over forty years. Born in another northern village in 1939, abandoned to an orphanage by age six, and working in the industrial city of Cherepovets by her late teens, Iuliia had a chance to leave rural life behind. In the Soviet Union, village life was not only very hard and poorly paid but—for all the backbreaking work villagers did so that their countrymen could eat—also demeaned and derided by city dwellers.

In 1955, Nikita Khrushchev, in a quixotic flourish, ordered that corn be planted all over the Soviet Union as a part of his new, post-Stalin, post-

---

1. A first version of this introduction was published in the *Wilson Quarterly,* in spring 2002.
2. All names of villagers and all local place names have been changed to help ensure the privacy of those who shared their lives and stories with me.

famine agricultural policy. Young Iuliia joined a work brigade from her factory, and found herself on the shores of a lake on the edge of a pine-and-birch forest, where she caught the eye of a gentle man who quickly fell in love with her soft beauty. Her girlfriends in the factory thought she was crazy to accept a marriage proposal that would take her back to the countryside. But she did. Telling anyone who asked that she wasn't afraid of hard work, she moved into a one-room cabin with her new husband's parents and brothers and sisters. The village was beautiful then, as it is today— hills rolling down to the shores of a lake, nearby fields full of spring and summer wildflowers, horses roaming freely in the swampy lands beyond.

Now, 40 years after making her choice, this is the life that fills the hours of her days. There is planting and haying and harvesting to be done, animals to be tended, and a cow to be milked three times each day. Meals must be cooked, the house cleaned, and firewood cut and hauled. There is no running water. There are almost no machines to help with the farm work. For most of Iuliia's life, the work for the collective farm had to be done first; the work that kept the family alive was done at dusk or pushed to the end of summer. Always there was the race to finish before the autumn rains rotted the potatoes or spoiled the hay. This is the life that numbed her hands, twisted her back forever, and brought her groaning to her bed at the end of a long day. It was hard and sometimes brutal. There was war and famine and family violence. But most of all, there was work. In 40 years, Iuliia and her husband took only one vacation together, to distant Leningrad for 10 days. That was it. How could they leave their farm? How could they leave their cow that had to be milked three times a day?

Farm life centers on the cow. It gives milk, and the milk is turned into cheese, butter, and sour cream. Every spring it gives birth to a calf, which can be slaughtered in turn a half-year later to provide meat for the long winter. In the symbolic lexicon of the village, a cow means wealth. (Indeed, after the Bolshevik Revolution in 1917, two cows were enough for a villager to be considered rich, and therefore suspect.) Most heavy farm labor is done to keep the cow fed, and giving milk and reproducing. For the cow the hay is harvested. All that time spent stooped over the soil in the summer sun, brushing away the swarms of flies and avoiding the bees, all the sweat of the day, is for the cow, as well as the many mornings and evenings looking up at the clouds for signs of rain. The discussions Iuliia has with her husband, the worries about a single teat that is having trouble, or about why the cow won't drink water or eat enough, or the risks of her being spoiled by the evil eye, or the nights of pacing before her calving—all for the cow. Lushka. Lushenka. So that day, in the summer of 2001, when Iuliia looked at her hands numb as wood and finally said that the cow would have to go—that was a big day.

In 1991, the Soviet Union collapsed, and Russia began its transition from socialism to protocapitalism. In the cities, old women stood in rows at the metro, selling anything from cigarettes and underpants to plastic bags and family heirlooms. Gangsters acquired money, roaming the cities in fancy cars and Armani suits, and indulging their taste for kitsch. New images and voices appeared in the media, luxurious new buildings sprang up in Moscow, and homelessness emerged as a social problem. A new instability shook what was once a complacent Soviet version of the middle class.

But what of the countryside?

In the Soviet village, socialism was embodied in the institution of the collective farm, or *kolkhoz*. In spite of petitions and protests, Solovyovo had its turn at collectivization in 1933, and villagers there spent the next sixty years working primarily for the state rather than for their extended families. In the period during and after World War II, stealing a turnip was enough to send a person to prison. Solovyovo's land (like most of the land of the Russian north) was best suited to dairy production. There were milking quotas to meet, and five-year plans to fulfill. And so the kolkhoz workers spent their days laboring together in brigades, doing all the heavy work required to keep a few hundred cows alive.

In 1992, just as Moscow was beginning its wild ride toward capitalism, Solovyovo's collective farm had a decision to make: What to do with its eighty-five head of cattle, now that subsidies from the state could no longer be counted on? The answer: Slaughter them. Sell the meat. Leave that enterprise behind, and concentrate on selling off the wood of the rich forests of the region. The result: In Solovyovo, as in countless small villages throughout the vast Russian countryside, the primary economy is now based on subsistence farming. The collective farm has not yet been privatized, although the villagers are beginning to use some of its land. Farmers in Solovyovo are still making do with the potato plots assigned to their families in earlier decades and with the tangled gardens around their homes. They hunt in the forest and fish in the nearby lake. They keep bees for honey.

For Russia as a whole, this subsistence life of the village has had several consequences. First in importance, villagers are relatively safe from the economic upheavals shaking Russia because they live mostly outside the money economy. One way or another, they produce most of what they need to survive. Conditions in rural Russia, home to about 27 percent of the population, are certainly harsh. Roads, telephones, telegraph, the postal system, and medical care have all deteriorated since the end of the Soviet Union. Salaries and pensions are miniscule, ranging from $20 to $50 a month. Still, this is money over and above a villager's basic needs for food and shelter. In cities, the same income barely manages to buy anything more than bread, kasha (grain), and tea for a month. Villagers remain insulated from the mixed blessings of a capricious money economy. When the skies do basically what they should, and health and strength remain, villagers need very little else.

Village life provides an independence that is bad news for political economists who see market expansion as the sine qua non of democracy and civil society. It gives a dismaying answer to those who ask, "Who is feeding Russia?" But as villagers make do with what their hands produce, as they feed their children and their aunts and uncles and cousins in distant cities (who fill up their villages in the summer and share in the work), they are providing a social safety net, perhaps the only one with any real meaning in post-Soviet Russia.

Dependence on the hands, then, is a form of independence. Until the hands fail.

The first time I saw Iuliia, it was a sunny day in the summer of 1994. The moment was very still and, for me, utterly captivating. She was returning from the fields with a small group of farmers, all in white kerchiefs and caps, and all carrying rough-hewn scythes and rakes. Iuliia is darker than some, quieter than most. She likes to sing Soviet hymns and old Russian folk songs; she can dance a rather complicated jig. She has a soft laugh. As fate would have it, I lived with her and her husband for a year and a half in their one-room house while doing research on social memory in rural Russia, the subject of this book. They told me matter of factly one day not long after we met that they would be taking me in "as a daughter." *Kak dochka.*

What I saw in Solovyovo was a world of great symbolic and ideological complexity. While growing up as modern Soviets, learning to believe in the "radiant future" of communism, and weeping desperately when their "father" Stalin died, the villagers maintained their own sense of how the world works, how problems are solved, how power worldly and otherworldly can be invoked. So although they grew up celebrating the Christian holiday of Troitsa (Pentecost) as a secularized "Day of the Birch Tree" in their local clubhouse, every year they would steal away, family by family, to the graveyard, bringing offerings to their ancestors, talking with them, invoking their aid in the harvest, becoming steadily more drunk and effervescent, and connected with one another and with the dead.

Year in and year out, even when it was dangerous because of the eyes of informers, they would seek out local sorcerers and healers, and women who could find animals lost deep in the woods because they knew how to talk to the "host of the forest," known simply as "grandfather." And always they feared the evil eye, effusive praise, or anything that pointed to personal wealth or distinction. They protected their animals and the newborn from the glances of strangers, covering their baskets of berries or mushrooms, hiding signs of wealth, never looking the stranger too long in the eye.

In this world that is very much its own, I have seen how farmers grapple individually and collectively with where they—as families, as villagers, as Russians—are going next. In Iuliia's family, a son recently moved from his village to the ancient, once-bustling port city of Belozersk with his wife and two children. The farm work was too hard, and the rewards were too few. Now he finds himself in a small urban apartment with no running water or central heating, hoping that he'll find work, but if he doesn't, that his wife's salary as a teacher will sustain them for a while. Iuliia's daughter lives with her husband and three children in a village twenty-five miles away and struggles endlessly with a full-time job at the local library, housework, the cow and calf and chickens she keeps, and a chronically sick son. For her family, there is never enough money and barely enough resources. Rural life is unforgiving in its demands. Leaving it can bring relief, but it can also bring uncertainty, as the social safety net that it provides becomes weaker or vanishes.

All over the world, there are societies that find themselves in similar periods of transition. All over the world, people carry with them a deeply cultural sense of who they are. And everywhere they ask themselves, "What next?" Since the fall of the Soviet Union, there have been two important ways of treating this very large question. The first way assumes that the "invisible hand" of the market will reach down and quickly turn Russia into something familiar to Westerners. As markets develop and grow, as competition expands, as corporate practices become transparent and "rational," Russia will become democratic. The rule of law will rein in the excesses of renegade moneymakers and politicians. Civil society will flourish. Russia will differ from America only in its preference for borsch and caviar over hot dogs and French fries, and a little ballet, a little Cossack dancing, and a couple of onion domes. Russia will become a rational capitalist society with a slight regional accent.

The second typical way of thinking about the Russian future has been to fall back on what anthropologists scorn as an "essentialist" concept of culture. The idea of culture has a long and controversial history among scholars, and one reason is that wielding the term carelessly can cause one to view the "other" as utterly different, that is, a separate, impenetrable gestalt. The Russian "other" has been seen, for example, as slavishly loyal to despots, as a collectivist with no ability to act individually, and as incapable of enterprise. Russian villagers carry the extra burden of how their own country's elite has seen them: conservative, irrational, mulish, and brutish (and, at the same time, the repository of the national "soul"). Russia through this lens, and especially the Russian countryside, is eternally separate and different.

This view would hold that where Russia is going is nowhere. Ever. This, of course, cannot be true, just as it cannot be true that there is a monolithic capitalist society out there that Russia is destined to merge with. It is true that Russia is changing. Even the Russian countryside—as rich and, in certain ways, as independent as its cultural traditions are—is changing. But how?

One day I asked Mikhail Alekseevich, Iuliia's husband, how he knew when it was time to plant the potatoes. "Go out onto the fields barefoot," he said. "When you feel the warmth start to rise from the earth, it is time to plow and to plant." From earth to foot, from eye to sky, this decision is made some time in the month of May. June, July, and August pass in fields and gardens, plowing and planting and weeding, and hauling hay and water, water and hay. The growing season is only about four months in Solovyovo; then the cold winds come and soon enough there is a frost and the leaves turn brown and there is darkness and rain. Once winter arrives, people settle into quiet rhythms; animals are penned up and closed in. As the winter stretches on, the vegetables gathered and preserved in the fall run out jar by jar; some of the meat slaughtered in the fall begins to rot; rats can be heard gnawing on the carrots in the cellar at night.

The growing season in Russia ranges from two months in northern Siberia to six in the south. Throughout Russian history, that time has had to provide enough not only to feed the village family but also to support the feudal landlord and the hungry empire. Although the Russian imperial court was as lavish as Versailles, the north of Russia is certainly not the center of France; because of differences in soil and climate, the force required to extract a Versailles from the Russian population was exponentially greater. The tsars who ruled Russia from the sixteenth to the twentieth centuries had little compunction about exploiting the serfs to increase their own wealth. In 1581, during the reign of Ivan IV (known as "The Terrible" and the first to assume the title of "tsar"), the serfs became indentured and were officially "tied to the land," having no freedom to move without the permission of their lord. Escaping serfs were retrieved as runaway slaves would be. Taxes, which were paid collectively through village communes, were exorbitant. Battery and sexual license were common. Neither the emancipation of the serfs in 1861, nor the series of reforms during the first part of the twentieth century, did much to ease the burdens of the peasant class. Although one of its stated intentions was to bring justice to the countryside, the Revolution of 1917 brought only more suffering and terror.

The months are short to grow potatoes, to grow grain, to grow hay for fodder, to feed the family in the village, to feed the animals, to feed those who have moved away . . . to feed the country itself. In the seven years that I have observed the Russian countryside, I have seen the steady (but not final) disintegration of the kolkhoz. I have watched villagers inch their way onto kolkhoz lands for their own haying, which a new law gives them the right to do. I have seen people retire. I have watched a post office close, a *medpunkt* (a tiny, seldom-used medical station) close, a local store close. I have seen people leave for the cities, with no intention of returning; I have seen others move into the village for good. There have been deaths from illness and suicide and violence. I have been to the graveyard for ancestor rites; I have watched scores of people visit a local sorcerer in search of healing for the sick or the lifting of curses from the accursed. I have heard tales of strange and wondrous beings that live in the forests where the mushrooms and berries grow. I have heard, in the winter, a quiet so quiet that one can hear the footsteps of a cat walking on the snow.

But mostly, I have seen mornings when a man and a woman sit at a table and look out at the sky and decide what needs to be done that day. I have seen them working. I have sat around a table with them as they ate and drank tea and rested from the labors of the day.

And now what do I see? A pair of hands, a worried look, a decision being made. When the cow is slaughtered (when Lushka is slaughtered), there will be no more milk, and no more butter or sour cream or cheese.

After the first frost of the year, there will be no more calves for the slaughter. And so there will be no more meat. No cutting hay in the summer. No bees and biting black flies, no more sweating and burning under the sun. No looking to the sky for rain nearly every hour of every day.

The village of Solovyovo, the home of the hands with no more feeling left in them, will have, this winter, one more family who looks at the sky in a new and different way. This family will no longer be a family of farmers. It will be a family of pensioners. Dependent. Changed.

Iuliia wrote me not long ago. "New Year's we will be home," she said. "Sasha and Zina will come. Lena's daughter Olia is growing up. . . . Now we have no more animals, only our cats Kissa and Kotia. Our little cow Lushka is already gone. . . . There it is, some news."

—*Spring 2002*

* * *

Karl Marx, whose life and works have had no small effect on Russia and its villages and all the hands that dwell therein, wrote tellingly in *The 18th Brumaire of Louis Bonaparte* (1869) of how the past imprints itself onto the present. "The tradition of all of the dead generations," he wrote, "weighs like a nightmare on the brain of the living." The past is a weight, and more than that, it is a haunted, ghostly weight. He goes on: "[J]ust when [people] seem engaged in revolutionizing themselves and things, in creating something that has never yet existed, . . . they conjure up the spirits of the past to their service and borrow from them names, battle cries and costumes in order to present the new scene to world history."

In a nineteenth-century world that reproduced brutal Napoleons, that recreated feudal injustices, and heaped new injustices in crowded industrial landscapes, Marx's longing—that there could be an unfettered future, free of history's haunting chains—made resonating sense. Why should the future not be free of the past? Why could it not?

As it happened, the social revolutions of the nineteenth and twentieth centuries counted on the fact that history's burden could, *in principle*, be lightened. The past could be forgotten, and once forgotten, it would cease to be reproduced. A new history could be written on the blank slate of humanity. What would it look like, this newly inscribed past, now cast hopefully in the future? Which utopia, which Edenic Island, borne of which dreamer's mind, would be the shape of tomorrow?

But the question is, can history's load be lightened? Can it be purified to timelessness? And if it can, what form does it take? One hundred years after Marx, Milan Kundera wrote of the tangled drama of twentieth-century Czechoslovakian socialism, that is, its formal erasure of history and formal forging of something new. In his Prague of 1968, there are crowds with fists raised in unison; there is the dull, sickly sweet caricature of state propaganda; there are photographs where denounced faces are erased, gone, light as air. Kundera (1984:5) asks about the "burden" of that historical, eternal return set against the great social experiment that he saw before him: "[I]s heaviness truly deplorable and lightness splendid?" Or is there something in lightness, in the ease of erasure, which is unbearable?

This is a book about memory. It is about a single small place, and the ways that place conjures its past into its present, and then casts its present into the future. It is about a Soviet place, a place where history was treated as a burden that had to be lifted. It is about the *difficulty* of cultural, social, and even economic erasure. And it is about the ghosts of ancestors, who come not only to haunt, but also to heal.

Anthropology chooses, as its methodological bias, to take long, hard looks at single places. Like any bias, this brings certain features into focus, even as it blurs and distorts others. The strength of the anthropological method lies, of course, in the patience with which it allows the chaotic whirl that is culture to settle into some semblance of deeper order. At its best, anthropology watches and listens carefully—allowing human agents to be complex and multidimensional. Then and only then does it map the mechanisms of social orders. In *Charred Lullabies* (1996:14), Daniel writes that his "purpose is not merely to show the manner in which a reality . . . is culturally and historically constituted, but how deeply so." My aim in this book resonates closely with his. I wish to speak of continuities in time—of social memory, as it were—not in the language of inevitable essences, nor in the language of neutrally negotiated, randomly constructed (and easily erased) realities. I wish to speak in terms of use, and action, and habit—and the weathered, eroded, cognitive and symbolic landscapes they forge. Because of the nature of my argument—which claims that memory is cumulative and layered, and, yes, weighty—this book will be full of evidence and voices, full of the *stuff* of social memory. There was no other way to write it: From earth, to foot, from hand and eye, to sky, and story, and song, and lament. From Iuliia's hands, to her voice, to her walk from then, to then.

I

Memory's Topography

I

Bezhala ia lesom dremuchim,
Bezhala ia roshchei gustoi.
Vzglianula na nebo, vzdokhnula;
I vspomnila dom svoi rodnoi.

I ran through the dense forest,
I ran through the thick grove.
Looked up at the sky, sighed,
And remembered my native home.

—RUSSIAN FOLKSONG,
SUNG BY ANNA PETROVNA, SOLOVYOVO

MEMORIES AS SOCIAL ACTS

* * *

Certainly, memories appear to be *things* sometimes—we can gather them up, we can put them in our heads and keep them there, or we can lose them. Reified memories have been used in various ways by various disciplines. Historians, for example, have looked to them for the stuff of historical reconstruction. As Fentress and Wickham (1992:1–8) vividly describe in *Social Memory*, historians have typically treated memory as the more-or-less valuable material that can be plucked out of people's heads, much as a piece of paper can be plucked from one's pocket. Oral history (or the history of people far from us and far from power who have not written their memories down) has until recently involved plucking the memories out of the heads of people who make a habit of making history look like myth (Cohn 1987; Vansina 1985). This should make the task of reconstruction inconvenient, but not theoretically impossible. Here, memories can be clearer or cloudier, more accurate or more obfuscated, but they are always held up to an objective standard with the goal of reconstructing historical truth.

If memories are things, we can gather them up and pour them out at will. We can recount these memories to other people, and thereby build up the society's storehouse of memories, and even claim memories as our own that we have never experienced. Memories-as-things are like this.

But what is the real epistemological status of memories that, if we are honest, never come free of cognitive, affective, symbolic, ideological, and cultural contexts? What do ten stories of the death of Stalin hold in them besides the fact of his passing on a day in 1953? What do ten stories of tears shed on that day—sitting on a rowboat or in a tiny rural classroom—have to offer, besides being individual snapshots of one day of remembrance?

Certainly, memories are more than two-dimensional *things*. They are more than the information that they convey. Within the realm of meaning that is the term "memory," distinct types have been classified, each representing a type of knowing, and each with its own insights into the human condition. According to various taxonomies, memory can be *personal* (or "autobiographical"), *cognitive* (or "semantic," "prepositional"), *historical*, or *habitual* (Connerton 1989:22; Fentress and Wickam 1992:3, 20; Olick and Robbins 1998:110). Memories can be images or stories recalled. They can be ways of knowing, or acts embodied. Recollection, as a human practice, is as vast as its functions are varied.

So, while the substance of memory can rightfully be treated as crucial (if mediated) *material* for historical reconstruction, memory per se has come to be understood more broadly by the social sciences as a *social act* as well as an individual one (Connerton 1989:13). Even as it gains particular meaning in a global context of postcolonialism and neonationalism, this insight is certainly far from new. Marx, after all, wrote of the ghosts of the ancestors and their weight on the minds of the living within the broader problem of social reproduction (Olick and Robbins 1998:107). More formally, in 1925, Halbwachs, a student of Emile Durkheim and his powerful concept of *le social*, published *Les cadres sociaux de la mémoire*, an in-depth study of the way in which memory is carried at the level of the group. Calling it "collective memory," Halbwachs (1925:109) treated the problem of group recollection as "a matter of how minds work together in society, how their operations are not simply mediated but are structured by social relations." Memories are not, he said, recalled in some "nook" of the brain (Halbwachs 1992:38), but "externally" among groups.

Over time, the characteristics of memory transmission, preservation, and function have come to be seen as part of the dimension of broader social phenomena: it is now understood that *we recollect when and where we perform other social acts*—in ritual, narrative, language, religious practice, and the details of social and economic organization. In such settings, the *stuff* of social memory is radically different from the content on the invisible pieces of paper in nooks in the brain. This sort of memory is performed and embodied (Connerton 1989). It takes place in the present: in its practice, it informs us of the social, political, ideological, and symbolic landscapes of today. The villagers of Solovyovo remember in a vast array of social acts. They tell stories. They use well-worn metaphoric figures. They turn to worldly and otherworldly powers in ways that are familiar to them. They travel through commemorative cycles. When Stalin dies, the story is told there ten times, a hundred times: the images, symbols, temporalities, ideologies, and emotions of that story are given life in a shared setting.

But why, in the broad and varied sense, should Solovyovo remember anything of its past, so much of it painful? (Could Stalin not, to our great human solace, be erased from the memory, rendering it light as air?) Why, indeed, remember at all?

CONTINUITY AND CHANGE

* * *

Anthropology labors, more poignantly than most of the social sciences, with the intersection of space and time. Having retreated from the grand, historical teleologies of the nineteenth century that had all civilizations marching in stages toward a complex, rational perfection,[1] the (moral) revolution of cultural relativity instigated by Franz Boas in the early twentieth century brought with it a detailed dedication to specific places: the Kwakiutl of northwestern British Columbia, the Nuer of southern Sudan, and the Trobrianders of Papua New Guinea. Fruitful as it was (and remains) to look exhaustively at single places for how a system makes sense

---

1. In the social sciences, Henry Spencer, Edward Tylor, and Louis Henry Morgan were important contributors to the idea that cultures (or societies) evolve, and can therefore be studied as part of a universal framework.

to itself, the concept of culture inherited a mother lode of epistemological baggage.[2] Cultures were seen as small, separate universes, where all parts represented the whole, and where all institutions conspired to maintain social stability. Being "monadic wholes"—indivisible, impenetrable, and interconnected—they existed outside of history and change.[3] They were "culture gardens"—frozen in timelessness (Fabian 1983).

And yet, things do change. No one knows better than anthropological fieldworkers in remote villages, distant highlands, or ancient cities— that relationships among families, groups, territories, states, the media, technology, and trade are always changing. Culture, such as it is, is a moving target. This is not a function of modernity (although modernity has been responsible for some near-universal phenomena, such as nationalism and globalization). It is a function of living in time as well as in space, a fact that culture garden theories—where the bulk of emphasis is placed on stability, rational function, and continuity—cannot account for. So although the nineteenth-century idea that things change in a particular, universal way never fully recovered its power in anthropology from the days before Boas, we have struggled to understand movement, conflict, struggle, and change. And we have struggled to shed the assumption that things need to make a particular, unified sense for them to be meaningful. Modern Russia could never be mistaken for a timeless culture garden; now, at the beginning of the twenty-first century, it rings with transformation (and the "rough beasts" of new social institutions).

And yet, it would be irresponsible to regard Russia—one more time— as a blank, history-less slate, swept free for the purposes of postmodern globalization. Social memory as a study provides a way of theorizing continuities in time without forcing cultures to be timeless (interconnected, impenetrable) wholes. It is able to do this because—as a general rule—it focuses on the *acts* of memory in the present, rather than the essence of cultures outside of time. As societies transition (as they are always in transition), there needs to be a language with which we analyze how some cultural forms persist and how others fall to the historical wayside. There are continuities in time—what are they made of?[4]

---

2. A good deal of which had derived from nineteenth-century Germany, where philosophies of the folk were part of nationalism. See Leavitt (1991) for an overview of the origins of the culture concept.

3. As elaborated in Leibnitz's theory of the monad. See Leavitt (1991).

4. The morality of the persistence of cultural forms is a separate question entirely, and

The field of social memory studies was born with the work of Maurice Halbwachs, who recognized keenly (and from the very beginning) that the recalled past was of use to the political exigencies of the present. With some notable exceptions, the field was largely ignored for decades until the 1980s, when interest returned in full force along with the advent of multiculturalism, the fall of communism, and "a politics of victimization and regret" (Olick and Robbins 1998:107). By then, nationalism—where the past is "used" for the sake of the present—had become an object of rigorous investigation for social scientists, along with the analysis of class and hegemony, the "politics of memory," and the "instrumentalization" of the past (Olick and Robbins 1998:107).[5] Social memory has recently been the subject of numerous studies by historians, sociologists, anthropologists, philosophers, and political scientists—each with their own disciplinary agendas. Theoretical consensus with regard to definitions, methods, and objects of study has not, however, been reached.

It has, nevertheless, become clear that memory studies cluster around the problem of continuity (or social persistence) and change. Why *remember?* Do collective memories act as the instruments of social cohesion and stability, as Durkheim would have argued? Or do they help to instigate change from "above" as, for example, the observers of nationalism would claim? Or are they meant to legitimate the identities of the disenfranchised, and bring about change from "below"? In fact, collective memories accomplish all of the above. In 1998, Olick and Robbins wrote a first broad overview of the field of social memory studies in which they provided an extremely useful rubric for categorizing the place of social memory. First, they asked whether social memory was, in a given case, part of societal *persistence* or societal *change?* Second, they posited that in contexts of both persistence and change, social memory can be: *instrumental*—of use to groups, typified in the studies of the invention of tradition (Hobsbawm and Ranger 1983; Herzfeld 1982; Handler 1988); and *cultural*—relevant with regard to systems of meaning; or *inertial*—

---

should be treated as such; sometimes it enables "resistance" and empowerment of the disenfranchised, and other times it enables the reproduction of exploitative social forms. Who or what is the bad or good agent in either case is a separate issue from whether these forms carry on.

5. The now-classic works on the theme include Gellner's *Nations and Nationalism* (1983), Anderson's *Imagined Communities* (1983), Hobsbawm's *Nations and Nationalism Since 1760* (1990), and Hobsbawm and Ranger's *Invention of Tradition* (1983).

part of customary practices that are generalized (and embodied) over time, as in the work of Connerton (1989) and Bourdieu (1984). Together, what Olick and Robbins (1998:129) call "six ideal types of mnemonic malleability or persistence" are summarized below.

	Instrumental	Cultural	Inertial
Persistence	Self-conscious orthodoxy, conservatism, heritage movements	Continued relevance, canon	Habit, routine, repetition, custom
Change	Revisionism, memory entrepreneurship, redress movements, legitimation, invented tradition	Irrelevance, paradigm change, discovery of new facts	Decay, atrophy, saturation, accidental loss, death

In Solovyovo—a village in a country engulfed in a state of economic, political, social, and symbolic transition from state socialism and totalitarianism to something surreally, inchoately new—social memory practices include those that encourage persistence and those that propel change. They are characterized by instrumental, cultural, and inertial modes. Institutions, large and small, have a great deal to do with some of these manifestations of social memory, and rather little to do with others. Language (in the form of narrative, exegesis, and habitual symbolism) plays quite a substantial role. In this book, I will concentrate analysis on the social memory modes that were most clearly manifested in Solovyovo while I lived there: *cultural persistence* (seen in commemorative practices, healing practices, some calendrical/ritual practices); *inertial persistence* (in lived-by metaphors, grammatical categories, narrative genres, social and economic organization); and *instrumental change* (in hegemonic assertions for power over calendrical rituals and commemoration).

Memory is a cultural act. Understanding memory, therefore, requires gathering cultural data in a way that avoids the essentializing problems of older cultural conceptions. This book rests on theories that treat cultural action and habit, particularly the work on construct and concept formation of Vygotsky (1962), the "lived-by" metaphors of Lakoff and Johnson (1980), the symbolic function of Sperber (1974), and the "habitual thought" of Whorf (1939). I rely on theories that see commemorative and ritual action as one foundation of social memory (Connerton

1989). As well, I look carefully at the relationship between institutions, power, and cultural meanings (Foucault 1969, 1971). Throughout the work, and inspired in great part by Anderson's *Imagined Communities* (1983), I emphasize the relationship between social memory and the communities that carry it, that is, categories of belonging of different sizes and dimensions from the local to the national, from the earthly to the supernal, from the intimate to the generic. For each of these categories, social memory serves a different purpose—has a different texture and resonance and emotional range. For each, memory can encourage either continuity or change.

A serious study of social memory requires attention to all of these factors: the institutional, ideological, cultural, and social/organizational. It relies, for this reason, on fieldwork that is as rich as possible, and demands an analytical framework that is flexible and multidimensional.

So, when we look at a single village in a country where, for seventy years, the state used memory as its instrument and rewrote it, replaced cultural heroes, reorganized work relationships, and tried to erase one kind of religion and replace it with another, we need to ask why some memories are stable, and others are not. We should ask why, even with the entire, impressive force of the state behind it, some kinds of memory were never wiped away. For that reason, a supple tool is required, one that can tell the difference between scraps and bits of memory images and moments, and the well-worn, much used topography of recollection.

Is light a wave or a particle? It took forays into quantum physics and the probability fields of wave equations to show that it could look like either at certain moments, but be neither. Metaphors are used in science because they can, when expanded, be stretched and bent to provide an ordered way of gathering and interpreting material. When they cease to be useful, they are put aside.[6] Is the Earth flat like a table? It is reasonable to say that most people now choose instead to think of the Earth as round like a ball, and seeing it as round like a ball has permitted us to watch it spin and rotate around the sun in an orderly fashion. In his landmark work in the philosophy of science, *La philosophie du non* (1940), Bachelard explored the ways in which these sorts of metaphoric concepts shape scientific models. They are the inescapable building blocks of sci-

---

6. This represents part of Kuhn's argument in *The Structure of Scientific Revolution* (1962). To cull a cultural perspective on modeling, symbolism, and science, see also Bachelard (1940), Althusser (1974), Lecourt (1975), and Foucault (1972).

ence, and one way or another, they become the very "seeing eyes" that are the organs of our scientific traditions.[7] Because of this, choosing them wisely is a weighty affair. Therefore, in honor of Bachelard, who, in the course of his life, went from being a philosopher of science and its founding metaphors, to a philosopher-poet of fire and dream and space, I offer an analytical idiom in the hope that it gives rise to analysis that is fertile (and many-toned) in depth, and in breadth.

MEMORY AS LANDSCAPE

* * *

> That we remember only by transporting ourselves outside space is therefore incorrect. Indeed, quite the contrary, it is the spatial image alone that, by reason of its stability, gives us an illusion of not having changed through time and of retrieving the past in the present. But that is how memory is defined. Space alone is stable enough to endure without growing old or losing any of its parts.

—MAURICE HALBWACHS, *THE COLLECTIVE MEMORY* (1980:157)

> I, like a river,
> Was rechanneled by this stern age.

—ANNA AKHMATOVA, *NORTHERN ELEGIES*, 1945 (IN HEMSCHEMAYER 1983:514)

Spatial metaphors seep into the language of dream and memory. They also seep into the language of social theory, although often in an unacknowledged way. They are, after all (*good is up!*)[8] embedded in the metaphors we live by.

There are two important ways that memory has been linked explicitly to landscape in past scholarship. First, geographical landscapes have been treated as the sites of memory, and therefore the sites of symbol. People remember places, and can remember them through culturally appropriate images. In *Social Memory*, Fentress and Wickham (1992:93n) discuss this "geographical sensibility," and link it, in particular, to agrarian societies. Most often, it is people's own local landscapes that bear meaning

---

7. From "The seeing eye is the organ of tradition," attributed to Franz Boas by Benedict (1943).
8. Lakoff and Johnson's (1980) representative example of a "lived-by" metaphor.

and history.[9] In a related way, there have been works that look at physical landscape as a place of symbolic reverie. Bachelard's lyrical work, *Poetics of Space* (1964), takes us to lived locations and describes the poetry of houses, corners, and hearths. Schama's *Landscape and Memory* (1995) is a historian's walk through the woods, down waters, and over rock, regarding these places in light of the symbolic features that fill them. In these sorts of works, the link between space and memory is essentially one in which space and place trigger cultural memory.[10]

A second way in which memory has been treated spatially has been in the notion of cognitive "mapping." Fentress and Wickham (1992:17) call these maps, as they have been described by others, "information-bearing representations"—whether maps of real places or those of "imaginary" ones like the skies or the underworld. In the mapping, social memory is supported. Here, it is the visual side of memory that is highlighted; there are places in one's mind's eye and those places can be recalled. The use of those places can be wide ranging: a zodiac can be used in navigation, but can also be filled with mythic tales of sociosymbolic import.[11]

Places are saturated with symbol, of course; and we have mnemonic maps "in our heads." These ideas are broadly accepted.

Overall, my use of spatial metaphors is more abstract than these. Linking landscape and memory for me is not a matter of taking snapshots of rivers and lakes familiar to the villagers of Solovyovo for the symbols they resonate with (although this will be a small part of what I do); nor is it only a question of offering cognitive maps of real or imagined locales. Over time, the narratives that I heard in Solovyovo came to look more and more like journeys along a *conceptual terrain*. These journeys were filled with recalled events (which I saw as milestones or landmarks), but, more deeply, they were marked by familiar conceptual "pathways." I began to see my task as twofold, where first of all I would seek to map the

---

9. But these landscapes can also be conjured at a distance (as in Halbwachs' work on the "changing sacred topography of Palestine") (Fentress and Wickham 1992: 93n).

10. See Basso (1996), and Feld and Basso (1996) for recent examples of this type of work in anthropology.

11. This take on memory and landscape is also related to the "theaters of memory" of classical Rome and later in the Middle Ages, where a scene with a series of visual images would be conjured by an orator who was required to remember an extended speech. Mem-

lay of the conceptual land; and second, I would analyze the deeper dynamics of that space in light of the fact that social memory is made of repeated action.

The material that I am attempting to frame is complex, as it involves the relationship of social memory to concept formation, grammatical categories, metaphors we live by, evocational systems, genre, discursive formations, commemorative ceremonies, social organization, and the production of social categories. All of these have been shown to have a direct bearing on social memory. In the next section, I offer a spatial idiom that will be used to speak of social memory in the course of the book that will effectively serve as a lexicon for the analysis that follows.

Seven Features of Memory's Landscape
1. *Landmarks.* In *Rethinking Symbolism* (1974:113), Sperber says that the human symbolic mechanism is, really, about memory. Symbolic representations are "opaque," he writes, and analyzing symbolism "is . . . not a question of discovering the meaning of symbolic representations but, on the contrary, of inventing relevance and a place in the memory for them." Symbolic figures resonate, and they resonate differently depending on the context. Stalin means many things in many contexts, but in Russia he is, generally, a potent source of symbolic evocation. May 1 is a day that has been associated with both socialist commemoration and agrarian religion. In recollection, it can be said that there are points of concentrated symbolic resonance, whether found in a figure, a day, or a historic milestone. I refer to these as *landmarks,* akin to what Halbwachs calls the "imago," or "generalized memory trace" (Olick and Robbins 1998:129). A first mapping of memory's landscape is a sketch of the symbolic landmarks that are returned to again and again. The death of Stalin is one such landmark in Solovyovo, as are collectivization, the destruction of the local church, the sighting of a UFO a few years ago, and certain activities of local sorcerers, among others. Like specific events, landmarks act as points of reference around which the broader landscape is referenced. This book will be textured throughout by their presence.

---

ory theaters and what they imply about popular conceptions of the meaning of memory is discussed in Yates's *The Art of Memory* (1966) and summarized in Fentress and Wickham (1992:12).

2. *Pathways.* Habitual action is at the base of social memory. I use the term *pathways* to refer to familiar lines of thought or action that are returned to. They are well-worn social relations, exchanges, and interchanges and are forged by the "dialectical interlocking of recall and social nexus" (Tonkin 1992:109). Pathways can be made of commemoration, ritual action, calendrical systems, and lines of narrative that share thematic, stylistic, or compositional structure. Genres such as the ones outlined by Ries (1997)—the litanies, laments, and fairy tales alive in Moscow's kitchens—are pathways of this kind. Pathways can be deeply wrought or superficial. They can be initiated by an individual actor or reiterated by hundreds of years of local knowledge. It is useful to speak of pathways in the memory for the same reason that it is useful to speak of concepts being channeled and deepened as childhood moves to adulthood (Vygotsky 1962): they are seductive and "good to think,"[12] perhaps, but they are not inevitable.

3. *Circles.* Circles are enclosed spaces. Within the landscape of memory, I use the term *circle* almost exclusively to refer to "social circles," or the categories and groups of social belonging. Tracing social circles entails addressing questions such as the following: How is a notion of an inclusive "we" formed? How is it articulated to territory, lineage, political groupings, and economic relations? What does it feel like when such groups are formed? What symbols resonate with belonging as opposed to exclusion? These are the questions of classical social anthropology, as exemplified in works such as Evans-Pritchard's *The Nuer* (1969[1940]). Here, I identify local social circles such as residential groups, lineages, extended families, parishes, and so on, as well as larger circles, including ethnic, political, and national affiliations. Social memory is enacted in the forming and the symbolizing of these groups in thought and language.

National and ethnic "identities"—as explored in a great deal of recent literature[13]—constitute one important feature of social circles. But, importantly, the establishment of a social circle is not subsumed under the problem of identity. When social circles come to life, they can cause social, symbolic, political, and numinous landscapes to transform, some-

---

12. The classic statement is from Lévi-Strauss's *Totemism* (1962b:62) regarding why some animals are eaten in a given cultural setting and others are not.

13. See Olick and Robbins (1998) for an excellent summary of this literature.

times through the medium of otherworldly powers (as in Durkheim's "effervescence"). This is a potent and multifarious process. In social memory practices, these circles (with their distinct characteristics) represent the carriers of memory, and are at the heart, therefore, of encouraging persistence or instigating change.

4. *Vector fields.* Landscapes are not only plotted in three dimensions. They can include features that are marked as vectors would be marked in mathematics and physics, that is, forces with the qualities of magnitude and directionality. A vector can attract an object to a certain realm, or push that object away. A simple use of the term "vector" within the course of this book is this: there are places in memory's landscape that are "good to think" and we are drawn to them. Other places are "bad to think" and we are thereby repelled from them. This includes not only the attraction to or repulsion away from a given symbolic representation (or even a given symbolic "pathway"), but all that is evoked around given representations and pathways.

But there are more complex uses of the notion of vector space within this book. One feature that will be treated at some length is the "vectors" that are embedded within Russian grammar, particularly within verbal prefixes. I will trace these verbal prefixes as they arise and cluster in village narratives. In all, this feature of memory's landscape is underlined in order to highlight the fact that journeys through memory include habitual motions in given directions. They are not static.

5. *Verticality (and horizontality).* In his exploration of imagined national communities, Anderson (1983) writes elegantly of vertical and horizontal "pilgrimages" of young colonialists to new lands and new affiliations. Vertical pilgrimages reached upward in rank or station (or, sometimes, toward the sacred); horizontal ones created solidarity of "equals." Such journeys, he wrote, were defined and refined by social landscapes that changed over time, and played a crucial role in the development of nationalism. Social landscapes allow journeys—in Turner's (1967, 1974) sense[14]—to high and low. The idiom of verticality, as a feature of memory's landscape, will largely refer to relative social status, how

---

14. Anderson (1983:53) uses Turner's notion of the "journey" (1967, 1974) as his way in to the problem of the social, spatial, symbolic journeys he calls pilgrimages. The language of vertical and horizontal affiliations is now mostly used in works on "social capital" (see Coleman 1988).

it comes about, and its consequences. But the "pilgrimages" to places of height and places of democratic equality will also be traced carefully. They come with comforts and dangers.

6. *Interdimensionality*. There are places within the topography of memory where other worlds of power enter into the sphere of everyday life (with their everyday sets of regular symbolic pathways, circles, etc.). As in Turner's discussion of liminality in *The Forest of Symbols* (1967), the journeys along memory's landscape can be suddenly jarred, and an entirely different physical, social, or symbolic space can be entered. The rules change abruptly and wholly there. The crucial matter of confronting and accessing (and falling into) daunting otherworldly powers is one of shifting dimensions. In this book, interdimensionality will come to play most importantly in discussion of a narrative place called the "world of wonders" and in healing practices, writ large.

7. *Layers*. There are ways in which memory's landscape changes over time in great, layered shifts. States change; ideologies change. Hegemonies, with their range of powers over mind and body, change. In Russia, there have been discrete periods of history marked by distinct ideological agendas—each more or less aggressively introduced by the state and its institutions. In each, the past was instrumentalized as programs of power were set for the present. Reactions to these efforts were varied: local practices were at times in harmony with "national maps and hegemonies" (Comaroff and Comaroff 1993:xxiii), and at times they opposed them in the form of defiance or quiet resistance. A Soviet commemoration, for example, would appropriate a holiday from the Orthodox Church, and villagers, in turn, would use the same day to regulate their relations with the ancestors. Could it be said, then, that the weight of the dead generations was lifted, light as air? In fact, rituals, commemorations, and crucial symbolic landmarks have been contested in Solovyovo. Archeological layers formed by the advance and retreat of states are traced in this book along institutional lines (Foucault 1969), as hegemony finds its way into the deepest pathways of social memory.

The lexicon that I have provided is meant to be a tool that allows complex material to be treated as a whole. Memory is social. Memory is bound to questions of hegemony, but is not defined by them. Memory is inscribed not only on bits of paper, but much more importantly, in action. Such actions are transmitted from generation to generation in ways that are quietly persistent—based, as they are, on habitual, uninscribed practices (Connerton 1989:102; Bourdieu 1977). But if they are marked by persistence or resistance to hegemonic forces, they are also marked by dynamism and creative problem solving and change. The study of social memory is a study that can ask—with some subtlety—about the weight of history and its lightness, and the possibility for transformation and change.

2

Setting the Village in Space and Time

Za rekoi, na gore,
Les zelenyi shumit;
Pod goroi, za rekoi,
Khutorochek stoit.

Behind the river, on the hill,
A green forest rustles;
Under the hill, behind the river,
A little village stands.

—RUSSIAN FOLKSONG, "KHUTOROK,"
LYRICS BY A. KOL'TSOV

THE VILLAGE QUESTION

* * *

In the lifetime of most of the villagers in Solovyovo, there have been wars, poverty, famine, backbreaking work for one's own livelihood and for the state, ideological upheavals, and a horrifying number of untimely, senseless deaths. Around their tables, in walks to field and forest, rocking along quiet waves in rowboats, and in the dusty air of their local store, Solovyovo's villagers spoke to me of the days of their youth, of the Revolution and civil war. They spoke with passion and vivid imagery about mass collectivization, and of the great scourge and pride of their lives, World War II. They remembered the famine of 1947 that left their bellies "puffed out," and the time of Stalin, his heavy hand and his aura of father-protector. They recalled with resentment the forced resettlement known as *ukrupnenie*. They told and retold many tales of violence: mass deportations, destruction of local churches and icons, the rape and murder of a young nun in the area, and other murders and other rapes. Death laced the corners of their stories.

But they also remembered life's joys: births and celebrations, communions and unions, songs and love, the sweet smell of the forest, and the sweet feel of well-earned repose.

Social memory is not a series of events, strung like beads on a necklace, one after the next. The death of Stalin, destruction of a church, or return of a soldier is part of a landscape of memory, where events are filled with various logics, rhymes, and reasons. In the same way that a "symbol" is nothing without a "culture" to house it, an event has no meaning in social memory without its context. In this chapter, I offer a brief introduction to the Russian villager as a historical and historiographical subject. My aim is to present the barest possible sketch of the material in which these farmers set themselves in time.

Eastern Slavic Farmers

By 800 BC, Slavic tribes—which perhaps originated north of the Caucasus —shared Europe with speakers of Baltic and Germanic languages (Gilbert 1993:1). In the sixteenth century AD, Ivan IV, "tsar of all the Russias" had extended the arm of Slavic rule deep into the heart of Asia. In the mid-twentieth century, the Soviet Union made up one-seventh of the Earth's land mass. In between these times, the Eastern Slavs known today as Russians have met with armies of Scythians (from parts of Central Asia), Sarmatians (Asiatic), Goths (Balts), Huns and Avars (also Central Asians), Khazars (from the Oxus River), Norsemen (who ruled Kievian Rus'), Teutons, Mongols (when, for two hundred years the Russians lived under the "Tartar yoke"), Lithuanians, Poles, Swedes, Turks, Frenchmen, Japanese, and Germans. Along the way, great empires rose up, declined, and fragmented, and formed again.

Throughout this time, and until very recently, the vast majority of Russians have made their living off the land. Until 1851, 95 percent of the Russian population was rural. The processes of industrialization and urbanization began in Russia in the second half of the nineteenth century, and in the short period between 1850 and 1900, the urban population of the country doubled, and increased again by 15 percent in the next fifteen years. Even in light of this vast urban migration, by World War I, 85 percent were still living in the countryside (Vernadsky 1969[1929]:242). Under Soviet rule, more than half of the population moved to the cities.

At present, an estimated 27 percent of the population resides in rural areas (Patsiorkovskii 2003; Kingkade 1997), but a far larger proportion is engaged in agricultural production.[1] In order to supplement food sources (and ensure survival during periods of economic upheaval), urbanites in greater Russia tend garden plots in dachas and accept goods from their rural relatives. This has profound implications at the level of the national economy, but agriculture is not only a fact of economic life. The relationship between humans and the land has been, over the centuries, fraught with a range of emotions in Russia—all of them mixed and many of them heady.

Indeed, the history of Russian agriculture (and the land on which it is realized) is a complex and, in many ways, a tragic one. The noted biochemist and historian of science Medvedev writes that this particularly tragic history is due to the "unique and extreme form of feudalism [that] survived in Russia until the middle of the nineteenth century" (Medvedev 1987:3). In fact, the feudal mode of production in Russia often operated much like a slave mode of production in the breadth of its economic exploitation, in the cruelty of its corporal punishment against wayward serfs, and in its making the villager available for fighting endless imperial wars and building imperial cities. Conquest writes, in *Harvest of Sorrow* (1986:14) that as European feudalism was waning, "[i]n Russia, it became more widespread, more onerous, and more inhuman right into the 19th century."

The violence of power cannot be explained—either at the personal or epic level—through any single causal factor. It is clear that modes of production vary in the ways that economic surplus is generated and used by different sectors of society, and in the degree to which inhumanity is a part of that process; to be "successful" (i.e., to be surplus producing), the feudal mode of production in Russia required a certain "squeezing" of the vast agrarian class. This is because, in a basic sense, the land in most of Russia is unsuited to large-scale agriculture. Pipes (1974:5) explains as follows:

> Like the other Slavs, the ancient Russians were primarily a pastoral people; and like them, upon settling down in their new territories, they slowly made

---

1. The Moscow GosKomStat supports this 27-percent number for the rural population for 2002 (Patsiorkovskii 2003:136). This statistic does not account for large numbers of people who spend a significant portion of their time in rural areas engaged in agricultural activities, but who are not officially registered as village inhabitants.

the transition to agriculture. Unfortunately for them, the area which the Eastern Slavs penetrated and colonized happens to be uniquely ill suited for farming. The indigenous Finns and Turks treated farming as a supplementary occupation, concentrating in the forest zone on hunting and fishing, and in the steppe on livestock breeding. The Russians chose otherwise. Their heavy reliance on farming under adverse natural conditions is perhaps the most basic cause of the problems underlying Russian history.

It appears that as long as the ancient Slavs were wandering and producing for themselves and their families, agriculture—when combined with hunting and fishing—made for a perfectly viable means of subsistence. As the Russian state developed in various forms over the centuries, along with a network of feudal estates, farmers were required not only to feed themselves, but, through their own labor, to support the ruling classes of the country. The poverty of the land made this a monumental effort. As Pipes (1974:16) writes, the particular "brevity of the agricultural season," was the cause of much human misery, arguing that with roughly half the growing season of farmers in Western Europe, the same production requires twice the labor. Russian villagers managed, nonetheless, to create incredible wealth for ruling elites from poor soils and an abbreviated growing season, and they did so for centuries.

The "Peasant" Question[2]
The tumultuous nineteenth century saw the birth of Russian industrialism, the first great waves of urban immigration, a well-developed militarism, and a social mobility that allowed new social philosophies to flourish. While thinkers in Russia—influenced first by Enlightenment philosophies and later by Marxist ones as well—tried to formulate ways of bringing justice to the Russian countryside, as discontent accumulated

---

2. The term "peasant" is problematic in the field of anthropology. The concern involves the fact that the "peasantry" as been treated as a timeless, monadic body that is either "rational" or not, or "noble" or not. Outside the parameters of this debate, it is significant that since the fall of the Soviet Union, the obligations that Russian farmers have to the state have changed dramatically. Therefore, whether or not it is appropriate to refer to these farmers as "peasants" before the fall of the Soviet Union, it is certainly not appropriate to refer to them as such after. During my fieldwork, villagers referred to themselves not as "peasants" (krest'iane) but as, simply, "villagers" (derevenskie). I will follow their lead and use the term "peasant" only when referring to historiographical materials or other such commentaries, or when quoting villagers when they choose the term.

Map 1. Northwestern Russia. Solovyovo is in the vicinity of Belozersk.

in every social sphere. Then, as now, there were no easy answers to the "peasant question."

Indeed, the history of rural reforms in Russia and the Soviet Union is long and tangled, made all the more complex because of the pronounced distance between the world of Russian farmers and that of intellectuals from urban and provincial centers. Unfortunately, the compassion that drove many members of the intelligentsia to fight for the eradication of serfdom and new systems of justice in land policies was not sufficient impetus to create a genuine understanding of the conditions of Russian farmers.[3] The heart of the matter appears to be that villagers

3. See Ries (1997:157–160) for a discussion of this point.

and the *intelligentsia* were strangers to one another. Conquest (1986:19) puts it succinctly:

> The Russian intelligentsia had taken two contrary views of the peasantry. On the one hand they were the People incarnate, the soul of the country, suffering, patient, the hope of the future. On the other, they appeared as the "dark people," backward, mulish, deaf to argument, and oafish impediment to all progress.

Any essay, treatise, or text on the Russian village contends with the fact that the Russian village has, for hundreds of years, been ruthlessly put in quotes by the intellectuals who seek to explain it. It is a prime Sperberian symbolic representation—it is fully opaque and takes its meaning from its context (Sperber 1974). If to some members of the intelligentsia, it was within the village that the great lessons of life could be uncovered (Tolstoy and Dostoevsky are classic examples of this position), the discursive purpose of the "peasantry" did not end there. To Marx, it carried primitive communism; to the Slavophiles of the last century, it held religious salvation; to the Populists (*narodniki*) of the same period it offered the generosity and community-mindedness of noble savages; and to Lenin it was the problematic locus of precapitalism (see Fanger 1968: 252–256; Etkind 2003; Frierson 1993; Figes 1997; Conquest 1986: 19). Reality, in each of these cases, clashed with idealized imagery.

The Russian villager, willing or not, would be a key figure of projection in the revolutionary period of the early twentieth century (Etkind 2003). Marxists and then Bolsheviks inherited the problem of "peasant" idealization; if Marx spoke of proletarian revolution, what was one to do about the rural farmer, who still made up the vast majority of Russians? Villagers fit neither the ideals nor the plans of Bolshevik revolutionaries, who were themselves creatures of libraries and salons and not of wheat fields (Frierson 1993). Their life was "idiocy," marked by "savagery"; villagers were not human, they were "scum" (Conquest 1986:20).

And yet, despite the symbolic configurations of village oafishness or soulfulness, the rural community, by all realistic evidence, was and is a body of the Russian population that has carefully and consistently calculated ways to protect local interests in the face of external pressures and demands. Holding the ultimate control over grain, Russian villagers have had a measure of real power and, like rural communities all over the world, have wielded that power not only in the form of rebellions (which were relatively rare), but in "everyday forms of resistance" such as withholding "labor, food, taxes, rents and interest" (Scott 1985:29; Fitzpatrick 1994:5). Such resistance took place over the centuries, and did not cease after the Revolution, even after the villagers were granted land through the Land Decree of 1918. In this sense, Russian agriculturalists have been not only an exploited mass, but also a defiant one.

Revolution and Collectivization

Defiance takes many forms. In rural Russia, the Russian Revolution certainly had support, even if the extent of this support is debated. It was the performance of the Bolsheviks after the Revolution that caused this support to waver and then to largely fail. After 1917 came and went, Russia (now a part of the Soviet Union) struggled for survival after having effectively destroyed its traditional ruling class. Agrarian production was needed as it always had been, but now in a context of renewed social unrest and devastating civil war followed by the "unprecedented" Great Famine of 1921–1922. There was a great sense of disillusionment among villagers, accompanied by the destruction of "the normal pattern of rural life" (Medvedev 1987:36).

The conflict between the urban revolutionary and the rural agrarian was complicated and intensified by Marxist theories applied to the Russian village. In the years of revolutionary ferment, Lenin wrote about class divisions that supposedly existed in the countryside. Within the village, he theorized, there were three classes in conflict: the *kulaki,* or "rich peasants," who were exploiting the "medium" and "poor peasants." These *kulaki* were the manifestations of protocapitalist development in the countryside (theoretically, they owned several heads of cattle, lent money, and hired poor farmers as wage laborers), and were, therefore, the enemies of a proletarian revolution. Within Bolshevik thought, the *kulak* who was "seen both as a nascent capitalist and as a dominant influence on the *mir* [village commune], was the fulcrum of [Bolshevik] fears" (Fitzpatrick 1994:29). If life can imitate art, it can also imitate theory: the notion that the kulaki must be destroyed as a class began in those dusty libraries where Lenin spent time theorizing, but by the 1930s ended in the mass deportation of over a million Russian villagers, many of whom were "shot or sent to the gulag" (Fitzpatrick 1994:83–84).

The reasons for this process—known as dekulakization—aside from the demonizing of Russian farmers in general and rich Russian farmers specifically, were centered around the early Soviet solution to the "peasant question," that is, collectivization. Villagers would be "collectivized" into village-based collective farming operations known as *kolkhozy* (collective farms) and *sovkhozy* (state farms). As socialist institutions, the land and materials of the kolkhozy and the sovkhozy would be collectively "owned," and workers would share the fruits of their labor. Unfortunately for planners, villagers resisted vehemently and sometimes violently against collectivization. Overcoming the kulaki became the particular focus of authorities. Their deportation was seen as instrumental in the process of bringing socialism to the countryside, since they were seen as the most vociferous opponents of the state's plan.

It was not only the kulaki who opposed collectivization. Joining the state-mandated collective farm was unattractive to many (although not all) farmers. As was their historical habit, villagers resisted state control in varied ways. For example, during the Soviet period there was a tax on milk of private cows, so villagers killed their cows and raised goats instead. They would also keep a single grandparent in a household working on the kolkhoz in order to keep the private plot reserved for families of *kolkhozniki* (collective farm workers), thus enabling other family members to do other work. Young men would get arrested to avoid working in the kolkhoz. Potatoes would be planted and relied on as a staple, because they are difficult to keep (unlike grain) and were, therefore, not appropriated by the government.[4] Many of the narratives presented in this book touch upon collectivization and dekulakization, key symbolic landmarks in rural memory.

The Problem of Social Organization

In certain important ways, social organization has changed radically in rural Russia in the past one hundred years. The emancipation of the serfs in 1861, the rural reforms (Liberal and Bolshevik) of the early twentieth century, and the adoption of the kolkhoz in the 1930s all served to transform certain key features of social organization. On the other hand, it appears that there has been a degree of continuity in the basic make-up of social life and production in the countryside. Except for the oldest few, the villagers in Solovyovo make their living through agricultural labor. For this labor, they rely on premechanized technology. Like the villagers of pre-Revolutionary Russia, they face the precariousness of the weather with a certain foreboding. Like those pre-Revolutionary villagers, they

---

4. These examples are drawn from Medvedev's *Soviet Agriculture* (1987).

work on family plots and distribute the fruits of their labor outward to those who have shared in the labor. They live in a world of exchange that is largely nonmonetarized. The rhythms of their days and years are bound in large part to the movements of the natural world. Their relationships to unseen worlds and forces—ones that can intercede in times of trouble—have also been marked by continuity to the past. Mass collectivization and industrialization at the national level did not fundamentally change these basic features of agrarian life. It is not surprising, therefore, that certain earlier forms of social organization have been preserved as well.

For centuries, the village has been a social hybrid in Russia, operating with a degree of self-definition and self-sufficiency, on the one hand, and economic and political controls at local and national levels, on the other. Such back and forth between an organization suited to small-scale agricultural production and one suited to serfdom and the exigencies of a powerful, centralized state, has made for particularly complex social forms. Echoing this point, Robinson (1969[1932]:70), social historian of rural Russia, wrote:

> The student interested in the realities of peasant life is hounded by a desire to assign each common interest and each collective function to the group which actually shared that interest and exercised that function; but to do this would require an interminable study, such as had never yet been made, of the actual practice of the peasants, as more or less modified and aborted by the agrarian laws, the interpretations of the Senate, the rulings of the local courts, and the actions of the local bureaucracy.

If the question was so complex in 1932, it is no less so today. Indeed, the convoluted quality of social organization has been intensified in post-Soviet Russia. In the village, social organization is today marked by chaos and confusion as the collective institution once known as the kolkhoz dies a slow death and social groups form and re-form. The question of land ownership, so crucial to any analysis of social groups in agrarian societies, has been blurred by the efforts at post-Soviet privatization, which has been slow and incomplete (Gambold Miller and Heady 2004).

Solovyovo's world is changing in this post-Soviet world. Indeed, social analysis of the village during the 1990s and now in the first years of the third millennium is a social analysis in and of transition. And yet, Solovyovo's world also sits "deeply" in time and space, to recall E. Valentine Daniel's remark in the introduction to this book. The changes and chances of policies and the names and biographies of leaders should be reckoned with in the course of any study on memory. But so should the constitution of its long-lived-in landscape.

SOLOVYOVO IN SPACE AND TIME

* * *

Passing through the northern Russian landscape, one sees clusters of houses huddled together—as if to guard the inhabitants collectively against the winds of ill weather and ill fortune. Each of these clusters is a Russian village or *derevnia,* and one appears every mile or two along the road. Inevitably, they lie near the curve of a river or on the shore of a lake and are made up of between ten and a hundred households.

Lying roughly at the northern latitude of St. Petersburg and the eastern longitude of Moscow, within walking distance of the Sheksna River and riding distance from the famous Monastery of Ferapontovo—Solovyovo, a tiny dot that appears only on local maps, was first mentioned in the Russian chronicles of the sixteenth century. By the late twentieth century, in the Solovyovo that I came to know, the sounds of car radios, television sets, and tractors were heard, and streetlights penetrated the blackness of the moonless night. But, in that same Solovyovo, the farmers would return home from their fields in bright white shirts, walking to the cadence of a day well spent. They would watch the weather every moment of every day—not daring to plan anything too far in advance—waiting for the moments of moisture, dryness, and frost, and the exact points of ripening and fruition.

Solovyovo is one of several villages situated along the shores of Lake Tikhonskoe. By the mid-1990s, only the villages that lie on the west side of the lake still survived. The others, many of them very much alive in local lore, slowly dried up and died over the decades. Solovyovo is the easternmost in this arc of villages and was, historically, one of the largest. As of 2004, it was still the third largest in that string.

The Solovyovo stop is the last one on the Belozersk-Solovyovo bus line. Once the bus driver came to know me (or, more accurately, knew that I was the guest of the Belovs), he would drop me off right at the house where I lived, and Mikhail Alekseevich would invite him in for a glass of milk or some tea. Before gaining that small piece of social capital, I would leave the bus in Vershina and walk the kilometer path that arches between the two villages.

Near Solovyovo's border, there is a crossroad in the path: to the left are the pastures set aside for the cows and sheep of Solovyovo and Ver-

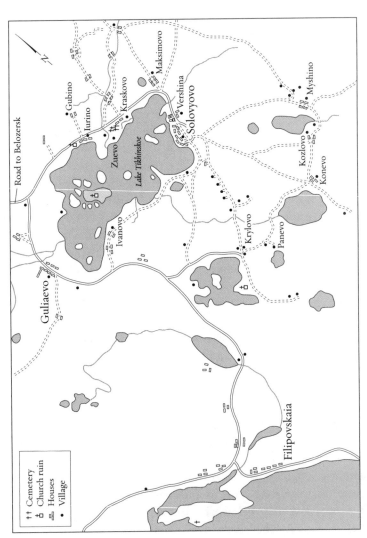

Map 2. Solovyovo and surrounding villages. Only villages mentioned in the text are named.

shina (thirteen head of cattle, five small herds of sheep, during the period of my fieldwork) and beyond that, forestland. Straight ahead are the potato fields and beyond them mixed forest and wheat fields. To the right, one can peer over a hill, beyond the sheep grazing in lush green fields near the roadside, and see the rooftops of Solovyovo. Beyond the outline of the rooftops are the banks of Lake Tikhonskoe. This is the end of the line: only water, field, and forest beyond.

When I lived in Solovyovo, the village had thirty-six buildings. During the cold winter months, the village was mostly inhabited by people in their fifties and older. This is a typical sight in the Russian countryside—the slow death of the village—and has been spoken of for generations (Gambold Miller and Heady 2004; Buckley 2000; Wegren 1995). The official population of Solovyovo in the winter was around thirty people, but in the spring, summer, and fall months, the village would fill up with friends and relatives of the permanent residents who came to help with farm work and harvesting, or to simply relax and enjoy the clean air, nearby lake, and gifts of an ample forest. In July, Solovyovo would bustle with children and young people, friends, and visitors.

The first building at the edge of Solovyovo is a large clubhouse, the center of cultural activities for villages in a five-mile range. In the winter, it is only open on holidays and special occasions, but in the summer it is open every night. The front room of the club has a pool table that is used by children in the early half of the evening and men in the later half. In the next room, there is a stage, where shows are presented, special dates are commemorated, dances are held, and young love is explored. In the back is a small library that includes classics of Russian literature and poetry (Tolstoy, Dostoevsky, Pushkin, and Lermontov are available, but no Solzhenitsyn, Akhmatova, or Brodsky). There are also classics of Soviet political literature. The librarian was advised at one point to burn the collection of Stalin's writings, but he couldn't bear to do so and gave them away instead. When I lived in Solovyovo, there was still a shelf of children's books dedicated to Lenin as a boy.

The village homes, or *izby*, are made of wood—in the style of log cabins—and are sometimes painted yellow, blue, or green, and often decorated with simple woodwork designs. In this part of Russia, the *izba* was designed to shelter not only humans. Indeed, under the protection of one long roof, there is a barn (*khlev*) on one side of the izba, and a home for a family on the other. Typically, the barns of Solovyovo house one cow, one calf, several sheep, a couple of chickens, and perhaps a rooster. In other villages, people keep pigs and goats as well. Second-story haylofts are common.

On the other side of the izba, in the section dedicated to housing people, there is an entryway, a large brick stove (*Russkaia pech'*), and usually one large room. People sleep along the walls, sometimes behind partitions and sometimes not. Every house is surrounded by its own garden, where villagers—even in the Soviet period—tended potatoes, beets, carrots, cabbage, squash, onions, berry bushes, apple trees, herbs for healing, and flowers for beauty and for the use of bees. Either in the family garden or on the bank of the lake, each household has a bathhouse where people can wash themselves and their clothes with water heated by an intense fire that is tended for hours.

No one in the village owns a car or a truck, so if someone gets sick, there is a long wait for the ambulance to arrive; the nearest town of Belozersk is an hour and a half away. Without running water, everything is slowed down, including cooking, cleaning, washing dishes, bathing, and feeding the animals. Even in the regional center of Belozersk, not everyone has running water, and people must bathe themselves and their children in public bathhouses. There are telephones in the village, but making long distance calls is difficult, as the lines are poor, and after rain or snow storms they inevitably break down. Village residents do have electricity, but it is unreliable. Every November and every March, the roads are impassable for a few weeks. In emergencies, people can ride on the postal truck (which runs three times a week) with the driver's permission. Villagers wash their clothes in bathhouses and rinse them in the lake by smacking and swishing them with the end of a long stick.

Now and then a truck or car arrives with guests or goods. Movement of any kind—especially such arrivals—brings the villagers to their windows, where they watch until the nature of the movement has been categorized. "Vania is getting water for the bath." "Fedia has gone for hay." "The gypsies have come with goods—what have they got?"

Just beyond the clubhouse, within sight of the village, are parcels of land allocated to village families. There, the villagers grow potatoes—the most important staple for people and a crucial part of animals' diets as well. The smallest plots are ten hectares, and the largest are forty. From these potato fields, there are several small footpaths that lead to hay and wheat fields and forestlands. When I lived there, villagers would go to these fields frequently during the summer months (primarily for the long period of the hay harvest), and less frequently in the autumn and winter (to retrieve the carefully stacked hay as needed). The forest is entered mostly in the summer and fall as well, for purposes of hunting, and gathering and cutting wood for household use.[5]

In the course of their daily chores, villagers spend a great deal of time walking. They walk to fields or forests that are up to forty-five minutes away, trudging over changing landscapes, such as fields of wheat, small patches of birch and aspen, fields of flower and clover, and clusters of pines. As the landscape changes, places are named and their histories come alive (e.g., here is where Aleksei Nikolaevich planted the pines for the landlord, there is the place where butter was manufactured, under those birches white mushrooms can be found). Walking, or while passing through landscapes, was often the "place" where stories were told, life lessons given.

For longer distances and heavier loads than simply scythes and rakes, horse-drawn carts and sleighs are still the most flexible form of transportation. Horses were distributed after the transition of the kolkhoz— people share their care, and thus their use. Harnessed to a traditional cart (*telega*), and under the weight of their famous wooden yoke, horses carry people or loads of hay, wood, or manure. In the summer months, they run along solid dirt paths only; in the winter, they can run quickly through the snow into the forest or over frozen lakes. For that reason, distances seem to shrink in the winter months: traveling over ice is faster than over dirt.

On an island in the middle of Lake Tikhonskoe are ruins of what for centuries had been the local church. According to scholars of the region,[6] the remains of a saint are buried in the soil. The church was destroyed after the Revolution, but the island still contains the graves of people who are very much alive in Solovyovo's memory. After the destruction of the church, a new graveyard was established for the region not far from the village of Kraskovo, approximately three kilometers from Solovyovo.

Most of the villagers spent their lives working as farm laborers, although some have worked as teachers, librarians and shopkeepers. Now

---

5. The few villagers who were still employed by the kolkhoz at the time of my research would sometimes work as loggers in surrounding forests.

6. Svetlana Adon'eva, St. Petersburg State University, personal communication, 1995.

mostly in or near retirement, the villagers raise their own animals and sow and reap their own food. The community lives almost completely by subsistence farming, with very little money and with very few links to the formal economy. As a mark of the success of the Soviet educational system, there were no illiterate people in Solovyovo when I lived there. Most residents completed only a couple of years of school before becoming collective farm workers, but in general they can and do read newspapers, books, and favorite magazines. All can recite (and many can write and improvise) poems; a few are exceptional storytellers.

Historical Landmarks in Solovyovo

Larisa Andreevna: We [were] stuck in work day and night in the kolkhoz. We don't know the white light of day. We didn't know what day, which holiday, anything. We don't take anything. That kind of work, when the war came, what did we do? Plowed with a plow; drag a plow with five or six people; we struggle [writhe] like dogs, with starvation, ripped, dirty. Don't sit, just think, "Would that the war would end. Would that the war would end."

Q: Which war?

Larisa Andreevna: There were all kinds of wars. Civil war, Finnish war, all kinds happened. This German war; it was no joke. And we were also young people. We spent our whole youth in war. Our boys.

The farmers I grew to know in Solovyovo—the same ones who told me stories about their lives and the fortunes of their families and about how the unseen mysteries of the world could be explained—were also historical actors. Nothing in my pre-fieldwork reading prepared me for the penetrating humanity in the stories of wars and social movements and displacements I heard in Solovyovo, and how those stories were read and internalized by villagers. A few local historical notes are in order.

Pre-Revolutionary Solovyovo was flanked by monastery lands on one side (where nuns lived and worked the land), and the lands of a single landowning family on the other. Solovyovo was couched rather comfortably in between these two spaces, where villagers also had access to a local lake, a nearby river, and a forest, and work for those times when extra income was needed. Although certainly no one recalled formal serfdom, villagers did speak at some length about the landlords who lived in the area after the end of serfdom. They almost never mentioned the Revolution, although they did remember the civil war that followed it. A single story was told about the "revolutionary idea" in Solovyovo, although many stories were told about the coming of the "communists" to the area and resulting changes.[7]

But war, as a more general theme, was a subject of great concern to villagers, and it became the focus of many conversations while I lived in Solovyovo. Villagers remembered wartime in great and rich detail. They had paid for wars with their bodies (as soldiers), animals, food, and labor. Men had been soldiers (and sometimes prisoners of war), and women had worked in war factories in distant cities and took over the work of men and horses in villages. Many other villagers were children during wartime, and recall their fathers leaving for war and coming back wounded or not at all. Some remember the sounds of German bomber planes; others lived with German prisoners of war in their villages who were assigned duties such as digging gardens or other farm labor.

In general, World War II, known in Russia as the "Great Patriotic War," brought tremendous movement to the lives of Russian villagers, many of whom saw the wide world outside of the village for the first time during the war. The war also brought the wide world to the village; evacuated people from St. Petersburg and other cities under siege were placed in villages like Solovyovo. There, the urban/rural dichotomy was, at least for a short time and in small ways, bridged.

The collectivization of Solovyovo took place between 1930 and 1933. Unlike other villages in the region, there was a great deal of dissent when villagers were first forced to join, then allowed to leave (without the an-

---

7. Mikhail Alekseevich tells the story as told to him by his father: "In Guliaevo, a few years before [everyone else], there was the 'revolutionary idea' against the landlord, against the tsar. Maybe oppression was stronger against them. Or it was harder to live there. In any case, the people from Guliaevo built a revolutionary rank. They called to the people of Solovyovo to 'Come on! Let's go against the tsar!' There, it seems there was such a situation in Solovyovo—people could do work on the side both for the monastery and for the landlord. They could work and so they could maintain their households more easily. They had no reason to go against the tsar. Because of that, the people from Guliaevo came and said, 'Since you are for the tsar, we'll come and burn you down.' And they came in boats. For that reason, the people of Solovyovo guarded the village in turns. So they wouldn't burn it down."

imals and tools that they had joined with), and then forced by circumstance to join again. Local resistance came with consequences: records show that six Solovyovo families were dekulakized. The story of one large family in particular, the Zakharovs, was told many times. This family was relatively rich and had a small home business for making the boiled wool boots known as *valenki*. This family was able to hire labor off-season to help with production. Labeled kulaki, these family members were sent off either to the Solovetskii Islands, according to one legend, or to Siberia, according to another. In the fifteen villages that made up the *sel'sovet* (village council) of Solovyovo, at least ten families were dekulakized and several other people were "repressed" in various ways. Homes were searched, property was stolen, and family members were arrested for "one wrong word."[8]

The famines of 1947, devastating to the bulk of the Soviet Union in the aftermath of World War II, was remembered many times and in many separate contexts in Solovyovo. Many local people died. I was told how people had eaten grasses and food scraps of various kinds during the famine, how animals were fed *veniki* (the leaves and tender branches of trees) from the forest to fend off starvation, and how strong men had died for the sake of children's lives. The famine was often raised as a subject within the context of broader discourse on how to live a moral life, a subject that I will return to in subsequent chapters.

Relative peace and prosperity in the decades after World War II brought some important positive developments to Solovyovo. Gradually, villagers began to recover from the war; they were paid for their labor at least in part in cash, and often in a mixture of cash and goods. By the 1970s, many were allowed internal passports (before that, Soviet law had chained them to the land in much the same way that serfdom had done so); and electricity came to Solovyovo (or, as I was told, "they brought light" to the village). At the same time, the village consolidation process

---

8. Mikhail Alekseevich had taken great pains to record the political repressions that took place in the fourteen villages that surrounded Solovyovo. From my notes: Solovyovo: 6 families dekulakized; 1 person repressed. Maksimovo: 3 families dekulakized. Kraskovo: 1 family dekulakized. Yurino: 2 heads of families dekulakized; 2 brothers from different families repressed, "probably for their tongues." Myshino: 1 family, confiscated everything, but did not send family away. Demshino: 1 man sent for six months; they didn't touch his things; one man sent for six months without being dekulakized.

of the period, *ukrupnenie*—which allowed electricity and relatively high technology to come to rural areas at the cost of abandoning small villages for larger ones—was generally resented.

The *Kolkhoz* after the Fall

By the time I arrived in Solovyovo for the first time, the institution of the kolkhoz had changed size and configuration several times since its inception—from two villages per kolkhoz brigade (work team) in 1933, to the pre-1991 form in which the entire sel'sovet of Guliaevo was only one brigade of Agrofirma Belozerska (as it was during the period that I conducted my research).[9] Fewer and fewer people in the region of Solovyovo are employed as land workers. The last three workers from Solovyovo left Agrofirma Belozerska by 1996: one young man found another job and moved to a larger village, a second was fired for drinking, and a third was killed in the winter of 1996 when a tree fell on him in the forest.

Over the years, the kolkhoz in Solovyovo was involved particularly with dairy production, but also with forestry, linen production, and animal husbandry. Corn was introduced to the region in the 1960s, but it was quickly understood that corn was not a suitable crop for the area. Today, kolkhoz lands still surround the village of Solovyovo, and negotiations for the use of these lands for grazing, firewood, hunting and gathering is still an issue, as it has been in rural Russia over the centuries (Robinson 1969[1932]; Pipes 1974; Medvedev 1987). Currently, the kolkhoz lands are not used to grow grain or flax for linen production; every year, villagers encroach on them more boldly for the abovementioned purposes.

9. Mikhail Alekseevich has meticulously recorded the "agrarian history" of the area around Solovyovo from the year 1928, when two villages near Solovyovo became a "commune." In 1933, Solovyovo's kolkhoz was only two villages large. In 1953, it united with all of the villages in the sel'sovet of Solovyovo (which constituted most of the villages in the southeast arc of Lake Tikhonskaia and the villages tucked farther into woods and past bogs). In 1958, that kolkhoz merged again with all of the villages of Guliaevskii Sel'sovet; by this time, most of the villages around the lake, plus other villages off the beaten track were included. The next major change came in 1991, when all of these villages became one brigade of Agrofirma Belozerska. Just after 2000, Agrofirma Belozerska technically went bankrupt, although the enterprise still continued to exist under a different administrative name and configuration.

As privatization was introduced in the early 1990s, the local kolkhoz went through some dramatic changes.[10] Most significantly, hundreds of heads of dairy cattle were slaughtered in the nearby village of Iurino and production shifted from dairy to logging. Agrofirma Belozerska is now struggling to keep itself afloat, and attempting to determine the marketability of local forests to investors.

The fact that the kolkhoz has changed so dramatically over the years, from an employer of nearly everyone to an employer of only very few, has encouraged an overall demographic shift in the area toward an older population. Although there are young families and children, particularly in the sel'sovet of Guliaevo, such families constitute a minority. Work prospects are less than optimistic and opportunities to move to bigger villages or to nearby towns are often welcomed. In Solovyovo and the surrounding villages, I saw very little evidence of the development of private farming. Villagers do sell excess produce and meat (as they have for years), but at a very small scale. This may be due to the notoriously bad land of the Russian north, which makes it very difficult—even under the best conditions—for farming to be profitable. It is clear that farming persists in a form that is almost entirely at a subsistence level.

Placing the Anthropologist

I was invited to live in Solovyovo by Mikhail Alekseevich and Iuliia Ivanovna Belov, a middle-aged couple whose adult children no longer lived in the village. For the entire time of my fieldwork between October 1994 and December 1995 (and in all of my several subsequent trips to the village since then), I lived in their one-room izba. I am exactly five days older than the couple's daughter Lena, and in many ways, the role that developed for me in that family felt most like hers: that of an adult daughter who has returned after marriage to visit her parents for a long stay. Mikhail Alekseevich and Iuliia[11] became my closest confidants,

---

10. The sociology, history, anthropology, and political science of these changes are now being written, albeit slowly. See Buckley (2000), Gambold Miller and Heady (2004), Patsiorkovskii (2002, 2003), O'Brien and Wegren (2002), Wegren (1995, 1997), Amelina (2002), Allina-Pisano (2002).

11. In Solovyovo, I referred to almost all of the year-round inhabitants by their name and patronymic. There are a few exceptions to this rule. The most notable exception was Iuliia Ivanovna Belov, whom I always referred to simply as Iuliia. Because she is such an important person in this work, it made sense that I would refer to her in the body of the text as Iuliia.

friends, "informants," and supporters while I lived in the village. Much will be said of them in the pages that follow. A few particularities are worth noting now.

First, although both had always worked in the kolkhoz, they had also worked in "culture" jobs, that is, Mikhail Alekseevich primarily as a teacher and librarian, and clubhouse worker, and Iuliia as a clubhouse worker. For these culture jobs, they were required to receive some higher education. Mikhail Alekseevich was born and raised in Solovyovo, and only left for two years of study in the nearby town of Ergovsk. Iuliia, as I described in the preface, was born in a village about a hundred kilometers away, but was orphaned at age six and raised in an orphanage.

Iuliia and Mikhail Alekseevich shared the trait of being kindhearted, *miagkie* (soft, tender) people, who had been raised in a rural setting. Their characters differ in many other ways, and their differences happened to be of great benefit to my research: Mikhail Alekseevich is an outgoing theorist, and is always ready to narrate a portrait of the universe and its workings. Iuliia is far shyer with outsiders and is pragmatic in her explanations about the world. Sometimes, when her husband would get an especially far-flung theory going, her response would be to roll her eyes in my direction, and clue me in that something was not quite intuitively right. He was very concerned with propriety in many different spheres (he'd been a loyal Party member, and now considers himself a faithful Christian), and so, for example, as he would read me Russian Orthodox prayers, she would take me aside later and find me an incantation that would work better to get the results I needed. In the orphanage, Iuliia had had an upbringing that was formally Soviet, and had internalized certain features of Soviet ideology that were more foreign to Mikhail Alekseevich. She also knew less about traditional culture because of this. On the other hand, it was Mikhail Alekseevich who had been a Party member—and a rather earnest one at that. Mikhail Alekseevich, Iuliia, and their family members and close associates made up my best and deepest contacts during my stays in Solovyovo.

Fieldwork in Solovyovo included gathering data on social organization, economic organization, regional and local history, sacred practices of various origins, the practices of traditional healing and sorcery, and the agricultural cycle and festival cycles of the village year. I also gathered folk material of several different genres including folk tales, songs, anecdotes, sayings, improvised rhymes (*chastushki*), and magic spells and charms. I also actively participated in the yearly cycle of farm work, and in celebrations, rituals, and social gatherings.

Interviews were critical to this research. In the course of fieldwork, I conducted interviews (sometimes multiple interviews) with most of the year-round villagers of Solovyovo, but also with villagers from the surrounding area. Interviews were usually done with a single person, but sometimes with a couple or, rarely, with a small group of people. It was not appropriate to conduct interviews alone with men outside of a public space, and for that reason this type of interview was rarer. The age of villagers who lived year-round in the area during my fieldwork ranged from 33 to 87. Most of the interviews were conducted with these year-round residents (and year-round residents from other villages), but some were done with people who live in the village for several months of the year only. The interviews were open-ended (my aim being to let villagers express themselves about themes that were important to them), but I set out to cover the following themes:

Personal histories and genealogies

Descriptions of historical events (in particular, the Russian Revolution, civil war, arrival of the communists in the area, collectivization, World War II, Khrushchev's agrarian reforms, Gorbachev's reforms, collapse of the Soviet Union, etc.)

Figures in history (political and social)

The otherworldly realm (religious practices of all kinds, including a particular focus on healing practices)

The yearly cycle and holidays

Historical teleologies (how events are given sense over time)

As important as formal interviews were to this research, I had been sent to the field with the words of my dissertation advisor, John Leavitt, ringing in my ears. Borrowing from poet Robert Duncan, he told me that the fieldwork method should "exercise [your] faculties at large." In hundreds of pages of journal notes, I strove every day to record the lived world of Solovyovo. These notes—and their ebb and flow of fact and intuition—became, ultimately, my richest source for the analysis ahead.

* * *

Solovyovo: Summer fields fragrant with clovers. Quiet enough in winter to hear a cat's footsteps in the snow. How is its landscape filled with the traces of living, acting beings? How does memory inscribe itself into Solovyovo's social space?

3

Being "One's Own" in Solovyovo

Memory is part of cognitive empower-
ing and a means to being; it is developed through social interaction; it is
medium as well as message.

—ELIZABETH TONKIN,
NARRATING OUR PASTS (1992:112)

INTRODUCTION: SOCIAL CIRCLES

* * *

The eye for physical geography seeks shifting patterns in physical landscapes, such as the places where hills rise and fall, where water drains
and flows, and where there are trees or grasses or wildlife. The eye for
social geography seeks clusters of people engaged in some shared activity, such as working together, living or sleeping together; distributing
resources; passing knowledge down or over; evoking transcendent
worlds. The shape of the social circles that form and reform creates a
telling landscape. In this chapter, I map social space with this in mind:
that "social identification and organization"—as they "tend to fixity"
(Tonkin 1992:110–111)—set the foundation for social memory. The categories that emerge in this chapter will serve as reference points throughout this work.

Before proceeding, there are three Russian terms that must be introduced. Together, they lie at the heart of modern Russian social organization, and will be of tremendous importance in the entire analysis of social memory that follows. The first is the term *svoi* (f. *svoia*, n. *svoe*) translated most directly as "one's own." Being *svoi* can mean being a member of one's immediate or extended family, a co-villager, a dear friend, a compatriot. The term *svoi* is a marker for belonging of a wide range of types. Throughout this work, I will refer to categories of belonging with all their range of sizes, shapes, and qualities, as "*svoi*-formations."

The second term, *chuzhoi* (f. *chuzhaia*), is the opposite of *svoi*. It refers to being a stranger—one who is a foreigner or outsider. It can be a person from another family or village or region or country. That which is chuzhoi is, most fundamentally, "someone else's," and the dangers associated with that which is chuzhoi will be treated at some length in the course of this book. Finally, *rodnoi* (f. *rodnaia*) is akin to *svoi* in its evocative range. The definition for rodnoi is first "own," and then "native; home; intimate; familiar." The root of rodnoi is the very productive term *rod*, or family line, which ranges in meaning from "family, kin, clan, birth, origin, stock, generation, genus, sort, kind." There is a relationship between the sense of being rodnoi, and that of coming from the same *rodina*, or motherland, or being from the same *narod*, or people. But the term is far from being simply descriptive of affiliation; it has a profound set of emotions associated with it. A person who is rodnoi can feel as close as one's flesh and blood, and there is perhaps no dearer term for a beloved than *moi rodnoi*. It is a word with earth and soil in it, as well as ancestral rootedness.

Each of these terms is broadly generative. Each comes with a set of feelings and associations. Each—with its particular pastiche of trust and belonging—expands and contracts according to the social context in which it is realized.

SOLOVYOVO'S SENSE OF *SVOI*

* * *

Residence in the *Dvor*

In Solovyovo, entering the home of a villager requires passing over several thresholds. One walks through the gate of the fence that encloses the tangled garden; through the front door that encloses the porch where tools, pails of water, just-picked mushrooms and berries and milk to be sold are stored; beyond the porch door which leads to the living space of animals and people—which is barred at night to keep out drunks and wolves; and finally one arrives at the door to the living quarters, the most important threshold that requires subtle rituals of protection. One knocks and calls out, "Anna Ivana! I have come to see you! May I enter?" The door opens to the figure of Anna Ivanovna (or Fedor Sergeevich or Larisa Andreevna), and beyond the figure is, perhaps, an entryway; a large brick stove, painted white; a large room; a table and some chairs; a couple of beds (partitioned away from strangers' eyes); an icon in the far corner, and—almost always—sepia-toned photographs of the long loved and the long dead.

In pre-Revolutionary, and then Soviet times, village households (*dvory*) like the ones in Solovyovo were inhabited by extended families, where a patriarchal family head (*khoziain*), his wife (*khoziaika*), his children (*deti*), and as time went by, his sons' wives and their children, all lived together under one roof.[1] When these extended families became too large and unwieldy through the natural process of reproduction, the residential group would split. At that time, a son would establish a new home for himself and his wife and children, usually in the same village. I heard such scenes described in the memories of Solovyovo's villagers, where one man told how his grandfather had cut a loaf of bread in two, "*Raz, popolam!* With one stroke, in half!" symbolizing the breaking of that household and the redistribution of its wealth and property.[2] While I lived in Solovyovo, several of the dvory had been inhabited by the same family line for generations.

In the lifetime of the current villagers of Solovyovo, marriage customs included a preference for, if not an absolute practice of, intervillage exogamy and patrilocality, where brides would tend to marry a man from another village (most often, not from the nearest villages but from those several kilometers away) and go and live with his family. In Solovyovo, I was told that the "best" villages to get wives from were ones like Filipovskaia and Ergovsk, both more than ten kilometers away. Although there were occasionally marriages between co-villagers, such unions were

1. Collectivization, in the minds of Soviet ideologues, should have "destroyed" the village *dvor*, making it secondary to a kolkhoz affiliation. When this did not occur, a 1935 Kolkhoz Charter "identified the household as the unit of entitlement in its provisions on the private plot and in the keeping of domestic animals" (Fitzpatrick 1994:112).
2. For a description of a similar rite as it was practiced in late Tsarist Russia, see Semyonova Tian-Shanskaia (1993:127–129).

considered less than ideal: first, it was "uncomfortable" for a young man to live in the same village with his in-laws, and second, it was suggested that a village is "like a family," and marrying co-villagers was therefore somewhat akin to incest. Increasingly throughout the twentieth century, there was a migration of young people out of smaller villages like Solovyovo and into larger villages, towns, and cities.[3] While I lived in Solovyovo, there were no young families residing there year-round (although neighboring villages did have young families living within them). Most households were comprised of a couple, or a widow or widower. All villagers kept gardens; depending on age and strength, some kept livestock.

In spite of this overall tendency for out migration, households regularly filled up in the summertime with temporary householders. Solovyovo's population was roughly thirty people during the winters that I lived there. In the summer of 1995, my khoziaika, Iuliia, and I counted 180 people who spent more than a couple of weeks there. Sons and daughters come along with their own children, as well as the sisters, brothers, aunts, uncles, nieces, and nephews of the khoziain and khoziaika. The household is fluid in these summer months, and although it is filled with mostly extended family members (of both the male and female lines), friends can come and stay as well. Anyone who resides under the roof for a period of more than a few days becomes a de facto member of the residential group.

Living together in a home carries with it, even for temporary householders, a requirement for participating in household labor and sharing resources; guests would arrive with goods to share (bread, tea, cheese, salami, sweets, cans of meat or fish, etc.) and ready to work. *Khoziaistvo*, or all of the tasks required to maintain a household, is also shared by all members of the residential group. Female householders would help with cooking, cleaning, fire tending, water hauling, cow herding, wood preparation, wood transportation, hay transportation, hay harvesting, potato planting, and potato reaping. Women were also expected to tend the animals (herding, milking, cleaning, helping with calving, shearing), and preparing food. Men would plow, cut down trees, heat the pechka (large Russian stove), hunt, make repairs of tools in the house or yard, and take care of the horses. They would build homes and bathhouses. Both men and women would garden, and gather mushrooms, berries, and healing

---

3. See Wegren (1995) for an overview of rural out migration in Russia.

herbs in the fields and forest. Out on the lake or on the shore of a stream, nearly everyone (but especially men and boys) would fish. In turns, families would pasture cows and sheep, bringing a book or some music to pass the time of day.[4]

Fulfilling these tasks is not only a pragmatic issue, but also a moral one. The khoziain and khoziaika bear the brunt of the moral responsibility to keep the khoziaistvo running smoothly. When obligations are not fulfilled, it is they who must answer to the dead ancestors, who can show their displeasure in a range of ways. Along with this heightened responsibility, the khoziain and khoziaika have more power than other householders when decision-making is necessary. Such decision-making includes both the small, daily decisions of how to maximize the available labor force to do all the many tasks at hand (given constantly varying weather conditions), and larger decisions such as those concerning slaughtering animals, going on trips, or making large purchases.

It is popularly understood that the khoziain has the last word in any decision, but in my village experience that was not always the case. Consultation is a crucial part of agricultural production of the kind practiced in the Russian north, and input from several sources is expected. Mikhail Alekseevich, the khoziain of the household where I lived, had more say than others (and more often than not, the last word), but no absolute say. Under normal circumstances, there was plenty of room for female voices and power. In fact, all householders—even friends who were staying for short periods—were allowed a certain weight to their opinions, even as they were expected to share in labor. This is a significant point: the household has a leader or leaders, but it also has many more-or-less equal voices. Decisions are made through group discussion and negotiation. Being a householder means landing in a social domain in which resources, work, and decision-making are shared.

There is one important residue of patrilocal patterns of residence: most of the female villagers in Solovyovo come from someplace else, and spoke to me many times of the difficult passage from their home village to a village of strangers. For them, if not for many of their daughters, patrilocality was a sometimes harsh reality. Arriving in her new home, a young bride was at the bottom rung of power in the residential group. She was

---

4. This practice no longer existed as of 2002. Several families have given up their cows in recent years, and the cows can pasture in fields next to the village (and do not require a herder).

given tasks of particular difficulty, to such a degree that it is sometimes not clear whether she is marrying a man or his residential group, joining it merely to become a new laborer there.[5] Even though patrilocality is not practiced today as commonly as it was in the recent past, conflict between mothers-in-law and new brides is quite common. In all my time in the village, I only once heard a woman make spontaneously warm comments about her mother-in-law. The feeling was mutual. Mothers-in-law would typically see their daughters-in-law as lazy, citing examples where their sons were required to do women's work. Often, they would intercede on the side of their sons when difficulties arose between son and daughter-in-law. Correspondingly, the son would typically offer no protection to his bride against the judgment or wrath of his mother; the bride's time in her new home could be a lonely one, indeed.

I was told that "good parents" would investigate the family into which their children wished to marry. As Anna Grigorievna explained, it was important to know not only the character of the young person, but also that of his or her "tribe."

> *Anna Grigorievna:* Before, it was such that they wouldn't let rich young men marry a poor girl. The bride needed to be rich. They avoided taking a far-away girl because you need to know all of her relatives. Her grandmothers, great-grandmothers, great-grandfathers, from which tribe/race/family the girl comes. If she was beautiful or ugly, [you need to know from which tribe]. If it's a good one, the girl will be good. . . . They considered if they were busy, hard working, if the family was a working one, not lazy.

The bride, in other words, does not simply marry a man, but does in fact, join with his residential group, where she is beholden to its requirements of work, sharing, and decision making. Arriving chuzhaia, she slowly comes to be considered svoia. If she is lucky, a feeling of warmth develops. Bearing children helps the situation for her, and failing to do so right away will elicit questions from the community. The children take the father's last name, and receive his patronymic. They are linked, in this way, to his family line.

---

5. This is evidenced in the comment of one man who told me of his decision to marry. One day his mother said to him, "Zhenis'. Nado pomoshchnitsu. (Get married. I need a helper)."

In general, it can be said that the household is a primary—although not singular—agricultural, economic, and social unit in post-Soviet Solovyovo, as is the case with post-Soviet rural Russia in general (Gambold Miller and Heady 2004). This is an interesting matter. In 1925, Chaianov published a detailed analysis of the economics of farming in rural Russia, in which he concluded that it was the family farm—dependent fully on the labor of family members for its survival—that was the most important economic unit in the village. Chaianov strongly opposed the ideas behind Soviet collectivization, and in 1939 was executed for his departure from the Party line. Collectivization eventually succeeded, but the tiny private plots eventually granted by the state to families were far more productive than the kolkhoz plots (Medvedev 1987:363–364).[6] The *dvor,* and the social circle that coincides with its outlines, has continued to be a crucial center of life-sustaining activities in the village, in spite of policies of collectivization in the 1930s, which sought to entirely wrest the economy into the hands of the collective farm.[7]

Who lives with whom (and, as a consequence, who works with whom, decides with whom, cooks and eats and trades labor with whom) is, in part, still patterned by the habits of patrilocal residence, where the dvor has tended to be defined around a man's biological family, and not a woman's. Most of the female villagers in Solovyovo come from ("are taken from") someplace else, and spoke many times of the difficult passage from their home village to a village of strangers.[8]

6. In 1987, Medvedev wrote: "In fact, private agriculture occupies only 1.6% of the arable land. Nonetheless, in the 1980s, it produces more meat, milk, and eggs annually than the total amount of these products produced by all sectors (1933–1939). Moreover it does this without any mechanization and virtually without horses." Overall, he demonstrated that "1.6 percent of the arable land in the Soviet Union produces around 30% of the national agricultural product in the Soviet Union" (1987:363–364). Contemporary studies reach a similar broad conclusion for the post-Soviet world. See Gambold Miller and Heady (2004) and Patsiorkovskii (2002).

7. See Gessat-Anstett (2001:136) for a demonstration of how, in contemporary rural Russia in the region of Yaroslavl, "kin-based forms of organization . . . have, throughout the 20th century, preserved their complexity."

8. In Russian, the verb that denotes a woman's marriage is *vyidti zamuzh,* or, literally, "to leave for a husband." In the tradition inscribed in that phrase, a woman's marriage means leaving the home where she was *svoia* and becoming *chuzhaia.*

The Family Line or *Rod*

Defined as the "generational line emanating from one ancestor" (Chernykh 1993:118–119) the rod, or family line, provides a model for group belonging that goes beyond the world of the living and into the realm of the dead ancestors. It is a powerful symbolic landmark in Solovyovo. The root term rod- generates several potent terms: there is rodnoi (blood kin), rodina (motherland), *priroda* (nature), *rodit'* (to give birth), *roditel'* (parent), *rodstvenniki* (relatives), and *narod* (people). A household contains part of a rod; a marriage continues the line of the rod.

The term rod, as it was used in Solovyovo in its various forms, carries with it a sense of deep and ancient belonging. The ancestors included in the rod are invoked for help both as individuals, and collectively in yearly rituals intended to bring fertility to the land. They also provide guardianship of individual households and have powers of intercession in the human world.

Names (both last names and patronymics) pass through male lines: Iuliia Ivanovna Belova is "Iuliia, daughter of Ivan, wife in the family of Belov"; her husband, Mikhail Alekseevich Belov, is "Mikhail, son of Aleksei, son in the family of Belov." Property passes down through both paternal and maternal lines. There is a tendency to associate the passing of land and houses with the male side of the family, but this is certainly not a hard rule. Religious icons and knowledge of magic tend to be handed from mother to daughter, but are also passed from father to daughter or son. I did notice a tendency for the children of daughters to come to the village for summers more often than the children of sons. And I also noticed that a sense of ownership of the household seemed to cluster around the brothers and sisters from the father's side (as opposed to the mother's side). All together, it was clear that there were no hard and fast rules with regard to descent along male and female lines.[9]

9. There are arguments to the effect that ancient Russian belief systems, including the "religion of the rod" were part of broader matrifocal tendencies, in which females and the female line held crucial administrative powers in social and religious life (Hubbs 1988:81). In this view, patrilinearity and patrifocality came about only after the church and state made considerable efforts to wrest religious power from the hands of women (Hubbs 1988:91). In pre-Revolutionary Russia, houses, garden plots (Watters 1968:143) and family property (such as livestock) were generally passed through the male line (Semyonova Tian-Shanskaia 1993:124, 126). Whether or not women were the focus of pre-Christian religious life, descent clearly occurred along both male and female lines in pre-Revolutionary Russia.

The question of descent regarding agricultural land ownership has been (and continues to be) an extremely complex matter in rural Russian society.[10] In Soviet Russia, land was not legally "owned," but private plots were granted to the families of kolkhoz and sovkhoz workers— plots that were, for all intent and purposes, passed on to subsequent generations. In the 1990s, the legalities of land ownership were in chaos due to the process of privatization and residues of the Soviet kolkhoz system. What appears to be clear is that the relative power of the male or female lines is secondary to the overall sense of belonging to the line of a given residential group. A house is a place. That place has its own line of history, its own line of ancestors who have been invoked within its walls, year after year. It is rooted in a location, and property appears to descend along that line of rootedness. Because residence has tended to be patrilocal, the land has tended to pass through the male line. But the subordination (or, at least, confrontation) of the human line to territorial space is of marked importance.

Extended Family Members (*Rodstvenniki*)

In terms of social groups in village Russia, it is worth making a distinction between more or less permanent members of a household and the extended family. The extended family members, or *rodstvenniki,* include family members from both the maternal and paternal side (and their spouses). Not all rodstvenniki are permanent members of a residential group. In terms of village social life, rodstvenniki become particularly important in the summer months, when even rather distant kin come to the village, stay for a while (becoming temporary householders), share in the large summer jobs, and leave. Important here is the fact that their work in the village allows them to receive the fruits of the harvest, and sometimes even parts of slaughtered animals. They receive goods, in other words, not as members of a household, but as members of a work group. Strictly speaking, this is not understood to be payment. It is simply fitting that kin members help with these large tasks, and fitting that goods are received from the farm labor. Interestingly, it is not necessarily the workers themselves who will be given a portion of the harvest. If a niece or nephew is sent from a nearby town to help on summer farm

---

10. An impressively complex portrait from the nineteenth century is Robinson's *Rural Russia under the Old Regime* (1969).

work, potatoes (for example) will be later sent to their parents as well as to them. The niece and nephew appear to represent their branch of the family. The extended family as a whole helps, and the extended family as a whole receives.[11]

Part of this is due to the fact that not every brother and sister of a given household will live in that household upon the death of the parents. They do, however, seem to feel that it is, in part, their own domain.

Certain tasks are more likely to require the assistance of extended family members. Specifically, help is given with the potato planting in the early spring, the *senokos* or hay harvest in the summer, the potato harvest in the early fall, and the wood preparation in the late fall. At these times, relatives will come from distant towns and cities and converge on the village for weeks. At that time they become temporary householders, and share in all the tasks outlined above. Their participation in the arduous tasks mentioned here gives them certain implicit rights to portions of the harvest.

Social organization in the Solovyovo clusters around the circles of the household, the family line and the extended family. But there are other groups—other social circles—that arch beyond the boundaries of the dvor and the extended family. The problem of Russian "collectivity," as a symbolic landmark and as a marker for a type of social circle, is one that has occupied the attention of generations of scholars.

Obshchina: That Which Is Common

It has been argued that the type of agriculture known in rural Russia is a direct, historical result of the poverty of Russian land (Pipes 1974:16). A system of village-wide interdependence appeared in ancient Russia, where groups formed that extended beyond the residential group and the extended family. Villagers learned to rely on each other as a matter of "practical necessity" (Billington 1970:19).

But the matter of communal action and identification (or not) in the harsh backdrop of the ancient Russian village has, for many reasons and in many different ways, been drawn into theological and nationalistic debates on the nature of the Russian collective, the Russian "people," and, even, the "mysterious Russian soul."[12] Aptly called by one author an "in-

---

11. See Gambold Miller and Heady (2004) for a discussion of mutual aid practices within three contemporary Russian villages. See sociologist Dershem (2002) for a discussion of support networks and their contribution to the sense of "satisfaction" for rural Russians.
12. For a rich ethnography of the symbolism of the Russian soul, see Pesmen (2000).

tellectual shibboleth" (Watters in Vucinich 1968:133), the sacralization of the Russian "collective" can be traced to the romance of nineteenth-century nationalism (with religious and secular roots) on the one hand, and Soviet revolutionary ideology, on the other.[13] This has made the business of clarifying social groups in the village context a complex, and, sometimes, murky affair. The shibboleth of the collective—as important as it was in defining Russian Revolutionary history (and as central as it is in Russian nationalist discourse to the present day)—is not my central concern here. When speaking of social organization in Solovyovo, it is necessary to distinguish actual social *groups* from actual *symbolic representations,* which resonate around the sense of the group, whether derived from the Russian intelligentsia or Soviet ideologues, or whether alive in the symbolic landscape of the village.

It is fair to say that if a certain degree of communal identification and action arose for reasons of poor land and a short growing season in ancient Russia, it was reinforced through the relationship that developed historically between the state, landowners, and agricultural laborers. The pre-Revolutionary institution of the village *obshchina* provided a practical bridge between these very different sorts of Russians. The obshchina, as journalist and ethnographer Lev Timofeev describes, "was a social institution which arose with the state's active support and functioned as a fiscal entity whose members were collectively responsible for the taxes levied against the obshchina as a whole" (Pisato and Zaslavsky in Timofeev 1985:6–7). It had other powers as well: in the obshchina, land was redistributed to villagers once a generation, according to family size,[14] and with respect to the relative quality of soil on given plots. This served to lend a community-based "fairness" to plot size; pragmatically, it gave large families the amount of land they needed to generate surplus for taxes. The obshchina also controlled the movement of villagers, often limiting emigration from villages in order to maximize local production. Furthermore, legal disputes were solved by the obshchina without reference to outside courts. Through the institution of the order-keeping obshchina, a special legal relationship was formed—one that made it easy

---

13. See, for example, Soloviev (1959) and Fedotov (1946, 1966), and for discussion, Etkind (2003) and Frierson (1993).

14. Family size was measured by the number of males in the family (known as *edaki,* or "eaters"), who were considered to be the significant laborers in a family. A Soviet reform to the distributional system was to count women as well as edaki.

for landowners and rulers to avoid face-to-face dealings with individual villagers. Through it, the centralized state and the landlord could treat the village community as a surplus-producing black box.

The word "obshchina" comes from the root, *obshch-*, one that is used to form words for all kinds of social intercourse (*obshchenie*/intercourse, relations; *obshchat'sia*/to associate with; *obshchestvo*/society, *obshchii*/ common). Obshchina rings with basic human interactions—the kinds of interactions that are understood to be at the heart of an ideal society. Because of this, even though the institution of the obshchina no longer exists, the symbolic landmark surrounding "that which is common" continues to be powerfully resonant.

In a sociospatial sense, the institution of the obshchina, in both word and action, traced a social circle where people were bound by a common responsibility to the landlord and to the state. Land, in the logic of the obshchina, is linked to a given family (a given *rod*) only for a generation. If a household "belongs" to a family, land "belongs" to the village over a span of time. The symbolic landmark of the obshchina bound the village social circle to a specific, common territory. It bound the disparate voices of villagers into a single voice when faced with dealings with the outsider-state.

Following from its institutional function, the obshchina grew to be, and to a certain extent has remained, broadly meaningful both within and without the village. The legal, political, and social isolation of the village caused city dwellers, rulers, and the intelligentsia to fill the symbol of the "peasant" and his obshchina with a plethora of imaginary qualities: some cheerily romantic, others soberly religious, and still others inspired by the fear and loathing of a distant other.[15] Because of this distance (whether made of romance or disdain), and because of the peculiar way that the idea of "peasantry" was circumscribed and made impenetrable by idea and by action, the obshchina became more and more fixed and opaque both in the conception of the state and in that of the rural community itself.

In terms of social organization, the obshchina was a fascinating institution. Given the fact that the suprafamilial obshchina was charged with

15. See Conquest (1986:20) for some of the more colorful language used by the Revolutionary elite to describe rural Russians—notably Khrushchev citing Stalin as having referred to them as "scum." For the romance of the Russian village, see Frierson (1993), Fanger (1968), Figes (1997:84–89), and Merridale (2000:29–32).

the redistribution of land, the concept of land ownership in the village resonated with both a sense of transience, in relation to the rod, and permanence, in relation to the village. The village layout echoes this: houses are clustered together, and outside the residential part of the village, individual plots are clustered together. When people work on their land, they work in close proximity—they can holler and joke with each other. If most labor was (and is) family based, the powers of decision making over the land as a whole was obshchina based.

Kolkhoz and Obshchina

After collectivization, the kolkhoz replaced the obshchina as a central village institution, and created a new suprafamilial group, one that pulled labor out of family-based groups and into local work brigades run by brigadiers and not village elders. A kolkhoz could be as small as a village or as large as an entire region. The larger kolkhozy were made of several brigades and centrally controlled. The will of the party was inserted in this system, as agrarian-workers were beholden to the (often wildly unrealistic) production quotas (Medvedev 1987). Historians have written about the fundamental difference between the obshchina collectivity and that of the kolkhoz: where the obshchina organization granted the family controls over production, the kolkhoz had little place for familial autonomy (Pipes 1974). Given that the obshchina-based organization had only cursory resemblance to the kolkhoz, Russian villagers of this century consistently failed to feel that the kolkhoz was "theirs" (Fitzpatrick 1994:14).

And yet, whether or not historians tell us that the obshchina and the kolkhoz had little in common as institutions, they are, in certain contexts, discursively interchangeable, as when Iuliia explained to me the meaning of obshchina: "In every village there was a kolkhoz. That's an obshchina. About forty houses. Sometimes villages." Not every villager would so freely trade the term obshchina for kolkhoz. On the other hand, a certain set of qualities could be said to animate the notion of the collective, whether referred to as obshchina, kollektiv or even sometimes kolkhoz. The symbolism of the kollektiv, writ large, will be returned to many times in the course of this work. The term has several crucial layers that add sense and resonance to the idea of group belonging. Cursorily, they are:

The kollektiv is linked to happiness and ideal social life.

The kollektiv implies interdependability.

The kollektiv is linked to a given territory.

The kollektiv, when formed, channels otherworldly powers.

For now, the most important general point about these symbolic resonances around the kollektiv is this: socially defined circles in the village exist that are reproduced in word and action. An obshchina is an institution, as is a kolkhoz; the symbolic landmark of collectivity has a separate (if overlapping) life. To the intelligentsia of several generations in Russia it has carried the weight of the idea of the Russian character. In the village, it carries a different load—one linked to special configurations of social and magical powers. In the next chapter, I explore in some depth the layers of resonance of "that which is common."

The Village Bounds

If the village once coincided with the institution of the obshchina—where the two overlapped neatly as social circles—it no longer did in the 1990s. Long ago, land stopped being redistributed by a council of elders, taxes stopped being levied or paid by a group, and village elders stopped having the right to control movements of villagers (even if the Soviet internal passport system took over that job, making it virtually impossible for most villagers to move to cities). The village also fails to delimit a kolkhoz; even brigades are much larger than a village territory. Does the village of Solovyovo exist at all in a social sense?

Certainly, a village is an important conceptual category. One's *dom rodnoi* (native home) is in a village, and deep attachments are made to the place of one's birth. When speaking of their native villages (*rodiny*), descriptions would ring with nostalgia. The village is where one's people (svoi) live, where one uses the familiar second person (ty) with everyone, and the region where one's dead are buried.

Villagers share some property, such as the horses that were inherited from the kolkhoz in the early 1990s. They also divvy up the small strips of land on the outskirts of the village—ones that had been too poor for the kolkhoz—for purposes of hay harvesting. Some work is shared at the village level, although rarely. In Solovyovo, there was one clear case where the village delimited a work group: at the time of the potato planting, villagers all help each other, in addition to the help given to them by their extended families. This was explained by the need to use the communally owned horses with maximum efficiency. Other than that, shared work involves families taking turns at given tasks. Pasturing was one such shared task, as was care of the horses (where families each give a portion of their hay and each are charged with a rotating turn feeding the animals and cleaning the barn). Modern habits of mutual aid among villagers are more or less in keeping with nineteenth-century habits, in the sense that the community members aided one another as household units.[16] As well, in Solovyovo as in other villages studied in recent years, mutual aid is still part of a "moral relationship" that villagers maintain with each other (Gambold Miller and Heady 2004:267–268).

During the Soviet period, the Party (and the kolkhoz) gave villages a means of parlaying their needs and grievances to the state through locally elected deputies. In the 1990s, there was an administrative leader elected for a nine-village region. When troubles arose, she would be contacted and results were often slow to manifest. In addition, villages chose a *starosta* (from the traditional term for elder, although without the age connotation today). In theory, this starosta should speak for the village when there are problems (such as flooded roads or downed power lines), but while I lived in Solovyovo, it was Mikhail Alekseevich who was chosen for this job and he was tired of that kind of public service (he had been a deputy in the local Soviet for many years and had recently grown quite busy with his healing practice). No one arose in his stead.

If there is only a very limited political body in the village, it has already been suggested that decision-making is sometimes done collectively, particularly regarding planting. Collective decision-making appeared to be a habit, even without institutions (like the obshchina or the kolkhoz) to support it. Villagers discussed the rains, the soil, the frost, and simply decide. "Working together," I was told, "is better."

The village per se also periodically delimited a unit of religious ritual. In funeral rites, a procession comprised of the casket, a cross, and lines of family members and mourners is led to the edge of the village. There, villagers do not pass the threshold of the village, but turn facing the village and throw a lump of dirt over their shoulder, and the person charged with carrying excess materials from building the coffin is charged with burning them at the village threshold. Although less frequent today, village pasturelands used to be delimited in early May with a ritual *obkhod*

---

16. See Gromyko (1986) as summarized in Howe (1991) for the systems of "collective aid" in nineteenth-century Russia.

(circumambulation), designed to protect cows within that territory from beasts and otherworldly forces.

Larger than the village, another suprafamilial group is the *prikhod,* or parish. The prikhod is a unit of social organization that still exists in the village conceptual world despite the post-Revolutionary destruction of churches. Associated with a given church, a prikhod typically encompasses a few villages. In the pre-Revolutionary era, Solovyovo's prikhod included Solovyovo, Version, and Maksimovo. Villagers from the same prikhod would attend the same church and be buried at the same graveyard. The prikhod appears to be linked to the practice of exogamy: one not only looks for brides outside a village, but outside of the parish. Seasonal holidays are assigned to *prikhody* (*prikhodskie dni,* "parish festivals"), where the prikhod makes for one form of local svoi.

Solovyovo's legal, political, economic, and social categories were in a state of fluidity in the 1990s. Nevertheless, a certain amount of continuity could be found in the broad conceptual strokes of social organization outlined above. If the village, the obshchina, and the prikhod are only cursorily linked to institutions, the sense of forming communities at various levels appears to be fixed in the memory, according to certain regular patterns. Among those patterns are the fundamental patterns of the giving and taking of vital substances of self, otherwise known as exchange.

BASIC ECONOMIC ORGANIZATION

* * *

On "All Things Being Equal"

What does one own in a village? And what does owning—and sharing—have to do with what it means to be, or not to be, "one's own"?

In their gardens, villagers in Solovyovo produce potatoes, cabbage, carrots, tomatoes, cucumbers, onions, garlic, beets, lettuce, sorrel, squash, peas, beans, berries, apples, herbs, and flowers with healing properties, among other plants. Most have built the roof over their head and the bathhouse where they clean and heal themselves. They keep bees for honey. They produce their own alcohol. People in good health keep cows, sheep, sometimes goats, sometimes pigs, chickens, and roosters. Solovyovo is on a lake (which—by the bucketful—provides all the water they drink and bathe with), and in that lake are abundant fish: bream, ruff, perch, and the highly prized pike. In the forest, there is game, including wild boar, elk, and wild birds, as well as perhaps a dozen sorts of berries and twice as many edible mushrooms. The forest offers wood for building, crafting tools, and heating. Sheep provide wool for spinning. The open fields grow grasses spotted with clover, which are cut and fed to animals.

The list of what must be bought or otherwise obtained in Solovyovo is shorter, but not insignificant. The farms and forests do not provide sugar. Nor are grains such as wheat (or the staple *kashas*) produced any longer. *Kombikorm,* a popular animal feed, must be bought. Gas and electricity must be paid for (although most heating is done with wood, which costs a small amount to cut down), as must certain hunting permits and taxes. Clothes must be bought, even if village women still spin wool in the traditional way. Radios, televisions, VCRs, and cars are the kinds of things that villagers want that only money can buy. Villagers also buy city-made furniture, as well, although they make and repair many of their own tools.

In between that which one labors directly for and that which must be bought, there is a large gap made up of all the things that individual households need, that they cannot or will not pay for. Old women living alone need their stoves lit for them. Some men are stronger and better at plowing than others, or are particularly good at slaughtering animals. Others have lots of time to fish. There are those who know the arts of healing, either through foods or through sorcery. There are women who keep cows and have milk, and others have none. There are times when a bathhouse needs repairs and other villagers can offer theirs. There is knowledge of gardening or the places for the best berries and mushrooms that is guarded like any form of capital. In cases like these, there is exchange.

Exchange comes in several forms. Some are formal, if not always monetarized. Goods and services can be offered in exchange for goods and services. For example, milk can be exchanged for specialty vegetables; a nephew who catches fish for his elderly aunt can be given food and shelter; in return for making healing potions, one villager receives produce, fish, or goods such as tea, chocolate, or beer; for plowing or slaughtering a cow, a villager can receive meat or vodka, which is used much as a currency (Hivon 1998), and which can pay for services such as grave digging and woodcutting.

Money, when it appears, comes from salaries for the younger villagers, and pensions that range in size depending upon the work that a person did during her life: culture workers get the least, *kolkhozniki* get more, and kolkhozniki who were war veterans of some kind get the most.

Money also comes from selling goods and handicrafts, usually in Belozersk or other villages. There is one very hard-working woman in Vershina who has two milking cows, and who gets on a bus once or twice a week to sell her milk and cheese in Belozersk, mostly through word of mouth. She rides the bus for free as a retiree, and in this way can make a little extra money for herself and her children. She is the only one in the three-village range of Solovyovo, Vershina, and Maksimovo who manages to do this, because of the huge time consumption that marketing in this fashion requires. There are young men who work in construction on the side, and sometimes they cut wood for pay.

Money is useful, of course, but can be an especially uncomfortable form of capital, particularly in certain contexts. There are two apparent reasons for this. First, the symbolism of "money" inherited a great deal of negative resonance during the Soviet period. Within the ideology of socialism, the lust for money (and endeavors to generate it, disdainfully called *spekulatsia* or speculation, even today) was seen as one of the special sins of the capitalist enemy. Dollars, the most stable form of world currency available to Russians after the fall of the USSR, inherited the mother lode of negative associations. Owning dollars made one a criminal in Soviet times, a *spekulant*, or speculator, and dollars still bear this underworld association.

The second reason for the negative charge attached to money is a deeper one that has to do with certain fundamental principles of exchange. Money is used in exchanges where debts are precisely calculated, and promptly erased. Money is comfortable where debt and the social connections it implies are uncomfortable. Within the context of the village, there are intricate webs of social connection: villagers are svoimi (one's own) to each other. Money (with its exacting ability to quantify debt and erase social connection) becomes problematic there, for reasons that will be clearer below. The principle can be briefly noted as follows: Money is particularly appropriate to exchange with if there is a great social distance between the traders; the closer the relationship between people, the more uncomfortable and socially inappropriate the use of money becomes.[17] Exchange of goods and services is something that is

---

17. Without contradicting this principle, money can be given, for example, from parents to children. Here, money is one gift among many gifts, and is not exchanged for labor or other goods. For a discussion of the ways in which rural pensioners give cash to children, see Buckley (2000).

done with categories of svoi ("one's own" people). Money is more appropriate to dealings with chuzhie (outsiders). Along with chuzhie, it carries associations of strangeness and danger.

In light of this principle, there was reluctance in the village to formalize economic exchange with money. When villagers occasionally sold each other milk or potatoes, they were at great pains to name prices. On the other hand, it was—in terms of one's reputation and status in the village—absolutely essential to reimburse people for their services. One day, a neighbor came to the house of Iuliia and Mikhail Alekseevich to slaughter a lamb.

> *Iuliia Ivanovna:* What will you take? Money, alcohol, or meat?
>
> *Zh—:* I don't need anything.

Zh— said that he needed nothing, but it was clear to all involved that they must pay him somehow for his service. Iuliia explained that she finally decided on a bottle of vodka and a kilogram of meat. Later I asked about Zh—'s statement that he needed nothing for his work, in light of his finally accepting meat and vodka.

> *Q:* So, when a person says, "I need nothing" [*nichego ne nado*], it's not true? Is it true when *you* say it to people who come for potions?
>
> *Mikhail Alekseevich:* Yes, all I need is the cost of the bottle.
>
> *Q:* How much is that?
>
> *Mikhail Alekseevich:* Around 500 rubles.
>
> *Iuliia Ivanovna:* And the bottle cap.
>
> *Mikhail Alekseevich:* And the bottle cap, around 250 rubles. [Pause.] But it is not for me to ask.

I saw in Solovyovo that exchange was certainly kept close track of. An outsider to the village would see countless examples of generosity. For instance, one villager has an abundance of fresh onions or berries and brings them by when she visits a neighbor. The host offers her tea and perhaps a shot of vodka or two. The next week, she may send *tvorog* (homemade cheese) to the neighbor. When produce was sold in the village, it was sold at rock-bottom prices (there even appears to be a certain pride in selling for the lowest possible price). When giving each other milk, the milk would literally overflow the jars into which it was poured. Tea was nearly always offered any guest who walks in the door. A guest coming with a gift was sent home with one worth twice the value. Giving looked, from this distance, like an outpouring.

Offerings were not always accepted. There were certain implications to accepting or rejecting the hospitality of various kinds offered. If I am invited for tea, acceptance means establishing (or reinforcing) a social link of some kind, which is often a good thing. On the other hand, some invitations were only formalities, and it was inappropriate to accept them. One family invited my hosts to tea constantly, but the invitations were always refused. Months of asking finally granted me an answer. The invitation was *radi prilichiia* (for the sake of politeness), and must be refused because of a comment once by the husband of that family that "the Belovs come for tea all the time." The implication that the Belovs had taken advantage of hospitality, leaving them in a position of debt, caused them to keep social distance from this second family. In head-to-head social confrontations, to "win" it is necessary to be the one who gives more. This could be called "one-downsmanship": spreading out one's surplus wins status in the community. That is, the "circle" of exchange groups appears to include this aspect of verticality. In short, vertical extremes (of wealth) are avoided in the village economic system in favor of relative social "evenness." Status is won by being an agent of redistribution (and not of individual accumulation).

As time went on, it became clear that accounts are indeed carefully kept, even without formalizing them through money: giving a basketful of green onions does not imply a return basket of potatoes, but it does create a debt which must be "paid" eventually. The debt is not one that is meant to be quantified and then erased, but one that will, in the future, continue to encourage interdependence on a local level. The green onions of today become labor on a potato field next year, which become help in extinguishing a bathhouse fire, on the next. The interdependence of villagers is fed and reinforced by such a system. As Mauss writes in his classic work, *The Gift* (1990[1950]:46),

> If one gives things and returns them, it is because one is giving and returning "respects"—we will say "courtesies." Yet it is also because by giving one is giving oneself, and if one gives oneself, it is because one "owes" oneself—one's person and one's goods—to others.

Exchange, most generally, is one of the mechanisms for summoning the "other" into the realm of the self. In rural Russia, the outpourings of one villager to the next are part of the procedure for making the subject a transindividual one. Becoming svoi, in large and small ways, is at the foundation of social organization in the Russian village.

There is a final general point with regard to exchange in this context. The unspoken rule that one should return more than what one has received is the hallmark of a broader system of exchange that, more deeply, tends to encourage economic homogeneity in the village community. The axioms of this system could be summarized as follows: *It is good to be generous with one's possessions; in terms of one's social status, it is crucial to meet generosity with equal or greater generosity.* In other words, a redistribution of wealth that gives rise to a rough equality between households is reified in an explicit morality of generosity. Howe (1991:17) writes about this logic behind practices of redistribution in pre-Revolutionary village life:

> It is assumed, usually correctly, that the individual can get ahead in a peasant community only at the expense of others, so that even "good luck" is suspect and a windfall may be given away to avoid envy. The peasant calculates his costs and benefits, but in a different currency from the small commodity producer.

It must not be assumed that villagers never wish to own beautiful things or receive more salary than their neighbor. The point is that such inequality of means can become a social liability. When generosity does not work to keep things more or less equal, there are other mechanisms that encourage homogeneity. Tattling on each other for infractions of permit laws has been practiced (and resented for decades). The envy that arises from inequality is not, however, a mere social unpleasantness; it is a particularly generative part of the workings of unseen worlds and unpredictable forces. Envy awakens unseen forces (such as *sglaz,* the evil eye) that can cause all forms of ruin. Social unevenness, in other words, sets the dark forces in motion that can and will topple the haughty.

In short, in Solovyovo, exchange happens in several forms, many of which involve no money. The preferred system of exchange is an informal one, where accounts are kept, but where there is a principle of returning more than what one has received. In this system, villagers are connected by the dynamic of debts (potential exchange) that they owe one another.[18] Such exchange is seen as a positive feature of social life, and—in its ideal form—understood to be marked by the qualities of generosity and hospitality. When there is social distance between families, exchange is avoided, and/or made formal. When outsiders (chuzhie) come into the village, the social distance to them makes monetarized exchange more palatable. In other words, with svoi (other villagers, in particular, ones with whom there are positive relations), one trades informally and with an eye for the tilted reciprocity of outward giving. With chuzhie, one is more likely to exchange formally and with an eye for equality, although even chuzhie can find themselves the recipients of the habit of generosity.

Exchange has related metaphysical aspects. Acts of accumulation (with the corresponding social inequality that they produce) increase the danger that surrounds the accumulator. Acts of redistribution (generosity, or *shedrost'*) confer power of two kinds. First, they raise the social status of the giver; second, such acts have a magical function that allows one to counteract unpredictable forces in the world.

In this local model of exchange, groups of various kinds are formed in the village in which there is a dynamic equality between members. Those who are svoi work together, exchange with one another, make decisions together, and (depending on the group) share given resources. The preferred style of exchange encourages a fluid homogeneity of means in the village, such that when inequality of means exists, the habit of tilted reciprocity as well as the explicit ideal of "generosity" tend to flatten its extremes. The style of decision-making encourages many voices. Work always needs many hands.

ON UNEVENNESS: HIERARCHY IN SOLOVYOVO

* * *

Within this system that rewards one for gestures toward evenness equality, there is room for social verticality. Below are a few of the social roles that come with an attendant social stature.

The term "khoziain" (plural *khoziaeva*) is defined as "owner, proprietor; master, boss; landlord; host." It means so much more than any one

---

18. This can be compared to the practices of exchange during the Soviet period founded around the concept of *blat* (influence). As in the practices I describe in rural Russia, blat depends on the actualization of goods and services through the connections between people. See Ledeneva (1998) for an analysis of Russia's economy of favors.

of those terms.[19] If the household head is the khoziain, the term is also used for anyone in charge of a given group of people, or a given territory. When the term is brought to its ideal culmination, the khoziain is not only the leader; he is the figurehead and emblem of the group over which he has dominion. The khoziain is integrally related to a community of *svoi*. He has moral leadership, and duties of heavy-handed fatherly discipline. No less important, he is a channel for otherworldly powers, ones that can protect and heal the entire community over which he has dominion. The usage of the term "khoziain" falls into three subcategories:

1. The khoziain of a household has special powers of decision making. Also known as *batiushka* or bat'ka, a household is seen to be his, and that of his father before him. Ideally, he is in charge, along with the khoziaika, of the workings of the household. Any failures are on his shoulders as well.

2. The khoziain of a larger group such as a factory or a town or, at its ultimate limit, a nation, are like the khoziain of a house, in that they are the emblem of leadership there. Like the tsars before him, Stalin was considered the "khoziain" of the Soviet Union. Such *khoziaeva* are ideally strong leaders. They rule with a heavy hand, and bring about social order.

3. Supernatural khoziaeva of natural domains, such as the forest (*khoziain lesavoi* or *leshii*), house (*khoziain domovoi*), barn (*khoziain khleva*), or bathhouse (*khoziain bani*), are in charge of their respective realms and must be supplicated and appeased periodically. The domovoi must be invoked before moving into a new house; the khoziain lesavoi should be asked permission before entering the forest. When such precautions are not taken, these khoziaeva (like the others, when they are not properly deferred to) can lash out against those in his domain. They can be visible or invisible and their forms change.

The term khoziaika, the female counterpart to khoziain, has less overall symbolic impact. A khoziaika is also in charge of a given domain, usually a household, but (in the realm of the otherworldly) sometimes a for-

---

19. See *Tolkovyi slovar' zhivogo Russkogo Iazyka* (Dal' 1911) for a sense of the richness and history of the term.

est or field or barn. However, she usually does not carry the extra weight of national leadership in her symbolic range. The symbolism of womanhood has a great deal of power, but the female khoziaika does not carry the ferociousness of her male counterpart.

The emblem of leadership from within (or perhaps, "above") a svoi-formation is the focus of a great deal of emotional and symbolic attention in Solovyovo. Such figures are not resented for their power. On the contrary, the khoziain, in its many forms, appears as a positive role (even if a given khoziain, such as Stalin, is hated or feared in given instances). For example, the role of the *barin* or feudal landlord is generally a positive one in the stories of villagers. Serfdom was abolished in Russia in 1861, but the sense that a powerful khoziain-like figure held dominion over a portion of land continued into this century and is alive in the narratives of several villagers. Relationships to a given landlord appear to have varied depending on the people involved. Solovyovo remembers the Polish family who had been landowners in the region: relations with the former barin were good enough (he would hire people for wage labor, and the work was well appreciated), but his wife was disliked for her nitpicking about use of the forestlands. She was murdered after the Revolution by a *durak* (idiot) who wanted her samovar. Other landlords in the region were decidedly well liked: one was known to give honey to the children in the villagers; another was appreciated for how he would work unpretentiously hard in the fields (in his "underwear"), along with everyone else. This kind of social stature is known, comfortable, and, in certain ways, seen as essential.

But there are certainly types of social and symbolic verticality (and the social agents who reinforce it) that are distrusted in the village. They are the ones that originate among the chuzhie. If the khoziaeva who are the figureheads of given svoi-formations are conceptually "comfortable," there is a layer of power holders (mostly administrators from outside the village) who are not. According to historians, the attitude of villagers towards the tsar was a warm one; he was a fatherly khoziain-figure—a protector and bearer of otherworldly powers. The *boiare* (members of the administrative class below the tsar) were, by contrast, widely feared and hated.[20] In the same way that villagers will, today, say that it was not Stalin who devastated the Soviet Union with persecutions, but those un-

20. See Cherniavsky, *Tsar and People: Studies in Russian Myths* (1969), for a characterization of this dynamic of love for the tsar and hatred/distrust for the court.

der Stalin, it was the boiare who were blamed for inhumane practices of the tsarist state. The khoziain-figure is understood to intercede on behalf of the "narod" (the people) to his administrators: in early centuries, those administrators were the boiare (and more local ones such as *zemskie nachal'niki,* or land bosses); in this century, they became the *kommunisty.* A three-tiered organization is here evident, filled by the roles of the khoziain-figure, the administrators, and the narod. The narod and the khoziain-figure are svoi to one another and have a synergistic relation one to the other. The administrators are chuzhie. And can be hated and feared as outsiders.

When the centrally organized Party was introduced into the village, not only was the "chuzhoi" administrative layer of power still a part of rural life, it became an intimate one as villagers themselves became Party members. In the post-Revolutionary village, there were local Party members, *deputaty* (representatives in the local Soviet), kolkhoz brigadiers, *agitatory* (Party agitators), *stukachi* (Party spies), and *predsedatel' kolkhoza* (president of the kolkhoz). These sorts of administrators and nachal'niki (bosses) did not come with a comfortable range of power. This was a hierarchy that was not defined by the internal workings of village social organization (khoziaeva and *starosti* of the obshchina), but by the arm of external, centrally controlled authorities. With the extension of that arm into the village, chuzhie landed in the circle of svoi.

Indeed, if there was little remembered resentment against the supposed *kulaki* for their relative wealth (they were still part of a village-level *svoi*-formation), there was a great deal of resentment against the Party representatives who sometimes betrayed co-villagers, and against town officials whose duties were dictated by the centrally organized Party. Many narratives reflect this resentment. There are very concrete reasons for this, as many people lost family members to the purges. One story vividly reflects the feeling for outsider/Party leaders. In one story, a man told how a "regional boss" who had "sentenced many innocent people" was left to die after crashing into a canal. "No one wanted to save him," I was told. "No one dared." This story reflects not only the specific hatred toward a specific man, although this is certainly clear. The head of the police was part of a stratum of leadership that is made of chuzhie. This sort of leadership is associated with fear and distrust, where part of the fear comes about simply because they are within the category of chuzhie—who bear associations of unpredictable, sometimes miraculous dangers.

GATHERING THE OTHER INTO THE REALM OF THE SELF

* * *

To conclude this chapter, I examine more closely the suppleness of the Russian self, through the suppleness of the sense of being svoi. It is this sense of svoi that, in its creation and reproduction, is a crucial part of the social memory practices outlined throughout the book. Svoi-formations are made of communities of family, village, nation, and "people." In the imagining, realization, and reproduction of these communities (with all the social and symbolic meanings they hold), the villager of Solovyovo becomes a social actor, agent, and purveyor of, variously, given state agendas and given instances of local empowerment. What are the features of svoi, then, when examined close up?

Grammatical *Svoi*

To this point, I have used the term "svoi" to indicate any social category of intimate belonging, but have made no attempt to regard its lexical meaning in any depth. In fact, *svoi* is a term with a very particular grammatical function and a wide range of uses. It is worth looking briefly at this grammatical function in light of its semantic flexibility.

Svoi functions in Russian as a reflexive possessive pronoun; its meaning shifts according to the actor in any given sentence. That is, *ia chitaiu svoiu knigu* means, "I read my [own] book"; and, *on chitaet svoiu knigu* means, "he reads his [own] book."[21] As ethnolinguist Kevin Tuite has noted,

> In its primary function as a reflexive pronominal (possessive adjective), svoi indicates coreferentiality between the possessor and the subject of the same sentence in which it appears. In other words, the choice of svoi signals the listener that s/he should seek the antecedent *within* the boundaries of the clause (or sentence).[22]

Given its reflexive function, svoi is nearly always found in cases besides the nominative. However, in one very important application of the

---

21. The ambiguity that exists in the English sentence, "Harry reads his book," where the book could be either Harry's or some other male's, is thereby taken care of. "Harry chitaet ego knigu" (ego, personal pronoun, "his") would mean that Harry reads the book of some other man mentioned earlier.

22. Kevin Tuite, l'Université de Montréal, personal communication, 1998.

term, svoi is used to modify a sentence's subject in a very specific way. *On svoi chelovek* does not mean "he is his own person" (as it would be expected by the pattern of the reflexive function), but rather "he is one of us." Tuite hypothesized that the "boundedness" of the sentence, which generally marks the pronoun's meaning (svoi is equal to the subject), becomes analogous to the "boundedness" of a social group:

> Drawing upon a metaphorical extension of this purely grammatical functional opposition (clause-internal versus clause-external co-reference), svoi has taken on the meaning of *social* interiority; hence *svoi chelovek* refers to a member of the in-group.

A grammatical category here creates a metaphoric template. Indeed, Tuite points out that this is an example where the boundedness of svoi to the edges of a given sentence is carried metaphorically to indicate the edges of a given social group. *On svoi chelovek* means that "he" is included in the category of svoi, and not simply that the subject belongs to himself (as it would mean if I said *eto svoia kniga,* or "it's my book"). That person is, in short, one's own. Boundedness, along with the concept of svoi, stretches outward.

Without claiming a direct link between the flexibility of the term svoi and the flexibility of social groups, I will say that svoi is a category that changes its proportions from small to large and back. *Svoia kniga* is my book, and it is bounded by the boundary of my self. *Svoi chelovek* is my person, whether he comes from my family, my village, my region, my country, or my overarching sense of the brother/sisterhood of humankind. Grammatically speaking, when he is my person, the "my" in that sentence becomes "our." He is included under the rubric of "we."

Creating a svoi-formation is, most deeply, about the gesture of pulling the other into the realm of the self. In other words, being svoi means that the other becomes "me"—on its way, making "me" into a larger unit.

Social *Svoi*

For the purposes of symbolic anthropology, the self must be understood analytically as a sociocultural construct. Its configuration therefore varies from place to place and from time to time, given a broad range of reasons from the economic to the symbolic. The strongly defined individual self known in the West is by no means a universal.[23] It helps the project of social analysis to imagine that categories of self differ, and can be highly flexible and context dependent. Of course, it also helps to look not only at the boundaries of social categories (such as the self), but their inner textures by way of their symbolic make-up.

Certainly, there is much emphasis on the needs of the group in rural Russia, just as the needs of an individual are de-emphasized. When entering a residential group, one's resources and one's tasks are defined by that group. Happiness is linked to group harmony. Semantically, it is awkward to speak of an "individual" who has an essential personality there. *Lichnost'* (from *lik*, face) is the closest term for that (and is also used to mean "a celebrity"), and is used rarely in the village. One's *kharakter,* or character, can be spoken of, but this character does not seem to be the object of obsessive attention, although a person can be described as soft or hard, nice or genuine, intelligent or silly, kind or cruel. Interestingly, a person "with a character" (*s kharakterom*) is understood to be, most generally, a difficult or socially awkward person. Character, in other words, comes negatively marked.

On the other hand, the self, as attached to an individual person, certainly has an existence in rural Russia. Aside from the connection between self and individual "personality," there are the deeper currents of how the self is symbolically bounded. I generalize that there are two defining modes of the self, modes that can be both positive and negative: the first one open, expansive, and soulful (and in excess is marked by physical and moral slovenliness), and the second, controlled and disciplined (and in excess marked by soul-lessness). The openness of the self can come about in many ways (drinking decidedly helps the "soul" to *raskryt'sia,* open itself up), and is linked to the explicit morality of generosity and hospitality (Pesmen 2000). On the other hand, self-discipline and

---

23. In anthropology, the subject of the degree to which "selves" and "identities" are culturally constructed, has been a topic of debate for decades. Whether exemplified by Marriott (1991), who writes of Indian "dividuals" (where selves are always in flux in relation to their environment), Yang (1994), who explores the layers of socially defined "personhood" in China (1994), or Murray (1993), who writes of the "Western" concept of self, a lively debate on the relative importance of the unit of the "individual" continues to unfold. A rich summary of recent anthropological work on the concepts of "self" and "identity" can be found in Sökefeld (1999).

control (*sderzhannost'*) are linked in their own way to the proper leadership of a family or other svoi-formation.

As an individual, one's actions have consequences back onto the self, and further onto the broader social sphere. Interestingly, these consequences often fall on the family-line and even the future rod, particularly with regards to misdeeds. I was told that destroying a church, for example, could curse the long line of an individual's descendants. An individual as a sociocultural unit also comes into existence when a person becomes the object of group-driven shame.

The Self and the Other: *Ty and Vy*

Even if we are to accept only the mildest form of the Sapir–Whorf hypothesis (Whorf 1939), that the habitual use of grammatical categories play some role in defining channels of thought, it is worth noting how the self and other are constructed in the Russian language. In "Structural Implications of Russian Pronominal Usage" (1979), Friedrich analyzes the second- person pronoun in Russian in light of how the habitual uses of *ty* (second-person singular) and *Vy* (second-person plural, formal) aid in forging categories of social closeness and distance. They shift for a given person even in a given discourse.

There are four basic relationships that can arise from a ty/Vy structure: reciprocal ty; reciprocal Vy; calling a person Vy and being called ty; calling a person ty and being called Vy. There is a great deal of subtlety to the use of these pronouns and the relationships that they weave. Mostly, the correct use of these pronouns makes social life more comfortable, but they can also be played with to notable effect. In the village, there are certain generalizations regarding pronominal usage that are worth pointing out.

The most important point to make here is that, generally speaking, all villagers are on a "ty" basis with each other.[24] In this way, there is a reciprocal sense of belonging to a socially equal group that can be more or less assumed. This does not mean that there is no way to show deference,

---

24. The exceptions to this rule include homeowners who are not understood to be relatives of established villagers, living or dead. This second category is referred to as *dachniki*—that is, those who buy a home in the village for the purpose of summer living only. Interactions with dachniki can be relatively formal and distant. They are also sometimes marked by social miscues: dachniki, for example, do not always greet villagers outside, a custom that is more or less obligatory in the social world of co-villagers.

for example, to one's elders. When respect is required, one uses the long form of a name (Aleksandr and not Sasha) and the patronymic along with *ty*. Children can add *tetia, diadia, baba,* or *deda* (aunt, uncle, grandmother, or grandfather) along with the short form of the name—producing, for example, "diadia Alesha"—to show proper respect to elders. People from nearby villages use a similar pattern.

Nevertheless, there is room for variation here. Vy can be used ironically or to insult someone with an implication of their social distance. There is also room for error, and there are those who are reputed to have a poor sense of naming etiquette.[25] Murkiness also attends a young bride who enters the home of her in-laws. Although she is immediately on ty terms with the members of the household, depending on how her relationship develops with her in-laws, she may or may not call them the close "mama" and "papa," but perhaps the somewhat less close in this context, *babushka* and *dedushka*. It will also take time to be on *ty* terms with other villagers. But this will certainly happen.

The use of close kinship terms for some villagers, along with the near-universal use of ty affirms what has already been suggested: that in certain conceptual ways, the village is analogous to the family. Ty is used for those with whom one is in a given svoi-formation. The residential group (which holds the family, in the broad sense of the term) is the first svoi-affiliation. The village is a second one. In keeping with the fact that social "verticality" exists in different degrees in the household and village setting, respect can be shown for certain members of a given group without resorting to the formal Vy. Nevertheless, within the village, the basically "horizontal" ty is used.

By contrast, Vy is used for outsiders and bosses. One may call a village boss (such as a brigadier) ty, but a city boss would never be ty, even if the boss in question were far younger than a villager. Interestingly, the use of Vy is associated with being "citified" and villagers can be mildly ashamed of their use of ty, calling themselves *nekul'turnye*, or uncultured, for widely using *ty* and being uncomfortable with the use of Vy.[26]

---

25. One village woman never called her husband Il'ia by the familiar form of his name, Iliusha, nor did she ever call her elders by their name and patronymic, but only by their nickname. The first error was seen as terribly sad and the second as terribly crude.

26. I called my khoziaika, Iuliia Ivanovna, Iuliia, ty. My host, I called Mikhail Alekseevich, Vy. Both called me Maggie, ty. This was the most comfortable compromise. Because of our age difference, it would have been inappropriate for me to call Iuliia by the short

Svoi versus *Chuzhoi*

Q: What does it mean to be svoi?

Mikhail Alekseevich: Svoi. By the place where one lives. And by pedigree. There, these two definitions. Either relatives or the zone where one lives.

It has already been suggested that the most abstract, probably most important concept in social organization is the notion of being svoi (one's own) versus being chuzhoi (someone else's, alien; strange, foreign). Svoi is not necessarily linked to any given kinship relationship, but certain relations imply it. If the reference is the village locale, then svoi would refer to householders and visiting kin and perhaps friends. In the context of the region, svoi refers to those from the *derevnia* (village) or prikhod. The context can broaden several times and svoi can refer to Russians or Soviets, even. Furthermore, a sense of svoi, it is clear, can accumulate. Whereas I had arrived in the village as chuzhaia, I was moved to have been greeted after an absence of several months, with "ty sovsem stala svoei (you became fully our own)." A sense of being one's own, of gathering and being gathered into a larger social sphere, is accompanied by feelings of warmth. It is a good thing, in this symbolic configuration, to live among one's own.

Creating a svoi-formation implies the production of bounded social groups. This activity can be done at various "levels." For example, in the household, the production of svoi brings about work groups. The production of svoi around the table when drinking together can serve to (for example) create a bond of friendship that will have implications of loyalty and sacrifice. Svoi-formation has a crucial symbolic function as well as its social function. In the act of svoi-formation, something is fashioned that is more than the sum of its parts. As we will see, such groups can battle the unpredictable dark forces in the world at large, and channel otherworldly powers. The svoi formed in the forest with invocations to

---

form of her name, Iulia, and since I was an outsider woman, it would have been inappropriate to call a man in my household, ty. I called most other villagers Vy, with their name and patronymic, and expected them to call me Maggie, ty, which they most often did. This offered warmth (from their end) and respect (from my end). Being called ty by people reinforced a general insider status. The fact that most villagers were far older than I made this rather easy. When Iuliia wished to tease me, she would call me Maggie Bat'kovna, which means Maggie, daughter of her Bat'ka (family head). This is the patronymic used for fatherless children.

grandfather forest can protect one from the dark forces that causes one to get lost. The svoi formed with ancestors at the graveyard during the festival of Troitsa channel in powers of fertility and healing. There is a sense of svoi that surrounds being a villager as opposed to a city dweller, or of being a Russian as opposed to any other nationality. The svoi of the rodina sends people to near-holy battle. The symbolic mechanisms at work in creating this larger force will be the subject of a great deal of subsequent analysis.

Svoi and the Land

> *Aleksandra Ivanova:* Now everything is destroyed. . . . The first offense was the collective resettlement from small villages to bigger ones. That was the most important thing that happened. It was very bad. Happened in 1972.

Soviet agriculture never really thrived; the subject of its failings can and does fill volumes. After the devastating period of war and famine in the 1950s, upon coming to power Khrushchev made certain concerted efforts at reforming agricultural policies on a large scale. Many of his policies were also poorly thought out (one of the more famous failings was his effort to bring corn to the northern regions). It had been a "dream" of his to create large, modern "agro-towns" that could bring modern development to rural areas, such as "schools, kindergartens, medical services, shops, clubs with cinema facilities, etc." (Medvedev 1987:402) Given that most villages in Russia were still very small (less than fifty inhabitants) (Medvedev 1987:402), this "dream" entailed a large-scale resettlement program, known to villagers as *ukrupnenie.*

Ukrupnenie was, perhaps surprisingly at first glance, extremely unpopular. It was brought up often in interviews. The following was a typical comment.

> People were unhappy because, for example, there in Krylovo. . . . The residents [in bigger villages] had put in those posts. To bring electricity [*svet:* light]. They lived beautifully there. There the land was very good. There were tons of berries and mushrooms! There were lakes! All of the basics of life were pleasant. And they couldn't put in the posts [for them]. If they'd had just the wires, they could have put in their own poles. For free. So it happened that people were torn from their places to carry their homes and build a new life again. It wasn't easy.

The deeper reasons for this dissatisfaction appear to be more complex than those cited above or, rather, they extend further than the above citation implies. Attachment to one's village of birth has to do with some of the most important features of social organization and rural symbolism. The ukrupnenie caused certain social patterns to be smashed, as people were "torn from their places."

Land has more than a little to do with a sense of svoi. As Iuliia told me, referring to the era of ukrupnenie, when outsiders were forced to move to Solovyovo:

> *Iuliia Ivanovna:* We didn't abuse anyone. Everyone was here. There was enough space for everyone. But anyway, somehow. . . . If people would start to fight over some petty thing, they would start saying, "Why did the leshii bring you here?" There were discontents. Because those [in the village] were svoi. Svoi among svoi, that is, villagers among villagers. They live friendlier together. Those who originated from Solovyovo lived much more as friends. There were no fights. There was enough of everything for everyone.

Perhaps the deepest form of being svoi is being rodnoi. People who are rodnye to each other have one of two connections: they are tied to the same family line, or by the land on which they live. These two notions are so symbolically close that the resonance from one nearly merges with the other. Rodina, the land of the rod, is kin and rodina is earth. When it is of the earth, a rodina can nearly smell with local soils; when it is Mother Russia, it is a vast expanse that one loves. Land has an intimate relationship to the concept of being svoi. Being rodnoi is a special form of being svoi, with an emphasis on the fact that that soil and kin are shared. The rodina, and the rod that fills its soils, will be the object of much subsequent analysis.

Russian villagers, like members of any society, form social groups in the performance of collective action. They create categories that distinguish between those who are included and those who are not. In this chapter, I underlined three points. First, where it is clear that group identification and group action are crucial in rural Russia, these groups are many. There is no single Russian collective (with essential qualities) that is linked to one Russian village. This is borne out in historical studies. Second, these groups are mostly all flexible: they form and reform and include both the world of living actors and beings from other planes. Finally, there is a great deal of power to the act of forming and maintaining these groups. Some of this power is seen to have an otherworldly quality to it, which explains some of the far-reaching emotional appeal associated with local notions of the "collective."

Clearly, there are certain basic features of social life in rural Russia that have "survived" the organizational tumult of the twentieth century. The focus on the family as an organizational unit, the economic, political, and symbolic features of local "collectives," and certain treatments of social verticality persist to this day, in spite of organized attempts to undermine their persistence. A specific insight on social space that will carry through this analysis is the way that the social body appears to strive for equipoise. This is not rare in agrarian societies; in rural Russia it becomes a broadly generative social gesture. "One-downsmanship" has social as well as metaphysical powers; letting extremes of wealth and poverty stretch out the social body has social as well as metaphysical liabilities. When configuring imaginary worlds, when turning to otherworldly powers to set the world right, when facing the prospect of societal transformation at the direction of the state, the question of how svoi-formations maintain themselves (and for what social/magical functions) becomes a crucial one. This is a first sketch of memory's landscape; as in Tonkin's sense, it is medium as well as message.

Radiance

INTRODUCTION: NARRATIVE LANDSCAPES

* * *

Iuliia said with a sigh, "It is good here in the forest." She and I had sneaked off to look for mushrooms one July day. The air was cool and fresh and quiet. Work was kilometers away in the village. We would let it wait. "Breathe in the air," Iuliia told me, "it's good for your health and good for the soul."

You go into the forest with prayers and incantations on your lips. Protect me, you ask the host of the forest or God, "from roaring thunder, from searing fire, from running beasts, from creeping snakes, from evil people, from the *leshii*'s eyes."[1] The space of the forest has the

---

1. "Ot groma gremuchego, ot ognia goriuchego, ot zveria begushchego; ot gada polzuchego; ot zlykh liudei, ot leshikh ochei . . ."

power to grant you blessings or to confuse and bewilder you—or to take your life.

In a similar way, the narrative imagination has its own forests, that is, places of affinity which can also be places of danger. The interviews I conducted with the people of Solovyovo and nearby locales yielded a tremendous wealth of symbolic and social data. When the necessary thresholds were crossed and conversations began, it was clear that my interlocutors had entered into symbolic worlds that were defined by their own boundaries, dominant metaphors, and affective associations. These narrative spaces were elaborate (and favored) pathways in memory's landscape.

In the next two chapters, I focus my discussion on two such narrative landscapes. The first I call the "radiant past" (*svetloe proshloe*), named to resonate with the "radiant future," promised for the day when communism would fully flourish for the Soviet world. The radiant past, however, finds its brightness and brilliance not in the days to come, but in days gone by; it harkens—in tones of lament and tones of fairy tale awe—to a better, earlier time. The second narrative space that will be featured in Chapter 5 is the world of the miraculous or *chudesnoe* (a *chudo* is a miracle or a wonder; *chudesnoe* is "miraculous, wondrous"). This world is narrated through stories of confrontations with otherworldly forces and powers. In it, the rules and logics of the everyday can be confronted with forces that have the power to transform—forces that can be violent or whimsical, absurd or deadly. Tracing the symbolic pathway grounded by this narrative landscape provides a first sketch of how confrontations with otherworldly forces occur in the village. Later, this discussion will provide the basis for a broader look at the (society-stabilizing, society-transforming) numinous forms and practices in Solovyovo.

In the telling of stories such as these, there is social memory. In the patterning, positioning, and reproducing of these stories, there is social memory that carries with it social purposes. Talk is a social action. Narrative, which is a particularly rich form of talk, has features that carry cultural patterning and conventions. As Ries argues in *Russian Talk* (1997), generic stories (and their performances) such as the ones offered here in fact have a great deal to say about crucial matters such as the construction of group identity and of the reproduction of and resistance to official ideology. In showing us the shape of radiant, miraculous worlds, they offer a template for how society has managed its brushes with catastrophe and will continue to do so, both from within and without its social circles.

Crucial here is the point that language, metaphor, and narrative are powerful (and omnipresent, and unavoidable) carriers of social memory. To recast social memory is to recast them, and this, it appears, is no simple task.

SVETLOE PROSHLOE (THE RADIANT PAST)[2]

* * *

When Was It Radiant?

I had heard the record play so often that I could repeat it in my sleep: "Things were better before." Sometimes "before" meant "in the time of Brezhnev or Stalin." Often it meant "before perestroika." But mostly it referred to a region in symbolic space, a locale in the past where people lived in social harmony. "Back then, we lived as friends. We worked together in harmony. People would go to each other's homes and visit. Women would spin and tell stories. We would sing songs and dance and work hard." This is not to say that, in other contexts, villagers would not lament their past hardships. But in this symbolic space, they expressed longing for something that seemed to have slipped from between their fingers, a dream that had appeared within their grasp and now had been betrayed.

The radiant past has no specific link to a timeline, no specific years that are implicitly golden; only the era, as defined in the imagination, is golden. In interviews and casual conversations, I found the "radiant past" tied to many overlapping eras, specifically, the "time of the *babushki,*" the time "before the Revolution," the 1920s and the years before Stalin, "Stalin's time," the years before World War II, the years after World War II, the period of the famine, and the period of relative prosperity of the 1950s. These periods are, in historical senses, radically different from each other. The "then" of the radiant past is clearly not a fixed one. Given this, how is it that the radiant past can be recognized as a specific locale in symbolic terrain, despite the different features of the years that it falls in? The logic that binds these varied historical periods is not necessarily a straightforward one. A radiant time is not necessarily a time when people had enough food ("the hungriest time was and remains the best period of my

---

2. To my knowledge, this phrase was first used in English by Parthé in *Russian Village Prose: The Radiant Past* (1992), to whom I am indebted for her insights on village prose literature (and for fascinating conversations while I was writing my dissertation).

life," said Konstantin Andreevich), enjoyed basic political freedoms, or freedom from war. What was, then, so radiant about this period?

When discussing the past, the world that is spun after the utterance of *ran'she* ("before") almost inevitably includes a type of a sociology of radiance, that is, descriptions and analyses of what people were like, what groups were like, and what leaders were like when life was good.[3] In this way, *the existence or nonexistence of radiance depends primarily on qualities of social relations.* There can be elements of material plenty in this idealized time, but they do not dominate or define the picture. In many of these narratives, the past is immediately contrasted with the present, and this helps to further identify key dichotomies and therefore key symbolism. Like the way in which we build and rebuild cities over the same fertile ground, this space is full of the resonance of different eras, different characters, and the colors and textures of different social temperaments.

Society in the Radiant Past

> Regardless of the difficulties of that time . . . it was and remained for me the best period of my life. There is a modern song with the words, "the river of my childhood." So you see, such was the river of my childhood.
> —Konstantin Andreevich

Konstantin Andreevich is a serious and unassuming man who worked for years as the shopkeeper in Solovyovo's neighboring village. Three or four times a week, he would put on a white work coat and walk a kilometer down the road to the store—where bread, dusty cans of meat and fish, various grains, hard candies, cigarettes, and vodka are sold—and wait for buyers. Ever since he had a falling-out with some of the leadership in the kolkhoz, he preferred to work alone. He and I spoke several times in that one-room store about subjects as varied as the best places in the forest to find mushrooms or berries, the meaning of political events, and his changing thoughts on religion and faith. While we spoke, he would lean over the wooden counter and play with his abacus, or pace back and forth as he organized his thoughts. Like his father before him, Konstantin An-

---

3. This is the aspect of the symbolic function discussed in Chapter 1—particularly the argument by Sperber (1974)—that concerns the placement of symbolic representations into memory using exegesis.

dreevich had been a communist in his time, and by his own account had struggled with what it meant to be a "true" communist—whose qualities included honesty, industriousness, loyalty, and service to the state. Now he was looking into religion, which required reading, asking questions, and reflecting.

Konstantin Andreevich told me that as a young man he had dreamed of being a writer—a striking rarity in his world. As the father of five children, his dreams faded over time, but he nonetheless kept journals and memoirs for fifteen years. At one point, he read an autobiographical text to me in which he described his childhood before the war:

> *Konstantin Andreevich:* Behind the garden, stretched long, even meadows. From time to time, planes landed there. One day, a plane landed so close that it almost scraped the roof of our house. Once in a while, on holidays, guests gathered at our house. It was loud and happy. We played popular songs from the time, like "Katiusha" and others.
>
> For us, the children, there was a lot of candy. Children, with fingers interlocking, would walk around the pine tree and sing songs, and grandmother would offer us treats one by one. On the whole, it was a happy time. Our parents bought us different sweets. . . . It was good for children before the war.

Konstantin Andreevich's reflections here were close in content to those of many other villagers. The radiant past (in this case located before World War II) is a happy and friendly place first and foremost. It is found in an idyllic physical and social setting. Furthermore, there is a sense that people in this past enjoyed a social "harmony" and peace that has vanished from the social life of the present. Where does this happiness come from? At a first, most basic social level, it appears to arise through obshchenie, social interaction.

Obshchenie and Happiness in the Radiant Past

While speaking of an indefinite time "back then," Valentina Ivanovna told me that the izba she grew up in could hold eleven people, and that if the *khoziain* of the household had brothers who got married, the wives might be crammed in that one house for a time, at least, and people would have to sleep on the floor. Bugs would settle in along with people so that "you just want to scratch and scratch." Nonetheless, times were good:

Valentina Ivanovna: We lived well [*khorosho*], in friendship, peacefully; we were all healthy. And now, everyone has gotten greedy [*zhadnye*]. To this one that; to this one that (you take yours, I take mine). We hate each other. What are you envious of? They are envious of everything.

Householders bore difficult circumstances in the radiant past, but were happy and, importantly, "healthy" in their interactions with each other. Valentina Ivanovna later brings radiance out of the house and into the fields, and, in effect, from the family to the kollektiv (and here she makes an interesting juxtaposition of the terms kollektiv and kolkhoz, layering the symbolism of kollektiv with a Soviet air):

Valentina Ivanovna: In the collective, in the kolkhoz, we lived. . . . We went [off to work] singing. Oi. Went to work with songs. And there, everything was peaceful, well. And now . . . [you] just have to have more [than everyone else].

In this broader collective, there were songs and peace. Now, again, there are selfishness and greed and acts that benefit the self at the expense of the group in a world (in a time) where, as she later said, "Everyone lives for him or herself, so that there would be more for me, and none for you."

Happy connections were characteristic of life before, whereas greed and envy exist now. This dichotomy lies at the heart of the distinction between the radiant past and the present it contrasts with: if the radiant past is marked by the social bonds that come about from certain kinds of interaction, the present is marked by self-centered acts. Bringing others into the social sphere of "one's own" is at the heart of social radiance; locking one's door, locking others out, as acts of private closure, are socially decadent acts of the present.

The happiness of the radiant past is linked to some very unhappy historical moments. Aleksandra Sokolova's father had been given a sentence of ten years in prison for having spoken against Stalin. As we sat and drank tea and I listened to this tale, the theme wandered to family baptisms and religious beliefs. Suddenly, happiness appeared. I ask Aleksandra Sokolova if there hadn't been a risk associated with being a believer. She answers:

Aleksandra Sokolova: No risk at all. Everyone believed in God. In the village, everyone went to church. It was happier then. We lived poorer. We went to each other's houses to sit together, taking whatever work we had to do.

Sometimes, it was work, specifically, that carried this feeling of happiness in the radiant past. Maia Bogdanova left the village after childhood to go to school in a nearby city and, in the late 1990s, she lived in Solovyovo for part of the year. She was a retired nurse, and had the best, most varied and most productive summer garden in the village. She herself was never a Party member, but is attached to many of the ideas of the Party. As a young person, like most of her peers, she was a member of the komsomol, and as she explained her time as a komsomolka, she entered the reverie of the radiant past.

> *Maia Bogdanova:* How active I was! We lived happily then. We had get-togethers . . . made up all kinds of concerts! We were active, young. I loved my life. We were always busy from morning 'til night. Not like now. We didn't have enough time. We were all happy. We all smiled. And now—you call this a life? Everyone locks his door! . . . We lived poorer, but we were all equal then. Because we were not only poor people. Then, you would walk. . . . [T]here it was all fields, fields, fields and all bread-grain and rye, wheat—there were peas, there was everything. Now, twenty-year-old children sleep until two in the afternoon. So, this is the way we're going to live richly? . . . I was a student in Cherepovets and I would come in the summers. We would get up at three or four in the morning. In the deepest darkness . . . I would walk home just to dry [the hay], it was evening and I would arrive from the senokos. . . . I think, "Will I go to the club today?" You just eat and go back to the club and then from the club to the senokos, without having slept.

Maia's happiness here is linked to shared, intense labor, a theme that is recurrent in village narratives (and one that is sometimes explicitly traced to the ideals of socialism). All villagers spoke of the backbreaking work that filled the hours and days of their lives—often in wrenching stories. And yet, this shared labor—even in its raw, painful forms—recurs in the radiant past. Maia loved her life. The link between shared pain and happiness has a logic to it, one that recalls the dynamic of social leveling.

Heightened Spirituality and Shared Poverty

Acts of generosity are also acts of redistribution. Earlier, there was discussion of how an explicit morality of generosity contributes to social leveling in the village, and that generous people are awarded social status. In the radiant past, another level of this problem is unveiled. As generosity marks a certain moral superiority, poverty, as well, particularly when shared, lends a *group* a heightened morality. Poverty has already been mentioned and implied in several of the passages, as it is linked to happiness. Mikhail Alekseevich made this dynamic between poverty and heightened morality clear when he said, "Poverty united people. Then there wasn't jealousy. There was one level. You will never see how people worked so well together after the war. We had nothing." And, further, he pointed out that there is a hidden spirituality in the lack of money and the lack of greed: "We are living now worse on a spiritual level, as well. From the pocket, from the pocket. Even before, when there was no God [in the Soviet period] we lived better spiritually. Now people only think about money."

What kind of "spirituality" is this? God is not required for it, and the presence of an atheist state does not impede it. "Spirituality" (*dukhovnost'*) in this not strictly religious sense comes from freedom from greed. Not only do the radiant past and the impoverished past live next to each other in symbolic space, they share a moral elevation. Although the radiant past can imply times of material plenty, the morality of being in a group can easily be linked to the morality of poverty.

Konstantin Andreevich echoes this point with his own reflections on the link between morality, spirituality and the poverty of the past where he describes the "happiest period of his life" during the great famine of 1947. "I remember well," he says, "for me this same most hungry period—during the famine, my memories about that period, for a little boy—was the most interesting period and that's all. It was as if there were some kind of inspiration in life then." And what was this inspiration linked to? Again, shared poverty holds within it a morality. Konstantin Andreevich makes it explicit that this is a "peasant morality."

> *Konstantin Andreevich:* Before, we somehow lived more happily. The mood of everyone was better, regardless of the hard life, it was better. It was more festive. We associated with each other more (*bol'she obshchalis'*). I don't know, either we started to live better. . . . It's a regular thing. When you start to live better materially, somehow that goes with the peasant morality that things will be bad. Television has played a real role. There is a lot of television. Everyone becomes disconnected [*razobshchili vsekh*]. Everyone is shut up at the screen.
>
> It seems to me that as I look at my whole life little by little, . . . that it is like this: That as much as life improves in the village, improves, right

away, people become more exclusive. They struggled more for things to be better. And already somehow started to associate less [*obshchenie men'she uzhe stalo*]. This is all because in difficult times, a person always reaches out to others. Everyone survives better.

The picture that Konstantin Andreevich paints is one of physical poverty and moral wealth.[4] It is a radiant past of social contact (obshchenie), and a present where faces are locked in the direction of the television screen. Konstantin Andreevich also hints at the problem of understanding the symbolic dynamics that take us from social harmony in the past to social decay and destruction in the present.

Freedom in the Radiant Past

Another prominent feature of the radiant past is the presence of personal, individual freedom. Freedom, or *svoboda,* appears in many contexts in village narratives, in a symbolic construct that associates it, again, with obshchenie:

> During the time of Stalin, we lived better than we live now. Everyone was free. There was everything everywhere.

> [We thought that] if Stalin lives and works a long time . . . we will arrive at communism. That means, we will all be free, everything will be excellent.

"We were free before" does not refer to the same symbolic complex of "freedom," as in the usual English use of the term. The standard renderings of svoboda into English are "freedom" and "liberty." But its etymological load is also telling. Its Indo-European root is *se- or *sue, the same root that forms the term for the social category, "svoi," or "one's own." Svoboda's linguistic burial grounds yield symbolism that takes us far from Western sense of the term for anarchical, self-centered acts. This freedom is one that is seemingly rooted in society and social intercourse. Etymology is merely a clue here. It allows an image of freedom (in its expression as a symbolic landmark in Russian Solovyovo) that is not mostly self-centered.

In the radiant past, "we got along, we were all equal, we were free." Symbolically, svoboda contains a vector that links the individual will to

---

4. In her chapter "Mystical Poverty and the Rewards of Loss" (1997:126–160), Ries confronts narrative logics that are strikingly similar.

comfortable belongingness in a group. It has the feel of expansiveness, and it appears to be located in the past. In her ethnography of *dusha* or soul, Dale Pesmen (2000:67) points to the sense of vast spatiality and freedom in Russia's ventures to otherworldly space. She writes, "Other worlds' otherness is often framed in terms of vastness and distances. Images of (opening or moving into) vast expanses, into physical, creative, and spiritual freedom . . . relate to *dusha*." Freedom and expansiveness of the intimate units of social belonging are integral features of the radiant past.

The radiant past, full of fields and flowers and song, amounts to a relatively apolitical way of speaking about a precarious political world. The political arena makes an overt appearance in the radiant past, as well. In certain cases, it was communism that was explicitly attributed with teaching people to live for each other and not for themselves. Iuliia, who was raised in an orphanage, was asked if she felt that she had had a Soviet upbringing. She responded: "Yes, of course, because we cared for/took trouble about each other."[5] Indeed, the promises derived from Soviet propaganda added certain elements to the world of the radiant past. But they did it in a backward manner: through a beautiful dream for the future.

Back to the Radiant Future

Most of the residents of Solovyovo came of age at a time when the messages of state propaganda were being offered via schools, Party organizations, orphanages, radio broadcasts, local Party organizations, and the films and activities directed by local houses of culture. Although villagers reacted to the Communist Party with varying degrees of cynicism and openness, the moments of nostalgia characteristic of the symbolic terrain of the radiant past were everywhere. Nostalgia per se is nothing rare when reminiscing about the strength and beauty of youth. But this nostalgia—ordered, as it is, by the template for a perfect society—has a role outside of that universal plaint.

Located in the terrain of the radiant past was a promise. By virtue of its explicit atheism, communism could not promise the afterlife in a traditional way and it could not promise the assistance of an unseen God.

---

5. Note that despite the shared visions of the radiant past, villagers varied in their approach to the role that the Party, specifically, played. Iuliia, from the above quotation, was raised in an orphanage, and eventually worked as a "culture-worker." Her view of the Party was relatively uncynical.

But it could and did promise a tomorrow that will be better than today—bright and better and the only teleology available: "I believe in the radiant future, and only in it." For the purposes of this discussion, the reverie of the radiant past blushes with this specific radiant future. The romantic, nationalistic images from particular war films and the songs[6] of the days of Soviet patriotism lent a specifically Soviet gloss to the radiant past—one where supreme sacrifice was committed *za rodinu, za Stalina* (for the motherland, for Stalin), and ultimately *za svetloe budushchee* (for the radiant future). Konstantin Andreevich speaks of his father and what he referred to in another context as the "beautiful dream" of communism.

> *Konstantin Andreevich:* He didn't pity himself. He worked, not pitying himself, for the sake of feeding the family, for the sake of everything there was—the beautiful future. Many acted this way. And what did they achieve? They achieved nothing. We were unable to arrive at where we wanted.

Emma Dmitrievna and Mikhail Fedorovich also spoke of the dream that a perfect future will arrive. Here, the radiant future takes on, unsurprisingly, certain of the qualities of the radiant past—specifically, its excellence and the equality and freedom of people living at this time.

> *Q:* They spoke of the radiant future. What does it mean?
>
> *Emma Dmitrievna:* For us, [we thought that if] Stalin lives and works a long time, . . . we will arrive at communism. That means that everything will be free [*svobodnye*, i.e., freedom], we will be equal. That everything will be excellent.
>
> *Mikhail Fedorovich:* Everyone believed and hoped. Only the very smart, very few . . . [said when Stalin died,] "Glory, to you, Lord. Now we can at least rest." All the rest cried and cried, "What now?"

By this logic, the radiant future, as promised by communist ideals, is located in the *past* and not in the future. There, everything will be (again) free and excellent. The radiant future is the mirror reflection of the radiant past. In the following exchange with Larisa Andreevna, note the near-seamless transition from the radiant future to the radiant past. Note

6. See Anderson (1983) on songs and nationalism.

as well the parallel qualities that they possess (happiness, contentment, celebrations).

> *Q:* Before, they said that someday there would be a "radiant future." What is that?
>
> *Larisa Andreevna:* They thought that we were going to live better. Much better. And life didn't appear to be so good, after all. And who of the youth thought before that we would start to live worse? No one thought it. They thought that we will live very well. Maybe happily. That we will have everything. After the war, life got better. We started to have everything. Everything was cheap. Our life wasn't bad. We all were content, happy, partied all the time. Celebrated holidays. Amused ourselves. That's what there was.

Tucked away in the radiant past is a golden future. When the villagers of Solovyovo reminisced about the past, they were accessing this dream and this inspiration. At the same time, there was, in their words, a longing for belief of any kind at all: "We always believed. Now there are no beliefs." It is no contradiction, in this logic, that there is, strictly speaking, freedom of religion now and that official atheism existed before. The past had goals and it had faith, both of which are conspicuously absent in the present.

Here, social perfection is located in a past that imagines a future. This perfection is accessible in the actions of social memory; it is recalled again and again, in detail, and with well-defined symbolic pathways at its base. It is a harmonious place, morally superior to the present by virtue of its poverty and by virtue of the group-bettering, as opposed to self-bettering, acts within it. It bears some of the resonance of the radiant future promised by communism. Characteristics of the radiant past vis-à-vis symbolism of the present are summarized below.

Radiant Past/Social States	*Present*
equality	inequality
obshchenie (n. social interaction)	*zamknutyi* (adj. closed up)
shared poverty	greed
happiness	lack of happiness

Radiant Past/Social States	Present
acts for group	acts for self
comradeliness in work	laziness
social connection	social disconnectedness
belief	no belief
"soft" people	cruel people
personal freedom/ease (svoboda)	lack of svoboda via individualism
radiant future	no goals/no teleology

The social order of the radiant past is one marked by social interaction and harmony and a certain internal freedom. The self is unlocked, and there is some boundedness around the group. The radiant past buzzes with social connectedness and social energy (in the form of dancing and singing, on the one hand, and good, clean, comradely work, on the other). These are vectors, dynamic in nature, that move out from the individual and into the world. They form bonds between people that feel unfettered. In the most primal sense of "svoi," the freedom of the radiant past is not about inwardly centered acts, but the inverse: it is about the gathering of the other into the realm of the self.

In addition, this idealized time period necessarily includes social evenness and a lowering or diminishing of the self for the sake of the group. This reflects the one-downsmanship of exchange described earlier. It is the overall tendency of the agrarian economic system to prefer social evenness to social verticality; it rewards status to those who redistribute wealth over those who accumulate it (see Foster 1965). In the radiant past, this preference was part of a utopian image of society, where societal perfections are located in the world "before" today.[7]

A first role of the radiant past in social memory is to provide a patterned template for social wellness and perfection—one not attached to

---

7. The Soviet *derevenskaia proza* (village prose) movement of the 1960s and 1970s reveals an idealized past reminiscent of the one that appears in Solovyovo's narratives. Indeed, Parthé anchors her study of this movement, *Russian Village Prose,* with the subtitle, "The Radiant Past," and writes, "If the past of Village Prose is full, radiant, and complex, the present is experienced as a time of loss, and the future is seen as a cultural and moral vacuum" (1992:63).

given times or places, but one that can be attached to any time or place. But the telling of the radiant past not only sings the song of fields and flowers and Edens. It also links Edenic places to social control. In a second, equally important role, the state finds its way into the radiant past.

Discipline and Frames and *Razboltannost'* (Disorder)

Countless times in interviews and casual conversations, "discipline" was invoked as the missing ingredient in the moral life of the present. By contrast, it was very much a part of the idealized past. Discipline, per se, is an act of individual will that keeps a person within a framework of behavior. *Distsiplina* is a foreign-derived word in Russian (entering the Russian language in the early eighteenth century) that seems to be close in meaning to the more native Russian concept of *sderzhannost'* (*s-* centripetal motion inward; *-derzh,* maintenance, hold, preservation, retention), or the quality of restraint. A contradiction emerges: bearing in mind that the radiant past has the qualities of evenness, social ease, and even freedom, this discipline and the social "frames" that maintain it function quite differently at a metaphoric level. They are the vectors that bear an inward force, like the inward-turning sderzhannost'. Discipline, Mikhail Alekseevich says in a comment about the army, "pulls you up from the insides." This inward pulling, this discipline, is seen as a necessary part of social life:

Freedom is good, but you have to have discipline anyway. And above all, discipline is needed in leaders.

> *Mikhail Alekseevich:* We don't remember repression. But it wasn't bad [if used] to keep discipline [*derzhat' distsiplinu*]. Now there is no discipline.

> *Anna Petrovna:* He understood that you have to keep discipline. Before, there was more discipline. In khoziaistvo and in general.

How is discipline maintained at a societal level? If a first way is through the inward-pulling will of an individual, a second is through the agency of the political and/or religious powers and the plans and frameworks that they set out for people.

> *Mikhail Alekseevich:* Of course, there has been a worsening of life conditions. That's for one thing. This is instability. This perestroika itself played a big role. [Before] we were striving toward something. . . . You

will work better if you are trying for that, . . . you won't carry everything out onto the street, you won't show everything. There was some kind of shame/embarrassment. So, you can't say that sin is what it was before. They got rid of sin. In the family, it was [said], "It's a sin [*grekh*] to do that, and that's not." So, now there are none. And the common political goals are taken away. And in each family, . . . "If you want to live, then turn around [get to work, move]." That's very bad.

Q: Why?

Mikhail Alekseevich: Because, if it happened right away, then after that, evenness. After *ramochki* [frameworks] [are gone], that's much harder.

Q: Which frameworks?

Mikhail Alekseevich: Ramochki, well, plan. The plan for unification of the khoziaistvo. The plan for education/upbringing . . .

Q: Ramochki?

Mikhail Alekseevich: Direction [*napravlennost'*] . . . in a defined framework. Pioneers can do this, but not that. And *komsomoltsy*[8] can do this, but not that—a framework.

The overall point here is that frameworks for social order no longer exist. It is important to notice, however, that a sense of sin (grekh is a religious term) and <u>shame</u>, on the one hand, and Soviet upbringing on the other, can equally be agents of this order. For purposes of the logic here, religious and political "frameworks" serve the same function. Generally, then, common societal goals that are formed into a framework create moral and political order. When these frameworks fail and when discipline fails, social order will be literally spun into chaos. A line is drawn between the past and the present, in which the loss of discipline is treated as the dominant force in the directionality of history. In interviews, this process was described again and again.

The raptures of the radiant past echo in some important ways the ideals of the future promised by the Soviets (social harmony and social equality), but by the logic of the radiant past, something went (and is per-

8. *Komsomoltsy* are members of the Young Communist League. Even in provincial areas, being a member of the komomoltsy could mean the difference between getting a desired job or not.

haps eternally going) wrong in the way history has played out those promises. Something caused the situation to flip out of control. Lack of discipline, or external social controls, is invoked as the cause.

Chaos and the Verbal Prefix *Raz-*

Things fall apart; the center cannot hold; the trajectory from the radiant past to the wretched present is one of chaos. In and surrounding the radiant past, the verbal prefix *raz-* showed up often in narratives enough for me to wonder why. A few words about the function of verbal prefixes in Russian are in order.

Verbal prefixes are a feature of Russian verbs that allow speakers to place verbs into the perfective tense. In verbs of motion, these verbal prefixes quite literally indicate whether action comes out of something [*vy-*], or goes by [*pro-*], or approaches [*pod-*], or arrives at the threshold of [*do-*], or marches through something [*pere-*], or circumambulates it [*o-*], or goes in and out [*za-*], or even disperses in a centrifugal manner [*raz-*, or *ras-*]. In these cases, the verbal prefixes tend to add a literal vector to the sense of the verb. "I went all the way to the store," is thereby distinguished from "I left the store," or "I popped into the store."

The grammatical plot here thickens. Because these verbal prefixes are also used with verbs that are not focused on motion per se, they can and do take on broadly metaphoric features. It can be said that there is practically no completed action without some marker for movement and direction. If *ia proshla* means that I have in fact walked by something or someone, *ia prochitala* involves no "real" motion or vector of "going by a book," but it indeed involves a metaphor of having done so. *Ia vyliubilas'* (I fell out of love) does not involve exiting from a literal threshold, but from a metaphoric one.

The ethnographic/linguistic point is this: *Since a subtle layer of directionality is embedded in every verb construct, speaking becomes a stage on which metaphoric landscapes are sketched.* Verbing is, then, a vectored and vectoring act where speaking necessarily entails wending one's way through small cognitive landscapes. These landscapes can be traced only through the metaphors people use as a matter of habit, and those embedded in habitual grammatical categories. There is a methodological point, then, as well. This type of directional metaphor can be traced in narrative. While most verbs have "unmarked" perfective forms (*prochitat'* is far more common than *vychitat'*), *metaphoric analysis can be enriched by noticing extensive use (or unusual use) of a given verbal prefix within a discursive context.* In light of this, I argue (in the spirit of Whorf) that these small movements can give hints as to some of the broader gestures in symbolic space.

When attached to a verb (or, of course, various participles formed from verbs), the verbal prefix raz- can mean that one object becomes many parts (as in *razbit' stakany,* to shatter a glass); that there is disassembly of a whole (*razdvinut' stoly,* to take apart a table); that action is extended into many different directions or places (*razbrosat'/raskidat' veshchi,* to throw things about); and it can mean centrifugal movement (*raskhodit'sia,* to move apart in many pieces).[9] This is the clearest image of raz- that I have configured: *It signals something that begins as a whole and moves or spirals outward.*[10]

Sometimes, that outward movement causes destruction. Indeed, the words for destruction in Russian ring with raz- (*razrukha,* destruction; *razrushenie,* havoc; *razryv,* explosion, rupture; *raznuzdannyi,* unbridled, unruly; *razlozhenie* [raz + *lech',* to lie], decay, decomposition, putrefaction, demoralization). In 1921, four years after the Bolshevik Revolution, Anna Akhmatova wrote: *Vse raskhishcheno, predano, prodano.* All is plundered, betrayed, sold out. *Raskhishcheno* is ras-, and *khishcheno,* predatory. In village narratives, raz-, in these and other forms, signaled the social destruction of the present when contrasted with the radiant past.

Like so many of her co-villagers, Inna Ivanovna Nikolaeva's life was not an easy one; she had been sent to a prison camp as a young woman for reasons that were not made clear to me. Our interview was extremely cautious, marked by a formulaic praise of the past. Whatever her reasons for exclusively praising the past, her story followed the familiar logic that happiness is in the past, and that the present is marked by theft and destruction. Such comments were repeated several times during the course of the interview.[11]

9. Examples here are from Pulkhina et al. (1979:388–390).
10. Pesmen, who also noted the special place of the verbal prefix raz- (in the case of her work surrounding the symbolism of soul), has defined it similarly: "Raz- is a widely used Russian prefix that conveys dispersing, spreading, or annihilation by creating an expanse outward from the center" (2000:67).
11. Given the Soviet fear of speaking openly with foreigners, Inna Ivanovna's reticence was far easier to understand than the openness of many of her co-villagers.

It was good before. Happy. We lived poorly and there was only a little money. We lived better even than now. Now everything is stolen [*razgrablennoe*]. How many cities were abandoned and destroyed [*narushili*]?

Inna Ivanovna's construction of a fearful present where things are stolen links theft and destruction (and the verbal prefix raz-) with the present. Raz-, and the centrifugal movement it implies, appears twice in the following segment.

Q: Do you remember the time (of Stalin)?

Inna Ivanovna: I remember. Of course, I remember. I remember when our Stalin died. We lived with four children and one mother. I remember very well when Stalin died, how mama cried. "Oi," mama says, "Now, without Stalin, we will die."

Q: You were afraid . . .

Inna Ivanovna: Well, that, there would be no discipline. Everyone was afraid that there would be no discipline. There will be *raskhliabannost'* [looseness, instability, slackness]. There will be *razboltannost'* [aimlessness, disorderliness].

There will be no discipline and everything will fall apart. *Razboltannost'*, or the state of being all flung about (*razboltannyi*: adj.-*annyi*: disorderly; vb.: *razboltatsia* to come loose, to get out of hand, to come unstuck; root: *bolt*, chatter, talk, dangle) is a term that was used frequently when describing social disintegration. Below it is contrasted directly with the disciplined society of the past.

Maia Bogdanova: After the war, things got better until 1985 when Gorbachev took power. This democracy came and everything fell apart [razboltannost']. I want no part of this democracy. All it was was people having meetings, going to demonstrations, and saying what they wanted. Russia didn't need this. Russia, more than anything else, needs discipline. It needs severity [*strogost'*], so that when someone says something, it is done. [Stalin] was severe/strict [*strogii*]. The country is like a family. If the husband does his thing (*dlia sebia*) and the wife does her thing, and everyone does their thing, no good can come of it [*nichego ne budet*]. We need it so that one voice is in charge, and that everyone does what that person says.

In the uncontrolled present, there will be no discipline and everything will fall apart. Razboltannost' is a term that was used frequently in the village when describing social disintegration of the present. *Raskhliabannost'* (*ras*+ *khliabat'*: to rock, sway, reel, to come loose, to be unsteady, to hang out) evokes a similar unhinging.

In both of these terms, the verbal prefix raz- signals the kind of destruction that looks like center-fleeing. This unhinging and center-fleeing is also seen in other—nongrammatical—symbolic figures. The following citation uses the raz- prefix, but indicates this sort of outward destructive motion in broader metaphoric terms: "Now our affairs are going nowhere (lit: *nikudyshnoe delo*), everything has fallen apart (*razvalili*). Theft. Carnality. Everything has been completely stolen (*vse perekrali*). It's all *khoziain*-lessness." Here, the adjective "nikudyshnoe" (lit. no-whither) adds its sense of spatial disintegration to the verb *razvalit'* (raz-: centrifugal outward, *valit'*: throw down) and to the idea of thorough theft (that all objects are leaving their rightful owners), and the notion of khoyziain-lessness—which (and this is the next stage of analysis) loosens the final lid of the disciplined past. All point to a present that is out of control.

Words like razboltannost', raskhliabannost', and razrukha are used, but it is the centrifugal movement that it bears that is important, and not the term per se. The verbal prefix "raz" hints at this meaning.[12] But the center-fleeing, destructive idea can be configured without this prefix, as in: "Before, we worked. It was a happy time, of course. . . . It was friendly. Friendlier. And now, I don't know how they work now. They work, they dangle/hang out (*kak boltaiutsia*)." Here, it is the verb *boltat'sia* that is used to connote the chaotic (and unhappy) period of today.

There is a subtle but rather important difference between the radiant past as described in its own terms, and the snapshot of it given when describing social disintegration. The former, as discussed in earlier sections, is full of life and stories and song and personal "freedom." It is also full of visual imagery (descriptions of people and physical landscapes). In the latter, the radiant past, one could say, darkens. As in a dim room, one can make out only silhouettes and outlines; details shrink into darkness. The radiant past shrinks to its outlines. This part of the radiant past is a place of discipline and order. People are well behaved there. The song of the

---

12. In *The Russian Mind*, Hingley (1977:46–47) speaks of the verbal prefix raz- in terms of one side of a hypothetical Russian "character."

past, the river of the childhood, turns into a litany against the present. There is a suggestion in this tone change that there are separate enclaves in the radiant past.

Indeed, what seems to be emerging is a battle in the vector field of the radiant past. Forces that spin outward are overcoming the internal, energy-gathering forces of distsiplina. The freedom/svoboda of the past— so praised in earlier citations—is also made of an outward spinning force; but since it is a marker of the *worthy* part of the radiant past, it will not be cited, in this sense, as a source of social destruction. The "freedom" of the radiant past (not to be confused with political freedom, which will be addressed soon) creates a tension with the requirement for discipline in the radiant past. What is the nature of this tension? In the following, I continue to investigate along this pathway, from radiance to darkness; from peace and contentedness to terror and fear.

Fear and the Dark Days of Radiance

Outside the discursive realm of the radiant past, the fear of the Stalinist period was discussed openly:

> *Petr Nikolaevich:* It was frightening. Then, you know how they judged you? They arrive at night, knock, the car is waiting, they take you and that's it.

> *Q:* Were people afraid to speak against the [state] power?

> *Fedor Sergeevich:* They were afraid.

> *Anastasia Ivanovna:* They were afraid.

> *Fedor Sergeevich:* Before, you wouldn't speak, like we're now speaking. No.

> *Anna Petrovna:* In general, in the time of Stalin, [people] were afraid to say a word. [A person] thinks and is quiet.

> *Q:* And were you yourself afraid?

> *Anna Petrovna:* Of course, we feared everything.

But fear also had an explicit purpose. Indispensable to order keeping in an idealized past was the agency of fear. Again, the sources of fear were different: there was fear of the state, fear of local authorities, and fear of

God and other unseen forces, but the status of fear is the same: an indispensable mechanism for social control. Once again a dichotomy is drawn: fear is a positive feature of the disciplined past, but is absent in the present.[13]

> *Mikhail Alekseevich:* The disconnection of the people from religion—
> that's a huge error . . . because, they destroyed morality of family and
> religious traditions. Anyway, "Fear God," they said often. If a person
> does something wrong, "Fear God." And here [now], whom do we fear?
>
> *Larisa Andreevna:* Of course we were afraid. We were afraid of every-
> thing. Afraid of everything. And everything was done—people were very
> careful in life. And now, no one is afraid of anyone! What we want, we
> do! You get money if you work, you get money if you don't work.
>
> *Anna Grigorievna:* Yes, that was the starosta [elder]. . . . The starosta
> walks [by] and everyone was afraid, respected [him]. . . . And now,
> anyone can walk, and this one, like with this Yeltsin. If someone sees
> him, he won't get afraid. No one will say hello.

Fear, as a symbolic construct in the realm of the radiant past, is linked to keeping order in an ideal society. How can we go around not being afraid? How can we not be awed by a higher power (such as God, the government, or the starosta)? Like discipline, which is an external constraint of behavior, fear also serves to keep people in line.

Social controls in the radiant past versus the radiant present are summarized below.

Present	*Radiant Past/Social Controls*
chaos	discipline
social injustice	political repression
raz-movement (centrifugal vector)	*s*-movement (centripetal vector)
fearlessness	fear (that produces physical and moral order)

13. Note that in other discursive contexts, fear is certainly a part of the present. The fear in the radiant past is a fear that produces order. The fear of the present is a sign of moral chaos.

If the internal mechanism for the preservation of radiance is discipline, there is an external mechanism as well in the person of the leader, the khoziain. Here, in the darkening part of the radiant past, he emerges again.

Discipline and Leadership

> *Larisa Andreevna:* In the Soviet period, the Union period, we lived better, because we all submitted and listened. Now, who listens to whom? Who? We don't listen! We don't submit to anyone. We do [*tvorim*] what we want. We lived very well. We lived very well . . .
>
> All the bitterness that we lived through. My God, we lived through this. It's wrong to think of it. Tears pour out of the eyes.

Sometimes villagers would tell me with a flourish that Stalin—with his hard, cruel hand—wasn't so bad, after all. I tried to look into their eyes and figure out which level they were speaking on. Were they baiting me? Sometimes. Were they speaking from some longing for national pride and order? Often. Were they more deeply referring to a *vozhd'*, a stern and god-like leader who could give them limits and guidance through the agency of fear? The residents of Solovyovo could, almost without exception, describe the legendary moment of Stalin's death, and tell of the tears that they shed upon hearing the news. What were you crying for? "How will we live without anyone to rule us?" Now that they know of some of Stalin's horror, they will often lay the blame on Beria or other such underlings: "Stalin didn't even know about these things!" Once I even heard a theory that Stalin had an evil twin who was responsible for all of the darkness of that time. How else could that which was so bright ("Our kind father, Stalin! Our great leader, Stalin!") be punctuated so regularly with a knife so black? In groups, the descriptions of the time of Stalin were made of a kind of symphony of dark and light, with comments running in parallel streams where darkness spills out along the path to the bright future: "How we lived better then! How we were joyous! *One wrong word and they could take you away in the middle of the night.* We lived in friendship and generosity! *Remember how they took away that woman—for one little rhyme—she never came back.*"

The schoolchild's phrase, "Thank you, Comrade Stalin, for our happy childhood," rings distantly in memory. Where is that happy childhood?

There are many leaders, many khoziaeva, from the khoziain of the family and household, to the khoziain of a larger farmstead, to the khoziaeva of natural and social spaces like forests or barns or homes, to the khoziain of the nation. Not far from the golden wheat fields in the radiant past stood Stalin, the great and terrible khoziain of the Soviet Empire for over three decades. His name was mentioned often as part of litanies and laments that things are not the way they used to be in the golden days.

When I asked people if they remembered Stalin, they would often answer that, no, they only knew him from the radio and films. People seemed to neither know nor love Stalin as a historical character. However, they were and are intimate with his idealized function; that is, the maintenance of group cohesion through heavy-handed leadership and the bestowing of bounty. Stalin was an index of that functional complex. So prominent in Soviet history, he was like the figure in an icon—powerful and useful and able to be turned to in times of need, but more or less interchangeable with other saints. He sits at the head of the national community as an opaque symbol, a two-dimensional image of necessary proportions and functions.

More specifically, Stalin and figures like him have two roles: first, to keep order with a strict/severe hand; and second, to bestow bounty from unseen sources. These figures are separate from the local leadership and are aloof from their machinations. Like any khoziain, the nation-khoziain, as I will call him, is a requisite feature of social life, but his function is attached to the national rodina, as distinct from any various local ones. In narratives on the past, he shows up prominently in two cases: first, in terms of his role as a protector against social chaos, and second, in the nationwide trauma of his death. These two roles were often linked—his death being seen as literally unsurvivable by the narod. The narratives of the death of Stalin are interesting in this discussion because they mark a trauma of national scale that scars the landscape of the radiant past. Although the radiant past is not always located during the time of Stalin's life, it is almost always located under the hood of that nation-khoziain's protection and grace.

When this nation-khoziain dies, the state risks dying. In the following quotation, the state after Stalin's death is plagued by murder and theft.

> *Valentina Ivanovna:* I remember how I came to work in the morning. The train went at four in the morning and work started at seven. We arrive and sit down there. There was no later train. We just arrived at the station and the radio said it was four o'clock. What's going on? Stalin is dead.

Everyone is in tears, everyone is sobbing. Many people were gathered at the station. And everyone cried. Everyone was pouring [tears]. On the street. During the time of Stalin, we lived better than we live now. . . . Such robbery didn't exist. Such murder didn't exist.

In this construction, Stalin's death marks the end of the radiant period. Freedom and social safety were replaced by the horrible question mark of social crisis. The fate of the nation is lamented, where the "dark" (here, unenlightened, ignorant) people bemoan their status as khoziain-less.

Antonina Sergeevna: When Stalin died, I was catching fish with the men on the lake in the winter. I went everywhere, everywhere. So, when they buried him, [in our] *sel'sovet,* where the post office is now, in that place, we sat. Sat and cried. We all are crying. We don't know anything. . . . "Now there is no *khoziain.* Now in the country, what will happen? What will happen now? And we are dark people [*liudi temnye*]." We said, "What will happen now?" Oi.

Similarly:

Iuliia Ivanovna: We cried. It was a great pity that Stalin died. Now who will stand and lead?

Laments such as these have broader echoes in Russian death rituals. There is a folk genre of death songs/laments of rural Russia called *prichitanie.* In them, the death of a loved one or neighbor is bemoaned, and the survivors are referred to as orphans. The requirement for such a lament seems to be that the dead was a member of a svoi-formation, and here, Stalin is likened to the *rodnoi* father and the people of Russia are, of course, the orphaned wards of the state.[14]

The nation-khoziain is a powerful figure in the realm of the radiant past, and his death is a profound crisis there. Outside the terrain of the narrated radiant past, the same Stalin—along with other outsiders—can be hated. As Konstantin Andreevich said, "no normal person" would praise Stalin or any other leader.

No person would praise Stalin and yet, the crisis of his death was at least as real as the way it punctures the landscape of the radiant past with

14. See Beznin (1993) for *prichitaniia* collected in the region of Belozersk.

its tears. Memory stops there and pays its respects, perhaps by bringing its own sorts of flowers. Whether or not Stalin was loved as a historical figure, the trauma of his loss is tied in the memory to out-of-control social disintegration. Villagers were not taught to blame him for the repression that they witnessed (and, certainly, all kinds of efforts were expended in maintaining Stalin's infallible, fatherly image). Some, however, out of extraordinary clarity of vision, were able to see beyond what they were told, and could say, "Glory to God! Now at least we can rest."

What could this be about? One could argue that the nation-state of "Russia" comes alive in the imagination only sporadically. The role of the state vis-à-vis its rural communities was from its outset in the early second millennium one of tax extraction and army enlistment. The state also introduced the Church and sent its emissaries off into the far reaches of the empire, although the results of that ideological effort were far from complete. How, under circumstances such as these, does the nation-state become, properly, a birth home, a rodina, a space that requires a khoziain? (Perrie 1987) If there is a nation-rodina, it will require a nation-khoziain. Rodina (like svoi, on which it depends) is a concept that is ready to expand and contract according to the exigencies of the imagination. The rodina does not always have to be a nation-rodina.

In the lifetime of the people of Solovyovo, the imagined nation came alive most tangibly in World War II. The very real German enemy that caused the very real deaths of an estimated 20 million Soviets was enough to form a circle around the imagined nation.[15] Stalin was required in this setting to be the khoziain; it was for him to bring inspiration (bounty) and order (discipline) to the people. Having been planted in this way in the imagination, his death, like the death of any great bounty-giver, needed to be mourned.[16]

In the radiant past, when the imagined nation comes alive (when Mama Rodina becomes Mat' Rossiia), it requires a khoziain, like any closed social space. Otherwise, going about their business of making an

---

15. Exact numbers for Soviet World War II casualties, military and civilian, have been elusive. A long footnote in the 2002 edition of the *New Encyclopaedia Britannica* (Royde-Smith 2002:1023) explains the sources of some of the discrepancies. Nevertheless, numbers that include broad demographic indicators support estimates in the range of 18 million to 20 million. See also Brown et al. (1982).

16. See Merridale's *Night of Stone* (2000) for the longing for Stalin in the context of the violence of World War II.

agricultural living, even in the imagination, folks would prefer to be left alone to their tangible social practices. This is not a minor point: The ways and whims of Moscow were certainly able to penetrate into the consciousness of the village. But there is much to suggest that its presence was rather more abstract and formal than anything else. People are attached to Stalin as a national khoziain, but that khoziain is a distant one. He can be the people's inspiration in a foreign war, or perhaps intercede in political arrests caused by bumbling local authorities. But he has no power over the domains in which people spend their days, hours, lives, loves, and deaths. For intercession in such matters, there are other places to turn.

And even in the landscape of the memory, the important qualities of the radiant past belong at the local level. Obshchenie, social intercourse, is a local quality. As is freedom.

Bifurcation in the Radiant Past and the Problem of *Svoboda*

Radically different resonances in the word "svoboda" give clues that the landscape of the radiant past is essentially bifurcated. I have shown how one meaning of svoboda inhabits the free-spirited past. It is linked to social equality and the safety and joy of social connection. It is also idealized as part of the radiant future.

But there is a very different svoboda; this "freedom" is reviled, as in an earlier quotation regarding discipline: "Freedom (svoboda) is good, but still you need discipline (distsiplina)." Freedom in this sense is dangerous because it threatens to undermine the social order. Svoboda (and its analog, *volia,* which refers to freedom and will) are described as negative features of the world today.

> *Antonina Sergeevna:* The best period was before Gorbachev. Yes, we began to live beautifully. Better, for many years. I don't remember how many years. Stalin died, then, after Stalin, things got better until Gorbachev. Of course it got worse. From what? They now gave us a lot of freedom/free will [*takuiu voliu dali*]. No responsibility. Anyone does whatever he wants. Anyone can steal from whomever. Anyone can kill anyone anywhere. They will hardly investigate here.

Freedom here is not that accompaniment to the ease of social connectedness in the past. It is, by contrast, the companion of social disorder (characterized by theft, murder and the lack of support for laws). It is something sinister. What was the meaning of freedom that carried with it such negative connotations? Below, Maia Bogdanova lets both uses of the term clash rhetorically.

Q: Was Stalin to blame?

Maia Bogdanova: No. Not at all Stalin. Stalin himself didn't know a lot of things. He himself didn't know.

Q: So what was it?

Maia Bogdanova: People in the leadership—the government. And do you think that now, Yeltsin doesn't know? He doesn't know. Yeltsin doesn't know a lot. And are you telling me that there are no repressions now? That now, they all say that we have freedom of speech. We don't have *any kind* of freedom. Before, there was freedom. If you weren't happy with something, you can write something up. There you can ask for help and they will figure it out. And now! No one will figure it out. Let them kill you! And no one will figure it out.

Q: Do you think that freedom of speech is important?

Maia Bogdanova: They gave too much freedom. A lot. And not there, where it's needed.

First, Maia Bogdanova tells us that freedom (expansive, interconnected freedom) was part of the past—something that we most definitely do not possess now. Next, she says that they "gave too much freedom." This is, clearly, that second, sinister freedom ("frameless freedom") that can cause the world to fall apart (through theft, murder, and lawlessness). In fact, "expansive freedom" and "frameless freedom" are confronted several times in interviews. For example, Valentina Ivanovna says that not only was there no "frameless freedom" before, there is none now (despite what they are told by the government):

Valentina Ivanovna: Of course, you couldn't say a word . . . and then we already understood that you shouldn't say an extra word. And now we can't. They say that now there is freedom of speech. No. Say something against [the powers], and they will lock you up.

We shouldn't be confused, she implies, by the rhetoric of the current national powers: things are no better now than they ever were "then," even if we acknowledge that bad things happened "then." Valentina Ivanovna quite enjoyed, as a rule, analyzing and critiquing both current and past leaders. But there was something almost sacred in her distinction between the ugly present and the radiant past. Earlier, she had spoken glowingly of "expansive freedom," and that in the time of Stalin, "Everyone was free.... Such robbery didn't exist. Such murder didn't exist." We should not think, she seems to say, that good and proper "expansive freedom" could ever be appropriated by the "frameless freedom" of current political discourse.

Larisa Andreevna also would not call the world of today a good or happy one. Freedom, in the following quotation, existed "before," but does not exist now. In that sense, it should be "expansive freedom," but we must look more carefully:

> *Larisa Andreevna:* Speak freely, what was that? If people were speaking for the truth, fighting for the truth. And if it was hooliganism, then they sent [them] away, took them from the path of the road. We survived our whole lives, and they didn't take any of us. No one was taken. Because we worked for honor and for glory. We fulfilled all the work honestly . . . without any discussion.

It was fair and just, "before," to throw people into prison, if they were being hooligans. They didn't do that to us, because we were righteous, and worked for "honor and glory." Her freedom is one that is, in a sense, taken into a Soviet discourse. As a religious woman, Larisa Andreevna knew firsthand what it means to need to keep her beliefs quiet. And yet, as a communist, a "believing" communist, she would not give up the honor and glory of Soviet ideals. Her freedom was a larger configuration, as it contained Soviet ideals that were part of the radiant past and its higher goals. When the two freedoms so clearly overlap, there can be no social disarray, can there? The freedom of speech ("What is that?" she asks rhetorically) is not something that people would even want, particularly. How can this contradiction be resolved?

It would be irresponsible, in this discussion, not to remark on the politics of "freedom" and the particular connotations of the term "freedom of speech" (*svoboda slova*). Soviet patriotism, gleaned from its various sources (and I would say again that the most powerful unifying idiom that brought it to life was not the bright future and the other promises of communism, but the battle against the Germans in World War II), was not discussed at great length in interviews, but it permeated nearly all political discussions in the village—while waiting in line for bread at the village store, or when gathered around the bus stop, or in each other's homes. The Soviet Union, people remind each other, inspired fear among all the nations. It was a great power, the first and greatest of the socialist states, the place where a unity of languages and cultures existed, and where one could find economic justice. It sent the first man into space and made landmark scientific discoveries, in spite of its (one could say) near-holy sufferings. Unlike America, people said, it was just to its minorities, and took care of its weak. All these were lessons that everyone could cite—regardless of the degree of cynicism with which they otherwise faced the Party and its legacy.

Although it is not my intention to analyze Russian nationalism—a rich and important subject that deserves full-length ethnographic study in its own right—it must be noted here, in the bounds of this radiant past, that the present will partly destroy the past for nationalist reasons. The West comes marching in, bearing (among other things) its native ideology. "Freedom," in one of its manifestations, is the way that the former enemy brags about itself. "Freedom" and "freedom of speech" are dangerous, not only because they threaten that one side of the radiant past (the khoziain should be keeping order!), but because people *feel them as words from the West*. The first associations with the word "freedom" (referring to political freedom) are often the new outrageously violent or sexual television programs from the West that now appear regularly. "Freedom" means the West taking hegemonic control. In the same way that other conquering nations bring in their "damned languages and customs," America—it is felt by many—has colonized with its damned "freedom." Liberty to an American is a noble truth. Even in the Russian backwoods, the term resonates instead with "libertine." Animals are free, people imply, but are humans animals? "How can we live without boundaries, without limits? How can we expect Russia to flourish without a strong guiding hand?" Svoboda is a large and old word, but when it is used in this context, it tightens and narrows—it's like an unknown relative coming in from a foreign country. It might look the same but it smells different. The expansiveness of "freedom" is fine in the context of the lyrical, idyllic, timeless world before. But "freedom," when it means "do whatever you want," is dangerous not only because of its way of loosening up the frames of order, but because—in the stretches of its borrowed meanings—it marks national humiliation.

NB

RETHINKING THE RADIANT PAST

* * *

Chaos and Control

It is tempting to speak of imaginary worlds in terms of dream worlds, perhaps because both worlds seem to be led by symbolically generous logics. You walk into a familiar room and its proportions slide. The next door leads to another place; it was a word that got you there, an image perhaps, an anxiety pulsing in the foundations of the house. This analogy serves an illustrative purpose: imaginary worlds are recurring. Not only do we walk over their ground again and again, but we do so in a dimension of suspended and twisted time.

There is no place in utopia for time. Indeed, physics teaches us that it is the very tendency that the physical world has to move toward chaos that lends time its directionality. Similarly, in village narratives, the radiant past is fixed in a forever-past. But fixed there, as well, are traumas of unleashed chaos. Like the logic of the familiar dream, we return along the convoluted paths of that trauma as we walk through the radiant past: things were perfect, then something terrible happened.

Forces are at work that first make that ideal world lopsided, and then propel it into movement. This is seen in narratives as a terrible crisis. The happy, outward-moving connections between people and the very act of broadening the self into the realm of the other give rise to a chaos that cries for control. Internal and external discipline are used to put controls on this chaos, but are unable to cease the flow of time. So here we stand, in the present—the eternal present—in a constant state of lament for that better time.

At a deeper level, the radiant past is marked by a vector outward, from the self to the other. This is the essence of social connection. In the radiant past, the soul is open and expansive, and this openness ties people into communities of svoi. The very same outward vector has a frightening side, as well. Social chaos (exemplified in the verbal prefix raz- but configured metaphorically in many other ways) causes social controls to be necessary. Some social controls are internal to an individual (distsiplina), and others come from the "frames" granted by state and religious systems. The most potent creator of order, however, very much alive in the radiant past, is the Stalin-like khoziain figure. He creates order from fear from above. The tension between the inner expansion that causes social connection and the other that causes social chaos is what propels time's arrow. We go from the radiant past to the lonely, destroyed present. And we keep doing it forever and ever.

What is to be made of this radiant world? Why is it told and retold in its shades of light and dark? In the radiant past, favorite gestures of social well-being are given a native home—a home never located *here*, but always *there*. One could argue that this radiant past functions simply as a discursive opiate that gives rise to social passivity. Many have argued, after all, that discourse reifies and reproduces the power of state ideology: If perfection is stuck in the past and inaccessible to the present, then somehow nothing can ever be really expected to change.[17] The acceptance (and even elevation) of poverty could be seen, in this light, as an ideological means of pacifying a sorry, tired, abused population. The villagers remain poor and slavish vis-à-vis the state, because any striving for betterment is capped and locked in the past.

Certainly, in its promises for a radiant future, the Soviet state actively enters the discourse on perfect societies. But, interestingly, this state never really explicitly controls the use of radiant societal images. Village narratives show that any life to the particular Eden that the state bestows on the imagination of the future is appropriated back into that of the past—where perfections promised for the future are locked discursively in the radiant "river of childhood." In other words, villagers take this ideological material and use it for their own purposes. Sometimes these purposes are reproductive of comfortable orders (in their acceptance of the hard hand of the state); sometimes they are generative of a form of localized resistance to orders (in their rejection of the greed, selfishness, and chaos that villagers see as externally forced upon them); and sometimes they are about a shared memory of loveliness and order, of expansiveness and freedom—entwined in a metaphoric pathway that is at least as poetic as it is ideological.

I see the radiant past as a ruler by which the present—emptied of its physical beauty and its social charms—is judged. I see it as active, in that it forces the issue of interconnectedness, on the one hand, and the need for external control, on the other. I see it not as static, but as generative of a tension between expansiveness and order. I see it as locked in a single time, but, because of its particular symbolic make-up (where the forces that connect also careen outward to cause chaos), as generative of

17. See Willis (1977), Bakhtin (1984, 1986), Bourdieu (1991), and Ries (1997) for discussions on the relationship between narrative and power.

a back and forth in time—a dialectic where there is social happiness and social weeping, lawlessness and iron hands.

To the extent that order is brought by a terrifying khoziain-figure the size and proportions of the state itself, the radiant past belongs, in part, to the discourse of belonging to a Soviet space. But it would be a mistake to see this way of looking toward a khoziain-figure for order and transformative power as new and exclusive to Soviet ideology. This question will be treated in depth later. For now, the radiant past will be treated as a symbolic landscape in memory that amounts to a social template by which all social states can be judged. There is where the grass grows far and wide. There is where one doesn't simply work, but one goes to work singing, hands "interlocked," loving one's life.

5

Wonders

I tak blizko podkhodit chudesnoe
k razvalivshimsia griaznym domam . . .

And how near the miraculous draws
To the dirty, tumble-down huts . . .

—ANNA AKHMATOVA, 1921[1]

MIR CHUDESNOGO (THE WORLD OF WONDERS)

* * *

There are memories of strange and miraculous things. What can be made of them?

The boundaries of the radiant past were relatively easy to define. In certain discursive contexts, the past is always better than the present. In light of this, the "radiant past" was defined in a simple binary manner. The task there was to draw out the particular dynamics of symbolism in that part of narrative memory. Other important narratives in Solovyovo—ones that define and reiterate key landscapes in social memory—are rather more elusive.

---

1. Translation by Hemschemeyer (1992:280).

When speaking of beings that inhabit the forest or lurk in the barn, or ghosts that fly in the night, folklore casts these stories into categories and analyzes them in their own terms (and often in a historical vacuum). It divides them by taxonomy, morphological structure, themes, and characters. Fairytales, which comprise a genre, are stories about unseen beings that pass into the world of the living. The field of Russian folklore has inspired some of the great currents in twentieth-century thought: formalism, structuralism, and generic studies.[2] And yet, folklore appears to be marked by an unspoken axiom: Purer genres existed before. What exists now—a mix of folkloric, Christian, New Age, Soviet-spiritual, and even belief in alien worlds—is seen as a murkier version of what once was.

Wondrous things of many different kinds happen. How are we to deal with the fact that fantastic things happen with many names, some of which are not neatly located in the catalogues of folk literature? Disparate characters enliven stories with diverse plotlines, but the point, as far as memory is concerned, does not end in chaos. Similarly to how Ries's (1997:51–64) *babushki*—lost on the way to buy sugar in Moscow—fill ancient folkloric functions, the village stories mix modern and ancient themes and deal, along the way, with basic problems of group identity, power, and contradiction.

For the purposes of plotting pathways in memory, I identify the boundaries of the world of the *chudesnoe* by understanding the narrative genre in terms of function, and not in terms of thematic content. In other words, even if a large part of the world of the miraculous is inhabited by fantastic forces and beings that come from Russian "folk culture," it is not defined by them. Rather, the miraculous is defined by what happens within that space—that is, it is defined by what it *does* and not by what it *is*. So what does it do?

In the broadest sense possible, *in the world of the chudesnoe, is a world where the regular, predictable aspects of time and space are suspended.* When one is there, one can expect invisible beings to come into view, sounds to ring out when there is no source, and time and distance to collapse as flat as an unopened top hat. For the purposes of my analysis, I am more concerned with the nature of this spatiotemporal malleability than with the characters that enliven it. Genre is the theoretical contract that says that meaningful orders of discourse indeed exist, ones with

---

2. Roman Jakobson, Vladimir Propp, and Mikhail Bakhtin, respectively, are the best-known Russian innovators in these fields.

broad societal relevance. The idea that this genre can be plotted as a topographical symbolic space shifts the focus from the boundaries of the discourse to its internal resonances, textures, symbolic configurations, and directions.

As in the case of the radiant past, this sketch of narrative space aims at understanding the way certain kinds of talk iterate and reiterate the relationships between agency—at individual and group levels—and power. In the language of memory's topography, I am mapping how interdimensional power of a certain quality is introduced into social circles.

The approach to the world of wonders is heralded by certain linguistic and gestural modes; narrative changes within its bounds. Paths through this symbolic space are sometimes light and easy (even comical), and at other times are threatening or deadly. Sometimes what happens in it looks like grace. This place where all dimensions are, as it were, up for grabs—has a lot to say about the workings of multilayered symbolic space—where equations are perched over zeros and chaos and surreal elegance ensue. Why would rural Russians head there—to that place?[3]

WONDROUS STORIES

* * *

More Wonders "Before"

Q: I heard that there was some story about Smirnova. Her daughter. Some story about her. She got lost.

Anna Grigorievna: Ah! That's Svetka.

Q: You heard it?

Anna Grigorievna: Yes.

---

3. There are some fine collections of stories about the fantastic beings that inhabit the Russian north. I have relied particularly on Cherepanova, *Mifologicheskie rasskazy i legendy russkogo severa* (Mythological Tales and Legends of the Russian North) (1996), and the well-known nineteenth-century collection edited by Firsov and Kiseleva, *Byt velikorusskikh kresy'ian-zemleplashtsev* (The Everyday Life of the Great Russian Peasants) (1993). In English, Ivanits's standard work, *Russian Folk Belief* (1989), provides an overview of the beings that inhabit local spaces (home, fields, forests, and waters) in village life in the nineteenth century. All of these works offer the transcribed stories of Russian villagers. I have used them mostly to check the representativeness of the stories that I was able to gather.

Q: What happened?

Anna Grigorievna: I don't know. She went to walk; she walked and walked. So, people also knew [how to communicate with other levels]. You come upon his tracks on the path. Where he walks, you will come across his tracks. Before, more of all that went around, appeared . . . All that.

Svetka Smirnova was a child some twenty years ago. In the context of this story, that is far enough in the past to be *ran'she*—a period before when people knew the magic arts and more of "all that" was evidenced in the world. Regardless of the fact that many of the fantastic stories that I heard took place "this summer" or "a few years ago," there was a general insistence that it was the past that housed the lion's share of wonders:

Iuliia Ivanovna: That was before. . . . Now you don't hear anything [about it].

Valentina Ivanovna: Now people have become craftier than the devil. Before, people were baptized, and now there are many nonbaptized. They are not afraid of the demons, or of the devil.

Anna Vladimirovna: Before, there were *domovye*.

It is not simply the fact that the past holds more wonders that is important here. Several times I was told that these beings—demons, *leshii, domovye*—existed before, but no longer exist today. In such statements, there is no general denial of the existence of otherworldly beings, but only of their existence in the present day. Below, Larisa Andreevna contradicts herself, first flatly denying the existence of the forest being known as the leshii—calling the whole thing stupid—and then giving examples of how the leshii "walked" in the past.

Larisa Andreevna: Well, you say that in the forest, there is something. There is nothing there. I don't believe anything from anybody. It's all stupid. It's a lie.

Q: People used to believe this?

Larisa Andreevna: They believed it before. And it existed before, a long, long time ago. At some [definite] time. Before these wars. Somehow existed. Everyone said that there, in the forest, the leshii walks around. Sings, walks. . . . [T]his was before these wars. And that was before, long, long ago. Old people who were sixty years old were there. Before, a lot of that happened. And now, there is none of it.

Q: So, for example?

Larisa Andreevna: There were all kinds of things. Some people lie, others [tell the] truth.

"People believed it before; and it existed before": It is the very belief that grants life to this other world. If that belief is in the past, then in the past (or, otherness in time) that world comes to life. Larisa Andreevna's logic is not atypical in any setting where the boundaries of discourse (in this case, the entry into a particular symbolic landscape) are shifted. The difference between the forest that is empty today ("There is nothing there!") and filled "before" with the roaming, singing leshii is a stark one. Once the journey into that symbolic space has begun, the terrain blossoms with imagery and movement.

How is it possible to know that this magical "past" is not the "radiant past"? If there was more magic "before," why not simply include that as a magical sheen that overlays the radiant past? There are indeed some points of confluence, most importantly, in concerns that focus on the problems of svoi production and maintenance (a matter for discussion later). However, in narrative, these worlds exist more or less apart from one another. In conversations, it would take a special line of questioning for me to get to the world of the chudesnoe at all. The symbolic topography of the radiant past was centered on the dynamics of social life, as a more or less closed system. The *mir chudesnogo* rips open that system and invites other "levels." It will become clear that these two imaginary worlds can overlap, but that they are in a functional sense, quite distinct.

Supernatural phenomena appear to inhabit the past in Solovyovo comfortably. The past is a better, although not the only, place for wonders. Important is the idea that that world—the world of the chudesnoe—is colored with "non-present-ness." Like with the radiant times, the chronology of such a past is not clear—it is "back then" and perhaps, more importantly, "over there." I would venture that *the use of "the past" as a construct here is primarily for the purpose of establishing this world's otherness.* A narrative gives clues that once a certain discursive threshold is crossed (expressed here as the boundary between the present and the past—but not exclusively so), the possibility of these wonders magnifies.

It would be a misunderstanding of the problem to let it rely solely on stated beliefs or nonbeliefs in fantastic worlds. True or not true, something out there is beckoning. Its form can change, its moods and humor can change—but it is summoning one to another place, aiming to lead one away.

Leading Away

The story about young Sveta got around:

> *Iuliia Ivanovna:* This happened to Mitia Smirnov's sister, Sveta, when she was young—six years old. Her mother yelled at her and she left the house. She went into the field and saw an old man. He called to her and took her into the swamp, where there was a small island. She slept there a night and spent two days. When they were looking for her they went to a special old woman [to help find her] . . .

> The little girl said that the old man took her away and played with her and fed her. This *babka* knows the head forest khoziain in charge of the planets and the whole region.

> The little girl was unnerved. At first, she was silent, stunned by the experience, but she was okay after that. It was the grandfather of the forest. He appears as an old friend or grandfather.

Spending even a short time in the forest of the Russian north—gathering mushrooms and berries or walking through it on the path to somewhere else—is enough to acquaint an outsider with the feelings of awe at the forest's beauty and the very tangible fear of getting lost there. The forest is, in a practical sense, a place where the stuff of food and shelter lies in wait. Villagers enter it regularly for its mushrooms, berries, game, firewood, tree branches, and "grasses" (botanicals used for healing). It is also necessary to go through the forest when headed for a distant village—though with an aging population, and with the ukrupnenie of the 1960s these sorts of journeys have become more and more rare. A longtime resident of a particular village knows the forest landscape by its hills, swamps, and patches of trees. Some spots have names, such as Belyi Mys (White Promontory), where there are good mushrooms and nearby cranberries in rust-colored mosses, or the forest patch called Pominova that runs parallel to the cow pastures, where blood-red raspberries are gathered. The forest can be catalogued for its bounties, but when you go farther—"idu, idu, idu, idu . . . (I walk, walk, walk, walk . . .)"—that map fades and even for veterans of the forest, there is a point of disorientation and intensification of the hovering threat of beasts (such as the bears, wild boar, elk, and wolf that inhabit these forests) and of other beings not so readily seen. The forest happened to be the setting for many village stories. And its host, with his whims of munificence and malevolence, was the seen, and then unseen figure who beckoned. The following narrative is a typical one. In it another child—this time young Antonina Timofeevna—is lost and then led away.

> *Iuliia Ivanovna:* She didn't tell you the story, Antonina Timofeevna?
> When she was a little girl, her mother once yelled: "Go to the devil!"
> [*Idi k cherty, k leshemy!*] Then Anna got lost and they couldn't find her
> for a whole day. On the second day, the father of Valov was out in the
> woods and heard someone whimpering. He listened some more and
> realized that it was a girl, a small child. Following the sound, he found
> Annia sitting on a dry patch in the middle of a swampy area of the forest.
> He asked the girl whom she belonged to and she said just that she was
> Annia. "Where do you come from?" "I don't know. Some small village."
> She was from the area of Myshino. [Valov's father] asked how she got
> here and she said, "Dedushka gave me his hand and I followed him."
> He took the girl home.

Stories such as the one above are indeed quite common.[4] Young Svetka goes toward the old man of the forest. Or cows wander off—moving not by "their own will," but by the will of another. Or a sheep is "led away," and only brought back with the intercession of a local specialist in the supernatural arts. Demons call to a young man who suffers from alcohol and "falling sickness." A young orphan is called to at night by the white ghost of her mother. Children and animals in stories are particularly vul-

---

4. In fact, I heard so many stories like these while living in Solovyovo, that I simply stopped recording them.

nerable to being lured from the here and now, that is, from the center of the living, breathing social circles.

This form of pulling away is not limited to the forest realm. Any number of in-between times or spaces can invite such contacts with otherworldly beings. As Turner writes in *The Ritual Process* (1969:95), some spaces and times—liminal in nature—are particularly marked by their potential to invite other worlds. Turner lists death and the womb, the state of invisibility, the state of bisexuality, the time of darkness, and the space of the wilderness, as typical of the sorts of liminal zones charged with supernatural dangers. In Solovyovo, stories where people are lured away take place in forests and graveyards, not long after the death of a close relative, at night, and while blindly drunk. In these stories, there is danger and magic at crossroads and thresholds. Through them, lessons are learned: One should never shake hands across a doorway, or walk into an unknown village or forest without incantations or other protective shields; and safety pins fastened to undergarments protect the body from the sorcery of outsiders.[5]

Lingering in the in-between space of thresholds attracts the forces from other worlds that can potentially lead you away into a surreal world. It is my argument that regardless of any given ritual, incantation, or holy object used to circum-protect[6] space, the real issue is the anxiety felt at thresholds and the meaning of the infusion of magic in these liminal times. Being led away is frightening: By paying close attention to this general trepidation, a view emerges that is rather closer to a topography of social comfort (and its absence) than to a semiotics of ritual. Why is the person fearful? And what is the shape of the disruptive powers that come calling?

Listening Ears

Valentina Ivanovna: There were many miracles. . . . Before, you couldn't curse at your cattle [saying], "The leshii take you away." [If you said it,] the leshii would lead [the cattle] away.

---

5. See Ivanits (1989:67–68) for protective strategies against, specifically, the leshii.
6. Perhaps, to "circumvallate": to surround with or as if with a rampart. See Ivanits (1989:49) for mention of "magic circles."

In Solovyovo's stories, words—and sometimes simply thoughts—are uttered. Then, these words are perceived by the leshii, or domovoi, or some other unspecified set of actorless ears. Something is uttered—even in private—and that which is uttered is heard or received. This can happen because these beings, distinct and indistinct, are everywhere:

> *Anna Grigorievna:* There is a host of the forest, a host in every [little] village. Of course. A host of the bathhouse. They are everywhere.
>
> *Q:* It seems to me that there are some words . . .
>
> *Anna Grigorievna:* "Khoziain, khoziaiushka.
>
> Permit me into the bathhouse
>
> To wash, to steam myself."
>
> *Q:* If you don't say these words, what can happen?
>
> *Anna Grigorievna:* Who knows what you can expect in the night?

Who knows what you can expect in the night in the bathhouse, graveyard, threshold, or forest? In stories of contact with otherworldly forces, there is an awareness that beings are out there waiting to make themselves known. They could be otherworldly khoziaeva or khoziaiki—they could inhabit the bathhouse or any little village, or gather in the dark forest at night. They comprise a whole range of named and unnamed creatures. Such a creature can, as Fedor Sergeevich told me, "appear as whomever he wants." "Something," he added, "is out there. Some kind of force exists." Fedor Sergeevich reminded me in several of his stories that "*chto-to est*'" ("there is something"). Some kind of force existed; the form was incidental: It could be God or it could be one of the *khoziaeva* or it could just be that amorphous force. There is *something* and it's "wrong" not to believe. There are two important points here: first, the supernatural world is a ready recipient for invocations (both intentional and otherwise); and second, The imagination of the chudesnoe little cares which ideology it springs from.[7] The forces that fill it are form- and name-seeking, regardless of whether they fall into any given ideological taxonomy.

---

7. Even if, with regard to other questions, the ideological source is indeed important. See Chapters 7 and 8 of this volume.

Readiness comes from the teeming supernatural world itself. But re-actions—where forms come into being and act in the world—are set off by (among other things) words. Words are uttered, and things happen. Mikhail Alekseevich warned Iuliia when she cursed using reference to the devil, "all words will be remembered." Curses such as, "The leshii take you away!", were common in the village. Usually, I was told, they are ut-tered in moments of frustration, without thinking ("without behind-thought"). So, after one man spent a long day working and his calf would not walk where it should, he smacked the calf and let out a curse, and *de-dushka lesovoi* caused the cow to disappear:

> Ded didn't like it that the man had sworn at the cow. For that reason, he hid the cow in the field. . . . The owner of the cow hit his own cow and the cow went out to the field. You should never hit a cow and hurry them through the gate, and never swear. You should say, "Go with God." Ded can either protect animals, or attack them, depending on the khoziain.

Stories in which curses were the operative words that awakened the attention of otherworldly powers were common. Yet other kinds of words were also ready to be heard. Just as a person can trigger the su-pernatural into action with misdirected curses, the correct attention to supernatural beings and forces—affectionate and respectful—can help a person, once lines have been crossed and magical space has been entered. When asking grandfather forest for permission to enter the woods, warm words must be used. The words should be, Anna Grigorievna told me, "totally affectionate—totally kind!" When she knew she would have to sleep in the forest alone at night, Anna Grigorievna herself would some-times invoke not only grandfather forest, but "mother pine."[8] She would say, "Mother pine tree, sweet one. Allow me to sleep here. Save, guard me. Allow me."[9] The tone of these words is warm and humble, and is sharply different from the sound of curses, such as "The leshii take you!", which can cause great harm. Sweetness and affection, regardless of the

---

8. The notion that trees have a spiritual presence is a part of ancient Slavic lore. See Propp (1995[1963]) for an example.

9. Esli zabludish'sia i nado tam nochevat', skazhi: 'Mat' elochka, milaia. Otpusti noche-vat'. Spasi, sokhrani menia. Pustite.

words of address chosen, bring about protection and patronage. The lilt of the phrase is clearly no less important than its content.[10]

Thus, depending on whim and circumstance, the treatment of an individual can vary in this form-finding universe: You simply never know if the manifestation that comes will look like a gentle grandfather or a nasty demon. Clearly, there are certain approaches that one can take to try and secure love and protection from the unseen forces, and certain intercessions that one can attempt once the more vengeful side of beings is brought out.

Yet regardless of the words uttered, there are certain states that raise the likelihood of contact with welcome and unwelcome miracles. A beckoning can take place in the space between waking and dreaming, between drunkenness and sobriety, and in the fuzzy world of the partially civilized forest. Many of these stories take place on a journey, that is, when a person is literally between here and there. A closer examination of this space is in order.

Journeys and Disorientation

One day, while transporting cream from one village to the next, a man named Vit'ka comes upon a stranger on the road. Fedor Sergeevich tells the story:

> *Fedor Sergeevich:* And I'm telling you that he left Nikitkin and passed by some dedushka. The [dedushka] said: "Take me where I'm going." And he sat that dedushka [down in his cart]. And so, they drove and drove, he says, heading somewhere. Then, he says, "The dedushka got lost somewhere and I was alone. And I went everywhere." He says, "I saw the ferry in the river." It's true, he went near the Sheksna River on the horse. The ferry, he says he saw. That's it. "And where is the horse?" "I don't know where."

Vit'ka was found on the second day, sitting on the road eating berries, his horse gone and having forgotten how he got there. Vit'ka's cart, which had escaped him somehow, was found far away, upturned and wedged between tree stumps. The men who finally freed the cart concluded that

---

10. Every time I asked about the words of a particular spell, they changed a bit. The practice of magic does not seem to rely on getting all the words exactly "right," but on the proper positioning of the invocation.

Vit'ka could not have placed it there himself, as it would have taken "in-human strength." The dedushka lesovoi was to blame.

Whether taking place in the forest or on the road, on the outer limits of a village or the world of the living, stories that include brushes with wonders almost always involve a journey of sorts, either by being lured "out there" or by enticing the unseen forces with one's distance from the center of things.[11] Again and again, as the stories are told, "I had gone for mushrooms when I saw a figure" or, "I was returning home from sell-ing cream when I chanced upon a man. . . ." The heroes in the stories are traveling between here and there; they are leaving the familiar and going into unknown worlds. What, most abstractly, is journeying? At one level, journeying simply entails leaving one's home, one's native village, one's *rodina:* Vit'ka leaves his village, goes into the forest, and opens himself up to dangerous contacts. But more generally, *a journey is any exiting from the comfort of being svoi*—being among "one's own" (to which the rodina is a related subcategory). Leaving the rodina is in fact dangerous because it involves leaving svoe.

In any case, a journey heightens the chances for encounters with the fantastic world where, as will be shown, time and space are up for grabs. Consider the following analogy: In the world inside a fish bowl, propor-tions of objects are regular and predictable. Looking out of the bowl—from that inside position—renders the proportions of the outer world monstrous. These journeys do something similar. They distort and dis-orient the experience of space and time. They can blot the memory. In Vit'ka's story, a journey begins to transport some cream, a village is left, a stranger approaches, and disorientation ensues. Memory is lost. Unre-membered distances are crossed. The physical world is literally and figu-ratively overturned by an "inhuman strength."

When journeying, when leaving the comfortable nexus of here and "us," confrontations with otherworldly forces have a striking effect on the regular rules of space and time. Many stories feature a stretching or surreal sliding of characters and landscapes. For example, Anna Grig-orievna told me how her sister—who often needed to go through the for-est to transport milk and cream—saw the leshii and "he was taller than

---

11. Journeys are a key element in the morphology of the folktale, according to Propp (1958[1928]). For a discussion on journeys in Russian tales, see Ries (1997:53n).

the forest."[12] In her story, which she tells with great animation ("Lord! Lord! What is all that? You can have a fright!"), the journey from town to town and through forest trees leads to encounters with the frightening other. This figure's proportions are stretched taller than the trees.

In several stories, figures appear out of nowhere. The commonest figure was the "dedushka," the grandfather host of the forest (who is known to appear as anything he likes), but there were also stories about demons, ghosts, and extraterrestrials. A key point is that, more important than the incidental *form* adopted by the inchoate forces out there, is the *process* of form-taking; it is that spatiotemporal gesture which is primary, and not the hands that fill it. The khoziaeva, and in particular the leshii, make a good case in point. There is no leshii, if the leshii must be defined by a given set of physical, behavioral, or even locational characteristics. Even the name of the leshii is unstable. In the region of Solovyovo, he is spoken of as leshii (from *les;* forest), dedushka lesovoi (forest grandfather), *khoziain lesa* (host of the forest), dedushka (grandfather), ded (grandfather, short form), khoziain (host, without reference), or khoziaeshka (hostess). In other parts of the country, he has still other names.[13]

There are some distinct attributes associated with each of these names: "leshii take you" is roughly interchangeable with *chert voz'mi* (devil take you); dedushka is a softer name, and he tends to either help you or play tricks on you; and the term khoziain tends to speak of his leadership role— you would ask his permission to be in the forest. But this division is not hard and fast. In general, he has no stable name; several names point to the complex of his function. But does he have a stable form? Clearly not. As Fedor Sergeevich said, "He can appear as anything you like."[14]

The khoziaeva of various spaces in these stories—particularly the leshii—demonstrate the multitude of forms that are available in the repertoire of unseen beings. They can be familiar or unfamiliar. They can be frightening or gentle. I have used the case of the leshii because his example is particularly vibrant. In the course of my time in the village, I heard stories about encounters with various hosts and hostesses (house, barn, and forest hosts in particular), devils, demons, ghosts, aliens, mermaids,

---

12. This exact wording is found in several of the stories about the leshii in Cherepanova (1996).

13. Ibid., 138.

14. The only physical description that I ever managed to get outside of the literature was that you could tell a leshii "by his brow," which is thick.

barn, mother pine trees, personified icons, poltergeists, and even a mud monster that appeared at twilight one night. Often, the form that the khoziain chooses is that of someone familiar, someone who is svoi (as Mikhail Alekseevich explained, "The grandfather of the forest . . . appears as an old friend or grandfather" or "in the guise of a friend"). Sometimes even Lenin and Stalin were attributed with omniscience and omnipresence. Names shift. All manifestations come out of nowhere and return there after an encounter. All present certain dangers, and some present certain graces.

The flexibility of space in the world of the chudesnogo is not only demonstrated in the forms of its regular inhabitants. It is also evidenced in the play of space-time itself, where landscape and distance are contorted and memory hazed. The leshii, crafty creature that he is, is not limited in his speed from here to there ("I was 1000 kilometers away!," said a leshii in one story after having been addressed, "Why did you call me for such trifles?")[15] But it is not only the leshii himself who twists time and space. The victims of the leshii's whim can also go great distances without being aware of it. As Mikhail Alekseevich noted, "The person being lured away might not notice anything [unusual] even if he were taken 100 kilometers away."

Now here; now there. The entry into the world of miracles obliterates distinctions of time/space. Anna Grigorievna told a marvelous story where a journey and some dangerous words led to a total expansion, then collapse, of time and space:

> *Anna Grigorievna:* I'll tell you about it. This happened in Iurino. That was the time of the war and there were evacuated people around here. And [among them] there was one lady [*dama*]. A woman. And she met a guy from Z—. . . . This young guy had come back from the war and was missing an arm. They shot his arms—Vit'ka was his name, I know him myself. But I never saw the woman. She met him. And so this Vit'ka arrived on a horse (they didn't used to have any cars) here to Vershina. So this Viktor came to see this . . . woman. She says, "Well, Vitia, take us to the club." Here in Vershina. He said, "No. I won't take you. If you have to go, walk!" She said to her friend, "Very well then." He said, "While you

---

15. This phrase, "Why did you call me away for such trifles?" uttered by the leshii, came up in several of the stories.

are walking to the club, I'll be in Z—already. Merin [the horse] will take me home. But I won't take you."

So he said, "I'm out of here."

And he left. And he left so that he went everywhere! Where did he not go? Which cities was he not in?[16] So, you see, she knew [the magic arts]. All the places he went to! He even rode along the rooftops. Which cities he didn't ride through! But the horse, on the horse—which cities didn't he walk in! Think about it! The woman knew what to do to him!

Q: So she did it?

Anna Grigorievna: Of course she did it! She did it with grandfather [forest]! With the host! The forest host! He did it to him. Where he didn't go [literally, to where only he did not ride]? And so, it was done to him [by the forest host] that these hours ended, and he was on his own road. In the forest there. In the forest near Myshino . . . so he would have gone through the forest and arrived. Only that, while the horse was good, he would come. [The woman] said to him, "You will see." [He said,] "As I stood on the road, it ended. It was done; it was all done. As I stood on the road, I see that I am standing on my own road in the forest." "There," he said, "Merin [the horse] dropped dead." "And there," he said, "I don't know. . . . I was everywhere."

And then he says, "All of a sudden, I look and I am standing on my road. In a flash. Standing on my road. Standing there and Merin the horse fell and died [*loshad' sdokhla*]." He went home on foot. And so. He was everywhere, but didn't go anywhere. And the horse died there. On his own road.

The girl had asked him to take her somewhere.[17]

---

16. Literal: He went . . . where was he not? In that one, in which city was he not?
17. This story, told by the best storyteller I have ever come across, is worth including in its original (and more complete) form. Except where doing so would obscure the meaning, I have transcribed the story to include regional variations in lexicon and grammar:

> *Anna Grigorievna:* Vot ia tebe raskazhu. Vot takoe bylo v Iurine. Tam byli tozhe, voiny byli—eto kak evakuirovannye . . . I vot, odna byla takaia dama. Zhenshchina. I vot, ona poznakomilas'—parenek byl iz Z— . . . I vot eta zhenshchina poznakomilas'. Etot parenek prishel s voiny. Ego ruki net. No emu ruku otstrelili—vot kakoi Vit'ka—ia ego znaiu sama. Nu, zhenshchinu etu ne videla . . . Poznakomilas' ona s

"Gde, gde ne byl (where, where was he not)?" The bravado of this man made him vulnerable, when combined with testing the sensibilities of a dangerous outsider. The result was a joke: the joke of being everywhere—in all cities, on all roads, through forests, and over rooftops. "You say you'll get there before me, well, you'll go everywhere and nowhere." The leshii, like other tricksters from other traditions, appreciates a good joke.[18] Even when the joke ends with the very serious matter of the corpse of a dead horse. First the jokes, then the tragedies.

Derevenskii Smekh (Village Laughter)

Perhaps it's not fair to say that this is humor. Yet it feels that way when the stories are told. People laugh. Even that poor dead horse was de-

---

im. I vot, kogda etot Vit'ka na loshadi priedet—ran'she mashin—ved' ne bylo. Na loshadi priedet. . . . Zdes' byl v tserkve—eto byl klub. Vot zdes' na Vershine. No—vot zdes', ona tserkov' byla. Vot etot Viktor priekhal k etoi devitse, zhenshchine. Ona govorit chto, "Ty Vitia svezi nas, mol, v klub. Vot siudy na Vershine." A on skazal, "Net. Ne povezu. Nado, dak, idi! A ia tebia ne povezu." Svoei podruge—ona skazala: "Nu, ladno." On skazal: "Vy poka do kluba idete, dak ia budu (v) Z— . . Merina dernu svoego, doma budu. No vas ne povezu.

. . . I govorit, "Ia ekhal. I poekhal. I poekhal dak ia gde, gde ne byl, v takom, v kakom gorode, ne byl." Vot che ona znala. "Ia," gat, "gde, gde ne byl." Dazhe po krysham ezdil. Ne znaiu, bol'she che. Vot, kakie, kakie goroda, ne ezdil. Na etoi loshadi. Na loshadi kakoi gorod ne idesh'. Sama podumai. Ona znala. Ona znala che emu sdelala. *Q:* Ona sdelala?

Anna Grigorievna: Sdelala! Eto ona sdelala s dedushkom. Eto ona sdelala s dedushkom! S khoziainom. Lesovym! Vot on ego del. Kuda, tol'ka ne ezdil. I vot, na skol'ko bylo sdelano eti chasy konchilis'. "Ia, gat, na doroge. Na svoei." Na lesu, tam. Tam les ot Myshina. Byl, vse derevni byli. Dak on by ekhal v derevniam doekhal. Tol'ka poka loshad' khoroshaia, s"ekhal. Ona, govorit: "Posmotrish'." Kak ia vstal na dorogu, eto konchilos'—eto sdelano—eto vse sdelano, che bylo. Kak vstal na dororge, vizhu na svoei doroge stoiu v lesu. Tut, govorit, Merin sdokh. Loshad' umerla. "I vot," govorit, "ne znaiu, gde, gde ne byl."

. . . A potom, govorit, "Vdrug, pogliazhu na svoei doroge stoiu. Migom. Stal na svoiu dorogu. Stal tut," govorit, "Merin upal i umer. On poshel domoi peshkom." I vot. On vezde byl, no nikuda ne ezdil. Tut i loshad' sdokhla. Na svoei doroge.

. . . Ona prosila chtob on ego svez siuda. *Q:* Eta devushka imela kakuiu-to sviaz'? *Anna Grigorievna:* Obiazatel'no!

---

18. See Radin (1969) for the classic work on the "trickster" figure in Native American societies.

scribed in a tone that was both ominous and humorous. A certain amount of explicit mention of the playfulness—or at least the whimsicality—of the various khoziaeva was described. Mikhail Alekseevich spoke of this several times, saying once, "Leshii have a kind of nature that they play tricks on you. They can materialize [like devils]." Another time he said, "The leshii likes to do things to amuse himself [*veselit'sia*]." Veselit'sia is a reflexive verb that literally means "to happy oneself." Even if no one is having any fun in some of these encounters, those form-finding forces are ready to laugh.

In a story that was quite funny, except for poor Shutov, the dedushka shows up again. This time, his attention was awakened by boastful words. The victim was drunk *and* journeying, two terribly in-between positions. He had bragged that he needed no ride to get home.

> This Shutov is dead now. Once, he went to another village—to Kraskovo. He bragged to the *predsedatel'* that he didn't need a ride home. "Not necessary. I will go by the lake, I live close by." "Fine," said the predsedatel'.
>
> He hears a noise. A horse is coming. On it is sitting a dedushka. "I stood up and the horse ran off." Sat down [*sel, sezhy*], looked, and saw that he was sitting in the snow, and that the horses had left. He had the feeling that he had sat on the sled. He sits and notices that his butt is cold. The horse was gone. [This was because he had] bragged—"I will arrive in a flash [*ia proidu migom*]. That he wasn't too drunk to go alone. The ded was joking with him [*shutil*]. How he had taken him for a ride [*kak dedushka prokotil*]! Lucky for him the weather was mild. I heard this story myself.

No great harm was done here; all Shutov got was a cold behind and a good lesson about watching where you boast.[19] The humor sometimes is more hidden, and has to do more generally with inversions of every-

---

19. Boasting (*khvastat'sia*: to praise oneself) is an interesting issue that has a place in the question of Russian self-definition. On the one hand, it makes sense that putting oneself above others would be distasteful in a world where equality and harmony are forever trying to be established on social and economic fronts. And yet, Russians (like Dostoevsky, just for example) have spoken of it as one of the more unflattering Russian "traits." Perhaps this is a case of our own taboos taking on a cultural reality, such as the idea that Americans only *think* they are prudes when in fact they are sex obsessed (Foucault 1986) or their problematic/self-contradictory notions of the "individual" (as in Riesman's *The*

day habits.[20] It is commonly held—and I heard this in a couple of stories—that after contact with the forest host, people are found with their clothes inside out. Andrei (in his early thirties and the youngest permanent villager) told me many fantastic stories, but only allowed a few of them to be recorded. One described how two girls got lost and encountered one dedushka or another. Here again are the elements of journey (into the forest) and being led away:

> *Andrei Konstantinovich:* Not long ago, let's say, I heard that there were two girls. . . . [The khoziain] carried them away. Into the forest. If he leads [someone away], he changes all their clothing around. On the left side. Turns it around. Dresses on, briefly . . . re-dresses them. Already on the other side up. . . . It wasn't long ago.

Interestingly, the theme of inside-out clothes also becomes the way to ward off the leshii, as in the following[21]:

> *Anna Vladimirovna:* So, Mania and I went to get *volnushki* [a red mushroom] this summer. I say, "Come on, Mania, let's pop into the swamp, see if there aren't some berries." We popped in and there were none there. "Let's go farther." We exited somewhere. We don't know where. Went from there, as we went there. We are walking, we don't know where. "Come, let's turn our clothes on the left side."

Regarding this symbolic landscape, there is an interesting dynamic here: not only is the whimsicality of backward/inside-out clothes the result of a meeting with the dedushka (a common story), but it can be the weapon against it. It seems that this is a case where the exception proves the rule. The mir chudesnogo has a property of upside-down-ness, of

---

Lonely Crowd [1950]). There is a similar opposite-side-of-the-same-coin-ness in Russian (explicit) self-definition, where they see themselves as a broad-minded and generous people, and likewise, a greedy and small-minded people. It is the axis that must be interesting. Boasting is charged because it falls into symbolically charged territory. We need harmony and equality to survive: Bragging is dangerous.

20. See Likhachev and Panchenko (1976) on *Drevnyi smekh*—ancient laughter; and Propp (1995[1963]).

21. Turning clothes inside-out as a protective strategy against the leshii is mentioned in Ivanits (1989:67).

whimsicality most generally. Again, here it is not the specifics of encounters with fantastic beings that is primary (putting one's clothes on backward or having them put on backward/upside-down), but the shape of the gesture (backwardness/upside-down-ness).

Once again, here is a world that is not only brimming with the powers of speed, transformation, and a certain degree of foreknowledge, but with trickiness, craftiness, and humor. Iuliia gives us a sense of this, describing the khoziaeva "for everything."

> *Iuliia Ivanovna:* Pershina got married. It was an elopement in Myshino. The husband took her away on the horse and sleigh. But the horse suddenly turned around and people fell off the sleigh. [The couple] had just left the village, [they] were by the club. They didn't live very well together. They say that some kind of ded joked. Before, they thought that there was an invisible person, ded. You can find a pile of wood [that you had stacked] in a whole other place where he always walks.

> *Q:* Is that the khoziain of the forest?

> *Iuliia Ivanovna:* There is a khoziain for everything. There's a khoziain of the field. Somewhere, these khoziaeva are different. Like the house khoziain. He starts to mess around (*balovat'sia*) if he is not content. Then, things get lost, things fall, and in the barn, too.

> You should say: "Khoziain of the house. We love you." He likes to be invited. If you don't invite him, or forget him or don't think of him, he'll start to make jokes [*komedet'*].

One khoziain jokes and things are thrown around a house. Another jokes and wood is moved from one site to the next. A third jokes and a marriage is ruined. If you neglect the khoziain of the house (and words of love to him), he can make your life miserable.

This back-and-forth between laughter and tragedy has reminded me of the many encounters that I had with drunkenness during my time in rural Russia; the ebullience that is forever ready to snap and darken into volatility. Some of the stories that described such upside-down-ness bordered on the macabre. It could be said that they are all like this. They are all like the funny house in an amusement park with its distorted mirrors—that are just not all that funny.

I have shown how lingering at spatial and social thresholds invites danger. Sometimes thresholds seem to take on a vicious life of their own. This appears to occur at the end of an encounter with the chudesnoe, concluding, as it were, on a dark and dramatic chord.

Crisis at Thresholds

Imagine the situation as Anna Grigorievna described it: A man is on his road and leaves on a journey. That journey is interfered with by bending and stretching space-time. He goes and goes everywhere and nowhere at all. After having traversed the whole world, the man is left at the very beginning of his journey, on his own road. And the horse, poor faithful Merin, drops dead. And it is over.

I have raised the fact that journeying is a symbolically dangerous movement (Turner 1969; Myerhoff 1974). How could it not be, in a setting such as rural Russia, where a strong, interdependent life exists inside the village, and outside of it there is a great unknown. A sense of svoi, as I've already discussed, accumulates. An outsider spends time in a village for a summer, five summers, ten summers, and three winters; he works together with the other villagers; and he drinks and sings with them. A sense of svoi grows on him. Rodina is where the best concentration of svoi is, or at least where svoi can be temporarily conjured. Journeying takes one out of that carefully crafted svoi nexus. The people whom I lived with in Solovyovo had once been to Leningrad; in thirty years of marriage this was their only vacation together. How can a cow be taken care of if you leave? How can you go away when the delicate set of conditions for successful agriculture never follows a calendar date? Familiar space and familiar time pull you home. And when you are away from the home (the rodina, that which is svoi) time and space change. Our going together even to Belozersk for the day would cause terrible nervousness in my host and hostess. They would fuss over what clothes I would wear, speak in a haltingly polite manner to their city bosses, accept no hospitality except from village svoi who happened to be staying there, tear through stores, panic over my crossing streets (I would say, "This, I know how to do"), give themselves an hour for the five-minute walk back to the bus station. And when the bus crawled home an hour and a half later, I would invariably hear, "Anyway, home is best." The dangers of the city as a particular symbolic construct—a time- and space-twisting construct—is a subject of its own. My wish here is to evoke the sense of danger in the practical matter of distance from the rodina.

In several of the narratives that enter into the world of the chudesnoe, the encounter with the miraculous ended with the equivalent of a dead horse lying on one's own road. Small and bizarre catastrophes. Yes, this is a world that stretches things, that laughs, that plays tricks—but the encounter with it can leave a particularly grotesque impression. In several stories, people, animals, and objects are literally stuck at thresholds after having been lured away—and there they meet their end, as in the case of the dedushka who caused a horse to pull its cart away so that it jammed between trees. ("It's stuck. You can't do anything.") Animals seem to suffer the indignities of these threshold crises in particular. A horse is led off "not by his own will," and is found wedged between two trees. A goat, Valentina Ivanovna's Irushka, is led off several times and found jammed between the boards of a fence. In a story of Fedor Sergeevich's, a bull was lured away by the leshii, managed to swim off an island and escape several times—including by jumping through a barn window—and was only found "in the underwood." His end was brought about by human agency, but his journey through the world of the chudesnoe was marked by what can only be called the bizarre passage through liminal spaces.[22] Thresholds are not only the *gateways* to miraculous worlds—it is in the nature of miraculous space to be found by hesitating at its peripheries; they toss one out with the flourish of the surreal.

POLITICAL WONDERS

* * *

Prikhodiat po Nocham (They Come by Night)

There is another kind of story that parallels the structure of the journey into the world of the miraculous. Although recounted without the luster of a fairytale, these stories involve words uttered in dangerous places that are somehow caught up by vast and unpredictable forces. They lead you off into a world that changes time and space—a world where all frames change, a world that throws you back into the everyday like it threw the corpse of that horse.

---

22. Life and death are other such thresholds. Stories of the hideous death of a local sorceress speak to the danger of that liminal space. Rites and ceremonies of the dead, as well as the role of the dead in healing, will be treated in detail in later chapters.

Petr Nikolaevich: It was terrifying. . . . You know how they judged you? They came at night, knocked, the car is waiting there, they take you away and that's all. It happened here. We had one *diaden'ka* [uncle; man]. From that house. His house stands there. Not long ago—in the spring—his sister died. They had gotten together to sow. They were throwing grain. And he couldn't hold it in and said that "this is not a kolkhoz basket [of grain], but a basket for parasites." Two Muscovites were there and they denounced him to the KGB. They came at night, arrested him and gave him 10 years. Sania S—'s father was also taken for a denouncement and also given 10 years.

I found the structure of arrest stories to be remarkably similar to other stories where one chanced upon otherworldly forces. Words fall on the wrong ears. Those terrifying creatures, the Kegebeishniki [KGB] come for you at night.[23] One idle statement becomes ten years of banishment. Where is the continuity with the everyday world here? There is no continuity. Another frame has been entered.

I had been concerned about including these stories in my account of the mir chudesnogo. There is certainly nothing strictly "wondrous" about totalitarian practices of the Soviet years. Furthermore, it is not my wish to reduce these terrible experiences to the level of metaphor, as metaphor is so often seen as ornamentation on the periphery of thought. It has been a recurring theme throughout this work that symbolism is lived by: In the model that I have chosen, we walk along its terrain as we would walk along any landscape. In our acts of consciousness, we may be able to choose among several terrains, but we have no choice to simply not walk. The mir chudesnogo is one well-walked terrain. In the same way that a *chudo* (wonder) becomes a *chudovishche* (monster), the mir chudesnogo can include stories aligned in the memory as whimsical, and others aligned as horrors. I do not believe that inclusion here diminishes the arrest stories. From the perspective of the land of the mir chudesnogo, I am simply pointing out some of the neighbors.

In another story, there is a horrific senselessness to the arrest of Antonina Sergeevna's father. Like the wayfarer who must ask permission of capricious hosts to enter the forest, her father was guilty of overlooking another kind of permission.

---

23. Ries's Moscow narratives contain discussion of these very forces that "stand ready to foil anyone's plans or destroy their happiness" (1997:113).

Antonina Sergeevna: They took my father. You know, it was his birthday. He was walking to the church in Iurino. There was still a church there. He had gone to the service and stood there like an *imeninnik* (one whose name day it is). Then he went home. The sel'sovet was there and in Zhirishenie. He went up to the front of the sel'sovet and there they pressed him to come over. They didn't let him go home. He was never home again. That was it. That was it.

Q: Did they search the house?

Antonina Sergeevna: Oi. So many times they searched us. There were many [complete] searches. They thought we had all this stuff. They would arrive by night. By night. *That,* I remember. That it was by night. They would come nights. That was my *ispoliatym* [bailiff]. From our own village was Pavel Filipovich. He was in the secret police. He was in the secret police. Someone from here. In this village.

. . . Of course, they took my father for nothing. For nothing. You needed permission to slaughter, permission. Father went [to get it]. Asked permission. And he [the person in charge] . . . said, "It's your own calf. Ivan Vasilivich, what kind of permission do you need for your own calf?" He put him on the spot on purpose. And that's it. He slaughtered [the calf]. For meat for himself. It was his animal, [but] it was forbidden to slaughter it. You needed some kind of permission. And they didn't give it. Said that [he didn't need it]. So my father believed him, and so they gave him three years. Didn't let him go home. There was a trial. We didn't know.

Q: You knew nothing?

Antonina Sergeevna: No! They didn't [say anything to] us. When they took him away, he wrote, "They gave me three years. Three years. I probably won't be home [again]." And that "[t]hey feed us badly."

He never came home again. Official permission was required from the bureaucracy. A form needed to be filled out. Without these humble invocations, all was lost. Ivan Vasilievich had been swept to that other world, by the "whirlwind," as it is known in Evgeniia Ginzberg's books about the camps (1967, 1989); the "house of the dead," as it is known in Dostoevsky's. In Anna Grigorievna's narrative below, the house of the dead could be the only name for the place where the family she describes was sent. Once again, "they" came in the night and took the family of the *bogach* ("rich one") away. Led him and his family away to the land of death.

Anna Grigorievna: What rich people? What rich people? [They would go] on the senokos and everywhere. The little ones banged and banged [worked alongside]. And he himself was digging with a spade. That meant that he was "rich."

Q: What fate did he have? Did they kill him?

Anna Grigorievna: They led him away. Led him away, [it is] not known where. Led him away, led him away, everyone they led away. Everyone. And the wives. Everyone. Everyone.[24] He worked with his father in the forest. And this was the son of the bogach ["rich one"]. They worked together there. They worked for the same kopecks. Natasha was at home, and he said that Natasha had just given birth. Everyone came here to us, loaded everything and took it away. We don't know where, nothing. They left all the cattle and ordered, "Pack up everything and climb on!" They told Kolia, "They took your whole family," as he said, the horse was driven to Cherepovets. . . . The wife was led away, took her with a little child. He died there. There, where they lived, there was some kind of typhus, a big [epidemic] one came, some infection. All were sent [to the grave]. My sweet one. No food there or anything. Her child died there and her Kolia died. And the parents all died. She alone came back. Lived in Belozersk.

Anna Petrovna's husband was also pulled away. It was never clear to me what he was supposed to have done.[25] One day, her cow was gone, and that indicated something more meaningful. Anna Petrovna, however, responded to this crisis of the everyday with her own kind of invocations. Like the woman who retrieved her lost daughter with prayers, or the animals that were found through invocations to the forest khoziain, Anna Petrovna's pleas fell on the right ears.

---

24. Ego uvezli. Uvezli, neizvestno kuda. Uvezli, uvezli, vsef (dialect variant for "vsekh") uvezli. Vsef. I zhen. Vsef, vsef.
25. Often, there was a difference between what a person had been accused of—such as speaking against Stalin—and what they had in fact done (threatened someone's job, had a fancy house, etc.).

Anna Petrovna: They took him away [*uveli*].

Q: They dekulakized your husband?

Anna Petrovna: They started to dekulakize him. We lived together with two brothers and two daughters-in-law. I didn't have any children, but the second daughter-in-law had two. And there were old folks. We separated everything and [the two of us] went to an apartment. The house wasn't built yet. In Myshino. It wasn't built to completion. That's when they took him . . .

Q: When did they come for him?

Anna Petrovna: The devil knows.

Q: How did they arrest him?

Anna Petrovna: . . . In the field. I didn't know that they had taken the cow away. Afterward, the neighbor said to me that they had taken away my cow. There, there, that's how it was. I went to the city and they wouldn't give me back the cow. She ended up in Srichen. Someone had already bought her. Oi. I can't talk about it [starts to cry]. I had just raised that cow!

Q: You didn't see your husband for two years? Where was he?

Anna Petrovna: On the island [a regional prison in the middle of the White Lake].

Q: He came back later?

Anna Petrovna: He came back. The house was built without him. I made the stove. He arrived and everything was done.

Q: Did he write to you from there?

Anna Petrovna: No, I didn't write. I had taken, written an official statement. And went through the whole village and had everyone sign it. See there, how I used my head! I wrote a statement about his behavior. That his behavior was good. I went into the brick house [the administrative center], and everyone had signed it. I took this information and they let him go. See how I thought that up!

There is a big blue house that stands at Solovyovo's only crossroads. It is the house of one prominent village family—blessed with many children—that had been dekulakized in the 1930s. I heard the story of this family and its disappearance many times. One sole member hobbled back from the camps in her later years, and people spoke of her as you would speak of a ghost. If the death of Stalin is a scar in the landscape of the radiant past, that large blue house stands in the memory as both a scar and a reminder. The echoes of its silence proclaim that the world of wonders—of inversions and time-space radicalism—is only one threshold and a few weighty words away.

"VSE-TAKI, DOMA LUCHSHE" (ANYWAY, HOME IS BEST)
* * *

What does the symbolic terrain of the chudesnogo look like? First, there is the question of leaving the familiar and entering liminal spaces. There are many ways to arrive into the world of miracles. Most of the stories that have been presented so far have involved journeys: into forests, into separate villages, into drunkenness, or into the night or dream world. Sometimes, confrontation with the miracle world can happen by simply awakening it—not by sending out one's self, but by weighty and dangerous words. Such words are snatched up and result in calling into form that which had no form, causing a chain of events that can be dangerous and even deadly.

If given symbolic spaces resonate with their own indigenous sets of metaphors, the boundaries between these spaces are particularly charged. The space between villages, the space between life and death, sleep and waking, sobriety and drunkenness, here and there, us and them, are naturally precarious places. If passing through them is combined with other dangerous things like uttering curses (like the man who cursed his cow just as she passed through the gate), or boasts (the man who boasted that he could return home alone and imagined the cart; the other man who boasted that he would arrive home before the stranger, and went everywhere and nowhere and lost his horse), the attracting charge is magnified. In this paradigm, one *falls* into harm's way. Certain conditions heighten the possibility for harm. Thresholds are charged. Regardless of the kind of threshold (physical, social, or symbolic), it is dangerous to linger there. The entry into the world of the *chudesnoe* necessarily involves a leave-taking of the everyday world. In the village narratives, this brings one into territory that has a surreal quality.

In addition, the miraculous world is defined by its otherness, by the ways in which space and time mutate within it. The beings of the world

147

of the chudesnoe, like the protean forces that make them up, display a range of qualities—from kindness and tenderness to unpredictable or vengeful cruelty. The various manifestations of the dedushka lesa, for example, make a good case in point. In his outward form, he can be familiar (one's own mother), unfamiliar (an unknown ded), imposing (huge, terrifying), or miniature. He can be benevolent (helping a lost girl out of the forest), vengeful (causing animals or people to get lost or sicken or die), or whimsical (putting people's clothes on backward, making a person see a horse and sleigh when there is no horse or sleigh). The identity of dedushka lesa, like that of other beings, is not fixed to a single name or form or place or character. Inhabited by beings such as these, the world is alive with the movement of mercurial forces—seen then unseen, recognized then foreign, benign then terrifying. Time, likewise, is mutable there—able to be puffed up with unending/world-crossing journeys (and this for a group of people who have perhaps never been more than a handful of kilometers away from their farm), or shrunk to nothing by forgetfulness ("He just sat and ate the berries").

The symbolic dynamics of the world of wonders look like a recounting of the kinds of ritual practice that take place in societies in general. According to Victor Turner (1969:96–97), the liminal spaces between here and there that have such power in ritual serve a social purpose: In their confusion, they level society's members to equality beneath the power of the elders. In Solovyovo, the story of journeying, told and retold, is a story of forces out there that can upturn everything. Individuals can try to protect themselves, but full protection is never possible. The urge to guard oneself from the form-changing beings and the faceless figures who can send a husband somewhere out to the whirlwind, never to return, amounts to a nervous pall cast over a life. When is it safe? The fact that stories of senseless arrest are told via the nearly exact narrative structure of stories of whimsical unseen beings indicates that it—life—is never quite safe. Frightful things can befall one from above—whether the "above" amounts to a forest sprite or the state. From the powers above, life's proportions can shift at any turn; as the powers lie in wait out there, every word counts.

If Turner is right, passing through narratives like these reiterates the equality of social actors under a category of power—sometimes personified, sometimes not; sometimes magnanimous, sometimes cruel—that comes from a categorically separate level. In the village of Solovyovo, this means that anyone can say the wrong word. Anyone can walk into a forest and watch dimensions slide. Anyone leaving the safety of the svoi and venturing into in-between worlds can be caught up by the whirlwind. This is the lesson to the study of memory: There are spoken places, told and retold, which cut a pathway that brings a sense of awe and wonder, on the one hand, and a landscape of anxiety and fear, on the other. This narrative persists because it is founded in stories that are lived by, that is, etched into a symbolic landscape supported by metaphoric and thematic structures. It is an orienting map in the darker, more awesome moments alone in the forest, or in the moments when "they"—the ubiquitous they—come by night. And from a deep place on the journey back to Solovyovo on a lurching bus, or quiet sleigh, or even as one foot follows the other on a path of hardened snow, it is the source of the sigh that, anyway, home is best.

Healing

Now there is war everywhere. How could that be possible? Now, in the whole world there is war. Isn't it true? In all countries, they are killing people. Oi. It's terrifying. It seems to me that with all these earthquakes—it's clear that there is a God. Mother Earth will not endure it. It's all of our disorder. Isn't it true? People are beating each other and so the Sweet Earth will not stand for it. Earthquakes and floods and other things—it's true, isn't it? The earth will not endure and is punishing, punishing people and causing them to fear, as if by a warning, "Remember, people." Why should they make wars?

Oi, would that Jesus Christ would come and save us—that God would come and make order. Now, we just need Stalin with a gun. Stalin we need, with a gun, to cause fear.

—MAIA BOGDANOVA, SOLOVYOVO

The time is out of joint, O cursed spite!
That ever I was born to set it right!

—WILLIAM SHAKESPEARE, *HAMLET*

SETTING SPACE RIGHT

* * *

Maia Bogdanova's words speak of a time that has gone out of joint. All of our disorder, our moral and physical disorder, has caused a state of supreme instability—to such a degree that Mother Earth herself will not stand for it, and in her fury sends earthquakes and floods to punish us. Maia's solution to these ills resonates with the discourse of the radiant past: bring in God, Christ, or Stalin to create order through fear, to save us from the rage of the Sweet Earth.

Much of the discourse on the radiant past concerned the process of social decay and how society can be repaired through the intercession of a powerful khoziain. In fact, when physical, social, and symbolic spaces lose their cohesion, that is to say, when they become ill in the broad sense of the word, there are more fundamental procedures that can be performed to go about setting space right. Healing, a form of spatial readjustment, as it were, requires tapping otherworldly powers.

Venturing outward into the mir chudesnogo is one (rather harrowing) way to come into contact with otherworldly forces of various forms. But what about in the known, familiar world? If we could somehow speed time and draw a map that traced the movements of the farmers of Solovyovo, we would see congested swirls of activity in the household and within the village limits; smaller knots out in the fields, down in the forests and swamps; spindly fibers stretching out into the area of the kolkhoz or into the city from time to time. The known social worlds are different kinds of space from the unknown, in-between worlds that were seen in the mir chudesnogo. The inside is different from the outside; home is different from horizon.

The narrative landscape that I called the mir chudesnogo involves venturing out into world and getting caught up by powerful forces that can be anticipated, and appeased, but never controlled. What kinds of attempts have been made to *harness* these powerful forces, to bring them down and channel them for local use? When out in the wilderness of in-between places, villagers in Solovyovo take their shields and hope for the best. But what about in the world where they spend their days; where children fall ill and families fall apart? While in their homes, villages, and churches, that is, in their known social spheres, villagers can be bolder. They can take matters into their own hands and use the unseen powers to maintain social harmony, on the one hand, and set things right, on the other hand, when they have gone wrong. This chapter focuses on that fundamentally local process. When Stalin and his state, and God and His heavenly kingdom will not, with one wave of an iron hand, pull in all the forces of disorder in the world, the village turns to its local experts in the art of calling in healing powers. This process is of special importance as it concerns the place where villagers hang their highest hopes when they are sick, trusting that some extraordinary force will come to change the very structure of normalcy—and grant bounties, miracles, and, in the broadest sense, health.

I should note from the outset that it was the healing practices I witnessed during my fieldwork in Solovyovo—in all their richness and apparent contradictions—that first caused me to shift my research toward the problem of social memory.[1] I saw how certain aspects of the practice

1. I had gone to rural Russia to study the "historical imagination," that is, the various

of healing through sorcery had persisted from earlier centuries, and how other aspects were completely gone. This pastiche of memory and forgetting was deeply telling. Why was it that some forms had persisted and others had not? Why was it that some symbols were reproduced into the twenty-first century, and others fell to the wayside? Through these questions, I was guided to the problem of where, in fact, memory lies—and I began searching inside the "social nexus" in language, metaphor, commemoration, and ritual. In this chapter, I sketch how otherworldly powers are accessed in rural Solovyovo. As in earlier chapters I focus on what I, in fact, witnessed there, and not the categories circumscribed by ethnographers and folklorists of previous generations. With an eye to how social circles form and transform, I use healing practices as a way to regard the limits and directions of human agency in the village. Here, social memory is cultural memory; in the performance of healing practices, there is a landscape of recollection—one that has, in striking ways, persisted through metaphoric, narrative, and ritualistic means.[2] In healing—so central, so essential to life in Solovyovo—social memory garners longitudinal momentum and force.

HEALING, RELIGION, AND MAGIC: LOOKING FOR TRANSFORMATIVE POWERS

* * *

> Among the peasants of Central and Eastern Europe elaborate magic still flourishes and children are treated by witches and warlocks. People are thought to have the power to prevent cows from giving milk, to induce cattle to multiply unduly, to produce rain and sunshine and to make people love or hate each other. . . . The richest domain of magic, however, is in civilization as in savagery, that of health.
>
> —BRONISLAW MALINOWSKI, *THE ROLE OF MAGIC AND RELIGION* (1965:105)

---

overlapping discursive formations that contribute to the telling of the past. As time went on, the act of speaking the past seemed to be simply part of the far broader problem of social recollection itself.

2. In the language of Olick and Robbins (1998), there are elements in the memory of healing practices that encourage persistence in *cultural* modes (via the "continued relevance" of the practices that support it) and *inertial* modes (via the "habit" behind the founding symbolism of the practices).

One of the great ideological achievements of Soviet rule was the aggressive advancement of science and its value into the consciousness of the people. With an impoverished, war-torn, and famine-ridden population at its base, and with a medieval form of agriculture to support it, there is no way to overstate Soviet achievements in science and technology in the past century. Healing, like so many other domains, was scientized in the Soviet Union.

The villagers in Solovyovo do go to doctors; this necessarily involves sitting on a bus for an hour and a half and perhaps staying in a hospital that, because of impoverished conditions, can be more of a death sentence than a place of healing. Many of them pay a large part of their tiny salaries and pensions for poorly regulated drugs. But doctors cannot and do not cure all that ails people. The local experts in healing, *te kotorye znaiut* ("those who know"), provide the sick with ways of going around doctors and their scientized versions of health and illness and into broader ones.

In the time I spent in Solovyovo, there were scores of visitors who came to the one-room home where I lived to receive potions from Mikhail Alekseevich. I grew accustomed to the disruption that this caused in the regular farmwork, and the sometimes harried objections that came from his wife over his use of time. It became part of my own job as a member of the household to run to the fields to seek out Mikhail Alekseevich, to replace him in his work at the clubhouse, and to make the unexpected guests feel at home. Some people would come with what would be classified as physical ailments that a doctor could not cure: in my journal were noted cases of cancer, skin ruptures, hearing loss, snake bites, sore arms and limbs, tooth aches, muteness, and babies with colic. For most of these ailments, Mikhail Alekseevich would recommend visiting a Western-style doctor, if that had not already been tried. Much of the help that was requested concerned more general ills, however. A person found himself to be tired, lethargic. A marriage was failing. A mother-in-law could not get along with a wife. A woman was visited by the ghost of a dead parent or husband. A cow ceased to give milk. There were signs of curses. Some of the problems that confront the local healer involved one person; others involved the larger units of families, and villages.

The problem of the maintenance of the community through healing practices leads this discussion into the well-trodden terrain of the anthropology of religion, magic, sorcery, and, most basically, of the shapes and outlines of social selves. A myriad of questions enliven this terrain, given direction and movement from a smaller number of ontological positions. Some approaches, historically, have come from disdain for the other ("How could they believe that?" *They, the strange. They, the irrational*); the elevation of the other ("How are they like us?" *They believe in spiritual beings![3] They are rational![4] They are explaining unfortunate events![5] They are musing over mysteries![6]*); or the elevation of community per se ("What is the unit of transcendence?" *The individual agent. The social body. The corporate self[7]*); the degradation of the state per se ("How is it all about the subjection/deception?" *The state makes you sick and saps your power and enslaves your class[8]*); or—most recently—the preeminence of the local ("How is it all about resistance/defiance?" *Local belief, religion, ritual grants you power[9]*).

Underlying these questions others echo, inchoate, in turn: What is power? What is order? What are the dimensions of a social body, a social soul?

3. "The elevation of the other": In the late nineteenth century, Edward Tylor argued notably that the "primitive" belief systems were unlike "civilized" ones not categorically, but only as a matter of degree. This was a revolutionary idea in its way: Here "primitives" (a term no longer accepted in any scientific study of humankind) were not "savages"; beliefs in spiritual beings (Tylor's "animism") were an early stage in a *continuum* towards like the "civilized" world and its beliefs in "souls." See Tylor in Lessa and Vogt (1965).

4. By the early twentieth century, Bronislaw Malinowski argued that the seemingly "irrational" beliefs of the other were, in fact, rational in their own way. See "The Role of Magic and Religion" (Malinovsky in Lessa and Vogt: 1965).

5. This focus on the need for explanation and exegesis as an animating force behind the world's religions is characteristic of the work of E.E. Evans-Pritchard (1940).

6. Clifford Geertz's famous "Religion as a Cultural System" (1973) relates the deepest functions of religion to the deepest needs to understand mysteries.

7. "The elevation of the community": Emile Durkheim famously claimed that "religious forces are in fact only transfigured collective forces," (1912:327) and this idea has generated many of the important insights in twentieth century anthropology, including ones that shone light on the work of healers. Notably, there is Lévi-Strauss ("The Sorcerer and His Magic") and Victor Turner ("On Witchcraft and Sorcery" in *The Forest of Symbols*).

8. "The degradation of the state per se": Marx was the beginning of this, but certainly not the end. In an ethnographically rich and historically graphic way, Michael Taussig's *Shamanism, Colonialism and the Wild Man* (1987) is one of the influential modern voices for this perspective.

9. "The preeminence of the local": There is room for Taussig here, as well for an array of contemporary anthropologists in this idea that religion is crucially a way of resisting the forces of the state. In a sense, this view reaches back to Durkheim's collective forces and *le sociale* on which they have their sway. See Judy Rosenthal's *Possession, Ecstasy and the Law in Ewe Voodoo* (1998) for a recent example of this view.

Healing has to do with power (worldly and transcendent), order (the pull for harmony, the push for exploitation), and dimensions of the wellness-seeking soul (the one seen attached to an individual, others seen attached to various sizes of social bodies). Healing, as I define it here, has ✓ to do with the regular procedures for fixing things, for setting them right. Healing practices point, then, to some of the most important gestures of social memory. They are what you do when you fix the world. They amount to, in Taussig's (1987:448) words, a "journey undertaken by the healer and the sick man into an underworld and up into the mountains across the sacred landscape of space and time." In this spirit, I ask simply that the healing procedure—so linked to people's direst fears and deepest hopes—be seen as a journey of its own, one that has a special importance in the landscape of memory.

Kuda Obratit'sia (Whither Does One Turn)?

> *Antonina Sergeevna:* Prayers? Who knows prayers? And who knows
> nothing? . . . It is necessary to believe. With your soul, you are a believer.
> We have no church now. No one goes. But still, we keep it in our soul.
> There is something [*chto-to est', ved'*]. And in fact, there is something. . . .
> There *is* something.

On the outside, the numinous in rural Russia—fed, as it is, by Russian Orthodoxy, agrarian beliefs and practices, Soviet ideology, New Age popular culture, and Russian tabloids with stories about alien abductions and teenaged seers—looks like an elaborate mess. Some of that mess has already been visible in the supernatural mix of the leshii, the alien, and the nation-khoziain in earlier chapters. Anthropology, which has thought through the subjects of religion and sorcery and magic for nearly a century with references to the problem of health and illness, offers theories that are more comfortable with (apparently) whole systems than with (apparently) disjunctive ones. Geertz (1973:127), in the most prominent definition of religion to come out of anthropology in half a century, underlines the idea that—whatever religion is—its task is to render "intellectually reasonable" a group's ethos. It is about moods and motivations, and systems of symbols and concepts. It is about the contemplation of the awesome. It depends, in this sense, on an intelligible rendering. Religion is there to make sense of things.

There are many dimensions to this reflection founded in the search for order and sense, and one can, in principle, imagine a case where a religion (or religious "system") is linked to every last part of social life, where religious specialists have power and influence; where the economic, political, sacred, and social worlds are all woven together, in a world without missionaries, state ideologies, pilgrimages to other lands, capitalism, or imperialism. Yet if such a system is possible in principle, it is not so easy to find in fact. Even in places where religion is vast, sweeping, and ancient and tied to every thread in the social fabric—economic, political, sacred, and social—like Hindu India, there are corners of the empire, hill peoples, local traditions, television sets, missionaries, outcasts, and ambiguities.[10] Belief fragments are strewn across the conceptual landscape.

But does there need to be some kind of systemic whole in the web of culture, to use Geertz's own metaphor, for there to be sense in the sets of practices and beliefs referred to as religious, including healing practices? Throughout this work, it has been my goal to pay respect to the symbolic diversity that enlivens life in one Russian village, and at the same time not give up the goal of uncovering local orders, such as they are.[11] The question then becomes, if order is not found at the level of ideology or even at the level of coherent symbols per se, where might it, in fact, be found?[12]

10. Leavitt (1992:42) addresses these series of questions in an overview of cultural holism in the anthropology of South Asia. How is it, he asks, that regional traditions can be treated deeply in the anthropology of India when they appear to sharply differ from (yet co-exist with) classic, unified Sanskrit models that have been the foundation for ethnosociological (Marriott) and structural (Dumont) schools in anthropology? In his own research in the Himalayan region of Kumaon, local religion (with its rural observances, lunar calendar, and the hierarchies of local gods) is articulated in complex ways with classical Hinduism. The answer to the problem of wholes and parts lies not in disregarding inconvenient data, nor does it lie in "proposing the abandonment . . . of the very process of informed speculation" (1992:42), as critical movements have suggested. It lies in "a more complex notion of wholes, parts, and the kinds of interactions that take place among them."
11. This has been an important project in the symbolic anthropology of Durkheim's intellectual descendants through Turner. See Ortner (1984:128–133) for a discussion.
12. In the study of Russian popular religion, the syncretic mix of Orthodoxy and agrarian religion has been known as *dvoeverie* (two-faithedness). This dvoeverie has been the object of great debate: How Christian is it? How "pagan" is it? How "old" is the paganism? How "pure"? In Chapter 7, I look more closely at how ideological sources overlap. For now, making the assumption of a syncretic mix does two things that get in the way of analysis. First, it posits an overarching intelligibility that does not exist. Second, it tends to encourage the exclusion of important data that do not "fit" into the system as defined.

Chto-to est'. There is something. On that, villagers agree. Something is out there with influence and force and the qualities of protection. There are forces out there, some named and some nameless. There are saints and there is a God, and there is the semidivinity of heavy-handed leaders. The leshii beckons and jokes and punishes in seen-then-unseen ways. Storms sweep the vast countryside; draughts wither it. Chto-to est'. There is something.

Villagers have another point of agreement. Fixing the health of a body, person, family line, family group, village, or country can be done in ways that involve invoking transformative powers.

From these most general points of consensus, I propose an approach to the problem of healing that is grounded in a local concept with far-reaching social resonance. It is a concept that arose ethnographically, but the effect of using it has broader theoretical implications. I posit this: To have faith in a Russian context means literally to put one's hopes in a certain direction. In Russian, this is called *obrashchenie* (plural *obrashcheniia*), "turning toward." This "turning toward," roughly equivalent to an invocation (or petition), is performed both in settings that are grounded in social life, and those that involve facing powerful, unseen forces. In a social sense, an obrashchenie is made to any authority: clerk, bureaucrat, Party member, or person in charge of the distribution of any resource. In the village, stories were told of obrashcheniia to local Party members or police when kinfolk were arrested. In folklore, there are obrashcheniia to the tsar to correct the injustice of a local authority (or, more recently, to Stalin, for the same thing.) The underlying sense of obrashcheniia is that they are what one does when one is beyond hope, given the regular course of things, when something transformative must enter the picture. If Anna Petrovna had not rushed through the village to get signatures for her husband's release ("Look how I used my head!"), he would have remained in the hopelessly distant world of prison. With her obrashchenie, she overcame the insurmountable, and recovered the irretrievable. Through the gesture of obrashchenie, there was a chance for hope.

Obrashcheniia are also aimed in the direction of unseen powers, wherever those powers might lie. They can be aimed at God, the saints, or unclean or clean forces. They can be sent in the direction of dead souls, grandfather forest, or to the khoziain of the house, barn, or bathhouse. They can be sent individually to relatives who have passed on, or collectively to the dead ancestors or to the healing powers of "mother-water."

They can be turned to for protection, healing, succor, or comfort, or for the proper functioning of the land and the farm.

In this chapter, I speak of healing in terms of obrashchenie. Healing (of this kind) is about turning toward transformative powers with the hope of pulling them in to the social sphere. This is healing; this is magic; this is religion. It encompasses a range of actors (worldly and other-worldly), ideologies (agrarian, Soviet, Christian), and social spheres (the person, group, village, land). The study of obrashcheniia is a study of a particular symbolic sphere very much alive in Solovyovo, but it is also a study of a specific social function that can tend, in its practice, to unify symbols from diverse origins.

In Asad's (1983:252) famous critique of Geertz's definition of religion, anthropology is called to consider the problem of religion not as a problem of meanings, but as a problem of power. He writes:

> Instead of approaching religion with questions about the social meaning of doctrines and practices, or even about the psychological effects of symbols and rituals, let us begin by asking what are the historical conditions (movements, classes, institutions, ideologies) necessary for the existence of particular religious practices and discourses. In other words, let us ask: *how does power create religion* (my emphasis).

How does power create religion? This serious reflection turned the study of religion, for many, away from the semantic and locally symbolic, and toward the crucial issues of the unfolding needs of the state and its ideologies, institutions, and movements. Much of what, in turn, happened in the study of religion in the next two decades, could be said to be implicitly or explicitly following that advice.[13]

A study of obrashchenie turns the equation further: I ask, in effect, how does *religion create power*? How does it let me (my body, my being, my family, my people) have some, too? In this sense (and in the spirit of recent works that have returned to ethnographic puzzles in settings at

13. Asad's critique of Geertz and his "heady" approach to religion mirrors Connerton's critique of the "heady" approaches to memory. Asad shifts emphasis to the state, and Connerton shifts it to the body (as a vehicle for the state). Epistemological questions should be open for debate, and epistemological positions should be ready for refinement. There is certainly enough room in anthropology to include questions of conceptualization and questions of state power.

least as ideologically complex as the Russian village), I bring the question of religion back to the local. Yes, it is about power, whatever that
is. It is about pinning one's hopes on radical transformations. It is about
setting space right. Of course, ideology is a crucial matter for understanding the ways in which religious institutions inform symbolic landscapes; this is a subject of the last two chapters of this book.[14] But for
now, I let people and practice and metaphor—the vehicles of cultural
persistence in social memory—speak first. And I let this landscape settle
into its own contours: deeply wrought, regularly reproduced, and not
easily, or lightly, forgotten.

A Note on Unseen Powers/Forces

Wondering about strategies for accessing otherworldly powers is not new
to the study of Russian folklore. In 1963, Propp first published *Russkie
Agrarnye Prazdniki* (Russian Agrarian Holidays), a seminal work on the
cycle of rites and holidays in the Russian agrarian calendar. Propp reaches
the core of the matter in a chapter on death. Why, he asks, are there several yearly holidays in which ritual dolls are burned in effigy? Did these
dolls represent, as many before him had assumed, gods and goddesses
that would be killed only to be resurrected later to ensure fertility? In following this line of questioning, Propp focuses on a deeper issue: Were
there "gods and goddesses" at all in the Russian world of the supernatural—as there were in other agrarian cultures (like those of the Romans
and the Greeks)?

Propp concludes that Russian agrarian culture is one of "forces" (*sily*)
and not of "gods" or "spirits" (Propp 1995[1963]:108).[15] In this controversial proposition, he appears to knock Russians down a notch on
the cultural evolutionary ladder, at least according to his detractors.[16]

---

14. The focus on obrashcheniia allows one to look at religious practice in Russia without
defining the problem in terms of the origins—including ideological origins—of symbols.
Obrashchenie is a social act that takes place in many different social contexts; some are
patently Orthodox and others are patently not. Methodologically speaking, I argue that
before attributing origins to various practices, it is useful to know what people are actually doing and how they describe this action. In Solovyovo, the gesture of obrashchenie
was certainly a symbolically potent one and a first tool in the explanation of religious practice. This chapter aims at enlightening this gesture. The origins of symbolism (and their attachment to hegemonic orders) will follow.
15. "Delo ne v dukhe, no v sile."
16. I thank Professor Svetlana Adon'eva of St. Petersburg State University for pointing

Evolutionism had survived as a dominant paradigm in Soviet scholarship; it fit well into a broader Marxist perspective. Propp's work included the stamp of this mindset. In *Russkie Agrarnye Prazdniki,* Propp draws from the Frazarian-type assumption that cultures go through a series of ever-maturing relationships to unseen forces. The process begins with beliefs in elemental forces that animate life forms; next, forces are seen to inhabit a place; then forces receive a name and can be figured and understood to have human traits; and finally more or less stable gods with names and functions are established (Propp 1995[1963]:108–110). A look at the yearly ritual cycle in rural Russia caused Propp to conclude that this final "step" had not been achieved in the Russian context. In his view, Russian villagers had no gods (*bozhestva*), let alone an elaborate belief in an abstract "God." Although he considered Russian these farmers to have anthropomorphized, protodivine forms, in other ways they were very nearly animistic.[17]

My own fieldwork revealed no evolutionary principle whatsoever. Yet Propp's crucial insight—that forces are not necessarily solidified into beings—concurs with what has been found in Solovyovo. The forces that would materialize into the leshii are always poised to do so; they take on and leave form loosely and sometimes lyrically. In Solovyovo, there is a diverse set of pathways to otherworldly forces, and a range of forms that those forces can take on. Sometimes they are much like those nameless forces "out there" (chto-to est'). Other times they are attached to a place, animating it with special powers (like the "mother pine" that was invoked in Chapter 5). In still others, they take on a name and a personality (ded, leshii, *sviatye* or saints, etc.), and can be dealt with as one deals with people. Sometimes they more closely resemble fierce, overarching khoziaeva (God, Stalin, etc.). Getting sick from these forces is more or less a single process, as is healing by them. If the unpredictable forces out there have made a person sick, or caused her family or her village to break

---

out this controversy to me, which lies in a complex web of ideological inference—that is, how is it that Europe's "weak link in the chain of capitalism," Russia, could be so essentially "primitive."

17. The Frazerian evolutionism that Propp refers to has been entirely discredited in Western anthropology, but it certainly informs discursive formations within the scholarship of the former Soviet Union. It is quite possible to draw from the insights of Propp without assuming this form of evolutionism and I endeavor to do so.

apart, or her country to go to war, or her time to be thrown out of joint, what can she do about it?

Here, I treat the process of accessing higher powers as part of a single analytical category, whether "derived" from Orthodoxy, communism, or Russian agrarian religion. Bounties from unseen worlds are, in fact, offered from various sources. What they share can broadly be referred to as a "symbolism of otherworldly powers."

It is worth noting that where scholars such as Propp use folk material gathered mostly before the Revolution, in my work, I regard symbolism in the context of the wide range of ideological forces that made their way into the village worldview during the course of the twentieth century. Categories emerge from the data. For now, the functional question is: How can one *turn toward unpredictable forces at work in the world*—forces that cause illness and the breakdown of social and psychological orders?

OBRASHCHENIE IN SOLOVYOVO

* * *

A Local Healer

> Creative figures—be they poets, prophets, even witch finders;
> whether they work with mirrors, medicines, or the written
> word—are experimental practitioners. They try to make universal
> signs speak to particular realities. . . . [T]hey seek to shape the
> inchoateness . . . into techniques of empowerment and signs of
> collective representation.
>
> —JOHN COMAROFF AND JEAN COMAROFF, *MODERNITY AND ITS MALCONTENTS* (1993:xii)

Mikhail Alekseevich Belov is by any account an extraordinary person. He was born in Solovyovo in 1939 as the youngest of eight children and is probably not even five feet tall ("My mother ran out of material for me!" he used to say). In addition to tending to his farm work and homestead, Mikhail Alekseevich worked as the librarian while I lived in Solovyovo, and over the years has also been employed as a teacher and an agitator for the Communist Party.[18] He was, in fact, for many years a member of the Party—even a deputy in the local soviet—and still earnestly believes in many of the Soviet values that were taught to him as a child ("They taught us not to steal and to work hard and to be honest.

---

18. Mikhail Alekseevich retired in 1999.

They gave us limits in life"). In recent years, Mikhail Alekseevich has been busy learning about Orthodoxy, and has been trying to help educate the village population about it as well, using gatherings at the clubhouse on Orthodox holidays as (often less than welcome) occasions to explain the meanings of holidays such as Easter and Christmas.

Mikhail Alekseevich is important in the context of his village not only because he is a gentle, hardworking man, but because he has practiced the art of healing through sorcery since the death of his father. His father, as villagers tell the story, received the knowledge of the healing arts from a local nun, who had asked him if he wanted to learn black or white magic, as she could offer both. Today, people visit Mikhail Alekseevich in a regular flow—from as far as two hundred kilometers away—at any time of day and without notice, to receive his cures. Most of the visitors are from other villages, but some are from nearby towns and (once in a while) cities. He uses as his tool the powers of what he calls "white magic," but his healing method is linked to the general method for spell casting in the practice of sorcery (*koldovstvo*), where incantations are whispered into water and that water is then taken by a client. The complaints with which people come to him range from cancer to alcoholism, from family problems to visitations by ghosts. He heals individuals and sometimes groups, and all forms of the sick and the cursed. Mikhail Alekseevich takes no money for this service ("You must not benefit from the suffering of others!"), but he accepts small gifts of gratitude: a bag of tea, a bar of chocolate, or a freshly caught fish.[19]

Mikhail Alekseevich is famous in the region, but he is not alone in his art. To "find a babka who knows" is one important way people in rural Russia order up protection against the unpredictable forces at work in the world—forces that cause illness and the breakdown of social and psychological orders. Mikhail Alekseevich, like his countrymen, is full of models of how to harness unseen powers, derived from a range of sources. He is a fine example of a person who wends his way through a range of symbolic fields in order to best access the protean forces in the world.

An obrashchenie works in the following way: After one of the types of problems outlined above occurs, a local expert in healing, *kto-to ko-*

19. To the supplicant, there is an idea that a token gift must be given to make the cure work.

toryi znaet (someone who knows), is approached,[20] usually a babka (older woman). In the case of Mikhail Alekseevich, the supplicant then comes into the entryway of the house and is asked to explain his or her problem in some detail. Sometimes the two of them (or the group of them, when family members come along) sit talking for a good, long time. Once satisfied that he understands and can explain the cause of the problem, Mikhail Alekseevich takes bottles filled with water and retreats to the corner of the house where his icons stand (over his bed).[21] There is no indication that facing icons is a general rule for healing procedures, but it does mirror the way that icons are used for healing in churches (and reflects a particular symbolic configuration that appears to dominate the thinking of Mikhail Alekseevich). Words are then whispered onto the water. Mikhail Alekseevich uses mostly "prayers" in a given order and invocations to particular saints. Sometimes he uses *zagovory* or incantations.[22] His prayers are his property as a healer, and were given to him by his father. In general, healing prayers and incantations are seen as property that must be passed down, not always from parents to children (most often from mother to daughter), but necessarily to someone. In the case of Mikhail Alekseevich, the prayers and incantations are kept secret, and this is understood to increase their power.

While preparing the "water," Mikhail Alekseevich sits alone on his bed, facing the icons. No door has to be closed but there must be relative quiet. He does not prepare the potions in a place where there is an open flue because the words can "escape" out of the house. After speaking the words onto the water, the bottle must be capped, again so that the words

20. This is the most neutral, safest way to refer to a healer: "someone who knows." The term *koldun* (fem. *koldun'ia*) means sorcerer, and has a negative connotation. Mikhail Alekseevich was called a koldun sometimes and it really bothered him, even though the core of his methods and means are the same as a traditional sorcerer. There are variants in meaning, regionally, but in Solovyovo, it was explained to me that a "person who knows" should not be confused with a *znakhar'* ("knower"), who is also a healer, but one who uses foods, plants, and herbs as his or her media.

21. As a divining and diagnostic tool, Mikhail Alekseevich uses a numerological instrument called a "pifagor," which he began using after reading about it in a newspaper several years ago. With it, a person's character (including weaknesses) is sketched.

22. The difference between "prayers" and "incantations" lies in the "direction" of the obrashchenie. The former is to the saints or God, the latter is toward a whole host of unseen beings/forces. Both put force into words and cast words in a direction.

do not dissipate. The client should not shake hands as he leaves the house, because the words will jump right back to Mikhail Alekseevich through that contact.

Putting a curse on someone—broadly defined in the village in terms of "changing another's will"—involves essentially the same procedure. There is still a pathology that must be dealt with, the straying husband or the unrequited love. Since cursing involves acting against the volition of someone, it requires more "crafty" measures in its methods (including placing the words on hidden or undetectable objects). Although much is made of their differences in the folk literature of Russia—roughly defined as the difference between white and black magic—in both healing and cursing, transformative forces are petitioned.[23] Further, common procedures (and, indeed, common symbols) enliven the sense of what it means to be well and whole, and what it means to be pained and ill.[24]

23. In one popular model of magic, "bad" forces—those that cause ill—are known as *khudye* (bad), *nechistye* (unclean), or *temnye* (dark), or scientized into *otritsatel'nye* (negative). Manipulation of such forces is *chernaia magiia* (black magic) or, more simply, *delat' po-chernomu* or *po-khudomu* (to do in a black or evil way/by black or evil means). In popular understanding, it is the koldun (or the *ved'ma*, witch) who uses these dark forces for causing harm. Good forces are less often spoken of, as a matter of fact. They are accessed via prayers to icons and "saints," usually. The use of such positive, often nameless forces in the paradigm of sorcery is called *belaia magiia* or, more frequently, this process is referred to as *delat' po-belomu* or *po-khoroshemu* (to do in a "white" or "good" way/by good, white means). The problem of "white" magic that heals and "black" magic that harms will not be a central problem in this chapter. The distinction is ethnographically relevant in certain cases but focusing on it here obscures the central problem more than it illuminates it. I am looking at magical practices as they are used to fix the world. For this reason, I shift from the existential matter of how helping one may harm another onto the functional question of how invocations (obrashcheniia) work and what they are for.
24. Mikhail Alekseevich was my most important teacher in these matters. By his own characterization, his interest was in healing and not harming. Villagers, who discussed his and his father's magical practices at some length, mostly (although not always) concurred. Although I could not be a witness to all of his magical activities, I was a witness to many (he would prepare the water in front of me, my bed—where I would sit and write—just a meter away from his and Iuliia's bed in the far corner of the izba where most of their icons were kept). No appeal to harm (and there were such appeals) was ever accepted, to my knowledge. Some petitions for love potions to lure a husband back to a wife were accepted. Mikhail Alekseevich would say that maybe he "takes a sin on his soul" for this, but does it to save a marriage, and therefore feels justified.

SETTING SPACE WRONG: HOW ILLNESS FALLS

* * *

> *Invocation in the bathhouse:* Like water from a goose, Let all bad substance fall.[25]

The experience of getting sick anywhere in Russia offers a crash course in the local healing arts and their logic. Advice will be plentiful, and much of it will be accepted. A form of bronchitis befell me during my first Russian winter, and I was treated with the following: honey in tea, honey compresses, raspberry jam in tea, vodka rubbed vigorously on my chest, mustard compresses (placed on the chest and back), and *banki* (where jars are heated with a flame and then placed on an oiled back to urge impurities out of the blood). In the village, the list of popular cures for common colds and the flu is expanded to steaming oneself in the bathhouse (and, if possible, being beaten with birch and other aromatic branches), and lying on the pechka, the huge brick oven in the heart of the village izba, with bare feet, and covered with heavy blankets.[26] In all of these methods, there is the idea that heat and sweat will carry illness away with them.[27]

But what about when a person tosses and turns in her sleep? Or when she eats poisoned food? Or when it is clear that she has picked up the substance of curses? The same logic applies: Something is bearing down on her. Some weighty substance must be released so that healing can come.

Illness and Weighty Substance

> *Anna Grigorievna:* I also had *kily* [a rupture caused by curses] on my hand. We also worked in the forest. I sat with a guy on the porch. In the winter. All of a sudden, my hand started to itch. Hand started to itch. Hand started to itch. I can't stand it. . . . It was kily again. I scratched my hand, [the kily] were like white peas. I squeezed out one and another

---

25. *Kak s gusia voda/ Vsia khudoba.*
26. In this volume, I do not treat in any depth the subject of healing with foods, herbs, and waters of various states and temperatures. This is an exceptionally rich subject that warrants full examination elsewhere.
27. As Konstantin Andreevich said, "[T]hey leave—the poisons . . . [T]here is sweat, and from the sweat, the [sickness] leaves."

appeared. I squeeze out one and another appears. And so I bandaged my hand. I can't work in the forest with an ax. I go to the forest. Fine.

There was this guy. And in his village there was a babushka who knew everything. But it's far away—thirty kilometers. We worked in the forest. [People] said to me, go to babushka Varvara." I went . . .

Someone placed [the kily] on. I know who. Or it was left off to go by the wind. Like that. I went to this babushka. . . . Nothing was better. I slept at her house; she lives alone. [Babushka Varvara said,] "[This girl] is suffering and so I will speak onto the vodka [*na vodku nagovoriu*]. . . ." [Then my hand] healed right away.

Someone lifts [the kily] off, and someone seats it. . . . [These words] had been seated on the wind [*sadili na vetru*]. Left off into the wind. Left off to [fly] along the wind. People cannot stand [keeping the words inside] . . .

"Someone lifts it off, and someone seats it" (*Kto-to snimaet, kto-to sadit*). These are the two gestures of magic and sorcery: to lay something on, and to lift it off. Anna Grigorievna, like most of the villagers in Solovyovo and the area, at one time or another described such a process. She was made a victim of words that had been let fly in the wind. Someone had put those words out and her body had blocked their flight. By turning toward the appropriate person, her ailment was lifted as quickly as it came.

There are two ways to manipulate forces: to "put them on" (*nalozhit'*, or, here *nasheptat'*, to whisper them on) something or someone (as in a curse), or to "lift them off" (*snimat'*). It can be said that the healer, whether claiming to use white or black magic, *snimaet*, "lifts off." The practitioner of harm puts them on. Both manipulate otherworldly forces for the purpose of manipulating the world. In the language of topography, they are manipulating social space that has a specific symbolic mapping, and which is imbued with formed and formless forces. What is the substance of these forces? Once again, the specific quality of a given force is blurred when faced with the question of what one does with it.

Although often left nameless (or referred to with the generic *khudogo*), a common term for bad substance in the language of sorcery is *porcha*, or, bespoilment, the stuff of spoilage. Porcha comes from the verb *portit'* (to spoil). Food spoils; a character of a person can become spoiled; you can spoil a child, as in English. The term porcha (in its magical usage) was understood and used freely by villagers.[28] It can act on a person, a relationship, an animal, the weather, even the way a garden grows.

Porcha comes to a victim by various means. Some involve the eye (*sglaz*), others involve words and their weight (*ogovor*), and still others come directly out of the fact of social inequality (through *zavist'*, or envy). *Porcha* is the result of having been glanced at with envy or praised in excess, that is, dangerous looks and dangerous words that tempt the forces out there. Looking at the various ways that porcha attaches to a victim is paramount to understanding the process of falling ill.

Topographies of Illness

What is happening when sickness occurs? Why does porcha (or khudogo) attach itself when and where it does? The following are five characteristics of illness gleaned from the stories of Solovyovo, described in terms of the shapes and dynamics of sociosymbolic bodies.

FORCES IN A DIRECTION

One day in July of 1995, Iuliia and I were walking along the path that would take us to the forest, past a field flooded with wildflowers where the cows graze during the day. Iuliia was explaining how you could go about casting a spell that would change someone's will. "How is it that people can do bad?" I asked. We had reached the edge of the forest and entered, stopped at a raspberry bush, and Iuliia began her answer:

> *Iuliia Ivanovna:* If I were to put a spell [*nalozhit' porchu*] on you, I would say an incantation . . .
>
> *Q:* Where I could hear it?
>
> *Iuliia Ivanovna:* No, I would put it in something that you would drink. You would begin to lose energy. You wouldn't know what from. You would go to a doctor and he wouldn't be able to do anything. If nothing is done, it wouldn't stop before you were in the grave.

There are concrete ways to send harm. Anyone who has been offended has means of summoning forces and directing them at a victim, and illness can come of this process.

---

28. Functionally similar, far more rarely I heard the substance referred to as "sin." Other times it was "karma."

Often harm is done unwittingly. Even if it is not my desire to hurt another, I can do so if my thoughts or words awaken dormant forces. In the following case, Valentina Ivanovna instructs me on how to protect myself against malevolent forces, this case the evil eye, or sglaz.

Valentina Ivanovna: So there are such people who can put the evil eye on you [*sglazit'*], look at you. Always wear a safety pin on your skin. You have to wear it so that it touches your skin.

Q: Why do people want to sglazit'?

Valentina Ivanovna: Some of them don't want to do bad, but it happens and that's it. There are such people. And there are bad people. A lot of them. We have here a lot of bad people.

A lot of bad people are out there filling up the air with their bad looks and bad intentions, and it behooves us to protect ourselves and be wary. Again, there are echoes here from Chapter 5 on the mir chudesnogo. Be vigilant, particularly with dealing with chuzhie liudi (foreign people) and chuzhie mesta (foreign places). Outsideness and in-betweenness are places of danger from which sickness can come and foreign glances sent toward a person are particularly dangerous.

In this regard, Anna Grigorievna tells the story of how she made an error as a young girl. She had traveled to another village—already a somewhat dangerous act—and allowed a stranger to praise her. Not only that, but she praised herself right back. "How could I have been so stupid," she said while laughing. She should have known that she was dealing with a sorceress while out there on the road.

Anna Grigorievna: In Kraskovo, I had a boyfriend. And we went to the store in Iurino, with his cousin. We popped into the store and there was a woman there from the guy's village. And she says, "Oooh! His girl has such white teeth!" (Laughs.) I had good teeth. . . . I said to her: "Well, I clean them every day!" I went home, and my teeth started to ache. *How* my teeth ached! I couldn't find a place for myself. Oi batiushka! And so, we went to the party [*beseda*]. What was I doing there? I can't dance! My teeth ache, teeth ache; there is no salvation. Oi. And my teeth are aching. Such a pain. Do you understand? They ached and there were no medicines. And I couldn't [relieve the pain] with anything. Fine. I went to

Solovyovo, and went to the house of Katia Ivanova, where they are building the house now. . . . And she said, "You, my girl, had better go to Uncle Alesha, that one, Belov. Bat'ka [the father]. Aleksei Nikolaevich. So I go . . .

He was working on a rake. It was winter. He was working on the rake. "Oi, oi, oi, oi! Uncle Alesha! How it hurts in my mouth!" "Anna," he says, "It's a big [pain]?" I say, "Big." So, sweetie, I am going around not seeing anything [*belyi svet*]. I don't see the road to walk. I probably had a temperature of forty degrees. And so I sit down. He is going to do it—I could see him looking up at me. This was at the house of Mikhail Alekseevich's father. He does it on me.

And from me, you understand, it is falling. It starts to be easier [*legche,* lighter]. You understand? Lighter. He says [to his wife], "Ekaterina, give some yeast. Give some yeast." . . . She gave me some yeast. She says, "Cast the spell [*nagovori*]." I couldn't eat, my sweetie! I couldn't put food down there. "When you arrive [home]," he says, "put the yeast in your mouth and climb up onto the stove." He said, "Lie down [on the stove]. And put the yeast in your mouth." And in that way, sweetie, I fell asleep. I hadn't slept for so many days. And in that way, I fell asleep. In the morning I got up, and there were no bumps, nothing!

And then, I went and spoke to my boyfriend, and said to him, "Oi! How my teeth were aching!" He says: "That babka Natasha in our village curses people [*sadit*] with kily! What were you thinking? This babka curses people with kily. What were you thinking with your head?" I say, "What do you mean, thinking with my head? I wasn't thinking. What should I be thinking? I am supposed to know that there is kily here?"

Babka Natasha sends curses. The beautiful teeth of a girl from several villages away were enough to inspire her to act. Excessive praise (ogovor), like the evil eye (sglaz) can wittingly or unwittingly cause porcha to attach itself to a victim by attracting the forces lying in wait. These forces are then sent in a direction. Mikhail Alekseevich made explicit the problem of directionality. In placing a curse, he explained, one "looks directionally, and adds in thoughts." These thoughts—perhaps of envy—are made to move in a direction. They become substantial. Once again, this is a symbolic vector, one that can be traced, among other ways, through Russian verbal prefixes.

The verb *nalozhit'* indicates directionality with the use of the verbal prefix *na* (onto). *Nagovorit'* is to speak onto, *nasheptat'*, to whisper onto. The language of the magic arts is laden with this gesture of "onto." In Russian, "laying on" and "seating on" amount to verbs of motion. They contain a vector, and through this vector it is possible to envision the trajectory of words or whispers as they are aimed at an object. And indeed, words and whispers—among other things—can be let out onto the wind to travel great distances and cause great harm, flapping up against the body of a victim. By the metaphors that found them, they have weight and are substantial.

In the deliberate practice of sorcery—one that is intentionally directional—it is necessary to use a medium when wishing to transmit the power of "words" from one place to the next carefully. Important here is the fact that as porcha is manipulated (placed on either wittingly or unwittingly, or, reciprocally, "lifted off"), it is first put into a form and then placed onto a medium. Mikhail Alekseevich usually uses water as his medium, but he also uses honey, yeast, and an ointment made from beef marrow.[29] These substances, he explained several times, "remember" words.[30] When wishing to do harm, a needle laden with words can be placed at someone's front gate (thereby affecting the entire realm of the household). A fruit can be spoken onto and then hidden in someone's kitchen.[31]

Why are forces sent? For a variety of reasons. Some of it is mean-spiritedness. Some of it is simply the chance negative discharge of a thinking being. Some of it—a large part of it, in fact—is envy. Sglaz, the eye on the other that wishes to see him down where I am, is given its power through

29. He does not sneak words into soup. Perhaps I should have already known better than to ask the question. In soup, the words would escape along with the steam.

30. This is, essentially, the principle of healing with "holy water" as well. Like other healing waters, it is either drunk or sprayed onto a person to cause healing. Water is made "holy" by association with religious words or objects. In the most straightforward sense, a priest can pray onto the water and sanctify it. Water can also become holy by having somehow touched holy objects. Water imbued with forces can bring healing, and in this sense, the healing procured through holy water can be considered a subset of the healing waters made by *babki* and other knowers.

31. See Ivanits (1989:103–105) for a discussion of "spoiling" on various substances.

the force of envy.[32] Envy, as a source of illness (both of the envied and the envier), deserves particular attention. It is a great, dynamic shaper of social space.

STRETCHING SOCIAL VERTICALITY

Emma Dmitrievna: A person thinks something bad or is jealous. For example, someone said about my calf, "What a good calf!" and that was it. Prayers healed it though.

Mikhail Fedorovich: A woman looked at our pig and it died right there.

Emma Dmitrievna: Envy pushes people to many sins. Mikhail Alekseevich can put them on [*nalozhit' porchu*]. Once in a bus, he gave his place to me. He had a thought, maybe just for a second [that he regretted giving that place to me] and that was enough. I had a temperature of forty degrees. He . . . has power. Maybe he wants to do good, but he is powerful and can do bad unwittingly. He does practice sorcery.

Economic exchange in the village has been shown to function at a local level through the principle of maximizing social horizontality and minimizing social verticality. In line with this, the radiant past describes a society that is perfect when everyone is even and equal, when it is bound through horizontal democratic unity and not through local verticality. In that context, putting oneself before the group, acting in self-interest rather than the group interest sets off the forces of chaos that break down society. Happiness comes from the sense of communal joy in interaction; only destruction can come of individualism and the social differentiation that it brings about. Differential capacities are a fact of village life, and do, indeed, result in more for some and less for others. Some boys are more handsome, and some girls more charismatic. One cow can be better than another, a child healthier, a basket filled with more mushrooms or berries, a profession filled with more prestige. Like most worlds that are dreamed of, the feeling of freedom and happiness associated with group cohesion and equality can only be a punctuated reality in village life.

Society is crippled at a collective level by envy, but such envy can also cause visceral illnesses in both individuals and groups. Mikhail Aleksee-

32. See Schoeck (1993[1955]:226–230) for a sense of the breadth of the phenomenon.

vich explains how this works: By virtue of being in a happy family, a person can attract envy and this can give rise to "a heaviness that bears down" on his family. That which should be "even" becomes strained with weight. Here, it is the relative success of that family—its "raised" social position, as it were—that attracts porcha to it in a structural way, independent of the intention to do harm. The configuration of social difference causes disease. It attracts porcha to it like a magnet. So when a woman came to Mikhail Alekseevich with a pain in her leg that prevented her from milking her cow, Mikhail Alekseevich identified her illness as having been caused by "envious thoughts" and "negative energy." The woman was the wife of a high-level official in a successful collective farm several kilometers away. Her social "height" (higher social status) rendered her vulnerable.

The deeper level of what is most often going on in sorcery (as in religion itself) is that of social management. In the early part of the century, Emile Durkheim moved the central unit of analysis in the study of religion up from the individual to the community, where the group's act of engaging in self-definition and realization came to be seen as the very source of religious power in its various forms. In this spirit, Malinowski (1965:110) concluded, in turn, that sorcery for the Trobrianders was a "conservative force . . . for the enforcement of customary power." In Levi-Strauss's *The Sorcerer and His Magic* (1963:183), magic finds its force by "readapt[ing] the group predefined problems through the patient." Turner's rich and comprehensive work on Ndembu magic summarizes the work of the healer as "less as curing an individual patient than as remedying the ills of a corporate group" (1967:392). Within the practice of sorcery, envy has long been seen as one of the manifestations of social regulation cast into the field of magic. Early on, Evans-Pritchard famously linked the two in *Witchcraft, Oracles and Magic among the Azande* (1937) and, much more recently Taussig (1987:168) adds the dimension of the colonial state, where the illness that results from envy is "a bodily attempt at inscribing a history of otherness within the body that is the self."[33]

In Solovyovo, as in many societies, being the recipient of envy was certainly one of the most commonly cited causes of illness. Even simply hav-

---

33. The quote continues as follows: "a tentative yet life-saving historiography that finds the dead hand of the past never as terribly alive as in the attacks by the spirits of the restless dead, or in the sorcery of the envious" (Taussig 1987:168).

ing work that inspires envy (anyone in a position of leadership that "raises" their stature above the group) makes one vulnerable to bespoilment or "negative energy." Here, of course, the unit of illness is not just the individual sick body, but also the sick group. In the dynamics of the social body in rural Russia, social unevenness is a sickness.[34] This is a disease of social structure, as if the very shape of inappropriate hierarchy were pathological. When the structure of social unevenness arises, a magnet for porcha appears along with it. Such porcha will ultimately destroy that unevenness with its weight.

Sglaz and ogovor are important manifestations of this essential structure. Both are caused by consciously or unconsciously testifying to vertical social distance. Beauty and perfections attract the weight of illness, and one way that they can do so is through the agency of one person's overly negative (envy) or overly positive thoughts or words (ogovor). The danger of praising effusively does not come from the positive words themselves, but from the way that they point to this social distance—a distance that attracts bespoilment.

SCARS ON SOCIAL SELVES

The doctors had called him a schizophrenic, but it did not occur to Mikhail Alekseevich that his client had a problem with chemical imbalances or the like. Most probably, he explained, the young man's awful state of affairs was the direct result of a childhood trauma that had weakened him.

> *Mikhail Alekseevich:* Maybe he was frightened [*ispugali ego*] as a child. Perhaps his father drank and came in and turned on the TV loudly and scared [*ispugal*] him. At a young child's age, you can ruin the child's whole life.

Villagers explained how children were more vulnerable to the evil eye and to excessive praise than adults. They were also more vulnerable to

---

34. Citing Foster's "Peasant Society and the Image of Limited Good" (1965), Howe (1991:18) writes of the nineteenth-century Russian villager: "An individual who seeks to acquire things and, generally, 'better himself,' attributes of 'consumerism,' traditionally was not simply 'bad,' but positively dangerous, motivated himself by *zavist'*, 'envy' and likely to incite envy in others. Alternatively, he might be a sorcerer (witch) or insane (bewitched), and was dealt with accordingly."

this sort of fright, called *ispug,* one that could "ruin the child's whole life." Such a fright caused epilepsy in Iuliia's mother.

> *Iuliia Ivanovna:* Mother had epilepsy from a fright that she had. Grandfather and Grandmother lived in Chushkovo. . . . [One time] after Grandfather was married, he pulled out Grandmother's hair. The skin to the pulp. And Grandmother screamed loudly and [my] mother was sleeping on the ceiling posts . . . near the stove, there. The posts above. . . . It was dark; there was no electricity. Mother fell. From fright. That is, epilepsy befell her. She had fits . . .

There was also the example of the boy who was afraid of his father for having accidentally cut open his new pair of boots while working with an ax. He was so terrified of the wrath of his father, it was explained, that epilepsy ensued. Eventually, I was told, the young man "died of shame," after having had seizures in public. An early fright can turn a child into a weak, nervous adult, but it can also have more profound psychological consequences: After the shattering ispug of having been raped by a local man, a villager girl "lost her mind" and would wander the village aimlessly, began "sleeping with lots of men," and was eventually sent to an asylum. After seeing a man's throat slit and his head roll, Vadim's behavior grew forever "odd"—hearing voices, seeing demons, and drinking to excess.[35]

With traumatic violence and frights, the space of the self is disfigured or scarred. The shape of disfigurement attracts porcha, which causes illness of physical, psychological, and social types. Ispug, the most common type of this violence, is seen to cause the breakdown of a person's physical, psychological, and moral health. The afflicted will display behavior that is radically asocial, whether involving "shameful" fits, promiscuity, theft, or simply a character too weak to live a full and healthy life.

INTERCHANGE AND EXCHANGE

Walking slowly and easily home one day after a long afternoon of work on the senokos, Iuliia suddenly asked me if I did anything to my eyebrows to make them dark. No, I said. She took my arm. Iuliia—who is natu-

---

35. By summer 2004, Vadim had escaped from an insane asylum, and no one knew where he was. His older brother Ivan, who had drunk excessively for years by then, had begun to see "demons" as well.

rally lovely—wanted to talk with me about her beauty secrets. She explained, "When I wash myself with water, I say, 'Like water from a goose, let all bad substance fall' (Kak s gusia voda; vsia khudoba). She then explained to me that even by shaking someone's hand you could pick up khudogo. "You never know. That's why you shouldn't look someone in the eye for long—ever. You can look at them, but not for long. You should look away. You can pick up khudogo that way, too."

Bad substance can, it's already been shown, befall a victim in many ways and through many means. Malevolence will do it, as will the structure of social relations. With a world teeming with the bad stuff of others, it is also enough to simply look at the outsider, shake his hand, sell him a fish, or pass by him on the road. Some substances can come to a person simply through social interaction. It is not necessary to share elaborate words or thoughts. Just passing by is sufficient. "Life's experience demonstrates," I was told by Mikhail Alekseevich, "that it's better not to come upon a person by chance on a path."

With scores of clients coming to Mikhail Alekseevich and watching the way he went about diagnosing a problem, I was able to see a pattern in his questioning of the people who had come to him. Once, I asked him to role play with me and he followed the pattern that had emerged in the course of the year.

> *Q:* I arrive, sit down and say, "Mikhail Alekseevich, I'm so tired. I don't even know why . . ."
>
> *Mikhail Alekseevich:* There, there. . . . Tire quickly, get very tired, don't sleep or anything.
>
> *Q:* Can you help me?
>
> *Mikhail Alekseevich:* I can in this case ask, "What do you work as?"
>
> *Q:* I'm a saleswoman.
>
> *Mikhail Alekseevich:* That's it. You work in a store as a saleswoman. That means that various customers come; one likes you, she was well served. Another one didn't like you. A third didn't get enough and started to get mad at you. There, and that one had negative energy . . .

In many conversations and casual remarks on the subject, the implication was that contact with people was potentially dangerous, and contact with lots of people could, in a cumulative sense, become very dangerous. When I would get sick in Belozersk or Moscow (or when I would return home to the village unable to sleep), this was interpreted as the cause. There were too many people around, too much energetic chaos, too many chances to pick up "bad stuff" and traces of "dirty things."

Economic exchanges are charged with the possibility of a more basic exchange of bad substance. Iuliia was angry because she had agreed to sell milk to a woman who had been unkind to her in the past by spreading gossip about her. This exchange, according to Iuliia, was the cause of the illness of her cow: "Believe it or don't believe it," she said, "ever since X has been coming for milk, the cow will not stand up." In a more elaborate example of dangerous economic exchanges, Mikhail Alekseevich told of an encounter that he had witnessed between his father and a local war widow who had many children and was desperate to feed them. No one would sell her fish:

> *Mikhail Alekseevich:* She herself came to my father, and even in front of me said, "Aleksei Nikolaevich"—she was such a bell-voiced one—"be as you like! If you want, be afraid; if you want, don't be afraid. But sell me a little fish. No one gives me any." Those who sold her fish, that was it. The fish just wouldn't be caught after that. There was a neighbor, for example. Deceased Pavel Ivanovich. And he sold Ekaterina Ivanovna fish and went onto the lake and [caught] not a thing, or maybe just a little bit. The fish stopped getting caught. It was very easy to notice.

The economic exchange of fish and milk set the seller up for potential danger, as do regular, cumulative exchanges with people.[36]

Just as obshchenie (or interaction) is at the heart of what is good about the *radiant past,* so is it dangerous in the world of the present. Interactions with chuzhie are more charged and more potentially dangerous than those with svoi. Just as contact with the wild, unwieldy world of wonders happens on borders, thresholds, and foreign landscapes, so does illness, which social in its source and where illness can come from just a single glance.

---

36. As Pesmen notes in *Russia and Soul,* money can be dangerous even to touch (2000: 130–132).

EXPLOSIONS OF WORDS

Sometimes, harm-causing forces are strewn about when there is no enemy, no social interaction, no social inequality, but simply for reasons of surfeit. Words have weight and are substantial. Words accumulate and land on things. Sometimes, the sorcerer—bearer of potent words—is oppressed by the weight and volume of his words. He is like a container, one that should be in harmony within the walls of self, but is filled instead with a ringing cacophony. He holds the words in, and then he can no longer "stand it." The words must be let out, fly where they may.

There were many stories where a possessor of words loses patience, and is forced to let the words out. Even if he does not want to do harm, the words must, absolutely, go somewhere. Pity for victims does not mean that words can be held in for long:

> *Mikhail Alekseevich:* Sometimes people just have this negative energy and have to get rid of it. There was a woman who knew [*kotoraia znala*] but began to feel sorry for the people that she had cursed and so instead, took her bad energy and spoke it all onto a turnip [*nagovoril na repku*]. The turnip instantly turned black.

For those who practice sorcery, it is a matter of particular urgency to get rid of their powerful words before death. In a dramatic case recounted separately by a couple of villagers, the sorceress Evdokiia was taunted by demons and kept from death because she had not given up her words. I was told that sorcerers must pass on their powerful words before death. Words here are not only substantial, but also valuable property. When Mikhail Alekseevich's father was dying, by passing the words on to his son—choosing him over other brothers and sisters—he was granting his youngest son a reward.

Important here is the way in which words are treated as substance, one that necessarily takes up space. Such words can either cause illness or be inherited and used by the next generation. The requirement to "let the words out" is akin to the pressure that occurs when water is heated with the lid on. Sooner or later, the outward seeking movement of the water molecules will cause the pot to explode. Like the radiant past, the social unit of the self here is a closed container. Like the radiant past, the lid can be blown off of it through the accumulation of center-fleeing forces.

Spatial Pathologies

The pathologies that have been addressed so far can be summarized in the following way: some pathologies are caused by malevolent intentions. A person can wish to do harm and call on a *koldun* or a *babka* who knows to help her. The koldun will harness forces and direct them at a victim. Harm can also occur structurally; that is, by inappropriate verticality in social relations where the very structure of inequality gives rise to illness. Other illness can come about structurally when a person is psychologically damaged in some way. Finally, illness can come about by the fluid dynamics of khudogo itself, that is, by words that must be released by one person only to be received by another.

Given what has been demonstrated in this section about the origins of illness, a few general words should be said about the named and unnamed forces. The means of falling ill here all involve a negative substance that accumulates on a victim. Where did the forces congealed into these forms come from? I have argued that these forces fill the unseen world and are ready to act on and react to the social worlds. One could hypothesize that they are seen to come out of (just for example) the elemental forces of nature itself, but I have no data to support or refute this. In the physics of these forces, it is the existence of the force and the dynamics of the forces when met with the concrete worlds that can be identified—but not the nature of the force itself. One thing is clear: Sometimes the forces spring from the thoughts of men and women. They pour not only out of the impressive goings-on in the natural world, but out of exceptional and dangerous goings-on in the social world. That is, *dynamics in the social world also generate forces*. A cloud of negative energy that surrounds a person (when put together with many other such clouds) can cause a cow to stop giving milk, a child to cry ceaselessly, or a garden to dry up. Evil, envious thoughts can kill. Sometimes forces are "out there," but other times they churn out of the active here and now. This amounts to power that is, again, local in its origins, and potentially in the hands of the individual. Not only can a person call on a local expert, but she can—as a social actor—make things happen herself. Harnessing these forces also includes harnessing that otherworldly power which is latent in social interactions.

When summarizing diseased space, once again, it is necessary to see the world as teeming, burgeoning with invisible forces that have the potential to act on this world. If one looks at the problem in terms of a symbolic terrain, it can be generalized that as these forces are generated, they can find form and take on a certain weight. The interactions between people in the social arena can generate this weight either by conscious manipulations of forces or simply by a structure of social relations that "prefer" social equality and react against inequality as if it were a contagion that must be expelled. Furthermore, it is possible to see such inequality as a scar in the symbolic landscape, as is the disease of weakness caused by ispug—one that attracts a certain degree of khudogo onto the sufferer.

It is possible to imagine that these forces exist in a dimension that is visible to the human eye. They could be seen swirling through the world—sometimes chaotically and other times almost lyrically. They could seen being generated as certain social relations called them into being, streaming together when attracted (or, indeed, beckoned) by any of the situations described above. They would, from time to time, congeal into hardier forms (from all of the various types of khudogo to the beings that slide into the human domains) and cause the breakdown of physical and social orders by their presence. Sickness is surfeit. It exists when these formed forces go to the space of a person, family, or community and settle there. Sickness is vibrantly spatial. It attacks person and place—all forms of social circles.

Healing involves correcting the social space that has gone wrong, whether that social space is that of the individual, family, community, or time itself. When involving the intentional manipulation of otherworldly forces, healing requires "lifting off" the weighty substance that causes illness. In the next section, I examine the central idiom for healing: that of lightening a load.

SETTING SPACE RIGHT: HEAVINESS AND LIGHTNESS
* * *

Evil words accumulate. Porcha, khudogo, and sin accumulate. Malice is, as I was told so many times, a heavy weight on the soul or the heart. Below, Iuliia speaks of the "sediments" on the soul of her mother, who died long before her time.

> *Iuliia Ivanovna:* So malice appeared in the soul. Malice. That she, of course, turned to [this woman] as a medical worker. Turned to her. But before, [abortions] were very forbidden. They prosecuted you for abortion. It was forbidden to do it. So. [Mother] knew that they would send her to jail. [Mother] is dying.

Q: And they send the medical worker to jail?

Iuliia Ivanovna: They send her to jail. . . . She was in jail, given ten years. But she stayed for less time. [T]hey let her go.

I saw her in Isakovo. When I went, I saw her. There was no malice at all. But in my soul, there were some traces [*usadok,* sediment]. Anyway, [I thought], "She could have done it. The abortion of my mother. Mother would have lived [if a professional had performed the abortion instead of trying to do it herself]. Well, [her death] wouldn't have happened."

Naturally, and clearly following the logic of this analysis, illness is often seen as a heaviness. This idiom is found in many stories thus far. Whether in the body's poisons (to be lifted off through heating the body and causing sweat), or on the person's "soul" or "heart," the accumulated weight of harmful substance creates illness. "Mne tiazhelo," translated as, "it's difficult for me," quite literally means, "to me, it is heavy." The language of illness in Solovyovo is marked by the language of weight and weightiness. For example, Mikhail Alekseevich says that envy, "will destroy the normal condition of the soul. . . . The person begins to doubt himself—something isn't right with him. It's heavy, there is a heaviness that oppresses [weighs him down]. It weighs down." It is the heaviness itself that is the sickness. It makes a person tired and lazy. It "oppresses" him or her. It "bears down."

Tiazhelo (heavy) in Russian is related to a series of roots, *tug-, tuzh-, tiag-, tia-, tiazh-,* and *tiaz-* with the meanings of tightness, stiffness, strain, grief, and burden (Wolkonsky and Poltoratzky 1961:371). In the quotation above, it is the sense of burden that dominates the word tiazhelo, akin to *tiazhest',* heaviness, weight, gravity, and perhaps *tiagotit',* to overwhelm, overburden, hang heavy on, be a burden. This pressure, or oppression, this bearing down is the mark of a heart or soul that is sick. When such weighty illness appears, it is time to seek assistance through some sort of obrashchenie.

When things are heavy, when "dirty things" have accumulated on the soul and left their traces, it is time to find a way to lighten the load. This is the heart of healing.

At six years old, alone in an orphanage, the ghostly visions of her mother terrified Iuliia. She told no one, and because she was afraid to get up at night to go to the bathroom, she would wet her bed. One day, a young woman came to the orphanage to work. It turned out that she was from the same village as Iuliia, and recognized her right away. In this way, Iuliia found something of a surrogate mother: "She would come and sit with me and hug and caress me [*gladit' menia*] like a mother would." Still haunted at night by the white figure, Iuliia decided to tell the young woman her secret. As the story goes, she went away for a weekend and found a babka who could prepare water with zagovory for Iuliia. The next time Iuliia saw the woman, the woman surprised her by spitting the word-laden water at her:

> *Iuliia Ivanovna:* Right in my face. I felt light/easy [*legko*]. As if everything fell right from me [*kak vse s menia slezlo priamo*]. I sit. It became light/easy [*legko stalo*]. Then, on the second day, once again. At home, she gave me this water to drink. In a cup, a cup. And said, "Drink." I drank it down. Seemed that I used the whole bottle. I didn't ask her where the water was from. And, in general, things became so light/easy [*tak legko stalo*]. As if heavy burden had been lifted from my shoulders. And to this day, I have not seen the image of my mother. She does not disturb me. I was not upset. I began to live the life of the orphanage, as they say. Things got lighter/easier for me.

The adjective *legkii* (from the root *leg-*; facility, ease, lightness) can be translated as "light, slight, easy, simple." *Mne legko* would mean that it is easy for me, it is "light" for me. When contrasted with *tiazhelyi*, its meaning is clear: *legkost'* is the complement of *tiazelost'*: lightness is the opposite of heaviness, ease is the opposite of burden. Thus, for every substance that bears down on a soul, there is the possibility that the soul can be free of weight. This is wellness.

When the *ded* took the kily off of Anna Grigorievna's teeth, she said, "From me, it is falling. It starts to be easier [*legche*, lighter]. You understand? Lighter." A schizophrenic man who came to Mikhail Alekseevich needed "a feeling of lightness [legkost'] and calm [*pokoi*]" which, Mikhail Alekseevich added, no hospital could give him. When washing in the bathhouse, said Iuliia, "The organism feels a lightness (*chuvstvuet takuiu legkost'*). . . . From the sweat, harmful matter is exuded." Wellness and illness are reciprocal.

Self-conscious magic can help harness or lift the substance of illness, but it is not the only means of getting sick or healing by lightening.

Whether dealing in curses or the forces "native" to a given person, contact with "heavy" people will leave traces of "heaviness"; light people will leave traces of lightness:

> *Anastasiia Ivanova:* For example, a bad person says words to me on this place. And it starts to ache, ache, ache, ache, ache. . . . There exists for a person that kind of . . . of essence, essence of his life. A heavy person, they say. So, for example, you planted plants, tomatoes, onion, or still something else. A person came, glanced, and all of your plants died. And there are also those who come and look, and the plants begin to grow, grow, grow, grow even faster. . . . And so, you sit with a good person, and you will feel free and easy, free, joyful. And sit with some bad person, heavy [*tiazhelym*], your mood is spoiled, bad recollections, a person can even get sick from that.

Healing by lightening a load can come by proximity to a "good" person. Such lightness can also be achieved in an inherently "light" place.[37] A place can be light, a person can be light, a healer can lift off one's burden and create that lightness. Spitting to the side after dangerous words or a bad, dangerous moment can do the same. Sometimes lightness can be achieved by the force of one's will.

Lightness and heaviness are central idioms in the thinking/feeling of bodily illness. But the bearing down of illness, the pressing down on the individual body, has an analogy in the social body. Envy brings illness because envy points to social verticality. Social verticality (when there should be horizontal, even ties) is also an illness of the corporate group. If this is the case—if the social body is warped and stretched (and heavily laden) by the extremes that self-centered acts bring about—then what are the mechanisms for treating illness at this scale?

The bodies—individual and social—fall ill and there are obrashcheniia to be made in the hopes for healing. Mikhail Alekseevich takes people into his home and listens to their long stories. They hope that, maybe,

---

37. Churches are considered to be such "light" places, which is one reason why their destruction during the Soviet period was such a grave matter. The other reason was the theft and disruption of the icons they contained, a matter to be dealt with in depth later. Places can also be "heavy" or "diseased." There is a story about how Belozersk had a dark cloud over it because of a history of kolduny in the area. It was a sick spot, just as the location of the monastery next to Solovyovo was a blessed and healing spot.

things will be better. Or that a loved one will die without so much pain. Or that some small or large miracle will happen: The cancer will leave, the nightmares will cease, the brutish beatings of a drunken husband will subside, the baby will calm her crying and sleep. This chapter thus far has offered many examples of these obrashcheniia, ones made to a neighbor or a friend, or to "that man" from "that other village," or to "that babka who knows." But there are also obrashchenie that are aimed in the direction of the *corporate* body. This is what happens when villagers turn not to Mikhail Alekseevich or that babka who knows, but inward, toward themselves.

FIXING THE SOCIAL BODY THROUGH *DOBROM DOBRO*
* * *

Mikhail Fedorovich: Jesus Christ said, "If you let bread out into the river, it returns with butter."

Emma Dmitrievna: If I do a kindness to you without self-serving thoughts, others [may] do good deeds in order to receive something back, [thinking] that "you must absolutely do something for me [in return]." I do this for you and you already respond to me. And what does "disinterestedly" [*beskorystno*] mean? That I need nothing from you. And I help you without any expectations that you will return something to me. . . . I [must] love another person like myself. Then, why do we make wars? If I respect a person, love him, how can I war with him? It's truly a high moral idea. . . . But materialists put the question, "Why do you talk about God?" Not long ago, one journalist wrote that if God is on high, why is there [the war in] Chechnya? Why doesn't He make it so that it didn't happen? But God, if He were to do that, He would render us all slaves. That means free will has been given to us. You can behave this way. You can behave this way. And what does God have to do with that? Because we are not slaves. And we are people. And we have a will.

"If you let bread out into the river, it returns with butter," says Misha Zakharov who, along with his wife Emma, were the only year-long residents left in the nearby village of Gubino while I lived in Solovyovo. The point he makes (and his wife elaborates) is that sending non–self-serving acts into the world causes bounties to return. *Beskorystnye* acts (those without mercenary motivation) are the essence of a "truly high moral idea." Misha and Emma explained this dynamic in terms of God and Christ, but the model they offered, that of sending good acts out into the world with no expectation of compensation, is general enough to have been brought up in a range of other contexts.

Dobrom dobro ("through good, good") is a mechanism for healing at the level of the group. It works like this: If Masha curses Tonia, Tonia must not return malevolence; this will not only harm Masha, but will harm Tonia as well. Tonia could sicken and die as a result of her own malevolent action. Tonia must instead send out good thoughts and deeds to Masha as a way of curing the illness that Masha sent.

Envy points to social verticality. People in heightened social positions sicken from the porcha that weighs them down. Dobrom dobro is a means of battling the evil thoughts, ideas, and forces that can befall one at any turn. If good and evil sometimes are treated, discursively, as enemies in an eternal battle, here good is not only more powerful than evil, but—unlike evil—is transformative of social space. That is, good and evil are not simply different kinds of forces; they are different orders of forces.

Certainly, dobrom dobro is not always chosen as the means to deal with acts of malice. There are curses, evil glances, ill-wishing mothers-in-law, romantic rivals, jealous neighbors and co-workers; there are baffled young soldiers sent to unfathomable wars. But as it lives in the conceptual landscape, the dynamics of dobrom dobro are deeply telling and deeply generative at a social level.

When it does make an appearance, dobrom dobro is understood to be the bedrock of a moral order, and does more than any religious symbol hanging in a home or dangling from a neck is able to do.

> *Maia Andreevna:* And if you wear an icon . . . [A]s if you can sin and the icon will save you. That's nonsense for me. Everyone does it in his own way. I consider that you have to rely on yourself. You have to look for good, before everything else, in yourself. Send out good to people, and it will return to you. I consider it that way. That it is all "good through good [*chto vse dobrom dobro*]."

The higher ground of dobrom dobro has a powerful underside: Disobeying its precepts can cause ill to befall a person. It is in this context that the logic of dobrom dobro is invoked most regularly. I saw it through the interactions between Mikhail Alekseevich and people who would come to him from time to time with the hope of counter-cursing someone who had done them harm. Such people expect to receive harming words from him but, as he explains, he will not do such work. Below, Mikhail Alekseevich describes what one client must do in response to the curse placed on her:

> *Mikhail Alekseevich:* You have to do good [*nado dobro delat'*]. Sometimes people come and say, "I feel bad, and I know who did it to me." Well, here's an example of two girlfriends. One wanted to get married [to a certain guy], but the second married him. She made it so that he would choose her. . . . "I'll make it so that you [don't] live with him." And so. If, in these cases, they say that I know [sorcery arts], then I say [to the person], "Who do you know? . . . Do you know the name [of the person who harmed you]?" "I know it." "So you. . . . He gave you words [curses] and you light a candle for his health. Well, a week or so, for his health— only, don't make a mistake! Only for the health." And if [they say], "He was mean/evil to me," I say, "Well then, only good with good [*dobrom dobro*]". . . . You can't get away from that. I am only for good.

Again, according to the principle of dobrom dobro (which he invokes), the way to cure such evil (here, harmful thoughts) is through good thoughts and words. "Don't make a mistake," he warns the supplicant, only wish well for the one who wished you ill. The ill wishes themselves, in such a context, can be converted into a dangerous poison. In an example of such logic far from the village of Solovyovo, a Muscovite who had been educated as a physicist, explained to me that her father had been bewitched by another woman and had left her mother. She warned her mother again and again to harbor no evil thoughts against this woman, not because this was a nice thing to do, but because such thoughts would be dangerous for her mother. Later, the Muscovite told me that the death of her own mother-in-law had come about for similar reasons: The mother-in-law had lost her husband to another woman and in October of 1995 had been killed in a car crash in front of the other woman's home. Her own evil thoughts were her demise.

Certainly, in the village, this logic is followed closely. Evil thoughts endanger not only the recipient, but the thinker. Iuliia explained this dynamic to me:

> *Iuliia Ivanovna:* One babushka wanted her grandson, Viktor Kuz'mina, to do some work for her and he refused. She got angry and *nalozhila kily*. He knows it was her because of the situation, and because he got the kily on

the same day [as their argument]. It was on his throat, and his neck was all swollen. He came to ded who said, "Yep, you've got kily." He fixed it. The next day, the grandson went and did work for the grandmother. You have to answer *zlo* (evil) with dobro (good).

Q: Do you good in order to protect yourself?

Iuliia Ivanovna: Yes.

Not only are the lives of given individuals explained by the principle of dobrom dobro, but generations of lives to follow as well. Acting against its authority can poison the life not only of an individual, but of an entire line. The grandfather in the following story was left with no heirs. His line was severed forever for his having failed to follow this most fundamental law of moral life of doing good with no expectation of reward, that is, failure to simply love others.

Emma Dmitrievna: Grandfather worked as the starosta [elder] in the church. . . . He was very serious. He was very severe. . . . Somehow it happened that he wasn't very happy. Why? Because he himself wasn't happy, and didn't make his wife happy. And with his children, it turned out that they were made unhappy. Why? Because he loved the older sister [of his wife]. And that one loved another and went and married the other. And he [said], "If not you, then your sister," and married her younger sister. But he didn't love her. Even though she was very beautiful and charming. She suffered greatly because of him.

Grandfather kept severity, of course, with his children. I will give you a vivid example. His son was eighteen years old. They were very good workers. They gathered flowers—there was a monastery and the sisters would gather flowers and healing herbs. They [the children] would bring them the flowers and the nuns would pay them. [The son] chopped wood, and with the ax, he split his new boots. Struck and split them with the ax. And he was so frightened [of his father], that he developed, as the people say, *poduchia* ["falling sickness"].[38] Epilepsy, right? From fear. What will father do now that the new boots were split with the ax?

So he started having falling fits. And he was already eighteen years old. One time, he went to a holiday celebration and, as my mother tells me,

38. *Poduchia* is a regional variant of *poduchaia*.

babushka said, "My dear son, you can't go." He would get the fit once or twice a month. And nobody knew. They hid it for a long time. So she told him, "Don't go. You are expecting [a fit], and it's better to not go." "No, I'm going. Everyone is going, and I'm going." And there it happened. From that shame, that now everyone knows, he couldn't bear it. He got sick, sick and withered, withered, and died. Twenty years old.

And the second son, he was on the lake, went skating and fell and that was it. There had been a break in the ice. He had no son. The second son was gone.

Three daughters were left. My mother's fiancé came to get married. Grandfather refused him. "Mama, I'm going to walk him out." And before, they would travel on sleds. He left the horse behind, pulled, grabbed [my mother] by the hands, and off he went. And took her away. I say to Mama, "Probably, you wanted to go." "If I didn't want to go, I wouldn't have gone." So, in the clothes she was wearing, she was taken . . .

Now, I want to say . . . if there is some kind of harm, there will be a curse. . . . And now, they say that they carry [the curse] and, more so, that the children suffer. The parents don't sin that [their] children will not answer for. . . . And so, [grandfather] had no love, and the most important godly law is what? Love those close to you like you love yourself. Love yourself, love close ones, love all people. Grandfather had no such love. He was the most important [person], didn't love his wife, and was severe to his children.

Emma's line was sickened by the disobedience of her grandfather to the "highest moral law" of loving another as you love yourself. The sickness was manifested in the ispug of her eldest uncle (and his death), the death of the second uncle, and the grandfather being left without a son and then losing a daughter to a young communist suitor (who eventually left that daughter behind, cursed by yet another woman). Death, suffering, and no heirs left to continue the rod: these were the consequences of disobeying the law of dobrom dobro. Living a life of good and loving acts is the way to health. Doing the opposite invites sickness to ourselves and that deepest extension of ourselves that is our line.

Speculating on the origin of this concept is tempting. It is certain that it is well embedded in rural consciousness. In its paradigm there are two kinds of forces, and one consistently wins out over the other. Good always wins. It is the trump of all forces. This differs from (one) Orthodox paradigm of good and evil, where good and evil battle to no end and with no winner. When I spoke with Belozersk's priest on this subject, he presented a model of Satan and respective forces in constant battle with God and respective forces: devils and angels in constant unending wars. This battle could be found wherever opposition to the Church lies, including (unsurprisingly enough) in the egos of scientists who glorify themselves and their ideas.[39]

The model of dobrom dobro has no such devils in it. Through the narratives, it cannot be determined whether it has Christian origins (turning the other cheek—that altruistic cornerstone of the Gospel teachings—certainly comes to mind), but it is clear that the idiom is invoked by people who believe in combinations of Christ, the leshii, communism, and sorcery. The theology of the Church is one thing; the theology of rural priests and their syncretic models is another. And dobrom dobro is, solidly enough, its own model for moral navigation through social life.[40]

For understanding idioms of healing, the importance of dobrom dobro lies in the broadly redistributive principle at its heart. If evil glances and poisonous words are made of envy, dobrom dobro is a neutralizer of envy. A kindness done is not only a moral act, but an act that discourages the vertical social extremes that would bring about illness. The mechanism of dobrom dobro lies in the acts of individual people, but the sphere over which the mechanism acts is that of the group as a whole, including current society as a whole, our descendents as a whole, us as a whole. The heaviness it lifts is all of our heaviness. Dobrom dobro clears that weight off; starts things afresh.

---

39. Even with this priest, who could speak eloquently on theological subjects, I found that later in the conversation these battling demons became leshii in the forest and apparitions that only the pure in vision (he, not I) could see. The priest had three versions of God and Satan: (1) God = force of creation; devil = force of destruction; (2) God is one (Satan has role in God's creation); (3) Devils and demons are the liveliest seen-then-unseen metaphysical beings. God is too far away to control all of the doings of the demons (see Leavitt [1992] on local gods and demons and their role as set against "great" traditions).

40. As Brodsky reminds us in his "Commemoration Address," in *Less Than One*, the business of turning the other cheek does not stop there; it continues with further generosities, such as giving away your coat (387–392). It is a redistributive principle ab absurdam. Absurd or not, as a principle, it wraps the social body in a separate logic.

SETTING SPACE RIGHT:
THE DEAD, THE *ROD,* AND THE *RODINA*
* * *

Ghosts walk through home, forest, field, and dream. They are envisioned as loved ones and strangers. They beckon sometimes. They admonish sometimes. Sometimes, they are silent and busy with what they had been busy with in life. If it is comforting to speak with the dead in moments of sadness or desperation, and necessary to honor them with toasts and offerings on appointed days, it is frightening to see them. Yet, in Solovyovo, there were many stories of how they walk among the living. Anna Grigorievna told how she saw the ghost of Il'ia Stepanov who died in a forest accident—a tree had fallen on him and killed him—when I was away from the village.

> *Anna Grigorievna:* There, I'll tell you. We went to herd the cows. This happened this year. Just now. One time. One of his [her husband's] turns [to herd the cows]. And dedka [Anna's husband] went to herd. I see the cows walking around. No. Not the cows. That's not right. That was another time. I walk and walk. Cry out, "Come on, dedka!" I am walking. I was speaking to my own [husband]. . . . I stooped down, lay down. Iliushen'ka is coming. It's the *muzhik* [husband] of the postal worker. The one who was killed in the forest. Iliushen'ka. Was killed in the forest. Marfa's *muzhik.* I look over; he's walking.
>
> So, he crosses the garden. I look. *It's not dedka!* It was during the day, [so] he had gone to herd the cattle. I haven't told anyone this.
>
> He walks, and fine, he crosses. And I'm not seeing dedka. It's Iliushen'ka. Fine. I walk. I bent down my head. He is walking; I am walking. It was far away, at the fence. I bent down [again], and no one is there. [I saw him] just a little bit.

The vital presence of the dead has many roles. One of these roles is to right social space that has gone wrong. Here, the dead are a healing body, where the agent of healing can be the individual dead (a grandfather, a mother, a friend who has passed), but is more commonly the collective dead, whose task it is watch over the living in their line (rod) and the land of their birth and death (rodina) and set aright the wrongs in the physical and social worlds.[41] The transformative obrashcheniia for healing are thereby turned inward, toward the community that is svoi.

Again, the territory of the place of the dead is one often visited by anthropology. Communities include the ancestors in active, vital ways. Ancestors and their ghosts can be malevolent or benign, healers or sickness makers, they can possess body, voice, and mind. They can demand that the debts to earlier generations be paid.[42]

Ethnographically, the life of the dead in the Russian north has been the subject of a great deal of research by Russian and Soviet ethnographers.[43] Described as "a strongly developed and well-preserved cult of the ancestors" (Cherepanova 1996:113), attentions to the dead in the include rituals that smooth the transition from this world to the next, and regulate the influence that the ancestors have on the living (Cherepanova 1996: 113) Indeed, that influence is seen as broad and sweeping. In *Russkie Agrarnye Prazdniki* (1995[1963]), Propp explains the entire structure of the agrarian calendar very much in terms of its ways of drawing power from the ancestors for the goal of investing the land with fertility. The dead that he describes are at the center of the equation of the living, where the entire yearly ritual cycle serves to build a relationship with them in the hopes that there will be growth and life in land and in love. Turning to the dead, an obrashchenie to the dead as a supraindividual group of otherworldly *svoi*, has a special kind of power on the living and their place, their land.

Parallel Worlds

Like the numinous in Russia in general, the views of the nature of life after death are enriched by several ideological sources.[44] It could reason-

41. Because separate ideological influences in fact converge on the symbolic space where the living face the unseen world beyond the grave, the matter of healing only scratches the surface of the problem of who the dead are in rural life. In the next chapter, I deal specifically with such multitextured symbolic spaces, including one space (on the day of the spring festival called Troitsa) that calls the dead in for assistance. The introductory points in this section serve as a basis for that investigation.

42. See Rosenthal (1998) for this fascinating twist on the sacred political economy that the dead see to.

43. For general references on the meaning and place of the dead in pre-Soviet rural Russia, see Zelenin (1991), Cherepanova (1996), Propp (1995[1963]), and Worobec (1994), as well as Chulos (1999) for a delightful look at the actual space of the afterworld.

44. See Worobec (1994) for an overview of nineteenth-century death rituals and a discussion of the problem of ideological sources.

ably be assumed that long before Christianity was known in the farms and fields of rural Russia, there were dead ancestors who could intercede in matters of import. The Orthodox tradition provides formal exegeses on the relationship between the living and the dead. In a standard reference book on the Orthodox Church, Ware (1991:258–259) explains:

> In God and in His Church there is no division between the living and the departed, but all are one in the love of the Father. Whether we are alive or whether we are dead, as members of the Church we still belong to the same family, and still have a duty to bear one another's burdens . . . , Orthodox are convinced that Christians here on earth have duty to pray for the departed, and they are confident that the dead are helped by such prayers.

Orthodox death is about resurrection (and, in less elevated language, about heaven and hell and an eventual merging with a family of Christians). Soviet death seems to be a very good and weighty occurrence when done for the rodina (here, Mother Russia) and, at one point in history, for "Stalin." Death in a Russian village is a complex affair. I argue—and Propp, I venture, would agree—that it is, generally, about that other, deeper rodina: mama rodina and her earth, her soil, the svoi of her space. It is to be expected that each of these concepts of death would be present in the minds and memories of rural Russians, and they are. Sometimes, in the village such musings would be hauntingly poetic.

> *Valentina Ivanovna:* So, they say that in any case, each person who has died, his soul flies there somewhere. But what kind of soul can you have there? If a person has died, he doesn't exist anymore. So many of these souls, perished, dead, that they wouldn't fit anywhere. I don't know. No one knows, no scholars know. There, we don't know, what those stars are that burn in the heavens. What are these things? The sun? The moon? How does all of this appear/come into existence? That there is a moon, that it is no longer there [there at night, gone in the morning]. That the clouds [appear and disappear].

Valentina Ivanovna goes on to tell of how, before, *chudesnogo bylo mnogo* (there was much of the miraculous). She spoke of going to the graveyard to remember *rodnykh* (the dead of the line) and of a magical healing well. Her materialist doubt of the existence of otherworldly souls was overlaid with mystery and the simple language of awe.

There is some consistency in villagers' views of the dead, vis-à-vis the Church. Certain formal elements of Orthodox theology concerning the dead were never mentioned, while others had filtered into common language. Orthodox notions such as that of "resurrection" were never invoked in the village within earshot, but the Church version of the journey of the dead (where the dead take three days to leave the home, nine days to leave the village, and forty to "fly up" to heaven) was mentioned several times. Certain Orthodox rituals associated with this journey were observed, as were "days of remembrance" outlined in the Orthodox calendar, but others were ignored, or "gotten wrong."

Quite present in the village, indeed, was the feeling that the dead (*pokoiniki*) are somehow still "part of the family" or, in other words, that their influence, as members of the family line, continues into the next world. This concept is broadly and deeply applicable in a rural understanding. The fact that this "family" does not refer to an "Orthodox family" per se (as in Ware's citation above), but to a more specific kindred svoi is relevant to the analysis here. That is, a person does not really have to be baptized in Orthodoxy to feel like a family member that one deals with after death. She does have to be part of the most intimate category of svoi. Such a familial relationship is a crucial one to the subject of healing—that is, *the dead who are a part of one's line have a role in healing that line, and the rodina of that line*. The special configuration of the influences of various ideologies is less important here than what happens when you shake them down: that is, the general gesture—the obrashchenie—one makes when one faces the powers of the dead. What follows is an introduction to world of the dead and its relationship to the living, specifically with respect to harnessing powers and healing. I begin, again, with pathology and move from there to healing.

The Presence of the Dead and Pathology

> *Konstantin Andreevich:* In a dream ded Fedia [who had recently passed away] said, "Kostia, I live on this star." Maybe you can consider it this way—that they live on a star. Different systems. A totally different image.

The home of the dead is a "totally different image," a world apart, a faraway star. Unfortunately, when the dead sometimes walk in this world, it is disturbing and a sign that something is wrong or unsettled or askew in physical, social, or metaphysical spheres of life. The dead, in general, should not appear; they should stay in their world and not disturb this one. Elaborate rituals (and ritual objects) are put in place to avoid such encounters.

When the dead do appear in unexpected and unhappy ways, they can come in dreams; sometimes they make noises or other trouble in the house.[45] Things can be flung around. Interestingly, an unhappy domovoi can also cause such drama, and this indicates a dimension of the deeper connection between members of the ancestral line and the *khoziain doma*, which will be explored in more detail in the following chapter. Such disturbances were noted earlier in a case where a woman's husband and her sister's and daughter's husbands had all died. Footsteps were heard and objects fell. These sorts of disturbances require protection, such as the placing of rowanberry (or sharp objects like knives or an ax) on a threshold.

It is significant that such objects of protection are placed at the threshold, that symbolically charged place in the physical-social landscape which wraps around the residential group and guards its svoi from the chuzhoi of the outside (here, otherworldly) world. Other funeral rituals protect the svoi-formations bounded by the limits of the village, taking place at the crossroads that are the village's border. Clearly, the essential (though shifting) distinctions between svoi and chuzhoi in the social worlds carry over into the metaphysical worlds: Although we protect ourselves from the unwanted attention of all of the dead (when unwelcome, they are all chuzhie), we only really harness power from the dead that in life belonged to some category of svoi. There is an important distinction between the dead-as-haunter and the dead-as-healer. Who are the haunting dead and why do they come? Three reasons for haunting emerged in my work.[46] For things to be right between the living and the

---

45. Worobec (1994:28) summarizes these ghostly disturbances, including historically great calamities such as "epidemics, or weather disturbances, such as droughts and hailstorms." Ivanits (1989:53) describes the actions of the unhappy domovoi: "[T]he *domovoi* would cause the walls of the house to creak, bang pots, tangle needlework, spread manure on the door and turn everything upside-down in the yard. This relationship between the domovoi and the dead khoziain has been explored in the literature of folklore, summarized in Cherepanova (1996).

46. A fourth reason that did not emerge in the data is explicated in Cherepanova (1996:120). These are the hauntings by *zalozhnye pokoiniki* (false dead). "The dead 'of one's own death' were counted as ancestors, grandfathers, parents, those who were not one's own became beings of a demonic nature" (my translation). See also Ivanits (1989: 47–48).

dead there must be a certain propriety in relations between them. And since the dead, after all, have access to benevolent and/or terrifying otherworldly powers, they get the last say on how things should be going in this plane.

LONGING FOR THE DEAD

Grieving for the dead in excess can cause them to come to the living in the form of a ghost, or in a dream. The ghost of Iuliia's mother came to her all those nights in the orphanage for that reason. *Toska,* or melancholy and longing, is often cited as the reason for such visitations. There are special magic spells to free one from the heavy lethargy of toska, a heaviness that not only affects the health of a person, but also can attract shades from the next world.[47] Similarly, if the departed cannot sever his bond with the living, such appearances can take place.

The barrier separating the parallel worlds of the living and the dead is a fragile one. Uttering words of invocation is enough to dissolve it. Here again, words—like thoughts and even feelings (such as toska)—can have a physical presence in the immaterial world of unformed forces. By themselves, they have the power to invoke the shadows of the other world. Like the beings that take on form in the mir chudesnogo, the dead are waiting and listening with open ears. Unintentional and inappropriate invocations rupture a barrier that should be respected and allow the dead to come in unexpected and potentially threatening forms. Rupturing barriers between this world and powerful unseen worlds is no way to draw healing powers from them. On the contrary, it is equal to pathology and will be manifested as pathology in this plane.

SOCIAL PATHOLOGIES

The dead will also come without being called; they can be drawn in when work is not being done properly or family affairs are off-kilter. Once again, their presence here is a sign that things are going wrong. The dead remain unwelcome in these circumstances (even if they are specifically turned to for help in the arenas of work and family life). As in the case above where the dead appear because there is a problem in the boundary between this world and the next, here the dead arrive because of another problem in "spatial relations" between the worlds. It is for the living to

---

47. See Adon'eva and Obchinnikova (1993) for examples.

keep things going well on farms and in homes. The view emerged that people should live in harmony, work hard, and not squander the land through lack of labor or attention. They have no right to fail to do their job. When they fail, it is as though they fracture the very topography of otherworldly space. As the "shape" of envy (social distance in a vertical direction) calls in the weight of illness, the shape of mismanagement of the land calls in the ghosts. Because of this, when Mikhail Alekseevich dreams of the ghost of his father scolding him for not taking care of his bees, Mikhail Alekseevich interprets this as a message that his father "wasn't happy" with his management of the farm.

The dead also appear if something is going on that is not to their liking in social relations per se. Here, it is the poor daughter-in-law who bears the brunt of ire that descends from the other world.

> *Iuliia Ivanovna:* Pershina's son and daughter-in-law came to stay with her after she [Pershina] had married her second husband [Stepanov]. The daughter-in-law slept on a bed, and in the night had nightmares about the first wife of Stepanov and felt her cold hand. It turned out that the daughter-in-law had a bad relationship with her mother-in-law [Pershina]. She told me about the ghost and refused to ever sleep there again.

The ghost appears as if drawn by the poor relationship between Pershina and her daughter-in-law, effectively driving the daughter from the scene. In these examples the dead come for the purpose of reproach and reprimand. In fact, this visit, which is a sign of pathology, is part of the much broader, positive role that the dead play in the operation of khoziaistvo, that is, the maintenance of the land and the family.

FAILURE TO COMPLETE DEATH RITUALS

Death rituals in rural Russia are packed tightly with large and small meanings.[48] From the placement of the body in the icon corner, to the dumping of the water in the home of the deceased, the inversion of all furniture there, covering of mirrors, placement of icons, money, and other

---

48. As they are all over the world. For an overview of the anthropology of death (with case studies from East Africa, Southeast Asia, Egypt, Sudan, and the United States), see Huntington and Metcalf's *Celebration of Death: The Anthropology of Mortuary Ritual* (1979). For a summary of Russian death ritual in imperial Russia, see Worobec (1994: 21–22).

objects on the corpse, and the order of the procession of the dead, the rituals of dying are full of precise gestures. Unlike many activities that are symbolically important in rural life (marked by ritual fragments and multitextured symbolic space), the business of death requires a series of very particular, ordered procedures. Everyone knows what they are and everyone does them, with or without explanations for what individual parts of the ritual mean. Failing to complete death rituals is another way of causing unwanted attention from the other plane. Several such examples were discussed of how ghosts would come if rituals were not correctly performed.

But aside from the mechanics of how and where the body should be buried, there is an important funeral rite that should be performed for the dead, which is relevant to understanding the healing function of the dead. Iuliia refers to it when she tells how they "throw the *zemel'ka* [little piece of land]." This rite has a place in Church ritual, but also in the deeply agrarian rites of rural Russia. *Predat' zemle*, or "committing the dead to the earth," should take place for the dead to rest in peace. Failing to perform this rite also risks visits from the "other side." Usually, this rite would require a priest to read the burial service (*otpevat'*, from *pet'*, to sing) in the presence of a piece of earth (*zemel'ka*), and for that earth to be placed on the grave of the deceased.

Here, as in the healing practices in general, words are substantial and carry with them weight and power. Because of the ideological complexity with which villagers face the meaning of death (essentially, is it about God, the rodina, or something else?), death rites are also complex. The dead will walk if this ritual is not performed, and yet, where were the priests who could have performed this ritual all those years? Indeed, the state's official policy on religious practice resulted in some inconvenient gaps in my data. Although many said that "singing the earth" was crucial, it is clear that priests could not always perform the ritual, as there were no local priests left to do so. Perhaps what is crucial in the rite is not the holy words of the priest, but something more basic to the structure of the rite. Indeed, given the fodder that nourishes its basic symbolism (land, ancestors, power), the rite speaks more about the positive function of the dead than the pathology that it guards against.

In terms of that pathology, I again regard at function over form. The essence of the ritual is that soil from the rodina of the dead must have words of power (priest's words, when available) placed on it; this soil must then be placed on the grave of the deceased. The function of these words (as explained in narratives) is to protect the community from the "walking" of that dead person. "Singing the earth" seems to have the effect of sealing the dead into the other plane, the "over there." The symbolic weight of the words keeps the dead in their place.

Other parts of the funeral rituals point to this notion that the dead should be excluded from first the house, and then from the village. For example, as the coffin leaves the village in the official procession to the graveyard, the villagers walk to the edge of the village, turn away from the coffin and in toward the village, and throw dirt over their shoulder. The last member of the official procession is a person who carries the excess materials used to build the coffin. As she reaches the edge of the village, and the coffin heads off to the graveyard, she sets fire to those materials. The smoke from the fire is watched; the direction it moves in is the direction of the next death to come. Endings are completed, and seals are set to keep the dead away from here.

In *Celebrations of Death* (1979:62), Huntington and Metcalf ask the question, "Why is the corpse feared?" Certainly, it is not simply because a corpse decays and that is repugnant to people. Not all corpses are equally feared in all societies; often the fear varies according to the rank of the deceased and his/her social connection to individual people. Rather, corpses are feared because they are still entwined with the world of the living, and yet have begun the passage to other worlds. They are liminal, "betwixt and between," polluted, and dangerous (Turner 1967).

In rural Russia, the types of unwelcome apparitions from beyond the grave share the feature of being related to tampered-with boundaries. Words and feelings must not be carried too heavily after the death of a loved one. The dead must be properly sealed in the world "over there" with rituals designed to set the stage for their otherworldly role. Finally, people must understand their obligations (a social, symbolic boundary), and not transgress the higher authority of how one must go about the business of living. It is for the dead to frighten us into submission if we fail at any of these tasks, or transgress any of these natural boundaries.

Apparitions occur, and, in an important way, the fact that they do is an indication that there is a difference between the mir chudesnogo that one fears and the chudesa (wonders) that one harnesses. This is a crucial point for the problem of healing. That difference is related fundamentally to internal versus external social spheres; that is, being local and familiar, and, most importantly, svoi, allows one to gather in power from other worlds. Being from the outside, or strange and chuzhoi, makes such powers threatening. When svoi is formed, even as it is formed into the reaches of the netherworlds, power comes.

Mikhail Alekseevich made the point above that it is one thing to speak of svoi (one's own) but to tread more warily when speaking of chuzhie (here, those from other families),[49] "Don't touch! Don't disturb!"[50] To a certain extent, this contrasts with what has been said before, in the sense that even one's own deceased family members can pose dangers and discomforts. What is important here is the fact that chuzhie pokoiniki, the dead beyond the realm of svoi, are less comfortable and more dangerous. They are not, in fact, the pokoiniki that one turns to for help; only the pokoiniki of one's own line (or the line of one's residential unit) are turned to in such a way. The link between the world of the living and the world of the familial dead is one that can be used for concrete purposes in certain cases. In the case where no such deliberate harnessing is taking place, it is better to keep these worlds apart.

The function of the dead is far from being simply pathological. The ancestor cult, introduced at the beginning of this section, has far more important matters to attend to than simply frightening the living.

Healing the Line

When things are very heavy for Iuliia ("when my grief is too great"), she turns to her deceased father-in-law, known to her as dedushka. Theirs was a close relationship. Before his death, he made it clear that he would help from the next world. Such cases occur, surely, that a particular departed loved one is invoked in times of need.

Most generally, it appears that the healing power of the dead is not only about comforting someone's heavy heart or even answering the specific prayers of a community. In fact, the scale of assistance that comes from the dead is far broader than any one individual and her individual needs. The ancestors have a khoziain-like role that puts the power of life into the land—the living must answer to the dead as children answer to their parents. The unit that these khoziain figures have authority over is not simply an individual or even an individual family (rod), but is as

49. See Cherepanova (1996:120) on different names for dead of svoi and chuzhie.
50. This suggests the lozhnye (false) dead discussed in Cherepanova (1996:120).

broad as the limits of the rodina. Their otherworldly space can, through a wrong word or feeling or gesture, appear to this world. But their otherworldly space has a function that far exceeds those mere appearances. As previously suggested, this function has to do with the maintenance of khoziaistvo.

Khoziaistvo is a word that means "housekeeping." It can refer to "keeping a farm working"—with all of the economic issues this implies— or "managing a home or family." Khoziaistvo is that ever-vigilant management of the land and the home that the khoziain and the khoziaika perform. It is what one does every day of one's life to keep oneself and one's family alive. One takes care of animals not because it is part of one's chosen profession, but because that is what one does. One watches the sky for rains and cold winds and frosts not out of curiosity, but because khoziaistvo requires such vigilance. The life of a farmer in such a stubborn and bad-tempered land is a life that requires constant intelligent decisions about the "greater picture," such as when to plant so that the crops will flourish; when to reap to maximize output and minimize rot; when to slaughter so that meat will not go bad; and when to cut, dry, and stack the hay. Khoziaistvo is the stuff of life, as it is, in fact, the stuff of death. If it is for the living to keep khoziaistvo, it is for the dead to add the otherworldly powers to make that possible. This is the essential order of things.

Intercession of the dead should be a steady one. It should not involve radical demonstrations of displeasure. This intercession comes about by properly remembering the dead and properly guarding their authority. But what is the form of that intercession?

The Dead and the Land: Intercession

The agrarian calendar, like the Orthodox calendar, is full of days on which to remember (*pomianut'*) the dead. They should be remembered on their saint's days, on the anniversary of their death, and on special days in the calendar. *Nado pomianut' roditelei* (One must remember the parents) was a phrase I heard numerous times as I sat down for a meal, as Mikhail Alekseevich raised a glass to his deceased mother or father. There were more days of remembrance than I frankly could take note of. On the holiday of Troitsa in early June, this remembering is brought to a certain crescendo. The entire prikhod gathers at the graveyard to tend to the gravesites of the deceased family members, to speak to them, to give an account of the khoziaistvo to them, to leave them offerings, and then to walk, grave by grave, hearing stories of the dead of other families.

Propp calls this festival a culmination of the attentions that one gives the dead throughout the course of the year (1995[1963]:29), concluding that it is the "force [sily] of [the dead] that is transmitted into the fields." Here again are the unnamed forces (sily), and the fields of the rodina. The two are linked. The symbolic juxtaposition of the functioning of the land to the powers of the dead shows up in the rituals associated with dead. The ritual of "singing the earth" while committing the dead to the soil relates not only to maintaining the boundary between the living and the dead, but to gaining power from one's own dead for purposes of setting social space right. And a good deal of "setting things right" here has to do with the proper functioning of the land. I asked Iuliia the obvious question, about what happens if the ritual of *predat' zemle* is not performed. She spoke not of damnation of that soul, but a certain damnation of the land.

> *Q:* What happens if a person is buried without the priest singing the words onto the earth [zemel'ka]?
>
> *Iuliia Ivanovna:* I don't know. It just seems that since we are peasants and work on the earth, it could be bad for the earth [to not sing on the zemel'ka].

In several of the activities of Troitsa, rites are performed that symbolically link the dead to the working of the land. First, one must tend the gravesite—pulling weeds and sometimes bringing flowers or plants. Then, one must eat food and offer food to the dead, leaving it on the gravestone. Finally, villagers take bags of grain and throw them onto the gravesite. When I asked about the meaning of this, I was told that the birds eat the grain and then they remember the dead as well.[51] By taking in nourishment, one remembers, and by remembering, one brings in power. Even the birds—flying out into the world and scattering their own thoughts—remember, and this brings power to the rodina itself.

Grain reappears in the funeral rites: A person must walk before the funeral procession and throw grain out for the dead to be carried over. Once again, a day of the dead is juxtaposed with the stuff of land fertility.

51. See Worobec (1994:17) for a description of bird symbolism in dreams as harbingers of death.

Russian ethnography from the nineteenth century tells stories of elderly people who would bow and genuflect in the fields and "ask the ground for forgiveness" before death, and it speaks of how villagers thought that when death was imminent, the body of the dying would emit a "smell of earth" (Worobec 1994:18). In Solovyovo, there was also a visceral connection between body and earth.

"The Rodina Pulls You"

"Rodina," a word that rings with nostalgia for one's country and the sweet safety of one's own mother, refers not only to the soil on which one was born, but the soil in which one's dead are housed. Maia Bogdanova offered some of the range of resonance of the term rodina (family, mother, home, land) and then spoke of the dead that should be contained within.

> *Maia Bogdanova:* Rodina? Well, it would be, for example, "mother."
> One's family. There, for example, my mother gave birth to me [*mat' menia rodila*], . . . as if in my home. This means that my house is found in my country. Well, surely, it is one's family. One's native place, as one's family, as one's mother [*svoe rodnoe mesto, kak svoia sem'ia, kak svoia mama*].
>
> *Q:* Does it matter where one is buried?
>
> *Maia Bogdanova:* Well, with us, father is there and mother is there. The native land/earth [*zemlia rodnaia*] as they say, takes everyone. People try [to be buried] nearby.

The rodina "takes everyone." It is the right and natural place to be. Valentina Ivanovna also spoke of the preference of being buried in one's rodina, and what to do if you cannot manage that.

> *Valentina Ivanovna:* It's better [to be buried] in the rodina? Yes, of course. Well, some are on the rodina, and others not, now. My mother is there, my father is buried on the rodina, in Krylovo. There the cemetery is all overgrown/forgotten. No one goes there. My son is buried here. When I die, I'll be buried here, too. Of course, it's not on the rodina. Well, they bring the earth, for example, so you must bring the zemel'ka here.

The general rule is that if one can, one should be buried in the rodina: "The mother made me, I return to the mother." Going to the graveyard on Troitsa, one joins generations of villagers in the area of the ancient prikhod. All of the dead are remembered by family members and friends together. All of the stories are told in a loud (and increasingly drunken) cacophony as the day wears on. The right place for the dead is with the living community.

This rule would be simple if it were not the case that people must leave their *rodiny* constantly. Women, in particular, have had this emigration set into the pattern of patrilocality. Most often they leave their rodina when they marry, and are thereby charged with maintaining the relationship with the ancestors of the husband's line. It is here that a two-dimensional diagram (we live in the rodina, we die there, the power of the dead is felt there) becomes three-dimensional and vector laden. The rodina, it seems, has a "pull." You leave it, and it calls you in.

General comments about the rodina speak of this pull. When you leave the rodina, you will still "ache in your soul."

> *Iuliia Ivanovna:* Rodina, it's like your home/house, in which you were born . . . Let a person live beyond the borders—still it will be in his soul. Still, he will miss it. Still, he will feel—that it is not his people [narod]. Let him know their language. Still, his soul will always ache, not in its place.

And only the rodina, in a real sense, will "pull you." The rodina has many shapes; Konstantin Andreevich, in a narrative, began with the broadest definition of rodina, and ended with the most local.

> *Konstantin Andreevich:* For me, rodina, first of all is one's native country [*rodnaia strana*]. We had this Soviet Union, it became, simply Russia. I never get pensive, that as a whole, it is the rodina. Well, "Rus', our Russia." Just like that, I think about it as one's own native corner. There, like our ancient Belozerie. Together.

> *Q:* Is it better for a person to live in his own rodina?

> *Maia Bogdanova:* Yes, I think that that's true, in one's own place. The real one. I am not pulled to any other place [*menia ne tianet bol'she nikuda*].

The rodina calls the living home, but it also calls the living to their own dead. This relationship can be invested with a great deal of emotion. It is not only that one ought to perform death rituals because it is the "proper" thing to do, but because it is terribly important to one's sense of broader well-being. There is some part of this remembering that is at its most potent when done in the place of one's ancestors.

In September 1995, not long before I would end my first long stretch of fieldwork, Iuliia and I set out on a journey to retrieve a small bit of soil from her rodina. The last time Iuliia had run freely in those streets was at the age of six when her mother died and she was sent to the orphanage; this was her first visit back in many years.

After being dropped off in the center of the village, we walked through the streets and Iuliia searched for familiar faces. There was no one, which was not surprising considering the early death of her mother and being sent away to the foreign hands of the state at such a tender age. We came across a street where the dirt road ended, and tender, green grass began. A few houses passed, and Iuliia pointed to a green wooden house: "This is where my house was. This one is a different one, smaller." My mind flashed with all the stories that I had heard of that home, full of beautiful sisters, drunken but loving grandfathers, beatings, and premature death from war and illness, and becoming an orphan, leaving, and belonging to no one anymore. We did not go up to the house; Iuliia did not know who lived there now. Instead, we went to the house where her cousin Genia had lived. There was a lock on the door and no one was home. Then we went to another relative's house. Again, there was a lock and no one was home. Finally, we found an old woman working outside one of the houses, sorting potatoes to store for the winter. Iuliia went up to her and I stood back, waiting.

After a few minutes Iuliia returned to me and said, "Everyone is dead." Iuliia kept asking questions of the old woman and the answer kept being the same. Genia was dead, Sasha was dead, her cousins were all dead. Some of the cousin's children lived in faraway cities. She did not ask how anyone had died, but only took in the news. Then she turned to me and said that she didn't think we would have a place to stay the night, and we may as well go back to Belozersk.

So we hit the road—it was a three-kilometer walk to the highway. We left and did not look back. Iuliia said, "I'm not going back. That's it. My soul was aching and now it has been calmed. I came to say good-bye to everyone and now the ache will pass."

Iuliia's journey to her rodina had been discussed for many months before we were able to find a way there, as well as to arrange for leaving the farmwork for two days. Iuliia's case was rendered especially poignant because she was such a young orphan (and because of the lonely turns her life took after her childhood), but the maintenance of such relationships—here bringing the dead into the sphere of the living through the rite of singing onto the soil of the rodina—is essential to all. This woman, who had lived nearly all her life away from her rodina, was pulled back there. Through the journey to her rodina, her soul could cease to ache.

Once again, given the preference for patrilocality, the rodina is often a faraway place for a woman. It was not uncommon to hear women sing songs about their village rodina. Sometimes they would weep, as Anna Petrovna did once when she sang the following:

> I ran through the dense forest,
>
> I ran through the thick fields of wheat.
>
> Looked up at the sky, sighed,
>
> And remembered my native home.

The rodina is where a woman was once treated as a treasured daughter or sister or friend. Through the course of her life, she returns to that village many times, and sometimes for long stretches. In the home and village of her husband, a woman is for a long time chuzhaia and treated as the lowest member of her new family. Only in time, and often after long years of arduous labor and loneliness, will she become a khoziaika of her new home. Leaving the rodina and adopting another home means acquiring another line of powerful dead. Nevertheless, a woman's own rodina lingers in her heart, her "soul." She will make such long journeys to visit her own village home, and, like Iuliia, her own dead.

The rodina pulls the living back to its soil, pulls the living back to its dead, and, pulls the living there to die as well.

Emma told me a story about her mother, who had been swept up by her groom in an elopement, defying her father's will and marrying a communist. It was years before she saw her own family again, during which she lived in a "foreign" village where her own husband would one day betray her. Gubino, the tiny village where Emma and Misha were the very last inhabitants, and where Emma's mother died, is surrounded by fields and then, a short distance off, forest:

> *Emma Dmitrievna:* Before she died, my mother grew more and more senile. She would go out at night and say, "I'm going home." And then she would head in the direction of the house she used to live in. I worried about her because she could go out in the dark and get lost . . . in the woods.

In nearly the same language, Iuliia described to me the way that her mother-in-law also felt such a longing. This woman had been a bride from Filipovskaia, one of the important villages in the nearby area where brides "ought to come from." As the story went, Mikhail Alekseevich's grandmother mother had said to his grandfather, Nikolai Alekseevich, "Kolia, get married. I need a [female] helper." So they were married and she bore many children (all of whom eventually left the village except for Mikhail Alekseevich), and had a long life with a good share of sorrows. It was for Iuliia to care for this woman when she was dying:

> *Iuliia Ivanovna:* When she was already quite old, my mother-in-law would get up and say, "I'm going home," and start heading in the direction of her rodina, which was over the lake. You are pulled to [*tianitsia*] the rodina. We would have to force her to stay.

Both Emma's mother and Iuliia's mother-in-law were pulled home-ward to die.[52] Over lakes and rivers and through dense forests, past thick fields of wheat. The rodina is not simply a place to live and die (although this is the explicit ideal), but a region endowed with a vector inward—a centripetal vector. Coming home, arriving back to the rodina appears to be part of setting the order of things right; allowing, in the broad sense, the dead to do their job in their native land. The pull homeward is a pull that answers that need.

---

52. In summer 2001, I witnessed the scene of another old woman leaving for her rodina. It was broad daylight, and she was wearing rubber boots and a pale green beret, and car-rying a small bag. Her daughter followed her outside to the crossroads but could not con-vince her to return. It was the granddaughter who finally managed to talk her into going home, after a long discussion that the whole village seemed to be watching through their windows.

It is clear that the ache Iuliia feels, like the ache of these other women, is a private feeling, but a social feeling as well. There, she was svoia. The soil of that land was her rodina, the land of her ancestors. Place and belonging link here as Iuliia sorrows (in a long, melancholy ache) along with the others from her rodina. This is also effervescence of its own kind: it is the ache towards something that draws villagers towards social cohesion.[53]

This pull—this very vector inward toward the rodina—where the living and dead can consort together, is very telling. Coming home to the dead establishes a sense of svoi. Creating a svoi-formation, as noted in Chapter 3, brings in power. United, we stand. In Chapter 4, I showed how an idealized form of this svoi, including how it should work and the benefits it provides (happiness, harmony, freedom). Extending the arms of that svoi into the world of the dead pulls in other powers, and most importantly, the power of fertility.

Setting Space Right: The Dead and Categories of *Svoi*

Rod and rodina are crucial categories in social life; the rapport between the worlds of the living and the dead is no exception to this. In this section, I have demonstrated how the symbolism of death contains three potent elements: the dead, the land, and the community of svoi. When they intersect in the symbolic landscape, the space of death becomes extremely potent.

Remembering the dead (and sometimes, invoking them) is the way that the living can access the powers of the dead. There are two categories of svoi that one must "remember": the familial svoi (and this takes place in one's home, around the table), and the local svoi of the rodina (defined specifically by the boundaries of the prikhod), which takes place in the graveyard. I argue here that remembering the familial svoi (svoi predki, svoi rodstviniki) brings that power to the residential family unit, and remembering the svoi of the prikhod brings power to the fields of the rodina.

---

53. See Durkheim (1995[1912]:403–406) for a look at the effervescence that comes with group mourning. This type of longing for the rodina is not performed in a group act at a given time. But it is felt and celebrated, as it were, by members of a group over the course of their lifetimes.

In this chapter I have shown s~~aw~~ how individual, familial ancestors can be invoked to assist the living: "When I have too great a grief, I turn towards dedushka in the graveyard and say 'Help me, ded!'" Failing in the duties of khoziaistvo can cause reprimands from these same personified dead (grandfather, mother- in-law, husband), as can failing to remember them in a ritualized setting or remembering them too much outside such a setting. The dead that haunt are personified dead. They are the mothers and fathers who are ignored, angered, judging, longing. The household as a unit of space that contains a unit of svoi is protected from these dead through ritual. Such dead ancestors can also be called upon for help, and the help that they bestow is directed at the ills of the unit of familial svoi.

The healer, embodied in the dead ancestors, can also be a supraindividual subject—that is, a supraindividual unit, acting on a supraindividual group. I once asked Petia Smirnov why it was that people married outside of their villages. "The old people weren't idiots. A village was considered to be one family." The village (specifically here, the prikhod) is another unit of svoi, another family, one that is serviced by the collective dead of the community. These dead are remembered as individuals, but celebrated ritually as a group in the festival of Troitsa where stories are told of the dead from grave to grave and family to family, and where, by the end of the day the stories of the dead merge into one great cacophonic tale. And it is then, in the echoes of that tale, an old woman walks, throwing grain throughout the graveyard, so that even the birds that alight only to fly off again will remember.

It is the responsibility of everyone to maintain the relationship with the dead, and for the dead to grant the power of growth to the land. Doing so, not only through ritual by taking care of one's duties in life (primarily through faithfully tending to khoziaistvo), the dead, in all their collective power, reciprocate: The crops grow, the seasons change, and life comes to the world again and again and again.

* * *

It was a day in December 1995. The dark of the Solovyovo winter was cast in grey, white, and dusty blue. My own memory reduces the day to an image or two or three: A large man, a small house. He bends down to walk in the door. "Mikhail Alekseevich. I've come to see you. May I enter?" He sits on a chair too small for him. He holds his hat in his huge hands. I am shy; I go to the back of the house as Mikhail Alekseevich—looking so tiny—sits down in front of the visitor. The man, a young man with large hands, had come to Mikhail Alekseevich because he wanted to kill himself. He was just back from Chechnya, where he had been a soldier: "What I had to do there. . . . My soul is out of place. How can I live now?" Mikhail Alekseevich gave him some water laden with words and told him to come back another time, when he wasn't drunk. They would talk. His load would be lightened, it was hoped.

This young man—this young haunted man who had returned from war—solved the problem of his call to death by journeying to a small man in a small village on the edge of vast forests and fields. This was the man who could whisper some words that just might have the power to put his soul back in its place and could call him back into the world of the living.

Religion creates power. With this power, ruptures are eased, crying stops, vitality returns, ghosts—living and dead—find their place. The obrashcheniia that make up religion call to supernal realms and ask that that power fix the body, the family, the land, or the place. All of these obrashcheniia imply that the supplicant lowers him- or her-self to the power out there, whatever its form. Help is beseeched. It is invoked, head bowed and hat in hands. Religion creates power through a humbling of the person. Memory is in the repeated gesture of this humbling, with the repeated set of expectations of lightening a load, leveling the group, and enriching the land so linked to the collective of the dead.

And so most ancient spells are forgotten in Solovyovo, but healing by sorcery remains. The Church was banished but healing by sorcery remains. The Soviet medical profession developed, and villagers learned to go to doctors; and religion and magic and sorcery remain. Social memory is in that known symbolic landscape that says, "This is how healing goes." There is a unity to that landscape that comes from a unity of purpose: There is illness; there must be health. Religion, as a description of a landscape of invocations, is the source of this healing.

And yet, as Asad reminded us, power also—in crucial ways—creates religion. Institutions, states, and empires are intimately connected to religion. Of course, it does matter, at a certain level, if one turns to a kindly father (or Father), or a forest sprite, or a demon, or the collective ancestral "we." It matters that these crucial images are layered and invested with different associations that have different functions. Memory, in other words, has an essential ideological component, a crucial way in which it is instrumentalized by the state and the powers that be. In Chapter 7 and 8, I explore social memory in light of the confrontation of *worldly* powers, as these powers attempt to shape the minds and hearts of men and women, and attempt to turn the direction of the obrashcheniia—coming, as they do, with the gesture of submission—toward themselves.

7

The Red Corner

Space, outside ourselves, invades and
ravishes things . . .

—R.M. RILKE, *POÈME* (IN BACHELARD 1964:200)

INTRODUCTION: LAYERS OF MEMORY

* * *

How did the Great Social Experiment fare? How did it change the landscape of memory? It educated with images of a great and radiant future,
it offered new leaders without the trappings of religion's dulling
"opium," it offered explanations, inspirations, and giddiness. When that
did not work, it droned with endless speeches and took children from
their homes to educate them in its precepts. When that did not work, it
took people away in the night, and battered them into some semblance
of animal submission. But do such methods work? Is this how hearts,
minds, and memory are transformed with any degree of efficiency?
When, I ask here, do the metaphors that are introduced by ideological
powers become "metaphors we live by," and when do they not?[1]

---

1. In both scholarly and literary works, images of the brutality of the Soviet efforts at re-

In Chapter 7 and 8, I turn my focus to locales in memory's landscapes that are laden with several layers of symbolic space. Like the space of healing, they are places where the symbolism has been derived from several sources that converge and sometimes battle for dominance. Here I underline differences in ideological origin, and strive to highlight patterns of dominance. Earlier, I likened social memory to a forged landscape. Vygotsky's argument (1962) resonates with this: that thought is canalized in stages throughout early childhood, and familiar paths of thought are tread to such a degree that they feel inevitable. The question of how and why given paths are chosen in the face of symbolic dissonance is the focus of what follows. It will emerge that there are cases where not only do local, anarchical powers win the battles for dominance in some important contexts, but the symbolic pathways forged beneath them are so deeply defined that they can shed the outer symbols that they once bore and still retain their dominance. In other words, remembering can happen without memories.

In their introduction to *Modernity and Its Malcontents* (1993:xxi), Comaroff and Comaroff write that ritual is "responsive to history." "Its constituent signs," they say, "are ever open to the accumulation of new associations and referents" and this very layering, full of contradictions" is the very source of ritual's "creative power." The next two chapters offer two broad examples of the problem of how ritual and symbolic paths are forged through multitextured symbolic spaces, some of which are attached to powerful institutions. The first is located in a physical space (the "red corner"), and the second, in time-space (along calendrical milestones). In the language of Olick and Robbins (1998:129), both examples deal with confrontations between social memory practices that encourage *change* through efforts at legitimation and memory entrepreneurship ("instrumental"), and those that encourage *persistence* via continued relevance and canon ("cultural"), and habit, routine, and custom ("inertial"). My aim is to show that these confrontations can yield varied results in varied contexts, where social memory sometimes looks very much like a hegemony to which villagers succumb, while other times, it looks like the resistance/persistence of a people who are deeply locally de-

---

shaping ideology abound. A striking overview of the tragic side of the Revolution can be found in Figes (1997). Smith (1996) presents the memories of Stalin's victims. Memoirs and pseudobiographic novels, such as those of Ginzburg (1967, 1989) and Solzhenitsyn (1963, 1974), provide extremely vivid portraits of life in the camps.

fined. So much has been said in ringing, essentializing tones, about the relative malleability and slavishness (or brave persistence or bullheaded stubbornness) of Russian villagers. I wish to use this discourse in this book as a way of letting the story unfold in its natural shades away from black and white. As in the rest of the book, I see this attention to detail not as an ethnographic indulgence, but as the one way in which the picture of memory—at a bird's-eye distance from the forest to the trees—can be mapped.

In this chapter, I regard a space that is "invaded by" one of the most powerful symbolic landmarks that I came across in my time in village Russia. The "red corner" is a physical space in the village home that is filled with meaningful objects, seen and unseen. The corner of an izba—specifically the one diagonal to the large household stove—is endowed with icons, the presence of the rod, and the domovoi. In analogous corners in public spaces during the Soviet period, it was endowed with portraits of Stalin. It is fair to say that the space of a corner is jammed with symbolism from a range of sources. The physical objects that reside there are tokens of the ideological systems that brought them into being (broadly, Soviet, Orthodox, and Russian agrarian). It is the nature of this particular hegemonic confrontation that as the sources of power accumulate, so does the power of the space itself in terms similar to those described by the Comaroffs. By the end of this chapter, the corner will turn into a symbolic "corner," and will channel power not only in its physical space, but in the arena of its metaphoric resonance.[2]

In Chapter 8, "Calendars," I regard a classic example of hegemonic confrontation: the implicit and explicit struggles for control over the calendar. The Soviet Union, like Orthodoxy before it, had endeavored to take milestones in the calendar (days of revelry, sacred days, days of mourning, days of planting), and claim them for its own. The "days not like any other," in their new Soviet light, should have taken on tags that

2. Sperber's (1974) treatment of the "symbolic mechanism," which shifts the focus of symbolic analysis away from the "meaning" of an individual "sign," and toward the field of resonances that accumulate around the symbolic representation, allows for a systematic analysis of this kind of heterogeneous symbolic mix. See Turner (1967:46) for an earlier voice about the need for a serious regard of symbolic cacophony that can stand for, in its "aggregate of meanings," a "unity and continuity of the widest . . . society." See also Bourdieu (1977) on doxa, hederodoxy, and orthodoxy, and examples of Michel Foucault's intricate studies of how symbolism modifies in time within and around discursive formations, such as the one found in *Madness and Civilization* (Foucault 1965).

associated them with new and newer ideological systems, so that when a villager walks through the year, she should have learned to take May Day in her heart instead of Easter; New Year's instead of Christmas; the Day of the Marines instead of the rowdy village fêtes. This mapping of calendrical milestones is intended to be a microstudy in battling hegemonies, using a small number of concrete examples.

KRASNYI UGOL (RED AND BEAUTIFUL CORNER)
* * *

When I began my work in Solovyovo, Iuliia would take me around from house to house and introduce me to her co-villagers. Along the way, I was also introduced to the implicit rules of entry into a chuzhoi home. Sometimes, I noticed, Iuliia was easily coaxed into a home after her polite ritual refusals. Other times, she would stick to the entryway and not pass through, despite what appeared to me to be sincere invitations. At first I was confounded, and (admittedly), a little annoyed. What could be keeping her from entering?

As noted in Chapter 3, the house wraps around a familial svoi and crossing the threshold there requires rituals. My apprenticeship in those early trips with Iuliia was a cognitive one (I learned how to ask to enter a home, and how to refuse entry more than once when entry was offered), but more deeply than that, it was visceral. Again and again, I watched Iuliia's hesitation to enter certain homes, how her feet appeared to be glued at the entryway. In time, I absorbed not only that habit, but the force of that habit: one that kept me, too, lingering at the threshold that separated svoi from chuzhoi.

The threshold is charged with significance in social, physical, and semiotic fields, so that you feel the space even if you do not see any given object on it. Lingering at thresholds—like lingering at any liminal space—can cause misfortune that must be protected against through invocations and talismans. The social and the symbolic meet at the threshold with a certain impressive force that causes it to be charged with ritual, symbol, and emotion. Threshold space is felt space, as is the corner.

The corner revealed itself as a place of particular symbolic intensity very early during my stay in Russia. On the morning of August 19, 1991, two weeks after I had arrived in St. Petersburg for the very first time, I was awakened by the telephone and the sobbing of an old woman. It was Tat'iana Ivanovna, the babushka whom I was living with. Sickness? Death? I came out from my room and was told that Gorbachev was very ill and would have to leave his post as president. Of course, so much more was buried in that phrase. Certainly, the long arc of Tat'iana Ivanovna's life had passed through several extraordinary times like this. I heard stories of living within the barricaded city of Leningrad during World War II (when hundreds of thousands of people starved to death), and how she had fed her husband with dandelion leaves that she had gathered at the botanical garden where she worked. I heard how her father had been exiled and killed for being a priest in the 1930s.

I got dressed for the day, and as I was leaving the apartment, Tat'iana Ivanovna, still crying, took me by the arm and led me into her room. It was almost bare. I noticed an icon, elaborately gilded, nestled into a corner. Tat'iana Ivanovna tapped my arm and gestured up to the icon. "Pray," she told me between sobs, tapping my arm and gesturing again and again up to the icon, calling on me to pray. For a woman whose sixty or seventy years spanned the entire history of the Soviet Union, and who must have prayed countless times before that same icon (watching wars, the starvation of her husband, the denigration of her beliefs), the answer of the question of *komu obratitsia* (to whom should one turn) in times of trouble, was to the image that lived in the corner of her nearly barren room. It took years of living in Russia to understand that within that corner space known for hundreds of years as the *krasnyi ugol* or "red corner," resided not only icons, but also the presence of the unseen *khoziain doma*, the force of the rod and even the faces of Soviet "saints." In the course of this chapter, these various beings will be disentangled (and, perhaps, re-entangled), and it will be possible to look at the overall effect of the powers of this space.

"Krasnyi" means red, or beautiful. While I was living in Solovyovo, the krasnyi ugol, the red beautiful corner, was adorned in almost every village home with icons. The icons were often placed on a special shelf (*bozhnitsa*), sometimes next to crosses and treasured possessions such as photographs and keepsakes. At the time of death, I saw how the deceased in a household was laid out in line (diagonally) with the icon corner (with her head under the icons) for three days. Ritual objects such as coins, soap, and a towel, and small icons were then placed on the body, and offerings and other ritual objects (candies, glasses of vodka) were arranged by the icons.[3] In earlier centuries, the icon corner was the "cleanest, neat-

---

3. In the home where I lived, there were no icons in the icon corner, but the television was placed there and was covered with decorative material. Often, televisions—otherwordly

est place in the house . . . [where] the most honored guests were seated, . . . [and where people] laid the body of the deceased" (Aleksandrov 1970:65).[4]

The red corner of a village home is a physical space where symbolic force is densely packed. Although the icons that fill corners are religious objects, the icon corner is not defined by its Orthodox religiosity per se. As Propp confirms, "Certain pagan, and, later, Christianized practiced are connected to this corner" (1995:25,n. 5). After churches were destroyed in and near Solovyovo and a generation or two went by, little was remembered of Orthodox ritual. But icons—by far the most powerful religious objects in village life—have remained a focus of supernatural powers. Heartfelt obrashcheniia are still directed toward them. The corner indeed holds the icon, but it could be said—and I endeavor to demonstrate—that it is not strictly the case that the corner of the home is powerful because the icon resides therein; but the icon is powerful at least in part because of its placement in the corner. In the course of the analysis, it will be clear that there is a certain reciprocity that takes place in that space. The microstudy of the krasnyi ugol presented here will be one where many objects and symbols of different origins converge in physical and symbolic space. The effect is cumulative. The icon, having left the corner, takes corner power with it. The corner, having been endowed with icons and more bears their special brand of force.

This power was and is of a mixed and manifold character. Regarding those icons (and amid the inchoate flow of their numinous images and objects) villagers passionately agree on one thing: Icons are indispensable.

ICONS IN CORNER SPACE

* * *

"You Have to Have an Icon"

Larisa Andreevna: It's bad to live in a house without an icon. There ought to be an icon. If you take an icon out of a house, everything leaves behind

---

instruments in their own right—are found in the corner of the room, again, placed diagonally. When I asked about the lack of icons in that space, I was told that since Mikhail Alekseevich had been a deputy in the local Soviet, he had been required to move them. While I lived there, the icons stood over Mikhail Alekseevich's bed, where there is some measure of privacy and where he can address them for healing out of the view of the public.
4. This is a description of the nineteenth-century icon corner in the village home from *Russkie: Istoriko etnograficheskii atlas*. See also Dal' (1911, vol. 2:470).

it. That's what happens. These people are now bad. Sick ones. Sorrowful ones. Drunkards. There is no cross in the house.

We always had an icon in mama's house. When I left, my mother-in-law also had an icon. Everyone has an icon in the house. In everyone's house stood . . . icons. . . And for him who carried out the icon, in that house, there will be no happiness. Only sorrow/misfortune.

Villagers told me again and again that icons in the home are mandatory. It is there so that "God protects better," says Valentina Ivanovna, "and that's it." Elena Andreevna concurs, with urgency in her tone: "You have to have an icon in the house. We consider that you have to have an icon in the house." More important than the performance of Orthodox rituals of any particular kind, is the dire importance of keeping the icon in the living space.

> *Antonina Sergeevna:* Prayers? Who knows prayers? And who knows nothing? The icon stands there and I don't take it away. That's it.
>
> *Q:* What can happen if there is no icon in the house?
>
> *Antonia Sergeevna:* Without an icon, as they say, oi, unbaptized; so that's all not good. It's something terrifying, even to say it with your tongue. It is necessary to believe. As if with the soul, you are a believer. We have no church now. No one goes. And in the soul we keep it all. There is something. And in fact, there is something. Let these icons be there. There is something.

Antonina Sergeevna knows no prayers, nor does she go to church ("no one goes"). But without an icon, something unspeakably terrifying may well be at hand. The icon in the home keeps the home safe, protected from illness and from terrible forces that can bring misfortune of all kinds.

The icon must be in the home, but (unlike for churchgoers in the city) it does not appear to be of great importance to villagers *which* icon is in the home. Maia Bogdanova, who had lived in a city and who had the opportunity to go to church many times, made the point emphatically:

> *Q:* Do you have icons? Which ones?
>
> *Maia Bogdanova:* Yes, well, that one, I have Nikolai here.

Q: Is it important, which icon you have?

Maia Bogdanova: No, no, no, no, no! There is no difference!

This point was not always made explicitly, but was implicit in the fact that people usually could not tell me which icon they had in the house (which saintly figure) or what given saints were "good for" (such as health or fertility). They would comment that their icon was big or small or beautiful or old (and the icons would spill into their dreams and visions), but not which icon it was or for what specific purpose.

Crucial here is the fact that, symbolically speaking, the icon is extremely powerful (its presence is nearly universally considered a necessity) but, in a Sperberian sense, it is opaque. It combines layers of resonance, but the level of analysis is not at the level of the visual sign. That is, it does not so much matter which saintly forms fill the icon, but that the icon is, simply, there. The presence of the icon settles the space in which it resides. Sets it right.

The question follows, then, what exactly is in that icon in the corner? What are those framed faces with the mournful eyes that look down at every village family? As a first step into the complex space that is the corner, I begin with a brief discussion of the theology of the icon. This requires regarding the problem not only in the eyes of villagers, but in the eyes of (particularly Russian) philosophers and theologians as well. Here, it is my aim to underline the symbolism of icon veneration as expressed by philosophers of religion—people who are enjoined with explaining religion in its official, ideal manifestation. It does not follow, logically, that the ideals of church philosophers would have any necessary relationship to how people worship. And yet, some common resonance does appear to exist.

Icons and Orthodox Theology
In the context of Orthodox theology, it would be difficult to overstate the centrality of icons in the practice of worship. The Orthodox icon has its roots in the theology of Greek Orthodoxy, which came to power in Russia in the tenth century AD. Given the prohibitions against idolatry in Judaism and Islam, it is not surprising that the use of images of the holy person of Christ were debated for centuries before finally being officially accepted by Eastern Christianity. The disputing groups were known as *iconoclasts* ("icon smashers,") and *iconodules* (or "icon lovers"). The

221

iconodules eventually triumphed and their triumph was not merely a theological one; it also marked the development of a style of worship centered on the visual image (Ware 1991[1963]:40).

Churchgoers in Russia are, indeed, icon lovers. Today, in Orthodox churches, the priest may or may not be heard or heeded in his sermon or his service (which is chanted in Old Church Slavonic, a language only vaguely comprehensible to laypeople). But the space around icons draws ardent attention, as people stand in front of them in crowds, they light candles under them, speak to them, and kiss them. Sometimes, they cry in front of them. They stare at the icon's face, the icon's eyes. Many turn to them for healing, succor, and hope, and for more than that as well.

In the debate between the iconoclasts and the iconodules, the point was made that icons per se were not being worshipped and adored. It was, rather, the truth that came through the icons that was venerated. Icons represented divine beauty, which was manifested on Earth through the agency of the icon. In this theological view, icons can be seen as the conduits for holiness, not as the substance of holiness themselves (and, in this way, iconodules sought to distance themselves from advocating idol worship). So, if icons are conduits, what are they carrying? If they are mirrors, what are they reflecting? The language used by theologians to describe the powers of icons centers around metaphors of light and those of passive envelopment: that is, the light or truth of icons clothe, flood, or immerse the worshipper (Fedotov 1966:33; see also Soloviev 1959:6).

In Solovyovo, there are hints of the notion that being in front of an icon can provide good "energy," a positive, freeing, lightening feeling that floods or envelops a person. Although not the defining rhetoric on the subject, comments such as the following were made (by women who had both spent long stretches in cities and had been to churches there).

Emma Dmitrievna: When a person stands in front of an icon, he is always converted into a peaceful mode; he is kind, he prays, he has cried, he asks for something. And around it, it's peaceful . . . In the church the old icons . . . so many people have prayed around them, there is so much good/kind energy, that just standing near the icon helps. Because there is so much kind energy.

Maia Bogdanova: If you go from the church, it is somehow lighter on the soul. That you remembered [someone]. As if you gave out [*otdal*] your spirit. It is . . . necessary for a person to find relief [*oblegchenie*, lightening] for their soul. Isn't it true? Not everyone can open his soul, as they say, right? And there you stand with your thoughts and you share and that's it. Even just in your head. As they say, you flood yourself [and are relieved] from pain.

In the exegesis of Orthodoxy, when an icon is seen and reflected upon by an individual, that icon is understood to be *felt;* that is, a part of the "grace of God" is said to flow through the icon and has an effect upon the worshipper. As Ouspensky writes in *The Theology of the Icon* (1978:185): "When we begin to strive with all our will power towards the beauty of the likeness . . . divine grace makes virtue flourish upon virtue, elevating the beauty of the soul from glory to glory, bestowing upon it the mark of likeness." In other words, the act of reflecting on the icon is felt to draw in a *transformational* power, that is, the grace required to transform man into God's holy image.

Indeed, it is this notion that humans are created in God's image that bears the rhetorical weight of the power of icons. Although being an artistic creation, one that is nevertheless highly regulated and supervised, icons have the power to draw individuals to their spiritually "true" images. In this line of thinking, the theologian Zernov (in Ware 1991 [1963]:42) wrote that icons "were dynamic manifestations of man's spiritual power to redeem creation through beauty and art. The colors and lines of the icons were not meant to imitate nature; the artists aimed at demonstrating that men, animals and plants could be *rescued from their present state of degradation and restored to their proper images*" (my emphasis). The figures on the icons, whether of the Virgin, Christ, or Saints, are seen as perfect aesthetic representations of spiritual truths. Only through perfect conduits can truth be transmitted. For this reason, their artistic fashioning is controlled by Church powers at various levels (Ouspensky 1978:197). Furthermore, the spiritual credentials of the artist must be established; a person insensitive to divine truths cannot portray them (Ware 1991[1963]:214). Through the perfect vessel of the icon, the act of reflecting upon these spiritually perfect images brings us closer to the image. Being like the image is being the true spiritual person. The veneration for images gives rise to a spiritual transformation that makes the earthly kingdom somewhat more heavenly (Fedotov 1966:355).

Note that, as here described, the access to divine truths is accomplished without the need of words or sermons. It is as though the human heart were made to respond to divine truths such as they are beheld in icons. They are "philosophy in colors" (Fedotov 1966:358) or "visible prayers" (Ouspensky 1978:211), where the sight of and reflection on the beauty of a particular image is what is required to grasp divine truths. In the rhetoric of Orthodox theologians, they are above sermons and above exegesis. If one is to begin to regard them sociologically, they provide, in their "democracy," a fundamental accessibility to divine truths—one that need not be carried through the will of a priest.[5] Zernov (1973[1942]: 31), indeed, stresses the "corporate nature" of the Mass in Eastern Orthodoxy, where the priest is little seen and little heard.

If a person can receive and come to reflect the divine image, so can a people. Dostoevsky, who was accused of being an extreme Slavophile even in the nationalist mind-set of his day, wrote often of the glorious destiny of "Holy Russia." When accused of blindly elevating the Russian people, he countered, "Our people [narod] is yet sinful and crude; its image is yet bestial" (in Soloviev 1959:50).[6] To him, the Russian narod had the potential to be holy and to reflect the image; but this was not yet the case. In *The Possessed,* Dostoevsky elaborated on this theme when he wrote through the voice of an idealistic young socialist grappling with the problem of the existence of God: "Reduce God to an attribute of nationality? . . . On the contrary, I raise the people up to God! And could it be otherwise? The people are the body of God." In this view, like the individual, the narod can receive divine grace as "streams of grace flood[ing] upon this sinful world purifying and deifying it" (Fedotov 1966:33). The arena of influence of an icon is, in this reading of the problem, flexible—able to expand and contract over various social units of svoi.

The theological point can be summarized that icons, when properly rendered, allow for access of divine perfections through the perfection of their image. Catching sight of such an image enables the transmission of a power, known in a theological context as "grace."

The notion that an icon can transform a person (or a people) toward some abstract, spiritual ideal was not clearly evidenced in Solovyovo. If icons can "flood" a person with some positive "energy," this energy does not appear to be transformational—at least not teleologically so. Icons can give one a feeling of "lightness," but do not "change" the spiritual

---

5. For specifically the icon's role in democratizing worship in the late nineteenth century, see Vera Shevzov's "Miracle Working Icons, Laity, and Authority in the Russian Orthodox Church," 1861–1917 (1999).

6. A similar point made in Cherniavsky (1969:195).

image of man to an idealized, divine one. Icons are certainly healing objects—and in that sense agents of change—but they are not fashioners of spiritual characters. Theology appears to wish for transformation of the spiritual self; the villagers wish to lighten the load.

Nevertheless, the theological notion that an icon acts over the body of a person, parish community, nation, or worldwide religious community mirrors a village idea that icons act over (protect and heal) a range of categories of svoi. This idea is also evidenced in the practice of ritual circumambulation (obkhod). Icons are used in Orthodox rituals where an arena of protection is delimited. In the pageantry of the Easter Mass, a procession of believers circumambulates the church with icons in the fore. In the village, the celebration of Easter is a distant memory. And yet, obkhody like the ones done in spring before animals are first let out to pasture, are indeed performed (with or without icons).[7] Protecting a social sphere by ritually encircling it remains a relevant solution to the problem of the dangerous, capricious forces "out there."

Another important feature of the icon as elaborated in Orthodoxy theology is the icon's specificity. Specific feelings ought to flow from specific icons. If the icon is of the Madonna and Child, and if the mother looks down at her child lovingly, knowingly, and sorrowfully—an icon known generically as Umilenie—the feeling that comes flooding toward the worshipper is one of tenderness. If the icon is of Christ—regal, judgmental, and potentially wrathful (the Pantocrator icon), one ought to feel awe and fear (Fedotov 1966:30). Specific icon types have specific functions. Certain icons of St. Nicholas are, first and foremost, for healing and miracle working.[8] In the broader, historical traditions of Russian Orthodoxy, certain particular icons are miracle-working ones. These icons are attached to epic stories (where their presence saved cities from foreign sieges), or beautiful odors can emanate from them, or they can cry tears of myrrh. They can heal, as well as destroy enemies.[9] The Orthodox calendar endows them with holidays, granting the images themselves the status of holy persons.

7. For a few years now, this circumambulation is no longer done in Solovyovo, but it is very much alive in memory.
8. Miracle-working icons are a fascinating theme unto themselves, and are reviewed in Shevzov (1999).
9. In one case in Novgorod, an icon of the Virgin is said to have saved the city from a siege of Tatars. Her icon was put onto the Kremlin wall, and was hit in the eye with an arrow. She began to cry and the Mongol raiders all went blind and were forced to retreat.

Within the Orthodox tradition, the images of holy persons take part in a functional semiotics of worship and invocation. In the village, though icons can be crucial elements in acts of obrashchenie, there appears to be very little speculating on the function of given types of images. As noted above, the point was made again and again that it was the possession of an icon per se that was crucial, and not which icon was possessed. On the other hand, specific icons in the village indeed have their own family and church histories. They are miracle workers; they have tempers; they save your life or kill you.

From the theology of Orthodoxy, three key features provided by icons emerge: (1) "floods" of grace with a transformative power; (2) specific benefits through particular images and respective histories; and (3) protection of circumscribed communities. In the village, traces of all of these features are found, although not all are emphasized. Clearly the icon protects a social body that can expand and contract in size, the icon is an instrument of healing in ways not dependent on the image on its face, and icons are personified at times. Importantly, however, the use of icons to bring about the teleological transformation of a person, people, or nation does not appear to have a life in Solovyovo.

Icons and Idols

Theology offers exegeses on the relationship between person and image. It tells us what should happen when interacting with its holy objects. We should feel awe, grace, new senses of spiritual light and beauty, an immersion in truth. We should feel fear. Standing in front of the icon, we should change fundamentally and directionally. Villagers turn to icons with an understanding that is informed, but not defined, by this.

Icons are images and they are objects. The question has emerged in the history of Russian popular religion as to the relationship between images/objects and worship before the Orthodox Church came to the countryside. This discussion has often been framed in terms of *dvoeverie*, the idea that Russian religious faith is double faceted—marked by a mixture of "paganism" and Orthodoxy. Although I believe it is an oversimplification to say that this faith is marked by a homogeneous mix of two elaborate theologies (one Christian and the other "pagan"),[10] the emergence

---

10. And one that I do not subscribe to. For critiques of the concept of *dvoeverie* (and the way in which it relies on false analytical categories), see Chulos (1995) and Levin (1993).

of the concept of dvoeverie has allowed academic discourse to flow to the (sometimes awkward) question how religious faith may not be purely (theologically) religious. To explore some of the broader associations to icons (ones that cannot be called theological), I turn to literature framed through the concept of dvoeverie in order to show how the icon broadens its symbolic resonance when one begins to regard the icon's function.

ICON/IDOL: ICONS AND "PAGANISM" IN THE CORNER

According to some historians, it was not until the sixteenth century that the Christian calendar (as a marker of Christian practice) was broadly accepted among rural Russians (Vlasov 1991). Connected with this, the acceptance of Christianity in Russia was said to be marked by pre-Christian ("pagan," in the language of the discipline) rituals.[11] As one historian puts it, Russian Orthodox worship arrived "in pagan wrapping," the very acceptance of Christianity by Vladamir I one thousand years ago, having been played out through a centuries-old agrarian ritual performed upon the conquering of one god by another (Froianov et al. 1992). As the ritual was described, idols of the conquered deity, Perun, were dragged by horses and then drowned. They were then replaced with images of the conquering Christianity. Although now converted to Christianity, the "transfer of deities" represented

> a kind of continuity of traditions, hallowed over the centuries and thus, a more painless adoption of the new faith, which (at least from external features) was a continuation of the former pagan faith. The [Christian] figures, like their predecessors the Pagan gods, were installed in one of the central places of the city, which clearly shows that they were made accessible to all (Froianov et al. 1992: 9).

Of course, more than one ritual in the center of a single city would be required for Christianity to establish itself. Several Soviet historians have argued that replacing "pagan" gods with Christian ones (in the form of saints) was a pervasive and long-term practice. In *Iazychestvo v Pravoslavii (Paganism in Orthodoxy)*, Nosova (1975:90) argues that such a replacement took place, without substantially modifying the func-

---

11. The term "pagan" is used throughout Soviet literature when referring to agrarian religion. This term is problematic, and I will use it when writing in terms of that literature, and not analytically.

tion of the non-Christian gods.[12] Although the dates and the details are disputed, there is general agreement that Christianity came to Russia at a time when the worship of gods and their idols was a dominant feature of religious practice and that icons—which contained the images of saints—took on the features of pre-Christian idols when they were used to protect and to heal (Nosova 1975:93,97).[13] The krasnyi ugol would be, by this logic, the locale where such idols were placed in the traditional rural home, and therefore were (and are) charged with this pre-Christian power.

Are icons symbolic variations of idols that represented the gods of a pre-Christian pantheon? Applied rigidly, this point has been disputed by Propp (1995 [1963]), who argued that there was never a pantheon of gods in rural Russia. Certainly, in the past there were names for deities attached to physical places or objects (Hubbs 1994). Regardless of the question of the existence of a Greek-style pantheon, it is possible to imagine that some of these personified beings were represented in and reified as objects.[14] It is also reasonable to assume that despite theological exegeses to the contrary, the icon has been partly precious *as an object* (one with a personality) and not simply as a vehicle of the divine. Whether or not in line with the position of iconodules, the physicality of the icons as objects (and, more so, the importance of their *beauty*) reduces the symbolic distance between venerating the Holy Spirit and venerating the object itself.[15] An icon that happens to contain characters from Christian history can certainly accumulate function and resonance from characters from other, earlier stories. The veneration of icons, like the veneration of images in general, has a rich symbolic past—one layer of which, it can be argued, is derived from the worship of embodied forces. That embodied force, person, saint, or deity has a name, a past, and a history of deeds.

12. "Fed by the traditions of multifaceted pre-Christian religions, Christianity in its essence converted old pagan gods into Christian saints."
13. For further discussions of the mixed nature of Russia's religious terrain, see Bernshtam (1992), Froianov et al., (1992), Balzer (1992), Ivanov and Toropov (1982a), Nosova (1975), Vlasov (1991), and Znayenko (1980).
14. There is certainly no evidence of such a pantheon existing today in the village of Solovyovo even if personified beings with power do exist. This is a disputed point and one that cannot be solved in the context of this work.
15. The discourse on "sensuality" (understood as the veneration of physical beauty) as a particularly Russian form of vice testifies to the importance of this theme in Russian thought. See Fedotov (1946:20).

Historically and evocationally, there is a relationship between icons and pre-Christian idols. Before icons of saints existed, there were certainly objects of power in Russian agrarian ritual. Most probably, these objects were personified and endowed with power (even if not manifested as gods of thunder, sun, and so forth). The crucial point there is that icons certainly carry powers as objects and as beings with miracle-working biographies. Icons, like idols, are venerated in profoundly physical and personalized ways. They are touched, kissed, gazed at. Their physical presence is required in homes. Certain icons take on personalities. But perhaps the symbolic feature to be underlined here is not the one-to-one correlation of icons and idols as they live and lived in corner space, but *the fact that corner space can fill a form with forces*. Nothing has yet been said, on the other hand, regarding the character of that form. To look for that character, I continue focusing on the corner.

Symbolically speaking, there are reasons to conclude that Orthodoxy has offered a substantial layer to the icon imagination. The images that it offered take corner symbolism into the realm of patriarchy and a God whose domain is the whole of the world, and, crucially, the limits of the rodina that is Holy Russia. Cherniavsky called the Russian leader the "most striking of Russian myths" (Cherniavsky 1969:2). That leader—part father, part god, part holy icon—lands in the corner as well.

TSAR ICONS

[A] Slav ruler [of the 11th century] thought he might be sinning in this reservation towards the universal suzerainty of the Emperor—the "visible ikon of the invisible King" (Vlasto 1970:284).

The symbolism of the icon extends to realms that are not, strictly speaking, religious. Throughout the history of Russia, state and church have been tightly bound. In Kievian Rus', the Moscovy of the Ruriks, the empire of the Romanovs, and, more recently, in the controls of the Communist Party of the Soviet Union, the political leaders of the Russian people were also—at least nominally—its spiritual leaders. In 1453, Constantinople fell to the Turks. The Byzantine Empire had been fading, and was falling to the Muslims as Rome had fallen to the European "barbarians" centuries before. Moscow, which had become the center of Orthodoxy after the sacking of Kiev in 1237, came to be considered the third and final holy city of Christianity, making Russia the seat of the "Third

Rome." When Tsar Ivan III married Sophia in 1472 (the niece of the last Byzantine Emperor), the tsar of the house of Rurik took the title of being the first tsar-protector of the Orthodox Church. At this time, the great power of the Mongols was waning in the Russian territories, and the tsardom was soon to be a force to be reckoned with. The balance of power in the region was to change definitively when Ivan III's grandson Ivan IV, known to Russians as Ivan Groznyi (the dread, the awe-inspiring, the great and terrible) became tsar. Under him, Russian territories were consolidated, the Tatar "yoke" thrown off, and the kingdom of Muscovy firmly established.

In Russia, state and Church were tightly bound for hundreds of years in the body of the tsar. Later, the abolishment of state religion in favor of the "sacred" tenets of communism was not so different, symbolically speaking. The resonance continued, one that linked the political to the sacred and one that, in its most blatant form, created a space in which people could believe in their leaders as they would in gods.[16]

There is much to suggest that the face on the icon resonates with the symbolism of a powerful leader. The Virgin Mary is a sweet and saintly image in much of the world; in Russia, icons are the kinds of holy objects that can also be filled with political avengers. In this section, I ask how a leader is symbolically construed in a Russian worldview and whether s/he can come to be contiguous with the icon.

The symbolism that resonates around a "tsar" or "leader" is not homogeneous: the visions of leaders and the symbolic resonance that follows them come in different forms. Like the contrast between the Umilenie and Pantocrator icons, there is more than one kind of proper leader. The resonance as a whole is fed by several key idioms.

A first idiom of the leader is his awesome, terrible power. In studies on the image of Ivan IV (Groznyi, The Terrible) in folklore (Perrie 1987; Rosovietskii 1984–1985; Oinas 1984), a portrait is painted of a bloody, cruel, psychopathic leader. Ivan IV shares certain "wandering" folkloric themes with Vlad the Impaler (better known as Count Dracula). Identi-

16. More than this, Russia's self-identity (in terms of nationalist discourse) would be tied to its degree of national "holiness." Literature on the birth of nationalism (Hobsbawm 1990, and Anderson 1983) points to the period of the latter half of the nineteenth century as a time of self-reflection and self-definition among the imperialist nations of Europe. Interestingly, when Russian nationalists of the imperial period mapped their uniqueness, it was along the lines of their "holiness" (V.I. Soloviev cited in Soloviev 1959).

cal atrocities are attributed to both of them (Perrie 1987).[17] The stories of Ivan IV include horrors (such as the murder of his own son and the destruction of the city of Novgorod) that are always followed by Ivan's lengthy and sincere tears of repentance. Yet the descriptive term for Ivan Groznyi does not mean horrible or evil. Rather, many Russian philosophers see it as an essential part of powerful leadership. As Soloviev (1959:24) writes, "Awesome majesty (*groza*) is the most important attribute of power: a tsar without groza is like a steed without a bridle."[18] Ivan's image is still one of a great (and even popular) leader. Perrie (1987:65) concludes in her study of his folkloric image, that Ivan is not condemned for these shortcomings, however: rather, he is admired in spite of them. Even his cruelty and terror are regarded as a necessary part of his campaign against traitors, which the narod approves.

Other leaders fit this pattern of cruelty and greatness such as Peter I "the Great" (*velikii*), whose atrocities—at certain levels—rival those of Ivan IV, and Catherine II, the "enlightened" tsarina who brought ever new heights of harshness and suffering to Russian serfs. Despite the misery brought to the Russian people at the hands of the monarchy, rural Russians in particular appeared to remain largely loyal to the idea of monarchy. The resurgence, in the 1990s, of monarchist loyalty in Russia is one demonstration that even at a literal level this attachment to a tsar figure has not faded into oblivion. The question of loyalty to the image of Stalin (at least within the context of discourses like that of the radiant past) explodes the metaphor to further horizons.

The icon of Christ the Pantocrator has the quality of groza. So do proper tsar-like leaders. The Christ in the icon is severe, judgmental and awe-inspiring. So were, by reputation, Ivan IV, Peter I, Catherine II, and Nicholas I, among others. The tsar leader and the icon share these qualities.

They also share attributes understood to be divine. Billington (1970: 98) writes that the "'true Tsar' was given divine sanctions in the eyes of the peasant masses." Just as surely as the tsar/leader is associated with

17. The two figures were more or less contemporaries and the history of both is marked by battles of Christendom against the Tatars and the Turks. Both were victorious.
18. Note that according to folklorists, a horse (*kon'*) in nineteenth century Russia is a masculine symbol (like the earth is a feminine symbol (Matossian 1968). Furthermore, in many folktales, a man "bridles" and "rides" his wife as a display of domination (Afanasev 1973[1945]).

groza, his is a holy presence. Soloviev (1959:20) puts it plainly: "The Tsar is not responsible to men but only to God for all his actions. His subjects must abide in humility and awe before the Tsar, whose power is established by God Himself and has a sacred character." For the purposes of this symbolic comparison, it is essential to recognize that—as for the icon—it is one of the leader's most important functions to draw in divine power. He does this by being a divine presence on "blessed" Christian territory.

There appear to be two distinct types of tsars: one terrifying and majestic; and the other gentle, pure, saintly, passive, and often feeble. This contrast was maintained and appeared to reproduce itself over the centuries (Hingley 1968:14). Cherniavsky writes of the meek, saintly leaders at great length in *Tsar and People: Studies in Russian Myths* (1969). The tender feelings that these meek leaders invoke (who—like the hemophiliac Tsarevich Alexei—are often victims of more powerful tsars and come to be prince-martyrs) are similar to those of the Umilenie icons. Whether mighty or meek, both types of tsars perform a common function in the hearts of Russians—to protect Holy Russia as a father would protect his children. Indeed, the tsar was described as the "father of the great family of the Russian people" (Cherniavsky 1969:130), and was known generally by rural Russians as *batiushka*, little father (Billington 1970:98). The notion that the tsar is seen as the father of his people, and that his is a divinely protective role, is broadly accepted. What can be questioned is whether that symbolic construction was transferred onto leaders that came later in Russian history.

The question about the existence of God and the effect that this should have on political organization were topics of intense debate among certain elements of the intelligentsia in nineteenth-century Russia. The Bolshevist period brought the destruction of religious infrastructure, and attempted to do away with superstructural features marked by religious belief. After the burning of churches and books and the persecution of professed believers of all denominations, one can ask how much of the "spirituality" of communism was simply a change at the most superficial level of the sign? As with the dragged and drowned statues of the defeated god Perun, it is possible to ask to what degree were old idols replaced by new ones that were given their own new temple in the center of town? In the cult worship of Lenin manufactured by Stalin, in the "palace of the people," in crossing oneself in front of a painting of Stalin,[19] and in an

---

19. Kevin Tuite, Université de Montréal, personal communication, 1998.

ability on the part of Russians to accept and even grow attached to groza, the answer would have to be that there is a great deal of continuity to pre- and post-Revolutionary Russia. As Richard Hingley describes, there is, as well, a marked continuity between Orthodox rituals that are reflected in the death rituals of Lenin, and in the iconic treatment of leaders' portraits in general (Hingley 1977:134).

Stalin, like the tsars he replaced, was also the figurehead of his people. He was the great terror inspirer and the great patriarchal protector. The cult of personality that he established in the Soviet Union demonstrated a refined sensitivity to Russian practices of veneration, where that veneration included both extreme tenderness and terror. But surely there is a difference between a leader, however sensitive he is to the symbolic "needs" of his people, and one that has the power to act as the conduit of God's grace.[20]

The symbolic link crafted between the nation-khoziain (whether tsar or Party leader) and the icon pulls the latter to the edges of the domain of the rodina. It grants the icon grace-bearing qualities and the ability to rage against dissenters. Both the icon and the nation-khoziain protect and wield power over their domain. Let us take this link and move it to Solovyovo. What do narratives tell us about the khoziain? In the language of villagers, does that khoziain live in the icon corner as well?

ICONS AND *KHOZIAEVA*: FATHER CORNER

Most deeply, most basically, most broadly in the sense of the trope, the khoziain lives in the corner. There, he hovers behind, inside, around the icon.

The symbolism of the khoziain is rich and dramatic, and has appeared in several crucial analytical moments thus far in this text. In Chapter 3, I outlined the role of the familial khoziain, including his rights and duties and the power associated with his role. The concept of the flexibility of his domain was also introduced, so that a family could have a khoziain, as a town or a country could. In the examination of the mir chudesnogo, the khoziain was seen to expand to the realm of the metaphysical world—where forests and homes and barns were endowed with their

20. Is there a symbolic difference between the father Stalin and the father tsar? Dostoevsky addresses this question in his chillingly prophetic *The Possessed*, where he paints a portrait of the doom that comes with a leader who lacks the spiritual qualifications for his role.

own khoziaeva—each of which had certain power over a domain. In the radiant past, the nation-khoziain, most specifically, the Stalin-tsar figure, was outlined and his role as the bringer of order was underlined. Social chaos and decay, destined to snap the Edenic *svetloe proshloe* into the arrow of time, accompanied the absence of such a khoziain. In the chapter on healing, a khoziain was one figure to whom people could turn in order to set space right. Specifically, the dead ancestors, the khoziaeva (and khoziaiki) of certain homes could be turned to as individuals; but the dead could also be turned to as a collective unit, with a collective power over the fields of the village rodina.

Thus far, the khoziain has been analyzed for his function, but not for the character of the symbolism that resonates around him. Aside from the metaphoric associations between the khoziain and the krasnyi ugol that are accumulating as this chapter continues, there are physical ones as well. Traditionally, the krasnyi ugol was associated with the family head (his seat of honor was found by the icons). In the context of this chapter, it is worth looking more deeply at the evocations of the term. Who is the khoziain who occupies that potent space?

Anna Petrovna tells the story of the khoziain of her household when she was a girl.

> *Anna Petrovna:* We had severe parents. Very. We had in our house twelve people. There were six sisters and two brothers. Khoziaistvo was good, there was a lot of work, a lot of wheat grew, we earned a lot. . . . We were fed, shoed, clothes were all good. There was a very great severity [though].
>
> I broke a window. A little one. And father threw me [and my brother] into the frost. There was *ice* there. My little brother says, "Come on, let's freeze, Aniutka. We will freeze and we will die." That's the kind of severity there was. We stood and stood on the ice.
>
> *Q:* Did your father forget you there?
>
> *Anna Petrovna:* As if it hadn't happened. He lay down to sleep, threw us out onto the ice because of our little guilt. There, we stood, stood on the ice—and no death of any kind [came].
>
> *Q:* Why didn't your mother protect you?
>
> *Anna Petrovna:* Then, mama didn't dare. He fell asleep and so mama opened the door and came to us. There was no death.

Q: He didn't want to kill you and your brother?

Anna Petrovna: He beat us, and so all kinds of things happened.

Q: Did he beat your mother, too?

Anna Petrovna: No, he didn't beat mama, and she didn't allow things to go that far. She obeyed all the time. There was a great severity.

Q: What did he work as?

Anna Petrovna: Simply a khoziain. He was a khoziain. Before, everyone worked for himself. For oneself.

Anna Petrovna's strict (*strogii*) father rings familiar. Such severity is an asset in the qualities of the Stalin figure of the radiant past—he creates discipline and order and certainly no small measure of terror. The khoziain has dominion over his house and the people therein. His word is law. He can be mercilessly severe, echoing the meaning (if not the language) of the groznyi (awe-inspiring, terrible) tsar. Like the tsar, his primary role is one of responsibility and protection.

When those functions are not fulfilled, there is an indication that men are not being "khoziaeva." As Elena Sergeevna explains, "Men used to be khoziaeva. Now, in the city, they aren't anymore and women have taken over. No good can come of it." More than condemning given men for their inability to do a certain kind of work, Elena Sergeevna generalizes that this role (it is no longer the svetloe proshloe) is left unfulfilled in the city now. The village, in her words, is the place where men are still khoziaeva.

But what other social positions does the term khoziain cover? A boss can be a khoziain of a factory. A *predsedatel' sel'soveta* (chair of the sel'sovet) can be referred to as a khoziain. But the most common use of khoziain outside of the familial unit and the metaphysical sphere is that of the nation-khoziain. This was apparent again and again in the radiant past—that Stalin had been the khoziain and that without him, the people were left in a state of terrible chaos. This khoziain-like quality of Stalin's was often contrasted to the lack of that quality in Boris Yeltsin, as Valentina Ivanovna remarked.

Valentina Ivanovna: We considered this Stalin as our kindred father [*svoi rodnoi otets*]. Thought that he was a good person, that he somehow knows everyone and helps everyone. . . . Now we have begun to understand things. . . . Yeltsin is not a khoziain.

Maia echoed the sentiment with, "I heard a politician say that Yeltsin can't be and will never be the khoziain of the country."

In a similar vein, the state itself is held up as, ideally, the khoziain. The term for state, *gosudarstvo*, is derived from *gosudar'*, the patriarchal lord of the land. In the context of the radiant past, says Mikhail Alekseevich, "The state was a khoziain. Took care of everyone." More recently (although still during the Yeltsin 1990s), Zina, a guest from St. Petersburg quipped that, "Our state is castrated." The castration of the state begged a pointed literary interpretation: that the maleness and therefore the khoziain-ness had been cut off.

The icon is linked to the khoziain figure by virtue of its power for protection, the fact that it is indispensable, and the awe-inspiring, terror-producing character that it sometimes takes on. The icon, by virtue of such associations, begins to take on the air of national khoziain figures. As the icon enters into affairs of state, so do affairs of state enter into the icon.

POLITICAL FATHERS, GRANDFATHERS, UNCLES

The potency of the "red corner" was not lost on Soviet ideologues. Soviet factories, schools, institutes, clubhouses, and public spaces were endowed with krasnye *ugolki* ("red corners" in diminutive form) where portraits or busts of Stalin (while he lived and reigned) or Lenin (until the fall of the Soviet Union) were displayed with banners, flowers, and ribbons arranged around them. Sometimes this krasnyi *ugolok* was in the corner indeed; other times it was on a table, covered with a red tablecloth, vases, and photographs of young pioneers and flowery keepsakes.[21] Faces of power, that is, of father figures went in Soviet corners, too. By putting Lenin and Stalin in corners, the hope was that some of the otherworldly power of that corner space could radiate to these very worldly men. This placing of Lenin and Stalin in patriarchal, otherworldly space was noted in the village. Here, Petr Nikolaevich and his wife recall the great, demigod-like leader that was Lenin.

Petr Nikolaevich: At that time, when Vladimir Il'ich was at the helm, we, of course weren't of age. We only knew him through the newspapers and

21. I thank Alexei Yurchak for this description.

books. This was the teaching in school. I studied for seven years. You open the first page [of your school books] with Vladimir Il'ich.

Q: What sort of person was he?

Petr Nikolaevich: He was like a *vozhd'* [great leader] and a teacher. And native father [*rodnoi otets*] for all of the peoples. Then, we only thought that.

Elena Andreevna: And there were many songs about Lenin. And many poems about Lenin. And the poem of Maiakovskii called "Vladimir Il'ich Lenin." There . . . were so . . . many poems, songs. I don't remember [them]. Just the saying, "Lenin lived, Lenin lives, Lenin will live!"

Lenin is eternal; Lenin is a *vozhd'* (great leader). Lenin is the father of all peoples. Clearly, the image of the khoziain-Party leader did manage to seep in to the village. Through newspapers, television, and books, Lenin and Stalin were patriarchal kin. Below, Iuliia refers to Stalin in his grandfather form (dedushka Stalin), the same khoziain form used in the forest (khoziain lesavoi is equivalent to dedushka lesavoi).

Q: People said "Father Stalin"?

Iuliia Ivanovna: Dedushka Stalin, more usually. If it was on a card, and they show it to you, and ask who it is, you say, "This is dedushka Stalin."

While I lived in Solovyovo, the clubhouse still contained several portraits of Lenin in prominent places, most particularly in the library that is located next to the room where pool is played. In this very most Soviet space on village grounds, such portraits raised no questions, even though they were located one room away from a display of religious books and drawings.

There were indications, as well, that the severe khoziain figure provided "inspiration" through the eye and ear. The figure present only in portraits and film reels takes on the role of "grace provider" and ties it therefore to the icon.

Iuliia Ivanovna: Soldiers/officers say that when they would go into battle, they would cry, "For the rodina, for Stalin!" That means, apparently, that his voice inspired [*vdokhnovlial*]. . . . [T]hey [heard it] on the radio.

On one occasion, Aleksandra Ivanovna stopped by and began speaking of her father's arrest for "political reasons." She insisted that the Stalin period was good. There was one point in her explanation when she looked upward as if looking into Stalin's face. It was odd and touching to see this face of an older woman, her false teeth not quite fitting her mouth, gazing up into the empty air with a fleeting expression of awe.

In the village, symbolic features of the khoziain, at a familial and a national level mirror features of the icon. They both protect and inspire. They are both indispensable (you are lost without them, sick without them, afraid without them). They can both be groznyi—awesomely majestic and terrifying. They channel healing force and brutish force. They are sometimes warmly parental, sometimes strict to the point of violence. They go, in metaphoric space, into the corner.

Icons and *Khoziaeva:* A Spatial Summary

The khoziain's role in healing, as in the social template of the radiant past, is to be the conduit for transformative powers, and to create order and protection. Whether the khoziain is known as grandfather or God, his powers embrace communities of svoi of various sizes and dimensions. This dynamic could be visualized as depicted in Figure 1.

Icons appear to be part of an analogous topographical paradigm, in certain ways comparable to the nation-khoziain in its function as a channel for protecting and healing powers. The icon in a closed space (that of the bearer, home, church, parish, the sweeping territory of pasture lands, the lands of a medieval city-state, the nation-state itself) is there to grant the special bounties of protection over that given territory. Like the na-

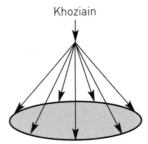

Khoziain

Communities of svoi within given territories
(a home, a local rodina, a national rodina, etc.)

Figure 1. Power enters via khoziain figure.

tion-khoziain, the icon can be "turned toward" (*obratit'sia*) for special favors that the mundane world will not grant (the healing of incurable diseases, the rescue from the awful, unforgiving tangles of bureaucracy). The otherworldliness that the icon provides us with is one that channels forces from other worlds. It is a receiver and distributor.

Generally, the power of the icon in a defined space could be depicted as directly analogous to the power of the nation-khoziain, as illustrated in Figure 2. The icon, like the khoziain figure, brings certain powers to bear over a given domain. These powers can be miracle-working ones, like the healing powers discussed in Chapter 6. On the other hand, dealing with the miraculous is not always such an ordered business. The unpredictable forms and forces that arose in the mir chudesnogo were not invoked, but guarded against. The mir chudesnogo, it was concluded, is not fundamentally about channeling something in, but about going out into the world and being confronted—in helpless wonder—with space-time flexibility.

An icon's function is that of pulling in powers. The stories about the mir chudesnogo are broadly about the powers drawing a person out. And icons, in their associations with fantastic powers, bridge these two contrasting idioms of contact with otherworldly powers. Icons in the village appear to be channelers, indeed, but can also add an unpredictable—sometimes terrifying and sometimes beneficent—set of forces into their midst. In this sense, the power that they bring in is not limited to the side of the khoziain figure that protects, and creates discipline and order. Sometimes icons, when turned to, explode the frame into a miraculous one. In the next section, I discuss such cases of icons that flirt with the rules of the mir chudesnogo.

Icon

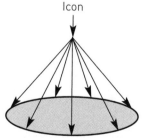

Person, home, barn, pasture, parish, city, nation

Figure 2. "Grace" enters via icon.

MISBEHAVING ICONS

* * *

Magical Icons

Stories of icons in the village—submerged, as they are, in a striking range of symbolism—press the boundaries of this study. They show up in dreams and as apparitions; they carry blessings and retribution. Narratives about magical icons were separated from the others here because they seem to represent, in their peculiar way, a kind of otherworldly harnessing that differs from both the typical topographical paradigm in the mir chudesnogo and from the model of icon-as-leader depicted above. It has been suggested that icons have a special power because they inhabit a symbolically fortuitous place. Here, I show how they take up some of their resonance in this very way, by standing between God, the King, and the farm, on the one hand, and deeply agrarian forces, on the other.

The icon of dreams and visions can, like the trickster leshii, ranges from the paternal and tenderhearted to the cruel and punishing. It can rage, grant health, kill, haunt. It can look at you, hovering, with enormous blue eyes, and then disappear, like a demon. The icon stories presented here have been divided into two categories: stories that tell of meetings with icons outside the everyday world, and others in which icons have a specifically retributional role.

Found Icons

Valentina Ivanovna had serious medical complaints. She had been to doctors and hospitals in Belozersk, but the medicine eats up much of her pension and the operations do not seem to help. She had been to Mikhail Alekseevich, who was periodically able to offer some relief with his spells and potions. The pain continued. A nephew would help with heavy chores sometimes, as would her neighbor, Raisa Aleksandrovna; but for the most part, she is alone with her three or four cats. Her only son died years ago. I visited her often.

From the time that I first met her in the summer of 1994, Valentina Ivanovna spoke of a healing spring. This spring was endowed with holy waters and she felt that it was her last hope for curing some of her more painful, chronic problems. Her nephew Mitia had a tractor, and she was planning to get him to take her to get some of the holy, magic waters. In an early interview, she spoke of the significance of this spring. It had to do with the fact that an icon had been found nearby.

Valentina Ivanovna: I heard that there is a swamp. . . . [I]t passes by
from the lake, probably, when it [reaches] the hill. Something like that.
I don't remember which year it was that someone saw it—I was still
young probably—[they saw] that there was an icon floating in a puddle.
A Mother of God [icon]. On that spot now stands a little chapel. That
chapel was in Krylovo on a dry place. And from there, they took away
this icon. It was so beautiful! They took it, carried it there.

An icon was found in a swamp and the swamp become imbued with
certain powers. Valentina Ivanovna goes on to tell how its healing powers work.

Q: Tell me about that place where you go to get water.

Valentina Ivanovna: It's in Krylovo. I've got to go this summer.

Q: Do you drink that water?

Valentina Ivanovna: Yes. Before, if a child was sick, they carried it home,
and put a coin in the well/spring.[22] . . . And from the *mezha* [a strip of
land, divided into two parts], they took some earth and washed the child.
They wash him through, and if it is his fate to live, in three days, he will
get well. If it is not fated, then in three days he will die. God knows who
decides this. We drank the water. One guy from nearby, two years younger
than I, lived in Panevo [with his family]. He had some kind of problem
with his spine. The doctors couldn't find the problem. We had gone to the
graveyard to remember our *rodnykh* [blood relatives; here, those who had
passed on]. We are walking back, and he says, "Valia, let's go find that
spring." In this spring, water never gets cold in the winter. Never, even
when there is a frost of negative fifty. We walked there in the summer and
he says, "I want to take this water and drink it." So there, he took it and
got better.

Q: Why was water holy in this spot?

22. There is a certain amount of ambiguity in Valentina Ivanovna's telling of this story. I
was able to conclude that the well (*kolodets*) that she speaks of is equivalent to the magical spring (*kliuch*) because of the "three days" that revealed the fate of an individual, which
she spoke of on several occasions.

> *Valentina Ivanovna:* I don't know. They found an icon there, there had
> been a church there, not far away on a hill. In our life, there are many
> mysteries that are as yet unsolved.

This narrative has several important features. Like other stories from
the mir chudesnogo, an icon is found in an out-of-the-way place.[23] The
water that it floats in becomes the means for healing, either by combin-
ing it with dirt from one's strip of land and the clothing of the ailing, or
by drinking it and waiting for the decision of one's fate. A church is built
in the environs, honoring the spot of the "miracle."

Interestingly, the water in this story does not only heal; similar to holy
water, it can heal or cause death. Its role is to resolve the problem of fate.
In this sense, contact with the holy icon is reminiscent of contact with
otherworldly beings from the mir chudesnogo. The contact is highly
charged, but one can never be sure of what one will receive.

The miracle of the icon found in the swamps near Krylovo was compared by Valentina Ivanovna to the story of an icon found near the famous monastery of Tikhvin, which she had heard about on TV.

> *Valentina Ivanovna:* They also found an icon in the water there, on the
> other side of the river. They also found this icon in water, on the other side
> of the river. They found this icon and began to build a godly temple on the
> spot. And they felled timber, came back on the second day, and there was
> no timber and no icon. And they looked, and it had been carried to the
> other side of the river. Who carried it there? Even the wood chips were all
> carried away. There were a lot of miracles . . .

The icon in this story had ("there were a lot of miracles") powers over
space-time. How else could it have moved itself and all the wood chips?
The icon's "will," despite being a "churchly" object, preferred its own
native home,[24] floating in its own swampy waters. The icon is construed
here as having a will of its own, beyond the will of the Church. It allies

---

23. The "found" icon (*obretennaia*) is an accepted class of miracle-working icons. See
Shevzov (1999:29).
24. Place has been an important component in the widespread veneration of icons, historically. Shevzov (1999:41) writes, "In the [laity's] estimation, a specially venerated icon
'belonged' to the place where it initially revealed its special character."

itself with a place in the physical landscape, endowed with its own holy character.

In a story told to me in the nearby village of Maksimovo by Antonina Sergeevna, an icon was first seen in a dream, and then found in another out-of-the-way spot.

> *Antonina Sergeevna:* I saw it in a dream. I saw this icon in the forest, in a bunch of dried branches. And this icon was lying there . . . with eyes like living ones. I see this icon—with its eyes turning there. In dry broken branches . . . [which fell] from the pines. . . . In this pile of broken branches, it was as if she were alive. I was dreaming it. So, in my dream, I didn't take the icon. I only saw it. And then I awoke. I say to myself, "Lord, what a dream I had." . . . I had in front of our summer house an attic. I went there [once], not knowing why. Before me, [my husband and his first wife] lived [there]. . . . I say, "In the corner, take a look what I have there." Everything was falling apart. I began to make order and look, and I see this icon. There, in the attic! In this house, exactly like in the forest. See, it's this icon. See, sweetie, such an icon!
>
> *Q:* Such an old one! Where is it from?
>
> *Antonina Sergeevna:* Where, indeed, my dear? And look—she has such eyes. Moving around as if they were alive.
>
> *Q:* Who is it?
>
> *Antonina Sergeevna:* I don't know, some kind of woman. A woman's face.
>
> *Q:* What does it mean that you saw it in a dream?
>
> *Antonina Sergeevna:* I was thinking that it was as if the icon were alive, like I saw it. And when I woke up, I thought "Lord!" And I didn't take it. I should've taken it. And then I did, you see.

This icon also has two homes. The first is the dream in which it is first seen. The dream icon lies under broken branches in the forest; it has living eyes. The second home is in the attic of Antonina Sergeevna's house—a house that she moved into after the death of her husband's first wife. This house was not hers (chuzhoi), and the attic of this house is also a liminal space. The icon there was recognized from the dream by its living eyes. The message that this dream had for Antonina Sergeevna was that she should "take it" and bring it home. In effect, she went out into the dream world, encountered a wondrous thing, and brought it back. The trajectory of her journey was neither the typical icon trajectory (pulling grace in through the instrument of the icon), nor the typical one of the mir chudesnogo (going out into the world and confronting space-time malleability). In a sense, it is a mixture of the two: She confronts space-time malleability, and she aims to possess it—to bring it home.

In another story, the local icon (the icon-khoziain) is dreamed of. This time, it is understood that it must be taken away.

> *Antonina Timofeevna:* We used to have a Bible and there were pictures in it. No one could read the Bible in Old Church Slavonic. The icon was from the Bible. Jesus Christ, Virgin Mary, Sergei Radonezhskii, etc. There was also Ekaterina Velikomuchenitsa—it stands in the cupboard. I saw in my dreams that the icon didn't go with the others, so I put her in the cupboard. And the icon stands, and I don't dream anything [about it].
>
> *Q:* Why doesn't the icon go?
>
> *Antonina Timofeevna:* Because I'm not a "Great Martyr."[25] Before, there were great martyrs. Many came through, lived in the monastery. And I didn't live there.

The appearance of the icon in the dream gave Antonina Timofeevna a specific message. Unlike Antonina Sergeevna's dream icon, it did not compel her to bring the icon in, but to take it out. It was unsuitable where it stood. The three icon stories that have been presented thus far indicate that the placement of an icon is a charged issue. The apparitional home of the icon is contrasted with its "true" home. Blessings of icons can be harnessed when their placement is right.

In the following story, there is another icon apparition that appears, this time in a ghost-like manner.

> *Emma Dmitrievna:* We were sitting, drinking tea in the kitchen. And I hadn't turned on the light; it was dark in the room. I bent over toward the corner of the window. And there in the corner, was a bag of *sukhariki* [dried sweetened bread]. And I felt that someone was looking at me. And

25. The title of the martyr/saint to which she is referring is Ekaterina Velikomuchenistsa.

I think with my mind, "Who could be looking at me?" We live on the fifth floor and in front of us is a school, far away across the street. And next to us, no one could be. But you always know when someone is looking at you. Who was looking at me, right in the face, because I. . . . In the darkness, I feel that someone is looking at me. But there was a curtain. But anyway, I feel that someone is looking at me, and that's it. But I took these sukhariki and I think, "I should look anyway." Then, I open the curtain and look out. And in front of me are two deep, blue eyes. They are looking at me. I got really scared. Only two eyes, for some reason, in front of me. And I stood under the icon. There was a double window frame. Between these two frames, there were such blue, deep eyes. I looked, then blinked . . .

Then I think, "What if it is really some special thing, a kind of blessed something or other. So I blinked, and then, I saw nothing more. I couldn't see anything more. And then, a friend said to me, "Come to church, my dear. Maybe you'll see there." And, in fact, when we went to church, I see two blue eyes on the fresco, in the church, on the beaten wall. The eyes were so similar. The same big deep eyes. Maybe it was some kind of angel. Maybe a guardian angel . . .

We carried holy water from the church, and also sprinkled it everywhere. I even did it in Kirovskii. Because they said, "What if it turns out that the eyes were not from God, but from a demon?" So I sprinkled water all around.

In the above account, there are again two icons: an apparitional icon and a "home"-oriented icon. The vision of the icon (those two living eyes again) parallels the very real icon eyes in a church fresco. There is a link between the two. But this icon also has, potentially, a dual nature—it can be angel or demon (and she sprinkles her apartment with holy water to be safe). This ambiguity is telling. Orthodoxy and its images and the apparitions that are fashioned from its images are not clearly "good" or fully trusted. Contacts with these miraculous forms are as ambiguous in their results as contact with any other being from the mir chudesnogo. Valentina Ivanovna's magic icon waters will not necessarily heal you; in fact, they may kill you. Emma's icon eyes could very possibly be demon eyes. The found icon can resemble other beings that come out of the mir chudesnogo in the capriciousness of their will.

In the preceding stories, there is a relationship between the miraculous icon (in dreams and apparitions) and a native icon "home" (the swamp, the church, the attic, the cupboard). There is a tension between the two locales. If the found icon has a topographical story, it is to come out of the world of miracles and settle into its native home. Contact with an icon in these settings may or may not bring good fortune (and the icon may or may not stay put). It is clear, in any case, that the icon that lives in the corner of the village home extends its symbolic reach out of the realm of that corner into the world of magical forests and otherworldly dreams. The symbolism of icons in villages extends outward from the religious object, to the patriarchal state object to the world of wonders. On it goes, next, to the retributional hand of the rod.

Icons and Retribution from the *Rod*

In the 1960s, the Soviet Union set up a series of initiatives to encourage youth to work in the Asian republics and help build the infrastructure for fledgling industries and agricultural enterprises there. The young people who went off did so as adventure seekers and, indeed, patriots. Emma Dmitrievna, from the tiny village of Gubino, just past the creek at Iurino, left for Kazakhstan as a young woman and taught literature there for several years. She was a moving storyteller, speaking with a gentle, warm pedagogical style. In the following, she explains a curse that had attached itself to her family line during a conversation with her husband and me about the existence of God.

> *Mikhail Fedorovich:* The communists appeared, . . . and already from all sides it buzzes, "There is no God. There is no God." That they destroyed the icon with an ax, there exists no God. . . . They started to say, "What are you doing?" "So what. There is no God. Not doing anything."

> *Emma Dmitrievna:* My father and three more men—they raised their hand against the church. They razed it to the ground. The icon. . . . Those who raise a hand against the icon will pay for it for seven generations. It's about karma. Father destroyed the church. He fought for the whole entire war and died at the end in Poland. He has no more heirs except for his sister's children. This is destroyed karma [*karma narushena*]. You have to take off the curse.

Early communists showed up regularly in tales of retribution. Sometimes they are punished by being led off to starve in the forest. Other times they are killed. Still other times—and more serious in the grand scheme of things—their descendants are made to suffer.[26] If you lay hands against the icon, the logic says, you and your line will answer for this sin.

Petr Fedorovich's father was one of the first communists in the area, and he was a guard during the burning of Solovyovo's parish church on an island in Lake Tikhonskoe in 1936. I was told more than once the story of the "four brothers" who organized this destruction. Participation in these destructive acts resulted in retribution:

> *Petr Fedorovich:* They destroyed the church and made tables from icons. They transported [all the valuables] on a boat and carried them out. A car was standing there—where the church stands. [Put it] in the car and took it away. And the books from this church burned for two full days. They burned Bibles. There was such a heap; the leather was a finger thick on some of the covers. For two full days, they burned books that are priceless. They didn't give away one single book. One special KGBeshnik participated in destroying all of this. And he didn't give any books. After this closing, my father guarded the church for two weeks, so that no one would steal anything. All the icons stood there, only the valuables had been carried away. And my father guarded this church. As he tells it, there were such jewels. Later, it was all destroyed. The local authorities started to destroy it. They began to break the floor. Take things to other people. And this happened to the people of Guliaevo. . . . The church had been a part of our kolkhoz. And Guliaevo was a small kolkhoz. And these [people], out of jealousy, burned the church. Burned it. And God punished them, all four brothers, and took them out of this life [*tot svet*].

Petr Fedorovich was a communist in his day, and a brigade leader. At the same time, he was able to lament the destruction of the church and the loss of its icons and treasures. His father had also been a communist as well as a "believer." For my purposes here, the fact that icon destruction led to the deaths of the communists is of primary importance. The icon appears to be one physical manifestation of a deep retributional

---

26. In summer 2001, I learned the terribly sad news that Emma herself had suffered a mental breakdown.

force. In Petr Fedorovich's story, the destruction of the church, with its holy icons inside, doomed the "four brothers."[27]

Whole family lines can be cursed. The deeds of a given generation are bound to the generations that follow, as they are linked to that generation's relationship with its own ancestors. The family line (rod) binds the generations. The retribution that came from the traces of wrong actions that Emma spoke of earlier (in her language, through karma) was reiterated by Mikhail Alekseevich:

> *Mikhail Alekseevich:* Life and experience determine positive and negative energy, not God. God decides whether to help a person or not, depending on how a person behaves and how his relatives behave. It's very hard to request help [from God]. God can't help right away. If a person's grandfather was a great sinner, there's a link between the dead and the living. A parallel world.

God is far away, but the deeds that tie you to your ancestors are in the fiber of your being. Here it is important to see the effect of the sins against icons—as metaphysical household khoziaeva on the family and its line.

There is another important relationship here. The retributional acts that come from the threat against icons, ones that can carry their rage into the generations, are directed against communists. It was the communists, of course, who had destroyed churches and icons, so it is not at all surprising that the icon figure will act against them. On the other hand, it appears that there is something deeper going on as well. The communists brought authority from the outside—authority that was essentially chuzhoi (foreign). Raising their hands against icons was not only an act of aggression toward a crucial symbolic object in the home, but towards the *local means of reining in power.* Many villagers ultimately became

---

27. An analogous story was brought to my attention in summer 2004. An acquaintance in Belozersk, G-, had come to Mikhail Alekseevich several times over the years for help. He was an amateur archaeologist, and had collected many different local objects over the years. Mikhail Alekseevich and Iuliia recently saw him and talked to him about the concern that among the objects he was "digging up" were pieces of churches. "Those who destroyed churches, they didn't survive: either they died or committed suicide." Some time after this conversation, G—, who in many other ways had shown himself to be unstable, committed suicide. Iuliia told me that "traces" of this remained on her heart—that it was somehow her fault.

communists. Larisa Andreevna, who spoke of icons in the most potent terms I heard, proudly accepted awards as a Party member and servant of the state. The problem was not the ideology of the state per se, but apparently its efforts at truncating the native means (my icon, my home, my village) of setting space right. The retribution that icons bring is often in the face of ideological challenges to the power of the local khoziain. Some of the raging of icons in icon space is part of a broader ideological battle—where the communists and communism's proponents (and their descendants) are made to suffer because they threaten the most local, most svoi of khoziaeva.

In this final example, taking the icon from the home causes such a rupture of domestic space that a woman's home is shaken, her life is threatened, and her heirs are lost. Once again, it is a communist who initiates the crisis. To cross the icon is to invite retribution of a particularly rageful sort. The rage, as Larisa Andreevna explained, emanates from the corner.

Larisa Andreevna: In the school, there was a director. My son went there and she would shake my son: "You tell your mother to take her icons out!" [My son] would always be quiet. [This director] took her own icon out of the house. They had in their house an icon out in the open in the whole corner. Huge one. And her husband worked as the salesperson at the store. Sashka. He arrives at home, and there is no icon in the house. They had a huge house. And the icon was such a huge, beautiful one. And she had placed the icon in the winter izba. She came home from school and [her husband] asked: "Where is the icon? . . . And who told you [to take it out]? Which khoziain turned up at the house and [told you] to take away a chuzhaia [somebody else's] icon? He told everyone, but not everyone takes out the icon!" He had a big argument with her; they fought so that she flew all around the house.

When they went to sleep, something started knocking in the front corner. The whole house started moving. They sprang out of the house in just their nightshirts, thinking that they were being bombed. So this is the kind of blow they received. They sprang out. Sashka ran all around, nowhere was there a sound. Everyone is asleep. "Bring in the icon, hang it where it was. If you even start to touch that icon again and put it somewhere, I will totally kill you, not considering that you are my wife. I will kill you for that."

So their daughter gave birth to a son with an arm as if it were one single one and the leg that doesn't reach to the ground. [Their daughters] don't live with husbands. Both of their husbands left them. One has a pair [of children], and the other has one mutant [*urod*]. The son is already suffering for four years; he's sick. The Lord punished. He punishes for everything. I will not take the icon from the house and sell it. You can't do that. I never will give the icon for rubles. And there—his whole family is punished. Everything is destroyed. The brother is only twenty-nine years old, and came home from work, lay down to sleep, snored, and died. There—that's how Lord God is angered. You should never do it. You have to tend [the icon]. I wash mine, cross myself, kiss it; the icon always helps.

In the above story, the powers that hover in and around the icon corner reach a certain crescendo. Here the locale of the icon is charged with far more than the face of an unknown saint by an unknown artist. It takes us into the far regions of the world of wonders. The function of an icon here is not only that of providing power to the supplicant, but that of guardianship and patriarchy. An icon must be in the house.[28] If it leaves the house, something unspeakable, terrifying, can result. The crime here is not simply against an object of religious veneration, but one that seems to reach into the deepest regions of the rod. Cross the powers of that figure, and you commit a crime against the family, the house, and the rod. In such cases, the unseen powers will arise against you, summoning themselves quickly and horribly to set things right.

This suggestion that there is a relationship between the khoziain, the rod and the icon yields more answers to the general question about the source of the powers of the icon. It is unlikely that the raging that Larisa Andreevna described came from a little picture of a saint that can channel healing powers because of its inherent holiness. Rather, it appears to have come from a type of *crossroads in symbolic space where powers overlap to their greatest effect.*

The powers of the rod, as I discussed in Chapter 6, include protection, healing, and fertility, which are granted in exchange for the dutiful fulfillment of the requirements of khoziaistvo. Raising hands against icons appears to cause the wrath of the very rod itself. Important here is that

28. It also must be in a church. In 2001, I was told a story about how, after many decades of standing in near ruins, someone climbed up to the top of the church in Iurino and stole the last icon in it. Right after that, I was told, lightning struck the church.

the crime against the icon is the displacement of the icon, that is, taking it out of its native "home" and realm of authority.

Thus far, the icon can be seen as a place of "grace descending" or of patriarchal khoziaeva (which are related to more standard forms of khoziaeva). There are other, related inhabitants of corners. These most likely preceded the icon in history, but through acknowledging their partial stewardship of the space, some of the more fantastic stories of misbehaving icons can be explained. Therefore, at this point, I leave icons aside. Icons go in corners, indeed, and their powers are vast. Before icons graced the krasnyi ugol, the corner was still a charged space. Earlier, I discussed the speculation that the krasnyi ugol had previously housed pre-Christian idols. Regardless of this fact, the corner seems to hold the powers of ancestors. This has already been suggested in the previous discussion on retribution, and in early descriptions of the krasnyi ugol as the place for deceased family members and offerings to them. In the next section, the corner will be regarded without reference to the icons that landed there only a few short centuries ago.

LOCAL *KHOZIAEVA* IN THE CORNER
* * *
The Entry Point of the *Rod*
In Bachelard's *Poetics of Space* (1964), a chapter is dedicated to corners and their poetry. What is this space that lies between this wall and that—between the ground and the covered sky? It is a forgotten space, he concludes—a spot of no-space and a spot for reverie.

The corner that holds the icons in the homes of rural Russia is a place that fills—rather than empties—the social space over which it has power. In fact, in this journey into the far reaches of that corner, it is that filling function that defines the icon space. The icon there calls in forces; it is judgmental, retributional. It is a holy relic, the probable equivalent to pre-Christian idols, the figure that appears in dreams and visions. It is a miracle worker. It echoes with the cult of personality of the state. This is that indispensable icon with mournful eyes and no name that grants protection and health to the inhabitants of a home.

But the icon corner is not only filled with icons. It is also, most broadly and perhaps most essentially, filled with ancestors and their manifestations as khoziaeva domovoi. These ancestors are invisible by most accounts, but there is still evidence of their existence in and around the icon corner and evidence that they share symbolic space with the Orthodox icon. This point is supported from three broad directions: from literature on Russian folklore that concerns the "cult of the dead" and the khoziain doma; from village narratives that discuss this subject explicitly; and indirectly—if quite clearly—from the symbolic character of the icon which resonates with that of the personified and invisible rod.

Here the khoziain returns once again in his final form—the one that takes us back into the world of wonders, the one that marks the bridge between the seen and unseen worlds that brush up against local places, the joker and rager, the most local of the otherworldly beings, the most svoi of those who arrive from supernal realms. In this section, I highlight three aspects of the khoziain-domovoi with the goal of making explicit this very deep aspect of the symbolism that converges in corner space: the function of the khoziain-domovoi, the spatial arena of his realm, and finally, his feature of mercuriality, one that allows him to bridge over to other forms. I begin, however, with an illustration: a being in the corner, the birth of a calf, an obrashchenie.

The Birth of a Calf: The Rite of *Naveshchenie*

Iuliia and Mikhail Alekseevich's cow, Lusha, is now, of course, gone. But my first spring in Solovyovo, after my first long winter there, was a big year for Lusha. She was calving for her very first time, and it was not clear how she would survive birthing. The question loomed: If she did not survive, how could the household survive with no cow and no calf? Another fear lingered that she would not turn out to be a good milk cow, and the family would be left with nothing but her meat to eat the next winter. Meat is not milk. Meat is transitory; milk flows and flows on with the long-living being of an animal.

As the day of the calf's birth drew near, Iuliia was excited and Mikhail Alekseevich was frightened and pacing. When the birth went by with no problems, and when Lusha began to produce fatty milk in abundance, there was reason for genuine rejoicing. A new life wobbled into the gray ends of winter.

Traditionally, a ritual accompanies the birth of a calf. It involves an invocation to the khoziain and khoziaika of the barn to protect and love the new being that has entered into their realm. Not everyone knows this ritual anymore, but Iuliia had learned it from her mother-in-law. In the ritual, the cow is milked and sprinkled with "holy water." A birch branch is waved over her. Then, one turns toward the corner of the barn and says:

Khoziain-father,

Khoziaika-mother,

Love and protect my Lusha,

As I water, feed and protect [her],

From the evil eye, from beasts,

From all evil things.[29]

We have returned to the corner and what do we find? Certainly no icon—not in this barn (although they well may have been found there in earlier times). But we do find unseen agents of protection and love to whom one can turn—agents whose powers extend over the domain of the barn. Mikhail Alekseevich and Iuliia explained the purpose of this ritual, known as *naveshchenie*:

Mikhail Alekseevich: You can turn to the *khoziain* of the barn: "Khoziain, father, love and guard our cow Lusha, little calf, Bessie,[30] lambs, Serok."

Q: Which khoziain?

Iuliia Ivanovna: Khoziain of the farmyard. Spirit. And there is a mother, too.

Mikhail Alekseevich: Khoziaika-mother.

Iuliia Ivanovna: There you ask, "Protect and love, I love [the cattle]."

Mikhail Alekseevich: Because if happens that . . . a khoziain doesn't like the cattle, then no matter what a person brings, [the cattle] won't live any longer.

Q: Has that happened?

Mikhail Alekseevich: As much as you like.

Iuliia Ivanovna: When the cow starts to give birth, I step in and say, "Khoziain-father, khoziaeshka-mother! Help, Lord, Lusha, to give birth. So that everything would be normal and good."

29. Khoziain, batiushka; Koziaika, matushka/ Liubite, i beregite moiu Lushu/ Tak, kak ia poiu, kormliu i beregu/ Ot durnogo glaza, ot zveria/ Ot vsego durnogo.
30. Bessie is not a Russian name; I had been asked to name the calf.

Q: Is God somehow linked to the khoziaeva?

Iuliia Ivanovna: Probably. I believe so. I look to the corner and speak.

Q: Do they live in the corners?

Mikhail Alekseevich: Not always. Everywhere.

Iuliia Ivanovna: I look in the corner.

Mikhail Alekseevich: When disagreements happen, or someone was there without a good [balance of energies, that one maybe the khoziain or khoziaika won't like that. And the cow starts to get upset, not eat, struggle with itself, not find its place.

The corner is here owned by unseen figures that have the names of khoziain and khoziaika. The khoziaeva are both feminine and masculine, they are charged with loving and protecting. They are supremely svoi. They linger in a space that is associated with the icon (and the Lord God, who appears to metaphorically hover somewhere on the side), but are not necessarily defined by the symbolism of that icon, as they are not defined by the authority of God. They must be pleased and appeased.

In this ritual, we glimpse the more general relationship between the villager and his corner. In the corner of this tiny barn, another set of beings radiates outward. Who are they?

Rod Functions in the Home

In the USSR's encyclopedia collection, *Mify narodov mira (Myths of the Peoples of the World)* (Ivanov and Toropov 1980:391), the domovoi or house guardian (khoziain doma) is described as follows:

[T]he spirit of the house. It was figured in the appearance of a person, often with the same face as the khoziain doma, or as an old person with a face, clothed in white fur, etc., closely linked with the well-being of the house, especially with the cattle: on this relationship—either benevolent or hostile—depends the health of the cattle (my translation).

Although certain features of these descriptions do not fully apply to the khoziain doma (or domovoi) as described in the homes of Solovyovo (the guardian's personification is rather more evanescent than it appears in this description), on the whole, the function of the khoziain domovoi is present here in his role as house guardian. Indeed, in village discourse, this function is underlined.

> *Valentina Ivanovna:* Before, they said that there is a domovoi in every home.
>
> *Q:* What does he do? Why is he in the house?
>
> *Valentina Ivanovna:* He guards/preserves/keeps [*sokhraniaet*] the house. Listens to everything and everyone.

What does a house guardian do? In later quotations, the health of people and cattle is mentioned in passing, and ritual invocations are made to the khoziaeva in their various forms to this effect. In fact, the guardianship role of the domovoi was often described through negative language. It is not so much that he maintains a home, but that he chastises the residential group for not treating him with the proper deference. As in the case of dealings with all other local khoziaeva, permission must be obtained before moving into "his" domain.

> *Iuliia Ivanovna:* In each house, there is a *batiushka* [khoziain doma]. In a new house, not everything goes well and the khoziaeva are upset [if you don't address] words [to them]. . . . You turn to the khoziain and say, "Take us in [*primi nas*]." [This is] the unseen khoziain.

In literature on folk culture in rural Russia, the house guardian is linked with—unsurprisingly—the ancestors. Indeed, in *Funk and Wagnall's Dictionary of Folklore,* the Slavic domovik or domovoi is described as:

> The one in the house: A Russian household spirit, ancestral and usually the founder of the family, who watches over and protects the inhabitants of the house, taking care that all is in order. He is an old, gray-bearded man, looking very much like the living head of the family. His correct name is never used; he is called "he" or "himself" or grandfather (Ded). (Ivanov and Toropov 1980:391–392).

Funk and Wagnall's domovoi is "gray-bearded," and appears in the form of the "living head of the family." If the domovoi in the stories presented here are not always so solidly and familiarly humanoid, the qualities of the *domovye* and the ancestors clearly converge: They are both guardians, they are both participators in the well being of a household, and, in general, of khoziaistvo. This is generally true in the folkloric traditions of rural Russia (Cherepanova 1996:119, 120). Stories that explicitly link the domovoi with family members and khoziaistvo were rare in the village. Nonetheless, Anna Gregorievna told one about how a mother double was seen actually doing work in the barn:

> *Anna Gregorievna:* I went into the courtyard. I look and my mother is walking. She is going straight in the courtyard. And with an armful of hay. To the cattle. And she simply walked out. And I went home. And my mother is home. She is sitting cleaning the grain. I say to her . . . I asked, "What, ma, were you doing giving [hay] to the cattle?" She made no response. And I arrive at home, and mother is there cleaning up the grain. She said, "I didn't go anywhere."

> *Q:* And that was . . .

> *Anna Gregorievna:* Uh huh. . . . That was the khoziaika of the house.

This khoziaika looks like the living female head of the household. She is involved, quite literally, in the business of khoziaistvo. This seen-then-unseen being that looks over khoziaistvo is reminiscent of the discussion of the role of the ancestors in the running of the home and the land where the link between the rod, the household, and the dead was established. Indeed, by extension, the domovoi shares certain of its features with pokoiniki (the deceased). If displeased, the domovoi "haunts" the world of the living—making noises, breaking things, making animals die, making "everything go wrong." This link is, again, made explicit in folk literature on the topic (Cherepanova 1996:136).

There are similarities in character between the icon and the domovoi as well. The domovoi shares with the icon the fact of its indispensability and the way that it must be "respected" by those who live in a home. Furthermore, like the icons from the last chapter, the presence of the domovoi (if not his form, which I will return to) is tied to the health and well being of a household and its human and animal inhabitants.

In addition, like the icon, the domovoi can—and perhaps by definition is bound to—misbehave. In ways similar to relations with other khoziaeva in the mir chudesnogo, this khoziain must be addressed and appeased and has a sense of humor that includes all kinds of trickery when he is not properly respected. This type of censure is discussed in folk literature:

> The domovoi can . . . tell how he is displeased, if [for example] he doesn't like the new daughter-in-law who has moved into the family (Cherepanova 1996:136, my translation).

In the village, several such comments were made—that the domovoi not only shows displeasure, but also enjoys creating it on a whim. Iuliia tells about how he starts to "mess around" (*balovat'sia*), how he likes to "make jokes" (*komedet'*) if he is not politely invited into the home with words of love or if he is forgotten. Things can get lost or fall from their places. Valentina Ivanovna says that he can either protect the house or not, according to his whim, and that he listens to everyone and everything, and "likes it when a person gets mad."

This quality of guardianship that extends to playfulness and then to vindictiveness is one that is familiar—again from the mir chudesnogo. As is, of course, his quality of mercuriality in time and space. As the guardian of the house, the domovoi has a few spots that are described as his native abode. Behind the stove is one popular place for the domovoi but, as we saw in the story of the calf's birth, the corner was the focus of attention for the invocations to the khoziain khleva (barn spirit). Mikhail Alekseevich draws attention away from the corner, and his wife brings it back:

Q: Is God somehow linked to the khoziaeva?

Iuliia Ivanovna: Probably. I believe so. I look to the corner and speak.

Q: Do they live in the corners?

Mikhail Alekseevich: Not always. Everywhere.

Iuliia Ivanovna: I look in the corner.

In *Mifologicheskie rasskazy,* as in Mikhail Alekseevich's aside, the locations where the domovoi is found include most of the ritually "marked" places of the household, like "the stove—the organizational center of the house, hearth, and in that way linked with fire; the threshold—the mythological boundary of the house; the basement and the attic—analogs with the higher and lower spheres in mythological semantics of the house as a cosmological model of the world (Cherepanova 1996:135, my translation). The *domovoi*—as the personification of the residential *svoi*—lives in all of the charged parts of the household, including the icon corner. The house has its spheres that are marked as metaphysical—including its thresholds and its corners.

In literature on Russian folk customs, the location of the ancestors in the icon corner is accepted, if in a somewhat speculative way. The corner where the icon now sits is the corner where ancestors used to be honored with elaborate rituals. As Matossian (1968:20) describes in "The Peasant Way of Life":

> When a stranger entered a Russian household he was supposed to take off his hat, cross himself facing the icon corner, and then greet the heads of the household. The jar that a family used to carry embers from an old stove to a new was broken and buried at night under the icon corner of the new house. . . . In the pre-Christian era the icon corner may have been the place where ancestral images were kept. Some Russian peasants believed that after a dead member of the family was buried his soul took up residence behind the family icons.

From the narratives in the village, it was impossible to draw general conclusions about the location of the domovoi as ancestor-guardian. It did not reside only in the red corner, as the icon typically does. Hubbs, in *Mother Russia* (1988:256), places the ancestors in the two charged spaces of the icon corner and the area of the pechka. The analogy made with the icon cannot therefore be considered hard and fast. In fact, it is not the business of this chapter to make hard and fast analogies, but to watch how analogies rub off on each other. The icon corner tends to house guardian-protectors; they can cluster there. Although the icon is rather more stable in the krasnyi ugol than these unseen khoziaeva, clues that the krasnyi ugol should, in general, house *ancestors* continue to accumulate.

For example, near the holiday of Troitsa, birch branches are brought from the forest into the home and placed in the icon corner. Citing Zernova (1932:39), Propp (1974:383) explains that these birch branches represent the "guardian of the household," whose job it is to ensure fertility. This practice lives within the memory of villagers in Solovyovo. Other evidence that lands the ancestors themselves in the corner is, of course, the practice of placing the dead there and placing offerings to the dead on their remembrance days. If the domovoi is an ancestor spirit of some kind, and ancestor spirits are found in corners, the domovoi can comfortably wander over there as well.

Unlike the icons, which also must be addressed and appeased—and which are also capable of a certain degree of space-time–defying mischief—the khoziain doma is only precariously visible. At most, he comes into cohesion at will, similar to the khoziain lesovoi. This mercurial quality is noted in folk literature on the subject, but is seen as a secondary point.

> There are several kinds of domoviks: the *chlevnik* [*khlevnik*], or barn spirit; the *ovinnik,* or kitchen spirit; the *bannik,* or bathroom [bathhouse] spirit. Every house has them (Ivanov and Toropov 1980:391–392).

Logically, this is an interesting point: the domovoi is here seen to be the defining being with separate "types." I argue that the primal forces, once again, have many ways of congealing and merging, one of which is into the name of the domovoi.

Not only can this khoziain presence be that of the bath or the barn or the home, it can take the form of people. According to literature, the domovoi can be zoomorphic as well (Cherepanova 1996:134–135)— appearing as various animals. I have no such stories to draw from in my own time in Solovyovo, but certainly the principle that the khoziain doma is not fixed to a given form (he can be human or animal) or even any predisposition to having a form at all, is perfectly in keeping with the analysis here.

There is another mercurial element of form that is quite important here: the village stories often include both a khoziain and a khoziaika. The fact that both the female and male khoziaeva are honored with invocations has broad implications. Generically, the male khoziain is the unmarked term for the leader of a household, forest, factory, or nation. In the village home, the gender of the khoziaeva is not exclusively male, and perhaps, it follows, not exclusively patriarchal. In *Mother Russia,* Hubbs shows specific cases where the symbolism of female power was lost over time, and she traces those losses to the advent of Church and state power. The overall suggestion is made that rural Russia was a great seat of local matriarchal power until the state and the Church made their way into the village sphere. This is an interesting hypothesis, if perhaps somewhat more simple than the data here imply.[31] It is possible to imagine that idioms of feminine power receded in the village, but they are not gone. The icon corner may be the place of honor for the khoziain, but when invocations are made, they go to the khoziaika as well. Her power is out there as well; she, as the guardian-protector, can appear as well quietly carrying hay and making sure that all is fine with the beings that she loves within her realm.

There are suggestions in ethnographic literature that the pechka (stove) is the female section of the home and the krasnyi ugol, which lies opposite the stove, the male corner (see Gromyko et al. 1989). There is no data to support this in my research, except for the fact that cooking is certainly considered female work. This semiotic take on space in the home is interesting, but once again, I am forced to conclude that the less rigid (and less semiotically delineated) explanation is more generally true: that *beings form and dissolve according to their overall viability in a given space in the imagination.* The krasnyi ugol, in its large and metaphoric sense, is the locale of many powerful resonances. Forces gather there, even when their outward forms carry contradictions. How is it that an icon can resemble Stalin? Or a domovoi? All of these hegemonic orders battle over their details, and the villager turns in the direction of the corner, and asks, please, dear khoziain, dear khoziaeshka, protect and love my Lusha.

Summary: Ideological Mixes in the *Krasnyi Ugol*

When speaking of the khoziain doma, discourse is marked by a certain mixing of metaphors—or so it appears. Below, Mikhail Alekseevich and

---

31. The rich imagery of female power that Hubbs presents is intriguing (she includes long discussions of female deities and yearly rituals associated with honoring them) but it cannot, alone, prove that female power used to dominate in the village. It is very easy to slide into the nineteenth-century concept that "primitive" societies that were "free" of the state were more "feminine" and more egalitarian than those of the corrupt patriarchal present (fallen, as we are, out of Eden and into the arrow of time), and that the state brought in patriarchy and swept all of this female power away. There are too many cloudy suppositions here: that matriarchy implies egalitarianism, that there can be only male or only female power concentrated in one society, and that only visible power is real power. Images of female strength and danger and power certainly persist in the village setting. If the images of Christ, God, and tsar are male images that have taken on a certain degree of outward dominance, it does not follow that female power has disappeared in a gesture of some hidden law of thermodynamics that power in the universe is neither created nor destroyed.

Iuliia work through an explanation for me. The khoziain doma is here a guardian, an object of invocation, an object of fear, one who appears from nowhere, one who is an angel, one who is a spirit, one who responds to icon rituals, and one in whom both the masculine and feminine can be merged into a single being.

> *Mikhail Alekseevich:* The house host comes with the house. If you don't do the ritual of asking for his good will (and taking the icon around the house), you can have problems. If you are not too bad people, you may have no problem with him. In principle, he can make everything go wrong. Your animals can die, everything can go wrong.
>
> *Q:* Does he show himself?
>
> *Iuliia Ivanovna:* He can appear as a person.
>
> *Mikhail Alekseevich:* Khoziain doma is like *a guardian angel.* It is a *dukh* [spirit].
>
> *Q:* Is there a khoziain in the barn?
>
> *Mikhail Alekseevich:* Yes.

In the following discussion, the khoziain doma can also refuse to love.

> *Valentina Ivanovna:* Before they said that there is a domovoi in every home. He can not-love the cattle. He can not-love a person.
>
> *Q:* In your family, did anyone ever see him?
>
> *Valentina Ivanovna:* No one ever sees him. He doesn't show himself.
>
> *Q:* What does he do? Why is he in the house?
>
> *Valentina Ivanovna:* He guards/preserves/keeps the house. Listens to everything and everyone. They say that he can get a person mad. He likes it when a person gets mad.
>
> *Q:* Is he clean or unclean?
>
> *Valentina Ivanovna:* I don't know.

The domovoi covers a range of symbolic representations, some of which belong to religious ideology: an angel, an icon, a little god, a guardian, a protector. But this is not all. Antonina Timofeevna, who spoke several times with me about the *interplanetetarii* (aliens) who were investigating the region of Belozersk with "war aims," included talk of icon corners in her description of the alien planet.[32] The figures that resided there as corner dwellers resonated with Soviet ideas and ideals: ancestors, icons, workers, and little gods.

> *Valentina Ivanovna:* Yes, they pray to the ancestors. Those who are very old—even one thousand years. Many supported the planet. Yes, they pray to them. In these churches they pray to them. Well, for example, we pray, there to that Saint Sergei, who spent his whole life in a church. Worked, there he is [points to the icon corner]. They pray to him. Here we pray in the same way. He is considered a good person. And there, where they live, they also consider. And they have many thousand-year-olds. It's like that, these kinds of, well, gods they are, like saints. They pray to them. And the people are ruled.

Workers belong in the corner, as well—thousand-year-old ancestor workers. Perhaps the ancestor workers are more akin to the domovye than to Stalin, whose supremely Soviet image can look out from that corner as well. Perhaps the ancestor workers grant, from that corner, the power of the collective svoi through the long line of the rod, where Stalin's power is that of a distant, oft-forgotten nation khoziain. The danger comes, of course, when that raging power is not forgotten. When he dips into the corner space to subjugate and punish a nation full of svoi.

This is a point that deserves to be underlined: If, in fact, it is the nature of the symbolic mechanism to accumulate resonances from various sources (Sperber 1974), and if the particular kind of symbolism that one is dealing with involves matters of otherworldly trust and protection as well as those of an order-producing, hard-handed state, it is clear that this territory can become charged with massive political power. Indeed, the image of the nation-khoziain bears not only the qualities of the guardian of the svetloe proshloe, the one figure with whom we can live in an Edenic

32. Antonina Timofeevna's entire story cannot be retold here. She had suffered a contusion while serving in World War II and raised a son alone. Her stories of contact with beings that were quite literally "otherworldly" were treated by some as crazed rantings, and by others as simply the truth (there had been many UFO sitings in the region). See Platz (1996).

society and without whom we fall into the arrow of time and corruption—but also has qualities of the vengeful icon saint; and those of the mercurial trickster beings who preserve and love and who kill and rage; and the rod, the deepest, most tangible form of otherworldly presence in this world, the one that is charged with keeping the world on track in the business of creation and life and death. When political figures appear in the imagination, this symbolic material can be used to great effect. Is the president of Russia a khoziain or is he not? Can his image inspire death on the battlefields of the rodina or can it not? He certainly offers the image of a strict and heavy hand. Can he extend his powers of guardianship over a people, answering their invocations with fatherly warmth? Or does he leave them, or punish them, for not exalting him (as in abandoning little Aniutka and her brother in the snow to die)? Which khoziain do Russians choose to trust? Is it possible to find a form of guardianship that can sit in a symbolically comfortable locale—one that is not volatile, not demanding of unquestioning loyalty, not so historically heavy-handed and cruel?

The political implications of this kind of khoziain—as one manifestation of corner power—are not the subject of this book. But it is important to remark that within this locale of power, this beautiful corner of honor, there are many possible routes, including some national and political ones, and others that are supremely and intimately local. It is striking that the corner was chosen as a place of power before Christianity came to Russia, and remained so after Christianity was subjugated by Soviet ideology. It is also striking that power flowed there, to accumulate on "top" of local images of the power of the rod and the khoziain and that such images became the defining thrust for that symbolic "space." This collective memory gathered in the corner, and from that corner it can and does shape collective images of the structure and mechanism of otherworldly powers. *Komu obratit'sia? Tuda.* Whither does one turn? There, to that mixed and manifold place.

8

Calendars

CALENDRICAL TOPOGRAPHY: THE POETICS OF REVELRY

* * *

While I lived in Solovyovo, days were counted in a limited range of contexts. The mail truck would come three times a week, as would the bus from Belozersk when the roads were dry enough or frozen enough to carry travelers. Bread would arrive twice a week and people from Solovyovo, Vershina, and Maksimovo would line up in the local store on the appointed days to be sure and get their share. Pensions came once a month, as did the salaries of the kolkhoz workers, post office worker, culture worker, and librarian. Another line would form at the post office on these days, and it could take an hour or so to buy an envelope or a stamp or a telephone coupon then because of the postal worker's slow manner and bad temper. People counted these days and set them aside as important. In small but significant ways, they oriented their time through them.

In my own efforts at self-orientation while living in Solovyovo, I often found myself falling into the question, "What will happen tomorrow?" The response was nearly always the same: "One mustn't guess what tomorrow will be." Tomorrow, I learned, is, at its base, a day that will depend on a million smaller factors, including combinations of wind, sun, heat, and dryness, and, of course, larger, unseen/unforeseen things such as illness, accident, or death. It finally struck me that perhaps farmers are not at all the conservative beings that city dwellers take them for. Perhaps these farmers who rely on the forces of the weather and the strength of their hands are the most flexible of beings. "One mustn't guess" means that all tomorrows are fluid, and all actions aimed at that day must be defined by creative approaches to larger problems: when to plant, when to harvest, when to slaughter. And yet, even in a place where time is marked by this pragmatic volatility, days are different from each other. As seasons ebb and flow, certain days hold power, others give instructions, some demand asceticism, and still others offer revelry.

Calendars order tomorrows; they organize timescapes and map them, and channel their fluid signs. They do not only tell us which days will be marked by revelry and which will be marked by tears, but they grade and rank these days. They lay out a topography of function and power. The fact that agrarian calendars are organized around the business of urging life out of the land is no surprise, as it is no surprise that centralized states and churches also order the year over which they claim dominion—granting milestones that elevate their status and maintain their position through deliberate manipulations. In settings such as rural Russia, where so many hoped that the conceptual terrain would be made of soft soils, tomorrows find their deepest function through the agency of social memory.

Calendars and Social Memory

> Try to imagine another type of memory, one which strives to retain information about the proper order rather than irregularities, about rules rather than exceptions. . . . Here it is not the chronicle or newspaper account that comes to the fore, but the calendar, the custom fixing this order and ritual making possible its retention in the collective memory (Yuri Lotman in Howe 1991: 42).

Anthropology has certainly formulated questions about the deeper meanings of calendrical habits. Referred to by Bourdieu (1977:97) as "one of the most codified aspects of social existence," the calendar is packed with lived symbolism, ritual action, elaborate (and deeply telling) exegesis, and without a doubt, ideological battles. In anthropology, one way of approach to the place and meaning of calendars has been to treat the year as a sort of semiotic problem that must be solved: where there is death in the winter, and in summer there is life; where there is a time for asceticism, as there is a time for sex and gluttony; and where there are times to honor society's laws, and times to invert them. Here, the procedure for understanding a calendar is a "decoding" one, where the yearly cycle encrypts ever-forming and ever-resolving mythic conflicts (see Connerton 1989:48): Nature to culture to nature; chaos to order to chaos again; darkness to light to darkness.[1]

A second, related approach treats the year not so much as a balanced (and balanceable) semiotic equation, but a drama to be lived through where particular human problems are solved. In Propp's (1995 [1963]) analysis of the Russian agrarian calendar, such an approach is evident— the year, then, is a journey on which we set in motion the wheel of life and death. There are procedures in this cycle to awaken the soil after the winter, bring the spark of life to it in the spring, and gather its gifts in the fall. Here everyone has a role to play in the calendar's ever-changing dynamic.

A third view of calendars sees them as containing the substance of social memory. In Connerton's *How Societies Remember* (1989), the calendar holds commemorative days that, in turn, hold the stuff of social memory. Because of the relationship of society to the state (and other hegemonic orders such as religious ones), calendars are constructed to embody narratives of group identity. For instance, I go to May Day celebrations, and I am a Soviet ("A day of Parades! Flags! Demonstrations, drink and song!"); I pass through a seder and I am a Jew (the long story of my people's wandering, the metaphoric link between the Jews' wandering in the desert as a people, and my own wandering in the desert of my soul).[2] Through the *habituated* performance of commemorative ceremonies, social memory is transmitted and reproduced (Connerton 1989:70–71). In this view, attention is shifted away from the content of commemorative rituals themselves and toward their form. Commemo-

---

1. See Geertz's "Person, Time and Bali" essay in *The Interpretation of Cultures* (1973) for an example of this approach.
2. I thank my uncle, Mark Siskind, for pointing out this reading of the seder.

rative ceremonies that make one day not like any other are regarded for the habits of collective performance that they instill—in other words, with reference to their role in sustaining and fashioning social memory. For Connerton, it is the collective identity per se that is here being fashioned and refashioned through the calendar. Hegemony and memory thereby merge in calendrical time-space.

For the purposes of this book, calendrical time is viewed as another sort of landscape in symbolic space. Calendars, as regular and revisited paths in that landscape, can be forged by hegemonic dicta ("February 24 will be the day to honor the Third Reich!"), or can be worn over time with the help of regular markers (the movements of the sun and moon, changing of the seasons, migrations of animals).[3] In this sense, they reproduce social orders. From Connerton's position, I take the point that social memory is indeed a kind of habit. It is the walking and rewalking along given historical paths, where the performance of that walk (and the lingering at certain commemorative milestones) is a way of instilling and re-instilling social memory. It is shared activity. I also take the point that the state and the Church can aggressively position themselves within that landscape in the attempt to shape collective allegiances and, eventually, collective memory. Nationalism and its corollaries demonstrate the power of this view, as in I'm a German! I'm a Serb! I'm a Catholic! I'm a Sikh! In the context of my investigation, however, social identity (including national and religious identity) is not necessarily always the primal cause of calendrical crafting. It makes sense that in state societies, hegemonic orders play a dominant role in defining the calendar. But even in places where the state has had a hard and heavy hand, there are ways for time to move along its own path. A certain independence is possible.

From the functionalist view exemplified by Propp, I take the point that going through the year and passing through its rituals is not simply a matter of saying to oneself "yes, this is us," although that is undoubtedly a crucial part of the problem. It appears that calendrical milestones are ✓ there not only as mirrors within which we regard ourselves (individual and group), but as occasions to intercede in the yearly cycle and, indeed, to set things right and keep them on course. They are occasions not only for social performance in general, but for intercession in the yearly cycle. In fact, I show how this very intercession appears to flow, in certain con-

3. The example is from Connerton (1989:41).

texts, from the act of group formation ("this is us")—or, as I have put it—svoi-formation.

I will only treat the semiotics of calendars cursorily. The calendar, in this view, tells a long story and contains a complete archeology of signs and symbols where archaic systems of cause can be revealed.[4] Soviet (and Russian) ethnography and folklore studies have provided rich renderings of these systems. Mapping social memory onto calendars, as I have proposed, stands at least one step back from the level of the ritual sign. Semiotic orders will not be expressly sought. Symbolic representations and their resonance fields will.

This chapter concerns spaces in the symbolic landscape that we return to—stages on which hegemonic orders confront one another. If the red corner is a physical space that bears a mother lode of symbolic power from a range of ideological sources, calendrical milestones also become the scene of confrontation between ideologies. In this context, I consider the crucial problem of competing ideologies/hegemonies in rural Russia and how, in effect, the calendar generally becomes one of the crucial battlegrounds in this confrontation. In the pages that follow, examples illustrate the degree to which the "powers that be" can battle over memory, but also the degree to which they are ultimately incapable of doing so. In light of this, the problem of calendars will be shown to have broader implications in the question of how collective memory is maintained and transmitted.

4. Because of the regularity of the natural calendar (there is always a solstice; there is always a new moon and a first frost, etc.), one might suppose that people are somehow urged into making order out of such regularity. This supposition, which need not be deterministic, can be supported by theoretical works cited in this book, such as Vygotsky (1962) and Lakoff and Johnson (1980). However, the tendency toward order is not the same thing as the *obligation* for order—and the notion that the signs manipulated in cyclical rituals *must* reflect perfect order and balance and therefore *themselves* carry a certain semiotic balance with them is by no necessity always true. In my study of calendrical ritual, I recognize that there are no necessary overarching orders to the world of meaning, but there is also no ultimate absence of order. Happening upon local semiotic orders can be seen as a great, if unassumed, reward. See Bourdieu on the semiotics of calendars and the "error" of the intellectualist theory (1977:97–98) Sperber (1974), for an epistemology of semiotics, and Ornter (1984) for a history of this problem in the context of anthropological theory in North America.

CALENDARS IN RURAL RUSSIA:
CONFRONTATIONS OF TIME-SPACE
* * *
Very much in the way that Bourdieu (1977) describes the mixing of
Berber and Islamic traditions enscribed in the Kabylia calendar, the complexity of the agrarian calendar in Solovyovo is visible in the layering
and overlapping of official calendars with local ones. The contemporary
Russian villager has four calendars within which she operates: civil, Orthodox (religious), Russian agrarian, and work-based pragmatic.[5] Each
comes with its own sets of rituals, symbolic range and tone, and "tem-
ples" and pilgrimage sites, all running along together through the year.
In the next section, I discuss each of the calendars, first separately and
then in light of their confrontations and overlappings. I begin, literally,
from the ground up, first describing the year as ordered through large
agricultural jobs—work that must be performed during the course of the
year in order to ensure survival (and ones that require a keen sensitivity
to weather conditions beyond villagers' control). Following that, I briefly
describe the organizing principles behind the traditional agrarian calendar, the Orthodox calendar, and the Soviet one. Each calendar contains
its own logic, its own holidays and "holy" days, and its own emotional
texture. It is certainly false, at one level, to separate these calendars. I do
it only as a point of introduction and will resume the questions of how
they inevitably overlap shortly. In the second part of the chapter, I map
the journeys to a few milestones in the agrarian year, with special reference made to the way in which commemoration (and, therefore, social
memory) is linked to the habitual act of svoi-formation at various societal levels.

The Shifting Calendar of Tasks

Winter—caught, as it is, on the dark side of Russia's polar tilt—is about
waiting. Its days are short and nearly without light; it is long and cold
and isolated and isolating. One dark day merges into the next, and people

---

5. Here, I follow the lead of Propp, who himself identified civil, religions and "traditional"
calendars (1995:24). To this, I add the calendar of work. The "civil" calendar is here both
Soviet and Russian, since the Soviet calendar is still the one that largely defines the state
holidays of the year. See Leavitt (1995) for his work on the Kumaoni calendar, which includes the poetics of work cycles.

pass the time waiting for spring, when life will snap into ordered motion. It was after having passed through this cold and lonely period that villagers began to smile softly and warmly at me when passing me on a pathway or greeting me at the store.

The only big jobs in the winter—besides waiting—are the regular tasks of caring for one's own barn and home. Once the lake freezes over, the horse and sleigh can easily get to the distant fields where huge haystacks produced in the summer lie waiting to be carried back to the village. Manure is hauled out of the barn and off to the potato patches. Lesser jobs are preparatory ones: tools are repaired, and clothes are knit and sewn. The duties of fire building, cooking, washing, and cleaning—all of which are time consuming and, in their own way arduous—never cease.

Starting in February, seedlings are planted in small containers in the house. They will be transferred to the house garden when the soil is ready. Certain days are singled out as "blessed" for the planting of given plants. Villagers would watch this calendar with a degree of attention, but did not hesitate to replant on other (not specially blessed) days if something went wrong with the seedlings. February, March, and April are months where preparations for spring accumulate. In May, seed potatoes are chosen and laid out on the floor of the izba as the day of the potato plant approaches. Some time in May, the waiting ends and the large agricultural tasks begin, ones that are absolutely essential for farmers' survival, and ones that anchor later discussions of calendrical orientations.

Potato planting begins when the earth finally warms after winter. This is the only job that I saw done "collectively" with the village per se—and not the extended family—as the work unit. Because of this, there were negotiations about when to begin the task, and more weight was given to trusted elders in the community. The collective nature of the potato planting seems to arise from the rather narrow range of weather conditions that are appropriate for the plant. It must be done quickly, and speed requires maximizing the labor of the three horses that Solovyovo, Vershina, and Maksimovo collectively inherited when the kolkhoz was partially dissolved. If families do the job alone, the horses stand idle for long periods. This is not only inefficient, but can cause the time of the ideal weather conditions to pass before the potato plots of everyone in the village are done. In order for the horses to be used with maximum efficiency, the work was done family plot by family plot and organized as a brigade: the horse plows, the potato is thrown in by one line of people, a mixture of hay and manure is placed over the potatoes by another line of people, and the horse makes a final pass with the plow to cover the seed potatoes. During the war, when there were no horses, plowing required "four or five women, instead." It must be said that this job is the easiest of the large, cyclical efforts, and is marked by a spirit of playfulness and joking. The weather is warm; the job is easy (except for the horses and the man behind the plow); the mood is light.

The senokos (hay cutting) is the defining labor of the villager in the months of June and July. In order to maximize output and minimize waste, daily work on the senokos is marked by a series of close calculations as to the degree of sun and wind and chance of rain; all of these factors have an impact on what work will be possible. In the home where I lived, every morning was spent discussing if it would be better to cut new hay or to dry and stack hay that had already been cut. Stacking at the wrong time can cause a whole day of labor to be wasted. Of course, this is not the sort of labor that one wants to waste—hours of hauling huge loads of hay over one's head under the burning sun. When weather conditions have been bad (too much rain for long stretches or not enough), tension fills the air during the morning negotiations and voices can be raised in panic. Villagers watch each other for progress, and fear also comes when one's family is falling behind.

Some families negotiate the use of tractors for part of the labor on the senokos, and this speeds up the job considerably. Use of tractors requires not only money (or vodka) and a certain amount of connections, but a strip of land that is even enough to allow for a tractor to pass over it. Consequently, most families don't bother getting help. While I lived in Solovyovo, the kolkhoz still owned most of the pastureland in the area, and work on the senokos still involved finding small pieces of land on the side of large pasture fields (along ravines, near the edge of a forest) where hay was cut by hand, dried in the sun, gathered into small stacks (*kopni*), spread out and dried again, and then re-made into large stacks (*stogi*). Making enough stogi for the year takes one and a half to two months in June and July, depending on the size of the family working together and the amount of livestock that the family keeps. Relatives move in over the summer to help with this work, and are fed and cared for and given vegetables and meat months later in unofficial exchange for their labor.

The senokos is hard and long and dirty. In the 1990s, each family had several sites where it cut and dried its hay; some were kilometers from the house. Villagers would head out for cutting in the morning and if the weather held, they could spend the entire day there drying the hay and stacking it. For weeks on end, work would begin at sunrise and end at the late sunsets of the White Nights—involving the combined effort of parents, children, and grandchildren. Flies and hornets plagued all participants, and the work was truly arduous.

When the senokos work ends, there is a brief period of relative rest. Favorite mushrooms and berries begin to appear in the forests in August, which will be preserved and eaten all winter long. Mushroom gathering, in particular, is a joy for all. It is a simple, sweet, forest joy that is indulged at this time of the year.

Regardless of the fact that individual families have their own potato plots, the decision to begin the potato harvest in late August or early September amounts to a collective one. Potatoes feed both people and animals. They can be stored and given away. They are the most important crop of all, and if they are harvested too early, they can be small; if harvested too late, they can rot from excess rain or frost. Deciding when to harvest them is a complex guessing game that involves constant negotiations with unpredictable forces, and no one wants to guess alone. One family begins—often a family with a respected elder—and the others follow suit. The rows of potato plants (which had been scythed down a couple of weeks earlier) are plowed. With the help of a wooden *lapatka* (which looks something like a short, thin canoe oar), villagers then hack away at the rows of potatoes with the considerable force of their arms and backs. The potatoes surface, and a next row of people dig them out of the softer earth and sort them into different piles. The job lasts for a few days, only, but in those days the village is empty. Everyone is out in the potato patches, which lie right on the edge of the village, past the clubhouse, one right next to the other. Everyone is together. The work itself is exhausting, but more bearable than the grueling work of the senokos when the sky is black with biting flies and bees.

When the potatoes are dug up, the bulk of the summer work is over, except for the regular garden work, which keeps people busy every single day. The next large concern is the preparations for winter, including the very substantial work of preparing firewood. This is a job that—like the *senokos*—has always depended on a somewhat fragile official relationship with outsiders for the use of natural resources. Villagers now can pay for a permit to cut a certain number of trees for use in their homes. They use gas-powered saws, but the trees are felled deep in the forest and must still be moved and piled by hand. This work is done before the first major frost, and only after that frost (when there is ice and snow) can the logs be easily transported from the forest to the village.

Jobs are set in this way: one large task after the next. The calendar, in this most pragmatic sense, is given form by the necessity to complete these jobs. While waiting for conditions to be right, villagers maximize the secondary jobs that are always present: work in the garden, work in the barn, fixing a broken fence or saw, and food preparation and storage.

With reference to these large and essential tasks, time is mapped according to the necessity for action. The calendar here is a flexible one, not beholden to any other calendar, whether Orthodox, Soviet, or even what can be referred to as Russian agrarian religion. Through the task calendar, the malleable is mapped. In the mir chudesnogo, space speeds and shape explodes along the symbolic cusps of everyday life. In the calendar of agricultural events, there is waiting, there are thresholds, and there is a dramatic leap into action. I underline this point: At its most tangible and pragmatic base, agricultural time gently and evenly flows until it snaps into vital action, and then back again.

Oftentimes, the tasks described above are mentally oriented by dates in formal calendars. The Christian calendar bears a certain weight of orientation, particularly regarding important changes in the weather (where a certain holiday will mark a frost or a day to let animals out of the barn for spring). The Soviet calendar can orient in a similar way. If, in the world of the farmer, the weather changes (frosts or rains come and go, soil softens and hardens) and tasks therefore change according to the whims of the forces "out there," there are orienting milestones provided by formalized calendrical systems.

Russian Agrarian Calendar

> The games of Sviatki, in the great majority of cases, strike the observer
> by the vulgarity of their mores and it is not without reason that the fathers
> of the church have called them diabolic. A good half of the games are the
> remains of barbarity, which strike the impartial observer by their cynicism
> without discretion. (C. V. Maksimov cited in Propp 1995[1963]:128; my
> translation)[6]

6. Propp (1995:128) responds to Maksimov: "The words 'barbarity' and 'cynicism' express the indignation of the author, but they explain nothing."

Because of the dominance of the Christian calendar for several centuries, it is impossible to separate the Russian agrarian cycle from the Christian cycle, in terms of the fixed dates of holidays. Most of the agrarian holidays, even the ones that appear to be the least "Christian," per se, now have Christian names. The distinction that I make is one of function. That is, the Russian agrarian calendar, even when set by the dates of Orthodoxy, is aimed at the workings of the natural world and its interactions with the social world. It is a calendar that is concerned with local issues. The Orthodox cycle, on the other hand, concerns the relationship between the divine world (as defined by Christianity) and the broader social world of humanity.[7] In this chapter, it also includes the fact that the Orthodox Church has been a great political force in the history of rural Russia, and takes on a quality of centralization. The Russian agrarian calendar as I refer to it *is preeminently local and deals with the relationship between a given community and a given parcel of land.* The Christian calendar is state centered and deals with the relationship between a state-defined community and a standardized Khoziain-God. This is as close to an operational definition that I will offer, given the not altogether organic nature of the distinctions I have made. Here I underline the fact that I do not treat agrarian calendrical practices as coming from an organized pre-Christian religion.[8] They are, at best, loosely organized, are made of disparate elements, and have changed over the centuries.

What general order can be made of the agrarian holidays en masse? In *The Peasant Mode of Production* (Howe 1991:45), anthropologist Jovan Howe cautions that the volumes and volumes of material on the agrarian calendar have not, until recently, been focused on the task of systematization, where "the interconnections between periods and rituals" are

7. See Leavitt (1992) for a discussion of the meeting of "great" and "little" calendrical traditions.

8. The term "pagan" (*iazycheskii,* in Russian) is often used to describe such a religion by Russian and Soviet ethnographers and folklorists. The term pagan itself, deriving from the Latin, *paganus* (dweller of the countryside) is not a particularly bad one (if it were not for the way that it was loaded with negative association), but it does speak to a historical, semantic completeness that I cannot acknowledge in this context. The functional definition offered here is an attempt to circumvent the complexity of the historical problem that the term "pagan" gives rise to. The calendar is agrarian not because it is found inside the countryside, but because it has to do with the specific interactions (and interventions) people have with a local parcel of land. Here, as in the previous chapter, I will use the term "pagan" when referring to discourse on the subject.

outlined. I will not attempt this task in any detail here, but will take the time to note a few regularities.

One fact jumps out immediately: The yearly cycle is just that, a cycle. It makes sense by looking at it as something round, and not as something linear and flat. If one were to take the line of a year and turn it back onto itself as a circle, several things about the agrarian calendar of rural Russia would be immediately evident. For one thing, the calendar is divided up into four quadrants that are necessarily aligned with the four seasons. For another thing, the calendrical milestones, unsurprisingly, cluster near the date of the solstices and the equinoxes.[9] Agrarian calendars appear to find such events as the comings and goings of the sun to be highly relevant. It is fair to say that these comings and goings are the organizing principle of this calendar, more than any other factor. The ten-day celebration of Sviatki (a masquerade-like celebration during rites that are performed to bring back the sun from its hiding) clusters around the winter solstice. The summer solstice arrives just about at Ivan Kupalo, at the height the period sanctioned for the coupling of young people. The spring and fall equinoxes are also marked by specific holidays (the rite of "bringing in the spring," and in the autumn, Pokrovskaia Subbota, an Orthodox holiday that doubled as a day to bring fertility to new brides). On the whole, it can be said that the movement of the agrarian year involves the specific problems of harnessing the life-giving powers in order to ensure reproduction of the land and the community. In doing so, villagers were "secur[ing] the annual renewal of life and thereby, the reproduction of the peasant him- or her-self" (Howe 1991:43).

The thrust of the year is one that is intended to urge out forces that are hidden (in the winter) and actualize the forces that are present (in the summer). According to Howe's argument, all calendrical activities are focused on managing the powers that will be required for reproduction in the land and the community as a whole.

As one of their crucial features, holidays in the agrarian calendar mark features in the volatile natural world. Through the calendar, one can

---

9. To make this clearly evident, it is necessary to shift the circle thirteen days, in that the Christmas date of January 6 is aligned with that of December 25. The shift from a Julian calendar (chosen by the outward-looking Peter the Great in the eighteenth century since it was the calendar of England at the time) to a Gregorian calendar (in 1918) is responsible for this lag. See Robert Massie's *Peter the Great* (1985[1980]:241) for the best explanation that I have seen of this shift.

know when there will be snow or a storm, or when it is best to plant potatoes or cucumbers. Some calendar days mark seasonal movements—
days after which it is forbidden to do something (such as swim) or sanctioned to do something else (like work on the senokos). Furthermore, the
calendar predicts the way the seasons will move. If there is frost on one
holiday, there will be a dry summer, for example. The list of these features is enormous. Most landmark days now come from the Orthodox
calendar, where, for example, a frost comes on January 24 ("Fedor
Frost"), on June 29 ("Day of St. Tikhon"), tomato plants will flower; or
on Christmas, if there is snow, nuts will grow well in the coming year.
The agrarian calendar is endlessly textured with directions and commentaries, designed to keep the natural flow of the seasons within the
grasp of local farmers. It is for this reason that I call this feature an agrarian one, even if the landmark dates are often founded by Orthodoxy. This
part of the calendar is one that aids farmers to harness the natural forces
that allow for reproduction and renewal. It is a calendrical feature that
is very much alive in the village of Solovyovo, and appears in several
places in the analysis that follows.

Orthodox Cycle

In previous centuries, the Orthodox Church exerted all kinds of efforts
in reining in the religious traditions of rural Russia—steeped, as they
were, in the precariousness of the agricultural cycle. It trained men as
priests (sometimes against their will) and sent them to the far reaches of
the empire, set up monasteries, and tied itself with the tsar and the state.
Even with these concerted efforts, the Church calendar took hundreds of
years to establish itself in rural Russia. In that time, it managed to give a
new face to many agrarian holidays: the winter solstice celebrations at
Sviatki became Rodzhestvo (Christmas) and Kreshchenie (Baptism of
Christ); the End of Winter Carnival became Maslenitsa (Mardi Gras);
and spring rites became Easter, Troitsa. Orthodoxy, in effect, pulled
people out of the fields and forests and homes where these days had been
observed before Christianity had established itself, and drew them into
the confines of the Church, where people were made to stand and listen
and quiet the rhythms of their song and dance.

It is certainly true that once the Orthodox calendar was adopted in the
village, it provided a new set of landmark days to interact with the ones
that were already fixed in the village year. New textures and tones were
added. New narratives were related through the story of the life of Christ,

the animating spirit of the Christian year (Propp 1995[1963]:13; Vlasov 1992:29).

The Orthodox calendar begins each year on September 1.[10] It includes landmark days that are fixed and others that change from year to year. By far, the most important of the Orthodox holidays is Easter, or Paskha, representing the resurrection of Jesus Christ. Easter sets the dates of several other great feasts, such as Palm Sunday (one week before Easter), the Ascension (forty days after Easter), and Trinity Sunday or Pentecost (fifty days after Easter), as well as the great fast of Lent (Ware 1991[1963]: 305). Other important holidays include days that honor a specific event in Christian history, specific famed icons, and specific saints. The calendar includes many fasts, some of them arduous. It attaches to certain holidays prohibitions against work. The Christian calendar sets order on the timescape by granting many milestones with various instructions attached to them. Most of these narratives come from the history of Christianity. Aside from what is taught in the Church, many of the stories have become part of local oral tradition (see Oinas 1984 for examples). The Christian year thus attaches villagers to a set of characters and themes that are broader than their local context.

Very little of my own data reflects this Christian storytelling. Villagers in Solovyovo were aware of many of the holidays with Christian themes, but almost never spoke of the narrative content of these holidays. I was present at the first group celebration of Easter in Solovyovo's recent history. It was held in the clubhouse. Each of the participating families contributed prepared food along with vodka. Mikhail Alekseevich, who had organized the celebration, dug into some books to find out the meaning of the holiday so that he could explain it to everyone. To his great frustration, as he went back all the way to Exodus, he could not get anyone to listen to his story. People were too interested in passing the pickles and marinated mushrooms. The Easter celebration ended in raucous dancing and singing, like most other celebrations in Solovyovo. The Easter narrative may have inspired Mikhail Alekseevich, but it did not seem to inspire anyone else.

On the other hand, bathing on a holiday or breaking work taboos on a holiday is felt by some as dangerous, and can be used as well as any other excuse to explain a sickness. Christian milestones appear to be

10. As does the school year, honored with the Soviet holiday, Den' Znaniia or Day of Knowledge.

treated as milestones with a certain weight. The days themselves are perfectly standard liminal spaces that deserve the respect of all liminal spaces. Whether they have a Christian character specifically is another question.

Civic Cycle

The civic calendar had much in common with the Orthodox calendar: Both were based on shared narratives of heroic leaders. In their history, both set out to reshape a preexisting timescape while attempting to insert new values along the way. Both aimed to exert ideological control over a large territory. In the morality play of the Soviet calendar, the heroes were mostly not individual people (although Lenin's birthday on April 22 was celebrated in the village in earlier years). They were—and this marks a difference between the Soviet calendar and the Orthodox one—"The People" and their doings and ideals as groups. Holidays honor mass movements (or movements claimed to be such) and revolutions. Soviet holidays also honored given worker groups of the population,[11] and, more abstractly, they honored ideals for humanity, such as worker solidarity. A small number of Soviet holidays during the year that were celebrated by all: New Year's Day, International Women's Day (March 8), International Day of Worker's Solidarity (May 1), Day of Victory of WWII (May 9), Day of the Soviet Constitution (October 7), and Day of the Great October Socialist Revolution (November 7 and 8). All of these holidays in post-Soviet Russia are still celebrated, with one exception: the Day of the Soviet Constitution. Correspondingly, a new Constitution Day (December 12) has been added. In addition, although celebrated on the same day, the Day of the Great October Socialist Revolution is now called "The Day of National Accord and Reconciliation."

How have these civic holidays been celebrated?[12] This story is very mixed, of course, and it is well known that fanfare for the Soviet holidays was, at least in part, forced. Nevertheless, in cities, many Soviet holidays brought with them some real fun and amusement: There were days off, sometimes gifts exchanged, and sometimes fireworks or parades. At

11. These days are still holidays. Game shows will have special shows where the participants are, for example, all "rail workers," and there will be misty-eyed toasts and special gifts and special pronouncements.
12. See Smith (2002) for a rich discussion of civic holidays and the state during the Yeltsin era.

the same time, in villages without the possibility for urban fanfare (and without the real possibility to leave work aside for an entire day), these holidays have perhaps never been as festive as in the cities. Nevertheless, there is evidence—as demonstrated later in this chapter—that Soviet civic holidays continue to exert a real influence in the landscape of Solovyovo's memory.

Soviet attempts at shifting the calendar did not stop at introducing new holy days and festivals after the Revolution. Culture workers (*kul'tra-botniki*) were trained in cities to amuse villagers with dances and other fun. It was perhaps inevitable that many well-established holidays leaked into the Soviet timescape. Culture workers would plan activities that co-incided with holidays such as Sviatki, and would set up masquerade balls. Or on Troitsa, they would write plays to honor the birch tree. The control that they exerted was, like that of the Church, one of tone. Through their efforts, many agrarian festivals survived, but in a radically changed way.

None of these calendars exists in a vacuum. The year is filled with around 365 days—a stage onto which many, many characters can play for a limited stretch of time. Overlap between these calendars is as inevitable as it is sometimes lyrical.

Overlapping of Calendar Spaces

Out of the blue one day during lunch, Mikhail Alekseevich began speaking of the khoziain of the forest and how he controlled the laws of the beasts of the woods. At first, I thought he was speaking of the forest inspector who gives fines to those who have illegally cut down trees (I had heard of such a khoziain before), and was amused and confused at the prospect of some civil inspector controlling the conduct of forest beasts (there was something oddly Gogolesque about the whole thing). Mikhail Alekseevich is, after all, something of a stickler for and lover of rules, and I wondered if he could possibly be going a little far this time. "Beasts don't speak Russian," I protested, "and won't listen to any of these rules!" Of course, it was my error once again: Mikhail Alekseevich was speaking of that other khoziain of the forest.

Mikhail Alekseevich: In ten days, on September 27 (Feast of the Exaltation of the Holy Cross), the beasts of the forest will be let free of all laws and allowed to hunt wherever they want. The khoziain of the forest lets the animals kill whatever they want—even each other. That's why horses in the village are locked up after that. The beasts are allowed to kill them. There is order everywhere like that; there is also order in the forest. The khoziain of the forest is in charge of this order.

Iuliia Ivanovna: But . . . isn't it because . . .

Mikhail Alekseevich: [Responding to Iuliia] The elements of the anti-Christ don't believe this.

Q: So you mean that not believing in the power of the khoziain of the forest is a sign of the anti-Christ?

Mikhail Alekseevich: Yes.

Iuliia Ivanovna: [Later, out of earshot of her husband.] After this holiday, it gets dark quickly and the grass grows badly. The nearby grasses are already eaten and the horses go farther and farther in this period when it's dark. Beasts, if they ate badly during the day, come closer for people's animals. They can even come up to the door. The wolves go together in groups of five or six. In the summer, the leshii controls them, but you can also say that there is enough food for them in the summer. Both explanations can be understood.

Mikhail Alekseevich's argument suggests some of the richness of the symbolic palette along the calendrical landscape. Here he argues that it is the khoziain of the forest who responds to this Orthodox holiday of the Feast of the Exaltation of the Holy Cross on September 27 by suspending all the laws of the forest. The agrarian forest khoziain is here waiting for an Orthodox holiday to assert one of his powers. To further thicken the plot, dissent on the part of his wife is categorized as "anti-Christ" talk, which turns the discourse back to Orthodoxy. Iuliia's later explanation for why animals are locked up after that date makes a good bit of sense in terms of the goings-on in the natural world. But she, too, makes this Orthodox date her reference point (and concedes the influence of the leshii). Three calendars here converge.

Such a rich and varied set of calendars creates symbolic complexity along the timescape of the year. Sometimes the effect of calendrical overlapping can be simple but noteworthy, as when I was told that the weather improves "after Victory Day," which is a simple case of weather changes being defined with reference to important celebratory days (as in "You must not swim after Elijah's Day" or "The first snow comes on

Pokrov"). Such statements are commonplace, and speak of that powerful pattern of relating the weather to milestone dates. The fact that a Soviet holiday (instead of an Orthodox one) can be the marked date of reference is no great symbolic leap.

Along the various timescapes, milestones are sometimes shared—even to such a degree that they merge into one. Often, a date is fixed by one calendar but the function it serves is fed by another. When this happens (oftentimes for broader, political reasons), it is still possible to look at the milestone dates in light of their broader presence in the symbolic landscape. What is the symbolic function of these days? How are they placed in the memory?

Political Overlapping

Looking at the calendars as a whole, there are certain general tendencies in the reworking of old holidays into new ones for political effect. First, historically speaking, were the Church's efforts at replacing the agrarian calendar with its religious calendar. As in the rest of Europe, agrarian holidays were Christianized in rural Russia, leaving remnants of their rites and symbols along the way. In this process of replacement and overlap, the rowdy winter solstice celebrations of Sviatki became the Orthodox Rodzhestvo (Christmas) and Kreshchenie (Baptism). The rituals of Maslenitsa (celebration before the spring period of fasting) merged with Provod Zimy (Leading Winter Out). Troitsa was founded on a day of remembrance of the dead and a birch celebration.[13] The day of John the Baptist (Ivan Kupalo) fell on the equinox, and its agrarian expression merged into the saint's day. The political benefits of re-fashioning existing festival days are clear. As in my discussion on icons and idols, the idea was to replace one set of venerated "beings" (marked by their own hierarchies and orders—here local) with another, the latter being defined and controlled by centralized religion and, given the particular history of the Orthodox Church, the state.

Claiming the calendar for the Church was not simply a matter of imparting a new meaning to old holidays (where a festival day is simply a vessel for collective cognition). It was also, importantly, a matter of changing the tone of celebratory days. It was specifically the "gaiety" of the agrarian rites that was then seen, according to Propp, as "diabolical"

13. See Ivanits (1989:5–18) for an overview of the nineteenth-century agrarian calendar and its relationship to the Christian calendar.

(Propp 1995:14). Conquering the agrarian holidays required modifying the tone of celebrations from one of gaiety and unrestrained emotion, to that of "asceticism, obedience and humility" (Propp 1995:14). This particular politics of tone will feature prominently in subsequent analyses.

This process was again repeated by the Soviets, once they came to power in the 1920s with an explicit program of ideological re-education (see Stites 1989). Soviet holidays were marked by three features relevant to the questions posed here. First, they indeed were placed on days that resonated with both the Church and the agrarian holidays. As Steven and Ethel Dunn wrote in *The Peasants of Central Russia* (1967:109):

> Some Soviet civil holidays, such as May Day and the anniversary of the October Revolution, seem to be popular and well established. Certain others, such as harvest festivals and the celebration of Russian Winter, have been deliberately encouraged and made to coincide with festivals in the church and popular calendars—just as the early Christians timed their holiday to coincide with the pagan festivals of the winter solstice and the advent of spring.

In other examples of this dynamic, the most festive of the winter celebrations, Novyi God (New Year's), comes at the time of Rodzhestvo, Sviatki, and Kreshchenie. It includes, like the Christmas of Europe and North America, the placement of a pine tree in the home, the singing of carols, and the gift giving of a Santa-like "Grandfather Frost." Like North America's New Year's, Novyi God includes excessive drinking and a loosening of social strictures.

Novyi God was a successful translation: The Soviet calendar managed to give the holiday a genuinely festive tone. Particularly in urban Russia, this is the great family holiday of the year. Interestingly, the state inserted itself in the economics of the festivities by sponsoring gift giving (during the Soviet period, factories would distribute gifts to children of employees through a costumed Ded Moroz). Rodzhestvo and Kreshchenie (marking the beginning and end of the Christmas festivities) are Orthodox holidays that refer directly to the life of Jesus Christ. Novyi God was able to take on the wild tone of Sviatki and family-based timbre of Rodzhestvo. It is a viable holiday in urban Russia in particular, and marks a successful de-sacralization of a religious holiday.

As well as commemorating dates that already carried resonance, the Soviet calendar explicitly pulled the agrarian festivals to the foreground, but did so with a certain twist. Rather than encouraging people to tell fortunes and engage in sexual play on Sviatki, *maskarady* (costumed dances) were arranged in clubhouses. Rather than burning the winter *chuchelo* (an effigy representing winter) in hopes of ensuring fertility of the land on Maslenitsa, and plays (with characters such as Ded Moroz and the fairytale witch Baba Iaga) and games in the snowy town square were staged. In the Soviet past, the chuchelo was burned (as it is today), but the ritual was not completed by throwing the ashes of the chuchelo on winter fields, the ritual act of Maslenitsa most associated with bringing land fertility in traditional practice (Propp 1974:376–377). A carnival festival was accepted by Soviet leaders and ethnographic references were to be encouraged (as one subtext of Soviet nationalism), but the rougher agrarian aspects were turned into a watered-down pastiche of non-Christian images. In this process, the superficies of symbolism were retained while attempting to eradicate its deeper resonances.

Importantly, Soviet recasting of holidays became occasions on which nationalist sentiment could be elaborated. May Day falls near the time of several agrarian rites in the spring (Palm Sunday, Easter, and Prepolovenie). It was transformed, of course, into a day on which the International Day of Socialist Solidarity was celebrated. In the village, these days could not carry the weight that they bore in cities, where there were days off of work, grand parades, and an atmosphere of drink and revelry. On the other hand, certain national holidays—particularly Den' Pobedy (Victory Day of World War II)—carry a great deal of meaning. This holiday can inspire great emotion, and is one of the few occasions where nationhood (as an "imagined community") is felt in a calendrical context.

Vying for days and series of days and sectors of seasons was and is a way to shape the loyalties of people: The politics of calendars is a subject of topical interest. Today, in post-Soviet Russia, new holidays are being introduced, such as the July holiday Den' Nezavisimosti (Day of Independence) in 1992, to commemorate the establishment of an independent Russia. In the village, this holiday has been greeted with begrudging comments such as, "Day of Independence? Independent from what?" Holidays like this go unnoticed—they do nothing to change the course of a workday. Some holidays resonate in today's political climate and others do not. This fact complicates the problem. If it were the case that we (the masses?) were all like grasses waving in the winds of dominant ideologies ("today I am a Christian," "today I am a Soviet," "today I am a Russian," . . .), taking in all the appropriate symbols and making them our own, calendars would be easy to analyze. But this is clearly not the case.

There is a degree of continuity—where new things are taken up without much fuss—and a degree of "resistance." But what is the cause of this resistance?

MEMORY AND NECESSITY

* * *

In this book, I have argued, both implicitly and explicitly, that some of the resistance to new ways (broadly put) results from the conservative nature of the metaphors we live by. If something is easy to think, and remains so, we will continue to think it (and talk, heal, organize society, and imagine with it) in our well-forged ways, ordering our mental landscapes along familiar ground. So, for instance, regardless of the ideologies that come in, the red corner has been continually filled with the power of the rod, healing has continued to take place through "lightening the load," leshie beckon as aliens do, and we are dragged to other worlds by khoziaeva of the forest or by the secret police who come by night. Some resistance to new ideologies occurs because they are not made of well-tread paths along the metaphoric landscape, and when introduced to them people are asked to "choose the path less traveled." And this, of course, makes all the difference.

But it is not only the metaphors which we live by that set the paths along the landscape of memory. Sometimes, paths are chosen out of what must broadly be called "necessity."

Are there primal causes, economic or otherwise, that can be said to generate and reproduce ideological systems? In Marx's materialist notion of production, the concept of "needs" is a generative starting point, where "needs" bring us first to the business of eating and drinking. Certainly, the farmers of Solovyovo organize much of life around this business, that is, ensuring survival through the practice of labor. But, as music has been defined as the silence between the notes, it is perhaps the silence between the moments of eating and drinking that reveal the quiet trajectory of deeper reason, or deeper necessity. Not all needs are material.

In fact, it cannot be said that life for the farmers of Solovyovo has ever calmly turned around the equation that labor ensures a living. No matter how hard one works, external and unpredictable forces can starve, kill, or send one to prison for one wrong word. "Needs" in Solovyovo surely refer to the business of eating and drinking, but also to dependence on fragile and volatile relations with unpredictable forces, guardians who must be appeased, and ancestors who must be remembered. Liberal uses of the term "need" allow even economic analysis to stretch into the domain of symbolism, granting that the business of eating and drinking does not cover all that we cannot live without—that existing in a human world makes us at least in part, "hunter[s] of more invisible game."[14]

If metaphors we live by set cognitive paths in the landscape of memory, perhaps there is a degree to which perceived needs—at physical, social, and metaphysical levels—ensure the survival of a given path in the landscape. Perhaps resisting new ways (and here, new calendar structures) comes about because, for one reason or another, the new ways do not fulfill perceived needs. Living by metaphors—the routes forged by the links between thought and emotion and language—is one explanation for the indifference to new pathways introduced by new ideologies. The question of whether the new pathways fill the range of human "needs" is yet another. Calendars, and the societal needs or functions that they fill (from the material, to the social; from the ideological, to the spiritual), are one route into the question of how social memory is set along certain definite pathways.

It is clear that in Solovyovo, under certain circumstances, one calendar is preferred to another. If there is a task that must be performed in the yearly cycle *in order to ensure or maintain physical, social, or metaphysical life, that task will be fulfilled regardless of which calendar references the date of that task.* That is, if a perceived need requires fulfillment, villagers will find a way to do so comfortably. The task will take on elements from symbolic timescapes that suit its fulfillment. Without flattening the problem to a crude functionalist outline, it must be possible to weigh why one choice is made and not another.[15] And, while weighing, it must be possible to then make general determinations about the social actors (and hegemonic battles) at work.

14. From Rumi's "Wean Yourself": "From an embryo, whose nourishment comes in the blood, move to an infant drinking milk; to a child on solid food; to a searcher after wisdom; to a hunter of more invisible game." In Barks (1995:70–71).
15. In part because of the way that North American symbolic anthropology was founded in reaction to a rigid functionalism, it is sometimes presumed that a careful study of symbolic action excludes the problem of social function. If the study of symbolism is, in part, about the pragmatics of symbols (what they *do* and not simply what they *mean*), there are points of reconciliation. See Ortner (1984:131) on the work of Turner and his theoretical descendants. Certainly, theories that treat action and practice (and their relevance and reproduction in dynamic, changing societies) have theoretical room for both function and symbolism.

For example, if the need is a physical one, such as letting the animals out of the barn as the warmer months approach, the date on which it is performed will depend on weather conditions more than it depends on the day chosen for that event by a given calendar. This is the case with the Orthodox saint's day, Egoryi Den', the day on which animals should be let out of the barn after the winter months and sent to pasture. The confrontation between calendars, and the ultimately pragmatic enactment of the task, are illustrated below in a conversation between Iuliia and Aleksandra Ivanovna.

Aleksandra Ivanovna: They circle the cattle [around the pasture fields] with an icon. We don't know any words, because no one passed anything down to us. My mother passed nothing to me, and I know nothing. She knew prayers. In my youth I also knew prayers, but now I only know one.

Q: When do you read prayers?

Aleksandra Ivanovna: I never read them. Why lie before God? No one told me anything. Mother said nothing. Mother died early. And they say that they circle the cattle, and I know no words.

Q: Well, do they circle the cattle without words?

Iuliia Ivanovna: No, you have to have words. You have to circle around the garden with words.

Q: [To Iuliia.] Do you also not know words?

Aleksandra Ivanovna: She knows, but she won't tell me, because I'm older than her. You can't do that.

Iuliia Ivanovna: Why? If I knew them, I would tell you. I also have cattle. Here, there is no such prohibition. . . . Now, everyone is his own shepherd. Everyone does it in his turn. . . . But you say simple words: "God bless you for the whole summer. . . ." You say simple words out from yourself. In order to preserve the cattle from beasts and people's eyes.

Q: Which day?

Iuliia Ivanovna: The first day that you let out the cow.

Aleksandra Ivanovna: You have to do it on Egoryi Den'.

Iuliia Ivanovna: Depends on the weather.

Q: When is Egoryi Den'?

Aleksandra Ivanovna: Sixth of April . . . May.

Iuliia Ivanovna: Depends on the weather. If there is grass, . . . usually we let them out in the middle of May or at the end of May. On this day, you try to bake a small loaf of bread and give it to the cattle.

The animals must be let out when the weather improves. Before, there was a requirement that an *obkhod* be performed before this took place with prayers and an icon and a piece of bread that would later be fed to the cattle. This was, in theory, to be performed on Egoryi Den', a date that Aleksandra is not even fully sure of. Because there is no longer any professional *pastukh* (cow herder) in the village, this collective obkhod is no longer performed. There is, on the other hand, a sense that "words" must be said for one's own cattle. The knowledge of these words is seen in the above citation as a kind of capital (it was always one person who knew the ritual who would perform it). Letting one's cattle out of the barn in the warm months must happen, and the holiday of Egoryi Den' is mentally marked for this event. Although the event and the ritual that accompanies the event almost never happen on this date, the idea that one's cattle must be protected with special words has not left the village memory. The overlap here leaves aside dates, but retains function.

This point is obvious, but it is a point that will help along the way as I describe how hegemonies confront one another. Often, a cyclical function will be filled without coinciding with the calendar date that the function is normally associated with. In such cases where the function to be fulfilled is a physical one, there is no going around the fact that the function will be performed, regardless of the calendar of reference. If no grass has appeared by Egoryi Den', no farmer would let out the cattle anyway. How, it was implied as I asked about this in Solovyovo, could a farmer be that stupid?

Some holidays fill rather straightforward functions that enter into symbolic realms. The winter holiday of Kreshchenie (Baptism of Christ) is a good illustration. The functions of this holiday appear to be two. First, on this day, healing holy water is collected for use during the year. Second, crosses are placed on thresholds and in charged places of the home for protection from "evil spirits" during the course of the year. The deep darkness of the winter solstice, the period associated with Kreshchenie, is a time when dangerous forces spring from the timescape. The

Orthodox calendar sets the date of Kreshchenie (January 19), but the holiday comes at the end of Sviatki, the agrarian festival in which there is special, sanctioned contact with otherworldly beings, as well as sexual experimentation and play for young people. Kreshchenie, like All Saints' Day that falls after Halloween, appears to "purify" after the dark, joyous, irreverent mess of Sviatki (Propp 1995:142–143).[16] The crosses and holy water of Kreshchenie are used in healing and in rituals of protection. Like the waters on which Mikhail Alekseevich whispers, they lighten the load. Like the safety pins put on an undershirt, they keep dangerous forces from settling on the self. This is how they "purify." The facts that this water is "holy" and that the forces are "evil" do not change their healing function, broadly defined. Sviatki is a festival period that beckons the sun back during the depths of winter darkness (Propp (1995:23–34). Kreshchenie speaks to the functions of healing and protecting, functions that have not been dispensed with over the years and remain attached to the rituals of that day.

But there are other functions that are more elusive than that of the holiday of Kreshchenie, and when that is the case, interaction between the calendars can be correspondingly more complex. Recent studies of the traditional ritual cycle of Russian villagers underline this less material portion of calendrical "needs," which highlight the "constant attention to the magico-religious aspect of living" (T. A. Bernshtam 1988:131–132, cited in Howe (1991:54)). Next, I regard the calendar in light of this part of social function that is not so readily seen.

Coalescing *Svoi*

In each of the perspectives outlined earlier (semiotic, functionalist, research into collective memory and identity), there is the possibility for extensive investigation. Here, I have chosen a measure by which to discuss the social and symbolic relevance of calendrical milestones and to organize my analysis. *What are the social circles that coalesce in the enactment of holidays and commemorative ceremonies?* By posing this question, I tie commemorative ceremonies to their social action and social reproduction. Here, the point is not simply "who we are," but what comes

---

16. Interestingly, "purification" also happened at the time of Ivan Kupalo, the festival of the summer solstice. During Ivan Kupalo, fire was understood to be a purifying element (see Propp 1974:390), unlike during Kreshchenie, roughly at the time of the winter solstice, which happens through ice.

out of the formation of svoi in a given context. Svoi can come in many forms, including from the familial to the village, social to metaphysical, and local to national. Previous chapters have highlighted the power that comes from forming a group. Holidays from different sources do this in different ways. In this sense, outlining *svoi-formations* is a key to understanding the outcomes in the battle of the calendars between different hegemonic orders.

I divide the following section into three parts. In the first section, I examine the summer festivities known as *gulianki* in light of their function of producing and maintaining belongingness at a social level, that is, social *svoi*. Although the realm is a social one, it will be clear that this process of congealing social groups that takes place on this sort of holiday has a magical function as well. Next, I look at the formation of the nation-svoi on the holiday of Victory Day. The year of my fieldwork allowed me to be present for the celebration for the fiftieth anniversary of Victory Day in World War II. Although not the only occasion where the nation-svoi is celebrated and narratives of national belongingness are passed on, it is a vibrant example of both the success and failure of the state at harnessing a sense of national belonging in the context of Solovyovo. Through this example, some of the hazards of this process in the post-Soviet context will be evident. Finally, I focus on the holiday of Troitsa, in which a sense of svoi is formed between the living and the dead—a practice with deep agrarian roots and one that has survived to the present day.

The holidays that I have chosen to discuss were actually celebrated in the village during the time of my research. Such holidays are few. With an aging population, few resources, and a changing technological climate, festivities are rare. But they are certainly not absent, and the ones that have survived the vicissitudes of time offer rich material for investigation. In each of the following examples, I regard the confrontation of different ideological systems, and trace the performance of the holiday in light of the confrontation. I mark the configuration of svoi that the holiday produces, and discuss the implications there with regards to the questions of symbolism and collective memory.

GULIANKI AND IL'IN DEN'

* * *

Along with the backbreaking work in the village at summertime comes a series of holidays in which there is dancing, singing, gang fights, and general rowdiness and irreverence. Such summer gatherings are generally known as *gulian'i* or *gulianki* (from *guliat'*, to walk). They exist today, if less common than in the earlier years of this century. Certain of the gulianki are linked to a given saint's day or to a day that honors prophets or icons, where each parish (prikhod) has its own summer festival day known as *prikhodskii den'*. Although there is an association in name with a given saint or prophet on the parish day of each village, people do not seem to assign any particular character to a village based on the central figure of its prikhodskii den', nor do they appear to identify in any other broader way with that figure. For as long as people can remember, villages have had their local prikhodskii den' in the summer. Solovyovo's is Il'in Den', or Elijah the Prophet's Day. Iurino's is Petrov Den', or St. Peter's Day. The prikhod, as discussed in Chapter 3, is most often made up of a few villages, and the parish holiday is shared by these villages.

In Solovyovo, Il'in Den' is the most festive day of the year. I was present for four celebrations of this day and each time it was a great, lusty party, where people dressed in their finest clothes and danced the night away, momentarily transported from the sweat and dirt of the senokos.

Common to other milestone days in the agrarian calendar, passing through Il'in Den' marks changes in the natural world. I heard several times that after Il'in Den', it is forbidden to swim. In a children's book on the calendar, I read that "After Il'in Den', mosquitoes stop biting" (Nagaev 1991:19). Again, in its purest agrarian sense, a calendrical milestone is marked by a change in the natural world.

Il'in Den' was, historically, one of the important village holidays. According to Matossian (1968:37), it was observed as follows:

> The peasants take a rest from their toil on July 20th,[17] the Day of St. Ilia (Elijah), the protector of cattle. They gather at the church in Staritsa,[18] where cattle are slaughtered and the meat is distributed to the poor and the parish clergy, as well as used for a common dinner of the people. The dinner meat

17. This is the old calendar date. August 2 is the date according to the new calendar.
18. A made-up village. This style is for some reason typical of the ethnographic accounts of the Russian village. A composite village is invented with composite characters such as "Ivan Ivanovich." Chapter and section headings read, for example, "Ivan gets married." I would guess that this follows from the Russian style of ethnography as an offshoot of folklore (and, essentially, national character) studies. The ethnographer is looking for the essential Ivan, one not "messed up" by contradictions.

is boiled in parish vats and laid out on long tables for all the adults of the parish. The priest blesses the beer [*kanunnoe pivo*] that the peasants have brewed especially for this day. Then they drink beer and eat pirogi at a picnic in the meadow.

By this account, the Day of Elijah the Prophet is set in the Orthodox calendar as a holy day with collective feasting and churchgoing. There is an association with honoring the "protector of cattle." In Solovyovo, there are no church services on this day (there being no church). In fact, nothing like the description above occurs in Solovyovo on Elijah's Day, except for the feasting. It is not a day of rest, nor is it a day to honor any religious figure. In that sense, the day is nonsectarian but, I venture, it is far from secular. For now, it is necessary to define the context and function of the summer festivities in general, because it is from its status as a prikhodskoi den' (and not from the specific "meaning" of the religious holiday) that Il'in Den' seems to derive its most immediate function.

Summer Celebrations: *Gulianki*

On the prikhodskoi den', gulianki form in the host village and guests come from other villages in the region to join in the celebrations. In stories that the villagers tell about their youth, the festivities can last for several days and nights. Valentina Ivanovna describes the fun below. Here the prikhodskoi den' of the village being discussed falls on Troitsa, a holiday that functions more generally (and quite importantly) as a day to honor the dead.

> *Valentina Ivanovna:* For example, it's going to be Troitsa, now. Troitsa. We went on Troitsa, [to the] Troitsa prikhod. There . . . my mother is from there, the village Ageevo. There the first day we partied in Ershovo. So there for a day they will party, everyone gets together with everyone else, those who are close, from ten to fifteen kilometers. Only after work they would party. . . . We walked around in the village, with the *khorovod* [dance circle], five or six people. As many girls. And girls in back danced first. . . . Then they . . . would dance the Russkii. They would play on the accordion and dance. Sang songs. . . . And on the second day, in another village. And we went there as guests. For a night or two. . . . Before, there was a parish [festival] like that. It was here, in Solovyovo. We had the Lupinskii prikhod. We had a church there. . . . They rode on horses, even. Oi. It was so good!

Revelry happens in the summer and with revelry comes the establishment of social groups, including marriage groups. This function, more subtle perhaps than it initially appears, is evidenced in many narratives about the summer festivities. Anna Petrovna's story below is a case in point.

GULIANKI AND FORMATION OF MARRIAGE GROUPS

At eighty-seven, Anna Petrovna was still able to recall every important event in Soviet history. In the 1920s, her husband was accused of being a kulak and arrested. In the 1930s, her village was collectivized, and in the 1940s there was war and famine. She never had children and would sometimes eye me, and say "bez detei khudo" (it's bad to live without children). She wore one earring and liked people to think that she knew how to cast spells and curses, and that she was well versed in the art of fortune telling, but there were doubts. One village story had her dancing naked on the senokos in some form of wild summer abandon. Her temper could be ferocious when she was crossed (woe to the woman accused of seducing her husband), and she has alienated many people, but I could not help but be fascinated by her odd humor and her long life experience.[19] By the time I met her, she had a habit of saying that she was waiting to die, which was the point of many of her visits to the house where I lived, that is, to tell anyone who would listen about how she wanted to just climb right into her coffin. The story below was a favorite of hers, a master narrative, perhaps. And it seems to have nothing to do with the spectacular arc of Soviet history that she witnessed.

> *Anna Petrovna:* I always went around in a hat. My older sister—we had five sisters—the older sister in our house was a real seamstress. Real one. She would always make me [clothes]—not in the village way. I stood out. Well, fine. We went out on Troitsa to party. Went out to party and he passes us. I didn't see him. And here, he knew one girl [who was with us]. He asks her, "Whose girls are these? [pointing at us]". . . . The [girl he knew] told him, and he said, "And whose is *that* one?" while pointing at me. She says, "Petr Ivanovich's from Iablochnovo." He says, "Oh, what a pretty girl!" He liked me. So, well. . . . Everyone was walking together. We got to the *gulian'e*, and he suddenly came up to me. I was sitting at the

---

19. She put human waste in the water bucket of the offending woman. It was not discovered until a pot of soup was being cooked.

edge. He leaves [the group and says], "Permit me, dear lady to dance with you?" And I say, "Please."

While I lived at home, he came to me twice. Then he said, "I will come for you on a certain day." Well, so. He arrived.

Q: How did he arrive?

Anna Petrovna: He came by horse in the winter. On a sleigh. My sister was at home in the village. And I had to get a chest, there were two chests, a lot of dresses. Such chests stand over there. There was a little wedding [*svadevka*]. He loved me very much. That one.[20]

Gulianki were, and to a certain degree still are, the place where love happens. I heard many love stories like Anna Petrovna's that were sparked during these summer celebrations. The function of the *gulianka* appears to be one of harnessing that love (and its corollary of lust) for larger purposes, providing, as it does, an occasion for young people of separate parishes to meet and eventually come together in marriage alliances. Recall that although it was possible to marry from inside the village, this occurred infrequently. ("Marrying one's own was rare. It happened, but it was rare.") Given the principle that co-villagers are more or less analogous to family members, this is not a surprising preference. For most of the older villagers, the gulianki that occurred in the villages of the region were the principal means by which young people would meet and marry.

Accompanying the goal of finding young husbands and wives from other villages, an air of sexual permissiveness pervades the gulianki, in spite of explicit village rules of sexual restraint. In his impressive study on nineteenth-century rural Russia, which includes broad insights on the agrarian calendar drawn from the study of hundreds of works by Russian folklorists, Howe (1991), citing Bernshtam (1988) describes some of the sexual permissiveness of these summer frolics, including young

20. On a visit to Solovyovo in summer 2001, I learned that I had seen the last of Anna Petrovna: she was finally unable to take care of herself (until that time, past ninety years of age, she had been cooking, lighting fires in her wood stove, taking care of her many cats and other pets, and gardening), and there were fears she would set fire to her home if left to her own devices. She was sent to a home for the elderly, and I heard that when her nephew visited, she would beg to be allowed back to Solovyovo. She died in 2003.

men throwing girls "on their backs, pull[ing] up their skirts, [and carrying] them out to the [dance] circle in their arms" (Howe 1991:59). Howe concludes that the summer festivities functioned as a time to ensure the reproduction of the village group—not simply about finding one's own love, but *ensuring the continuance of the line at a collective level.* He writes, "[H]arnessing of the collective (reproductive potential) of the newly nubile girls was a condition for reproduction of the communal structure" (Howe 1991:64). The gulianki, with their sexual permissiveness, were the means to this very crucial end. The question of whether this function has been carried into the present will be reserved for later treatment. For now, I note that although there are no such formalized debaucheries on the gulianki in Solovyovo today, there are plenty of tales of sexual exploits of one kind or another. Young people still gather together in the summer evenings—along the shore of the lake and in the stables—raising the eyebrows and the wrath of the village *babki* (old women, grandmothers). As Anna Petrovna curtly put it, referring to the girls who sit next to the boys in the stables: "Those are not girls. They are prostitutes." Her own naked dances are conspicuously lacking in such declarations. What can this sort of contradiction reveal more generally?

AGE GROUP FORMATION: YOUNG DEFINED AGAINST OLD

It cannot be imagined that the sexual permissiveness of the gulianki was ever accepted by the older generations. Even today, young people are watched with eagle eyes, and their behavior discussed in great luscious detail by the babki. It is enough for a young woman to speak to a young man or walk down a path next to him to create a scandal. This became a problem for me, as I was seen as a marriageable *devushka.* Interviews with men were only comfortable in public space. I made my share of mistakes. The biggest was going mushrooming in the forest with an outsider who was visiting from Belozersk. For this, I received a cold shoulder from Iuliia until I had the presence of mind to ask her what I had done. "You'll understand," she sniffed, after chiding me for my impropriety, "when you have a daughter of your own."

In the context of such prohibitions, it would seem odd that these festivals were (and to a certain extent are) occasions for a consistent debauchery. How could such social strictures give way in that summer context? An answer was provided for me when I was complaining to my friend Tamara, who had grown up in a village in the region of Belozersk, about how I couldn't make a move in the village without scrutiny. She put it most succinctly: "It is for the babki to make rules; it is for young people to break them."

At a profound level, this explains the contradiction between established mores and behavior during the gulianki. By keeping their eye on young people, the older generation is fulfilling its function. By breaking the norms, the young people are filling theirs. Howe writes (1991:64):

> [H]arnessing of the collective fertility (reproductive potential) of the newly nubile girls was a condition for the reproduction of the communal structure. Parents could not forbid their daughters to join the khorovod [dance circle], despite the sexual license likely to occur. . . . The acts of young people, no less than of the adults, fulfilled the purpose of life, were essential to establishing the cosmic rhythm necessary to a continuance of the social order, and therefore, had a sacred role.

The gulianki are a period of acceptable disobedience to one's parents with the greater goal, according to Howe's hypothesis, of ensuring the reproduction of the local community, that is, the local social svoi. It is more than disobedience; it is a larger, "sacred" duty. This sort of sanctioned irreverence appears later in the analysis with regards to questions of land fertility, and gives us hints as to the magical function of the establishment of social svoi.[21]

It is important to underline that the summer is a time for generating sexual energy. The autumn, according to villagers and folklorists, is the traditional time for marriages (see Hubbs 1988:79,115; Matossian 1968; Semyonova Tian-Shanskaia 1993).

Love and lust are not the only prominent characteristics of the gulianki. The gulianka has another striking feature that is not unrelated to its function of forming marriage alliances between villages. Along with affairs of the heart comes a sort of informal militarism that tends to reinforce the social category of the prikhod.

---

21. Exemplified in India in the festival of Holi. See McKim Mariott's *The Feast of Love* (in Singer 1966:200–212).

DRAKI AND VILLAGE AGE GROUPS

Q: The fights were between prikhody?

Konstantin Andreevich: It was probably that way. I think that fights were not in the time of the tsar. That all arose in the twenties in the time of the Soviet power. By the stories of my father, this tendency of hooliganism was in the twenties.

Draki, or gang fights between the young men of separate prikhody, occurred throughout the years of this century despite attempts at suppressing them by local authorities. It was, as Konstantin Andreevich put it above, a "tendency toward hooliganism" (which, as far as ethnographic accounts go, appears to have preceded the time of Soviet power) that has been a regular feature of village social life.

As a rule, young men from one parish show up in another parish, often during a gulianka. There is some kind of challenge and a fight begins.[22] I was told several times that accordion music would accompany the fights (meanwhile, touching the accordionist was strictly off limits). Some men spoke of the days of their youthful fights with nostalgia. Pyotr Smirnov, in particular, spoke glowingly about the exploits of himself and his father ("Before, my father was the ottoman [gang leader]"), and how his village of Myshino proved, again and again, to be the strongest. To most, however, the theme was not very amusing. In extreme cases, lives were lost in these shows of village rivalry.

Such draki diminished over the years, but did not end completely. Every year I was in the village for Il'in Den', there were fights of varying degrees of seriousness and violence (and always instigated by "outsider" boys from the prikhod of Iurino). One year while I was there, women came out in the middle of the night and grabbed the wooden poles that the young men were bashing each other with. A contemporary of mine in Solovyovo instigated a fight in his youth that sent a local boy to the hospital with knife wounds. Such fights are expected to continue in the years to come.

Q: And are there [such fights] today?

Mikhail Alekseevich: They happen, they happen! . . . [Now the boys] are little. . . . They'll grow to age sixteen and they'll fight.

22. See Ries (1997:65–66) for a discussion of urban drinking and brawling.

Alliances would form between prikhody and, over the course of the summer; fights would break out between "enemies" that shifted from village to village. In spite of their similarity to organized aggression, it appears that the fights did not take place for reasons of personal vendetta. After the fighting, the boys would generally remain friends. In fact, the fighting appears almost formal; it is simply what one does when one arrives at the appropriate age. It is linked, that is, to an age group activity that sets prikhod against prikhod.

Indeed, with their many differences with regard to detail, the fights have in common a sense of rallying around one's own (svoi). They provide a clear example of prikhody being defined against each other. Here, Anna Grigorievna speaks of fighting in order to protect "one's own":

> *Anna Grigorievna:* And they chase them out. Chase them out into the wheat. Drive them out. Or drive them out into the forest. They run away.
>
> *Q:* And they didn't beat the girls?
>
> *Anna Grigorievna:* If you are going to participate, they'll beat you.
>
> *Q:* The guys?
>
> *Anna Grigorievna:* Yes! If you jump in for your own, you will fall there where they are and they beat you. I'll speak for myself. I was really feisty. From my village. . . . They beat my guy and all at once they threw him down. They beat him there on the earth. They all run. I say, "Run!" He tore himself away and ran. I was strong; so I run and they are beating him with a stick. . . . I was sorry for ours. They were from my village, so. They knocked him down. Could've killed him.

The category of the prikhod is reified further through these fights when one looks at the perceived "cause" of the disputes. Although not exclusively, the draki often were sparked during the gulianki. When I asked several people about why this was the case, I was told that this was "because of the girls." The fights would take place, and the winners would "get to dance with the girls." With her pre-Revolutionary material, Bernshtam confirmed this rivalry in the citation above ("the lads of different villages fought over the girls" [Bernshtam 1988:237 in Howe 1991:59]). It was not, of course, only dancing at stake. The foreign (chuzhie) guys were coming to find wives, and this was dealt with violently at times.

Anna Grigorievna: That one was from Iurino. That big house where
Fedia I—lives now. There was a dekulakized [*raskulachen*] man. That was
Fedia P—. They were all sent away and there [in the camps] they died.
They had five daughters and one son. And so this one from Iurino shot
him point blank. These ones from Iurino would come here. They would
arrive here to fight. This guy only wanted to get married, and his
betrothed was already here. Had arrived already. The girl had come to
guliat'. So there, they shot him to death. That's how they fought with the
guys from Iurino. And they came on Bogoslov and shot him. Lisa, the
guy's sister told me. Five girls, [the parents] had, and one son.

The category of gang allegiances thus coincided with the category of marriage alliances. Where preferred mates came from outside of the prikhod,
so did battles between the young men of separate prikhody, with the
stated cause of these battles being "the girls."

It is important to note that although there is no longer a church in the
area, and most of the villagers did not grow up going to church with any
regularity, the prikhod still shows up as a social category—a local svoi—
in the context of these fights and in the stated preference for mates outside of the prikhod. Memory happens here at the level of social action, if
not in the presence of the church structure that originally defined the social category in question. The gulianki are the site of that memory.

On these occasions for drink, lust, and battle, a further current can be
identified: The gulianki serve as a socially sanctioned occasion for irreverence. In them, explicit rules of social life are inverted, and official hierarchy is treated with disrespect. As I have already commented, sexual
unions are permitted in spite of the disapproval of parents; dangerous
fighting is not assuaged. Besides sex and war, the gulianka is, in this way,
made of many separate acts of thumbing one's nose at authority. And this
also appears to have a "sacred role."

Irreverence

Muza Mikhailovna: It was a splendid place. Lakes, such brilliance. The
water shines blue. And the river was much wider then. Deeper and wider.
From this side of the river, there is the forest; and there, from our side were
fields and meadows. Flowers all around. And there, the young people got
together. From Guliaevo, there now, Ivanovo, Beryozovo. From Guliaevo
to Solovyovo. And from Ergovskii region. The guys with accordions and,

next to them, the girls sang *chastushki* [rhymed verses]. . . . The girls and guys were together. They hang out all night. Laughing in uproars. Totally laughing.

If a first function of the summer gulianka is to provide an opportunity for young men and women of different villages to meet and form marriage alliances (reinforcing the marriage categories through the enactment of gang fights), a second function is to provide occasions for laughter, and more generally, irreverence. During the gulianki, young women are irreverent to young men (and vice versa); young people are irreverent to parents, to the local authorities, and to ideas of the ideological establishment. I look at two sides of this irreverence with regards to gulianki in general: First, the content of the songs and chastushki sung on the occasion of the festivities, and second, the way that the gulianki acted (whether consciously or unconsciously) as a form of resistance against outsider control of villagers. In that sense, the gulianki form not only a reproductive svoi, but a "village" svoi. They create and reify intimate and local social categories.

THE *CHASTUSHKA:* SEXUAL AND POLITICAL OBSCENITIES

The chastushka, a sung rhyme of four lines and often improvised, has a noble history in the annals of Russian studies. In countless volumes, these fragments of oral tradition are recorded for posterity (although often cleaned up considerably when immortalized). They come in tones that range from the sentimental to the blasphemous. They address themes of love, war, sex, and politics. In one local story, a chastushka that fell on the wrong ears caused the singer to be sent to the camps. In the context of the problem of calendrical timescapes and battling hegemonies, the chastushka plays an important role: If the gulianki are, in part, occasions for irreverence, the chastushka is one of the principal means of being irreverent.

In the stories of Solovyovo, young men and women would gather together on summer nights to party, trickling in from the different houses in the village. Some would walk from other villages; others would be staying with relatives. Traditionally, the gatherings were outdoors, including in front of people's houses, at the lake shore, and out in the fields.

Music begins, often just a few simple accordion chords, and people step up to dance and to sing. During the gulianka, one singer is featured at a time. She emerges from the crowd and dances, circling the area, and

then stops in the center of the group and sings a chastushka, often gesturing along with the words to one person in particular. Another singer
takes a turn. Sometimes there is back-and-forth between two singers,
who are working the crowd and trying to score with the better song.
There are well-known chastushki that appear all over Russia and ones
that are improvised. The performance of the chastushka is full of stomp-
ing, howls, and squeals of laughter. A really good chastushka can make
a grown man—a soldier, sailor, or convict—blush.

In the chastushki, humor emerges as the most powerful weapon with
which young people face the battle of the sexes. Women, in particular,
wield sharp tongues in the gulianki,[23] and it is through irreverent humor
that barbs are cast toward men. From the benign and ridiculous to the
patently obscene, a well-performed chastushka brings howls of laughter.
In one well-known chastushka, the boyfriend makes creative use of domestic pets to improve his knowledge of romantic matters (and I do believe this is the toned-down version):

> My sweet one doesn't kiss, but says, "Later, later!" He climbs up onto the
> stove, and practices with the cat![24]

The themes of chastushki often included incredibly creative descriptions
of the powers and perils of male and female sexual organs. They bring
farm animals into the mix. Always, they bring light-hearted laughter.[25]

Obscene songs are certainly not exclusive to the farmers of Russia. In
fact, there are certain regularities of genre in this regard, with the rites of
many ancient agrarians (Propp 1995:129–130). The obscenities and "inversions" of established norms of modesty appear to be part of a broader
phenomenon. Throughout *Russkie Agrarnye Prazdniki* (1963), Propp argues that the laughter one sees during solemn occasions (mock murders

---

23. I witnessed far more biting humor among women, but more investigation would be
required to determine if this is generally the case. Anecdotally, it seemed to me that women
bear the brunt of the brutality of village life. Violence against women is a topic of great
importance, and one that cannot be dealt with in the context of this book. I will note that
the narratives that I gathered on the subject are horrifyingly wide-ranging and diverse.

24. "Menia milyi ne tseluet/ Govorit: 'Potom, potom!'/ Zabiraetsia na pechku/ Prak-
tikuetsia s kotom!"

25. These chastushi were difficult to record properly, and it was awkward to ask for explanations out of the context of the gulianki. It was certainly not for lack of trying, and I
am hoping that further research will be possible.

and burials in several of the holidays) during the rural year, mark regulatory practices regarding the land's fertility. Laughter, in other words, calls life into being:

> The concept of the reproduction of life in nature was connected with rituals of an erotic and phallic character. . . . [T]he sexual freedom and jokes which were canonized by custom . . . [and] accompanied and reinforced the laughter, and this in turn reinforced its magical influence on the fertility of the earth (Propp 1974:405).

Irreverence regarding sex and relations between the sexes is a prominent theme in the chastushki. Such inversions of explicit mores regarding chastity and modesty appear to resonate with the overall tone of the gulianki.

Sex is certainly not the only taboo to be treated in these songs. As the argument goes, fertility is urged through the creation of laughter. This laughter is not only merriment, it is a type of inversion in which respected societal norms and hierarchies are turned upside-down.[26] The laughter of the chastushki also appears to be concerned with societal norms in a broader sense. Certainly this pattern is evidenced in Solovyovo. The chastushki deal with love and lust, but also with power and, along the way, with a very particular kind of self-definition.

Propp gives an example of an ancient rite in the village that hints at the political side of irreverence. Here he writes about one rite of Sviatki, the inversion festival par excellence in rural traditions. In this rite of "social satire," a "game" is played where marriage is simulated with the feudal lord, or barin (1995:131). Although this rite in which the local barin is mocked and a communal reproductive act is simulated no longer exists in the village, the crux of the matter—that opposing oneself to hierarchical outsiders gives form to a local svoi with reproductive powers—appears to endure. Chastushki of a political nature certainly do.

Given its status as a truly popular genre, it is not surprising that someone got the idea that chastushki could be used to convey political messages. Indeed, chastushki were introduced during the Revolutionary years by "shock brigades" of poets and musicians as part of an effort to create rural support for the Communist Party and its programs. Appearing be-

---

26. See Likhachov and Panchenko (1976) for a look at the role of humor as source of social inversion.

low are a few chastushki dated around 1930 from *Umnozhai urozhai: Kolkhoznye pesni i chastushki* (von Geldern and Stites 1995:142).

> Hey, Fiodor and Malania/ And Avotia and Pakhom!/ Let's strike up a merry song/ About the sowing season!

> Hey you, Vania, best stretch out/ That accordion past your ears!

> Why should you be sowing from/ Your grandpa's basket in these years!

> Take a gander in the barn—/ Ain't it mighty nifty?/ How that newfangled machine/ Sorts the grain so swiftly!

Although these translations clearly cannot render the authors' (no-doubt) energetic attempts at getting the genre right, they do give a sense of the inappropriateness of using such a genre to summon people to establishment views. The farmer is supposed to realize how great a thing mechanization is, and be (accordingly) grateful for the Party's role in it. On the other hand, cozying up to authority is perfectly out of character for this genre and would be roughly the equivalent of using American rap to get people to vote Republican. More typical of the chastushka genre is the following from the 1930s:

> This hammer, this sickle—/ There is our Soviet Emblem!/ If you want to, reap!/ And if you want to, forge!/ Anyway, you'll get dick (or "Get it up your—")![27]

And when Solovyovo sings of the powers that be, it sings in equally irreverent—and knowing—tones.

> I went into the kolkhoz/ With a new little skirt!/ I left the kolkhoz/ With a naked little ass![28]

The *kolkhoz* was certainly not a broadly popular development in the village of Solovyovo and the *chastushka* was a way of airing this dissent.

---

27. "Eto molot, eto serp/ Vot on nash sovetskii gerb!/ Khochesh'—zhni, a khochesh'—kui/ Vse ravno poluchish' khui!"

28. "V kolkhoz poshla/ Iubka novinkaia! Iz kholkhoza poshla/Zhopa golen'kaia!" Or in its variant form: "Kogda v kolkhoz poshla iubka novaia/ Iz kolkhoza poshla/ zhopka golaia!" When I went into the kolkhoz/ [There was] a new skirt/ When I left the kolkhoz/ [I had a] naked little ass!

Valentina Ivanovna, who recorded the above *chastushka* (which showed up in several variants), offered the following commentary by way of explanation:

> *Valentina Ivanovna:* It's true that people didn't want to go into the kolkhoz. Nobody. And then, we. . . . [H]ad the war not come, without the kolkhoz we would have lived better. Each person had everything on their own. Everyone had everything on his own, horse, cow—before the kolkhoz. Everyone had everything on his own.

When the kolkhoz came to Solovyovo, Valentina Ivanovna told me how the villagers petitioned against it—signing their names in the space of a circle so no one could know who had signed first. The chastushka was, politically speaking, an opportunity to speak one's mind in the village context. It is used in this way today. Valentina Ivanova penned the following:

> *Valentina Ivanovna:* Yeltsin sits on a birch tree/ Chernomyrdin on a pine!/ To what, did [such mother—ers]; Reduce Russia?[29]

In the chastushki, no theme is sacred, not even the most dangerous political theme. The following chastushka was recorded in my notes from the village, but was known all over Russia:

> Guelder rose, guelder rose!/ Stalin has no underwear!/ Rykov has them!/ As did Peter the Great![30]

The danger of these themes did not silence the songs. In fact, in the context of the gulianki, the "naked asses" and underwear-less Stalin of the chastushka were not only political commentaries that used obscenities to underline their points. I would argue that the chastushki were and are a way of distancing the village and its local order from the center of power. In them, there is a sense of "we the villagers" being formed in opposition to political outsiders. In the following chastushka, the "naked ass" returns along with an important reference to the attempts that the state had made to introduce "culture."

29. "Sidit Eltsin na bereze/ Chernomyrdin na eli!/ Do chego, [takie materi]/ Rossiiu doveli?"
30. "Kalina, kalina!/ Net portkov u Stalina!/ Est' portki u Rykova!/I to Petra Velikova!"

Culture was wanted!; Trousers were sold!; I was left naked-assed; But culture was created![31]

Let it never be said that the villager is incapable of ironic abstraction.[32] Aside from voicing discontent, and doing so with a certain degree of subtlety (despite the naked asses popping up everywhere), the level of irony in chastushki such as the one above appears to manifest a deeper sentiment directed to the powers at large: Leave us alone. The following incident that took place in one of the local clubhouses underlines this sentiment.

Q: Is it sometimes easier to sing a chastushka than say something directly?

Valentina Ivanovna: Yes, yes, yes. Of course. Before, everyone sang these kinds of ulcerous songs.

Q: When it was forbidden to say things directly?

Valentina Ivanovna: Yes! And sang songs. Created chastushki. . . . Sang them. I remember these swearing songs. It was forbidden, but they already started to stop these songs. We were in the forest, at a [wood] preparation site. . . . Well, the guys from Pendinskii. Vaska. And we gathered in the club there. Gathered and well. . . . There, that one went to dance. And they [sang] swearing songs. And one woman was going around, and this one woman had five or six children and no husband. And they stand there, and before people weren't dressed [well] and were stopped [arrested] for such songs. . . . He sang this song about her. A policeman grabbed him, and she [said], "Don't touch him!" They started to stop [arrests for the singing of such songs] . . .

Galina Alekseevna: So that they wouldn't sing such . . . songs. So that they would be singing cultured songs.

31. "Zakhotelosia kul'tury/ Pantalony prodala!/ Golozhopaia ostalas'/[No] kul'turu navela!"
32. As Pipes indeed comes quite close to saying in *Russia Under the Old Regime:* "The peasant of old regime Russia had what anthropologists like Levy-Bruhl used to call a 'primitive mind', an outstanding quality of which is an inability to think abstractly" (1974:157). Although arguing this for the purpose of praising the villagers' down-to-earth qualities, it clearly reinforces the (objectionable) stereotype of the rural Russian as an irrational and timeless innocent. See Figes (1996:98) for a similar critique of Pipe's view. Also, see Fabian's *Time and the Other* (1983) for an overview of how the social sciences have fixed "primitive" others in a forever-past.

The local villagers make fun of a woman without a husband and that woman defends the villagers against the police. In the logic of this story, outside authorities are attempting to bring "culture" to the village —civilizing the villagers by handing them new "genteel" norms where one does not sing "ulcerous" songs to unwed mothers. In this "civilized" world, one arrests such singers. In the telling of the story, the village doesn't want this type of civilizing, thank you very much.

There is more to the political side of the gulianki, with regard to direct attempts by the Soviets to control village behavior. The memory inscribed in the calendar is not only located in the imagination. It is also located in "real" space. The presence in villages of Dom Kul'tury or Houses of Culture is a testimony of the Soviet efforts at controlling village action by attempting to gather villagers into controlled space. Gulianki were traditionally outdoors and irreverent. They now exist in and out of the peripheries of local village Houses of Culture. In the next section, I examine briefly the space of the clubhouse, and the way politics were played out there.

IRREVERENCE AND THE STATE: THE CLUBHOUSE

Attempts at taming and civilizing had a specific site in the village context. The clubhouse was brought into existence as a place where villagers could get culture of a specific sort. In the clubhouses, professional kul'trabotniki (culture workers) were charged with planning activities in the remote village areas, including celebrations of the new Soviet holidays, dances, plays, "agitation" of Soviet ideals and atheism, and, importantly, keeping watch over the successes and failures of the kolkhoz. In villages, the clubhouse was the locus of all these activities, from light-hearted dances, to admonitions for poor kolkhoz returns. A cheap, easy, symbolically poignant way of making a clubhouse was to simply lop the cupola off the top of a church, take out the icons, give the whole thing a good paint job, and add some posters about the value of labor and perhaps a krasnyi ugolok—a "holy corner" dedicated to party slogans and images. The church, the reiner-in of godly powers and power provider from otherworldly planes was transformed into the local house of imported Soviet culture.[33]

33. By contrast, for a look at the resacralization of a Soviet space in post-Soviet Russia, see the example of Moscow's Christ the Savior Church in Smith (1997).

Gulianki were to take place in the clubhouse. Dances and songs were to be transformed to citified ones. Religious holidays were to be left aside and state holidays honored. The reasoning for putting such celebrations into controlled space was not without a certain real logic, given the "hooliganism" of the gulianki. Mikhail Alekseevich speaks of this rationale and how he responded to it as a culture worker.

> [So that there wouldn't be] murders, and, finally, [other] unpleasantries. For that reason, so that it would be easier and that these things wouldn't happen, they wouldn't let the clubs open on religious holidays. Let them be outside! Less responsibility. They didn't let us—the club workers—open the clubs. But, to the degree that I was convinced that there was nowhere else to go—the church was closed—I opened it. Didn't listen to the predsedatel' of the sel'sovet. . . . They're going to celebrate anyway.

If the purpose of the clubhouse is, one way or another, to control festivities, Mikhail Alekseevich was dutiful in opening up the clubhouse and having the crowds come in and not beat up on each other. On the other hand, by doing so on the day of religious festivals (and by this he means *prikhodskie dni*), he is continuing to reinforce their celebration. Even with the most loyal intentions as a culture worker, Mikhail Alekseevich was aiding and abetting the enemy timescape.

There was much to battle. The clubhouse, it appears from narratives, was not seen to be a very fun place to hold a gulianka.

> *Valentina Ivanovna:* We would gather *besedy* [lit: discussions; here, gatherings], if we were bored. Not like now, there in the club. Who wants to go to the club? You have to have music. We had the music [called] *italianka,* well, the accordion. There was the accordion. We gather together and leave the village [and go to the] bank of the lake. In the village[s] Panevo, Styopanovo, Konevo, Krylovo, we had—there were many young people. . . . [W]e had no clubs. If at some time we needed to make an evening party, we got together. . . . There were these poor women. [One of them] lives alone. Her husband died. She had three or four children. There, we bring to her . . . gather together, bake pies there. . . . In the summer, we left and went onto the bank [of the lake] . . . in Krylovo. The bank was beautiful, good. . . . There we played, danced [*pliasat'*, rural style dancing], with not just one accordion[, but rather] a few. How it was joyous!

Even Antonina Timofeevna, speaking of that ideal other planet (from which the aliens have come to investigate), told me that on their own planet, the aliens do, in fact, sing, and celebrate holidays. But they have no clubhouse.

So far, the gulianka has been described as a summer festival that involves singing, dancing, sexual play, finding marriage partners, drunkenness, and gang fighting. Socially speaking, it provides a forum for forming marriage alliances, and, in its tone of irreverence and in its resistance to being "tamed" by the clubhouse, it reifies a local village svoi against external authorities. In both cases, it forms categories of svoi that are both local and intimate.

Is it possible that political obscenities have something to do with sexual obscenities? I have already hypothesized a link between the two. On the occasion of the gulianki, prikhod is set against prikhod, creating an occasion for local self-definition ("this is us"), and by doing so allowing exogamous unions. Youths are set against parents, and this opposition ensures reproduction. Girls are set against boys, and the obscenity of the remarks between them encourages, according to Propp (1995), fertility of the land. And what of political obscenities? Surely, they set outsiders with power against the local svoi. Is it possible that the common thread, that of the creation of a local communal svoi, is the most powerful thread that runs through the days of the calendar? Does the political here become intimate, such that by making a local svoi, a local social unit is solidified, reified, and given form? Does this bring otherworldly, life-producing powers in?

IL'IN DEN'

In the summer of 1996, there was no doubting that the Zh— family's haystacks were bigger than the Belovs'. When I visited them one day on the strip of land where they were working, their haystacks could have towered over the ones that we had completed earlier in the afternoon. Ivan Nikolaevich, in his sixties, stood atop the enormous stack and directed operations. His grandson was lifting the hay with a pitchfork three times his height; daughters, working in their bikinis, were hauling hay from smaller stacks toward the larger ones; granddaughters raked loose hay into small piles, making sure none was lost. As they labored in the hot sun, the children and grandchildren goofed around with their patriarch; teased him as he bragged to me from atop the haystack that they had finished all their work already ("And you mean you haven't?" "He's deceiving you! Ivan Nikolaevich! We're going to leave you up there if you don't start behaving!").

It was no surprise that their stacks were bigger and better than ours. Ivan Nikolaevich Zh— and his wife Anna Alekseevna had many guests with them that summer. Sixteen people were sleeping under their roof— some in the dark, breezy attic area, and many others on the floor. As Ivan Nikolaevich said to me one day as he drove me home from the senokos on his wagon, "The house is filled with my daughters and my grandchildren. They came to help with the senokos. Here, there is enough meat and milk and vegetables for everyone. You can't say the same in the city."

On and off, the Belovs do have many helpers: a niece came with her husband from Belozersk; there was a sister in her seventies (who would tell me about how, during the war, the women had taken the place of horses at the time of the potato planting); another cousin and his son; their son, Sasha; and me. But it was never the same as with the Zh— family. The Belovs struggled with distant, bad pieces of land (caused by a combination of their lack of assertiveness and a village habit of leaving the worst parcels of land to families that did not work exclusively for the kolkhoz); they are physically smaller than most of the other villagers; and, worst of all, they have no large family to help. The Zh— family finished its work on the senokos a couple of weeks before the Belovs.

The summer work is family and extended family work. Labor is shared, and the fruits of labor are distributed out into the family line. In this way, potatoes from Solovyovo may head for nearby towns and cities such as Belozersk and Cherepovets, but also to distant cities and even countries: Petrozovodsk, Murmansk, Tver', Sakhalin Island, St. Petersburg, Moscow, Moldova, Latvia. On Il'in Den', that very fruitful family line becomes secondary to the village (and what used to be the parish) collective. The gulianka on Il'in Den' expands the svoi-formation of focus from a lineal/familial one to a suprafamilial one.

The trajectory of the holiday reflects the shift. Celebrating begins in the home, and ends in a collective gulianka that includes all members of the local community, visiting friends and relatives, and "outsiders" from other prikhody. The next section provides a general description of the holiday festivities.

WHAT'S IN A DAY?

According to Konstantin Andreevich, Il'in Den' is supposed to mark the end of the period of the senokos. But, as he told me in 1996, "With the weather the way it's been this year, it's as if it just began." Depending on how the senokos is going that year, the day will be more relaxed than a regular day. In the first year I celebrated with the village, the senokos was going rather well and the day was nearly free of farm work. Seven people were staying with us. Men fished and took it easy, and women cooked and gossiped. The next year was a much worse one overall, and we spent nearly the whole day in the fields. So did many other villagers, since the day was bright and hot and fully suited to senokos labor.

Working on religious holidays is, according to Orthodoxy, forbidden, but that prohibition was not observed by anyone, as far as I could tell. The pragmatics of the summer of 1996, in particular, meant that not a single workday could be lost. Here the calendar asserts that the pragmatic concerns come before any other factor. On the other hand, there is also a prohibition against taking baths in the bathhouse on religious holidays, and this one was fairly strictly observed. Some children would not go swimming on the day, telling me "it is forbidden on a holiday." Others swam. Generally, it was commented, as I remarked above, that summer swimming should end after Il'in Den', and that if a person swims after the holiday, he can get sick.

There is a looseness in attitude, in other words, regarding Orthodox prohibitions. Although certain acts are known to be forbidden, if they conflict with overriding pragmatic concerns of farming, they will be ignored. On the other hand, there is the sense that Il'in Den' is a landmark date, and that changes in the natural world and the human relation to it should shift, accordingly, after having passed through the day. This is a feature of the agrarian calendar and it is in evidence today.

In the early evening of this holiday, after the cow is milked and all the animals fed and watered, the table is set with the finest foods the farmer has. Iuliia and I would often speculate on menus for days before working out the exact content of the Il'in Den' feast; I remember that the fate of one kohlrabi plant was determined months in advance of one particular Il'in Den'. Traditional salads of fresh vegetables, fresh fish, cheese, pies and cakes, cold soups, and jars of jam are brought to the table, as well as berry drinks, and vodka and other spirits. The visitors—friends and relatives—gather around the table in their nicest clothes and are seated. The dinner begins with toasts to the company, the hostess, and any poetic theme anyone can come up with. People drink and then eat; drink and eat. An hour or two is spent this way.

At some point, music begins wafting into the house from outdoors.

This marks the next phase in the celebration, where individual families start drifting outside into their yards. It is from within the boundaries of individual family yards that music is first created. Someone starts playing the accordion or balalaika, and people chime in with chastushki. Later in the evening, people will head over to the clubhouse, but in the fresh early evening air, the celebration is under way in family yards.

The village of Solovyovo is very small. In the early evening of Il'in Den', it rings with these pockets of music. Screeching accordions, feminine whoops, song howls, and laughter. Soon, these private celebrations expand into collective ones.

Indeed, in the next phase of the evening, people walk from yard to yard, visiting each other. After dinner on my first year there (1995), Ivan Nikolaevich was sitting on a bench in front of his house with all of his daughters. The daughters are all city women and were wearing urban-style dresses and heels. Despite this level of sophistication, they all knew the chastushki and would sing them out, inviting me to sit with them and chew on *semechki* (sunflower seeds) and join in the laughter. The next year (1996) the singing began, again, on the street. This time it was in front of the S—'s large yard; people had come out to honor the bride and groom who were visiting from Belozersk. There was also singing in front of other yards. At this phase of the celebrations, crowds form. Larger movement begins.

The trajectory of the holiday celebration thus begins in the family home and goes to the outside yard. People linger there with their songs and then begin movement from house to house. The next phase brings them all together in collective space. Eventually, it is time to go to the club and families head in that direction. In 1995, Seriozha from Moscow—the husband of a young woman who had spent all her summers with her grandmother in the village—began walking with his guitar toward the club, and a crowd of children and in-laws followed him. He had played in a band in Moscow and was determined to do some performing for the village in the evening. The next year, another villager walked with his accordion to the clubhouse. Walking and playing is reminiscent of the traditional gulianki. Here, however, the goal is to gather in an inside space: the clubhouse.

Once in the clubhouse, people begin their celebrations shyly. In the first few Il'in Den' holidays that I spent in the village, Mikhail Alekseevich would set up chairs around the periphery of the large room in the clubhouse where there is a stage, and where he and his wife used to put together plays that demonstrated the virtues of atheism. People would come and sit in chairs, family by family. Accordion music would begin, but it always seemed to take a while to stir things up. As things slowly would get going, one woman at a time would go before the crowd, pulling out her finest chastushki from girlhood. These chastushki are not sung only by *devushki* (young women), but by the matrons of the village. If the official composition of the village is aged, this summer collective mixes young and old. It is clear, however, who is really in charge. Older women who had once gone to gulianki to flirt with their favorite local boys, now assert their place in the collective with chastushki such as the following:

They say that I'm an old crone/ But I don't believe it!/ Well, what kind of crone am I/ If I can still shake it like this?[34]

These older women are no longer the vessels for reproductive force that they once were, in the sense that they are no longer childbearers. But the force of their voice is considerable. They are the reigning matriarchs of oral tradition; through the power of rhyme and irreverent laughter, they carry forward the svoi-forming function. It is for them, it appears, to carry not only the memory of these rhymes, but the memory of self-definition that is produced during the gulianki.

In a videotape that Serezha made of the festivities in 1995, the evening progresses as follows. First, people sit soberly against walls decked with posters honoring veterans of World War II. I sit in the corner next to Andrei, and try to get her tape recorder to work. In the next scene, there is dancing by one individual woman, then another woman, and another. In a video flash, the floor is full of people. Taped music of Russian disco comes on and the babushki who had been doing the traditional dance movements try out the citified ones. By now, the floor is full of young and old, men and women. People are dancing alone and in pairs; sometimes in larger circles.

For hours, there is a subtle battle of music inscribed on that videotape. The accordion has a large and active following. Chastushki contests begin and the dancing grows more expressive and wild. Some of the young people are quite good at performing, although one granddaughter who is exceptionally good seems to be performing in irony. Russian disco gets

34. "Govoriat chto ia starukha/ A mne ne veritsia!/ Nu kakaia ia starukha?/ Vo mne vse shevelitsia!"

its share of followers, and songs like "Russian Vodka (What Did You Conjure Up?)" have people dancing in a large circle with whoops toward featured dancers in the center. Even the anthropologist is in this circle. Anna Petrovna grabs her shirt as she dances by, and whispers something into her ear.

Serezha from Moscow, still armed with his guitar, elbows his way into the battle for musical dominance. He sings well-known favorites (such as "Conductor, Don't Hurry!"), but jazzes them up so the babushki have trouble singing along. Katia makes an earnest attempt, as does another woman who spends only summers here. These are the two local queens of song. In front of the camera, they have their hands on Seriozha's shoulders and sing out as loudly as they can—which is very loud.

Disco, accordion, and guitar are all instruments of revelry. The clubhouse contains this revelry, but not rigidly. People filter in and out. Men gather on the porch to drink, and other groups start playing music outside of the large room where all the activity takes place. Men play pool in the pool area. Children on the verge of puberty, all friends still, zip in and out of the main room. Some girl likes some boy. There is much to discuss, in that regard.

In my first Il'in Den', a crowd of guys showed up from Iurino, which historically had its own church and its own prikhodskoi den'. The guys looked somewhat hostile, but tempers were eased somehow. Iurino was, of course, one of Solovyovo's traditional rivals. While I lived in Solovyovo, Iurino still felt like a foreign place, where the dogs are fiercer, the women steal husbands, and the men beat their wives with more vigor. It appeared that this is what one thinks of the familiarly foreign.

In short, the festivities continued all night long. There is movement in and out of the clubhouse for the entire evening. The movement reaches a certain pitch and frenzy. When the sun finally sets around 11 p.m., people go home, to each other's homes to continue drinking and conversation, down to the river to make a bonfire, or down to the stables in pairs to find love, perhaps.

Summary of Gulianki and Il'in Den'

Il'in Den' is a holiday that was originally set by the Orthodox calendar, but the sacredness of this day appears to have no affiliation with Church meanings. Although historically it had its own traditional celebration in the village, one that is linked to honoring the protector of cattle and distributing meat to the poor, this function is not fulfilled today.

On the other hand, Il'in Den' has been and continues to be the prikhodskoi den' of the village of Solovyovo. The prikhodskie dni functioned historically as part of a broader set of summer celebrations in which young people would meet and eventually marry. Furthermore, there was a magical side to this function: Through the summer gulianki, marriage groups were reified along with local village communities through the production of svoi-groups. Producing a svoi-formation does not only create a social group, but attracts otherworldly powers of fertility in its making. As part of this process, sexual and political obscenities were used to define the local group, and generate fertility. Sexual and political self-definition are therefore part of a broader process of generating local power, of strengthening and furthering the village rod.

In this century, local culture workers were charged with the task of ideological education, where part of that education was the introduction of new Soviet holidays, and another part was to bring the celebrations into a space where they could be directed by authorities. Clearly, Il'in Den' was not only a Christian holiday, but part of a broader range of summer agrarian holidays with a crucial task: that of fertilizing the community and on the way, the land. In this sense, the survival of Il'in Den' is a failure on the part of the re-education process, as the holiday was not forgotten. On the other hand, the culture workers succeeded in reining the celebration in to the space of the clubhouse.[35] Where there is a Soviet failure in the timescape, there is a Soviet victory over space. Which part of this function carries on in the celebration today? Although it cannot be said that the first function of this holiday—to create sexual unions that are neatly matched between prikhody—survives today in full force, the air of sexual permissiveness and irreverence has survived. There is still the creation on this day of a larger communal svoi, one of the very few occasions in the village year on which this happens. In this communal svoi, there is no agreement over the favorite style of celebration (Seriozha's guitar or Ivan Nikolaevich's accordion), but the night is celebrated

35. However, in summer 2001, the outside singing and dancing took a much larger part of the celebrations than it had in earlier years. There was a virtuoso of a chastushka/pliaska performance with Katia Smirnov and a 70-year-old visitor from Guliaevo, where men's and women's clothes were exchanged, and horses were simulated and sex was nearly simulated. Upon reaching the clubhouse, and seeing the still-empty room with chairs lined up against the wall, Katia said, "Let's go back on the street. Something about the air here. You can't really sing. You need to sing outside, under the sky." So the fate of the space of Il'in Den', it appears, has not been resolved as of yet.

in a spirit of shared revelry. The sexual and political obscenities with their broader magical functions survive intact.

I have suggested (with the help of Propp, Howe, and Bernshtam) that on the summer gulianki, a social svoi is formed—the very forming of which brings in magical powers. The politics of the gulianki are interesting, and must be regarded with a careful eye. It appears that the obscene, irreverent chastushki that are such a vivid part of the gulianki serve as a way to voice resistance against outside powers. Surely this is the case. But it seems important to note that, by the overall logic of the gulianka, it *is not the resistance to the outside world but the self-formation that is of central importance.* It is this *self-definition* that bears a crucial function. The resistance, it appears, is at least somewhat incidental to this most serious function, one that, by the evidence in Solovyovo, survives to the present.

VICTORY DAY AND STATE REMEMBRANCE DAYS
* * *
The War Comes to Solovyovo: Two Voices

> *Valentina Ivanovna:* I remember how the war started. I was born in 1923. The war began on the twenty-second of June. I remember on the second day, we went to Konevo to party. I remember it as if it were today. All of a sudden, the guys were partying and men arrived for them on horses. From here, from Solovyovo. They brought them notification. "Go! The war has begun!" Everything was over. All of our gulianki. Of course, everyone went from house to house saying, "The war has begun." There, from the twenty-second of June, the war began for us.

> *Larisa Andreevna:* The war happened. Those whom we went out with were sent to the war. Not one returned . . .

> We waited. We waited and they wrote us. One guy wrote me. [Sasha] wrote for the whole war, telling me to not go out with anyone. "Don't get married. Save yourself until I return. Wait. I will come back from the front. We will be eternal friends." . . . He loved me madly. Madly, he would come to me, before the war . . .

> Then I got a letter saying, "Tomorrow is peace, and they killed him today." His sister came to me. She told me. That Sasha had died. My mother cried more than I did.

And Sasha, my brother, was a soul-friend of his. They both died. My brother Sasha and this Sasha died. No one came back. It all stands here in my heart. You talk about it, and there are bitter tears. You have to live your whole life. . . . So, in that way, you weep. . . . Sasha will not return. In that way, I remained for my whole life a suffering one.[36]

These two citations echo with some of the loneliness of the twentieth century's most extensive scourge. It is for historians to explain why the Russians lost those millions of lives during World War II. The inferior war technology of the Soviets, the focused bombardment of Russia by Germany (which had no western front for the first years of the war), and Stalin's great mismanagement are cited as reasons for this vast devastation. Here, svoi is far from local. A calendrical festival that conjures this war can, along the way, provide modest insights into the workings of Russian/Soviet nationalism, a sphere of discourse that instrumentalizes memory by linking the social role of the local ancestors to national agendas, in much the same way that the dead of Yugoslavia were used and manipulated, as described by Verdery in *The Political Lives of Dead Bodies* (1999).

In this section, I discuss the way World War II is held in collective memory through the vehicle of Victory Day, commemorated on May 9. On this day (as on several other Soviet calendar days), a national svoi is created and elaborated. As with other holidays on a national scale, it does this through narratives of shared history. Unlike other Soviet (and now Russian) holidays, this holiday has been "successful" in the village in the sense that it is honored to this day. I begin with a look at the calendrical arena on which the holiday day falls.

May Days: The Height of Spring
In springtime, in early May, farmers wait for the potato plant (watching for the thaw, watching the sky, feeling the soil for warmth). Festivals take place along side this waiting period. Easter, the most important of the Orthodox holidays, falls most often at the end of April or the beginning of May. The Orthodox spring calendar also includes the Holy Week before

---

36. This story was pieced together from one interview with Larisa Andreevna. Some of the parts are out of order here, for the sake of clarity.

Easter and holidays thereafter (such as Prepolovnie, twenty-four days following Easter).

Of course, Easter did not originate with Christianity. Paskha, the Russian term for Easter, betrays its roots in Judaism's Peisakh (Passover), one of the holiest times of the Jewish year, and, a day of storytelling (and "ethnic" svoi-formation). At the same time, the deepest associations of the Orthodox Paskha do not seem to be Judeo Christian. Falling, as it does, during the height of spring, and dealing, as it does, with questions of death and resurrection, it is not surprising that the European version of the holiday bears many non-Christian associations, from its ritual objects (such as eggs) to its ritual focus on seasonal re-birth (Hubbs 1988:71).

The festival of Radunitsa is recalled in Solovyovo to a small degree. I was told that on Radunitsa, children would get up at dawn to see if the sun *raduetsia* (is joyous).[37] If the sun was "happily" jiggling, a good year was ensured. Reflecting the overlap between these two rites, one ostensibly Judeo-Christian and the other pre-Christian in origin, was the fact that I heard of this rite of checking the sun for its happiness with reference to both Easter and Radunitsa. In May, the important Christian and pre-Christian holidays appear to overlap.

Along with Radunitsa, many other agrarian holidays occur in early May. Egoryi Den' on May 6, discussed briefly above, was observed as a day to let the cattle out of the barn for the first time in the spring. This holiday is no longer observed collectively even if, in general, the notion that the cattle must be protected in their journey out of the barn still makes special invocations required. In a strictly agrarian sense, the weather of Egoryi Den' divines the weather pattern for the coming spring months: "A warm Egoryi Den' and spring begins" (Nagaev 1991:13).

In Solovyovo, there are a few Orthodox and agrarian festivals that are remembered in May, but only one holiday is actively celebrated collectively. And this is a Soviet one.

May is, of course, a great month for Soviet festivals, beginning with the International Day of Workers' Solidarity or May Day, a day that nearly all Russians I have spoken with wax nostalgic about.[38] During the

---

37. The connection made between the name of the holiday and the term for happiness appears to constitute a folk etymology (Svetlana Adon'eva, St. Petersburg State University, personal communication, 1995).

38. Now called "Prazdnik Vesny i Truda" (The Festival of Spring and Labor).

Soviet period, it was a great festival, indeed. In the cities, there were always huge, festive parades on this day, and people would go out drinking and carousing and would holler along with the party slogans blaring on loudspeakers.[39] Factory workers would march with banners and cheers. The holiday granted two days off work. In the village, where the scope of this fanfare was not possible, May Day was more humbly celebrated in the clubhouse. Days off have little meaning for farmers, and May Day is no longer celebrated today.

Victory Day, a second great Soviet celebration, comes on May 9, and honors the European allied victory in World War II.[40] This victory signaled, in official party discourse, the moral victory of the Socialist Union over the "aggressive, adventuristic course of imperialism" (Shvets 1987:155). As the holiday is explained in a date book for Party members:

> The victory of the Soviet Union in the Great Patriotic War was deeply in order. . . . The war and its prevailing victory once again supported the prophetic words of V. I. Lenin: "They will never conquer a people in which the workers and the peasants in the majority knew, felt and saw that they defended their Soviet power—a work(ing) power which they fought for that thing, victory of which they and their children are provided with the possibility to use all of the blessings of culture, all of the creations of human labor" (Shvets 1987:153–154).

Unlike May Day, Victory Day is still celebrated today. With all the tension surrounding spring renewal, other functions are fulfilled on Victory Day that still resonate with the other Soviet holidays of early May. The holiday appears to have two functions. First, on this day that the village shares narratives of common suffering during the war, and a nation-svoi is produced and re-produced. Furthermore, it appears that the type of celebration of Victory Day is in line with the general tone of agrarian spring rites, where the dead are honored and power is brought to the community through this remembering.

---

39. Not all were "sincere," of course. See Yurchak's "The Cynical Reason of Late Socialism: Language, Culture and Identity of the Last Soviet Generation" (1997b) for a discussion of the "white noise" of Soviet ideology in the late Soviet period. The festive atmosphere of the May Day celebration does not seem to have been diminished by this lack of patriotic fervor.
40. Prazdnik Pobedy sovetskogo naroda v Velikoi Otechestvenoi voine 1941–1945 gg.

VICTORY DAY IN SOLOVYOVO

> You can tell any number of alternate stories of the Patriotic War—
> all of them crucial to its meaning—but in the end there is no mini-
> mizing the reality of Russia's loss, the deaths of millions, the truth
> that lies behind the military myth. The people's grief was over-
> whelming. It is not easy, ever, to bury wartime dead. In a culture
> based on earth, bones, and belonging, the quest to lay the ghosts
> can take a lifetime.
>
> —CATHERINE MERRIDALE, *THE NIGHT OF STONE* (2000:233)

The first spring I spent in Solovyovo marked the fiftieth anniversary of
the end of World War II. Victory Day has been an important holiday in
Russia since the end of the war, doubling as a day to honor and mourn
the dead and to exult in Soviet victory. This half-century mark was special. In 1995, Yeltsin's government was paying particular attention to the
proclivities of provincial pensioners—all of whom had lived through the
war. This group had proven a difficult one for Yeltsin to win over. By
working at stirring up national feeling on this holiday, Yeltsin could also
hope to gather support for his own devastating war against the break-
away republic of Chechnya, a war that was notorious for taking local
boys in the region and sending them away to their physical and psychic
deaths.[41]

As Victory Day approached, many films about the war were shown on
television. Such films offer a range of images of the war: from sentimental love stories, to heroic sacrifice stories, to the movies that masterfully
depict the human tragedy of the war. People know these films well. There
are saccharine musicals among them, but even the most sentimental of
the movies touch something genuine. People cry when they watch. No
one is without personal losses caused by this war, most of which changed
the entire course of people's lives (e.g., no father, dire poverty; no husband, living alone or in bitterness). The emotions that lie within the symbolic landscape of this war are possible to call up, and thereby possible
to harness for broader purposes.

---

41. Young men from the urban intelligentsia (the children of the people who vote for
Yeltsin and other "democratic" parties) often get out of military service through the payment of an appropriate bribe. Rural and "provincial" children have no such connections
and no such refuge.

In the Solovyovo region, Victory Day was observed in two ways. First, on May 6 and 7, there were medal presentations for those who had served in the war effort, including women who had worked in factories. Mikhail Alekseevich prepared two such presentations, one in Solovyovo and the other in Iurino, six kilometers away. Next, on May 9, there was a get-together at the clubhouse, where people brought food and drink and danced and sang to the music of an accordion.

Perhaps fixing the importance of this date in the local memory, I was told that "after Victory Day, the weather would improve." Once again, a calendrical milestone causes a change in the weather. Here, a Soviet milestone filled that function.

The May 6 medal presentation was held in Iurino. Villagers gathered under the bright blue sky on benches outside of one house. A metal plate lay on the ground, setting up a small square where people could dance. One could imagine the thousands of times that feet stomped out chastushki rhythms in that spot over the years. The official part of the presentation was gleaned from several different sources, including poems, and historical and original material. Much of it was done in the form of rhymed lines. Songs were sung about the war and fallen lovers and victorious armies, and the audience was full of tears. One by one, people got up and received their medals.

The next day in Solovyovo, there was another medal presentation, this time in Solovyovo's clubhouse. The main difference between the two was that I know the people from Solovyovo fairly well, and I knew the stories that caused their tears. Larisa Andreevna's lost love. This brother or that husband or father, lost. I was particularly touched by the tears of Anna Vladimirovna. The day before, Iuliia had mistakenly told her that she wasn't going to get a medal at the ceremony, and Anna Vladimirovna responded by saying that she couldn't care less and that she wasn't going anyway, that during the war she worked for herself and not for the war effort specifically. But when the time came, she sat in the front row, and I saw her eyes redden and fill with tears as she went back to her place with her medal (of course, she got one), her head high and her mouth turned down in a proud and sorrowful frown. A smiling, toothless baba, Rita (sent to the camps for ten years for stealing a turnip from the kolkhoz to keep her children from starving) sat next to me beaming at everyone, her eyes shining. Valentina Ivanovna sat on my other side, and she cried as well with her medal. She had told me earlier that people did not believe that she had worked in a factory in wartime. So here was her proof.

Veterans received a gift in addition to the medal: a wall clock. The people who received the medal for services of various kinds during the war received a gift of 10,000 rubles (a jar of *tushenka,* or cooked meat, cost 7,000 rubles then). Katia Smirnova sang marching and sentimental war songs, such as "It Is Victory Alone That We Need."[42] Her throat tightened and more than once she could not finish her performance.

On May 9, there was a large celebration for Victory Day in the sel'sovet of Guliaevo (where the dogs are more fierce and the men are more drunken), but I decided not to go. The rumor was that villagers there had brought together twenty bottles of vodka, and I had seen enough drunkenness in the past several days to want to skip this display. Solovyovo had its own celebration of the fiftieth victory anniversary. We gathered again at the club, about eighteen people all together. There were six bottles of vodka consumed and some *samogon* (homemade alcohol). The first toast was to the victory. There were other toasts to those who came back but perished later.

Evgenii T- had met the Americans on the Elbe at the end of the war. He had suffered a contusion, I was told, and now, drunk, he made little sense as he slurred his words and jumped from one idea to the next. He spoke with some fondness of the Americans. One black man whom he had seen at that great meeting on the Elbe had understood Russian. Three years later, on a summer's day, Evgenii hung himself in his Solovyovo home. Konstantin Andreevich V-, whose father had gone to war and come back an "invalid," spoke of remembering the German planes flying overhead. There was dancing, again. Bear-like Petia dragged me to the dance floor and told me that by not drinking vodka, I could never understand the Russian soul. His aunt, Anna Petrovna, was drunk and sad, crying for her departed husband, Stefan. Everyone had forgotten her, she said. No one cared for her. She had gone to the cemetery this morning, as did several other villagers, to visit her husband's grave. Drinking, toasts, and stories of the dead were the order of the day.

Iuliia drank more than I had ever seen her drink. And she told the story of her father's disappearance in the war. And her mother's fall from the rafters as a child, her epilepsy and subsequent death, and the beginning of Iuliia's own life in the orphanage, among the lost children of war.

---

42. Words and music by B. Okudzhava.

The festivities on and around Victory Day solidify the shared experience of war. The collective memory is in the telling. The fact that such stories are told each year lends a certain permanence to this process of narrative, if not to the content of the narrative. But this war was not only about private suffering. It profoundly changed the lives of village Russians, not only in the sense that individual lives were lost for a "common" cause. It also stretched the sense of belongingness out from within the confines of a local village arena to a national one. Here the Soviet Union came alive in the village imagination in a very tangible way.

THE OUTWARD PILGRIMAGE OF WAR

When I asked villagers about current politics in Moscow, answers varied as much as they would anywhere in the world. One common thread, however, was the idea that the village is distinct from Moscow: that the affairs of Moscow do not ultimately have much effect on life in the village. So, as the Leningrader Tat'iana Ivanovna wept and prayed in front of her icon for three days during the putsch of 1991, the village was slower to react. Iuliia spoke to me of the reactions in the village:

> *Iulia Ivanovna:* Afraid, we weren't afraid. We watched and were waiting to see who would win, but we weren't afraid. This was the center [where everything was going on]. It wasn't our affair. We were just afraid that they might take our men.

"It was not our affair." The local category has great strength perhaps because most of the important categories of life (regarding production, reproduction, supernatural) are still local for the farmer. Wars send villagers from the comfort of their local categories of belonging, out into the world.

Indeed, villagers left the village en masse during the World War II, many for the first time in their lives. By doing so, they were necessarily extending their circle of social interaction from a small, local one, to a vast, national one. Soldiers left for the front, and some of them saw foreign countries for the first time. Yet it was not only male soldiers who left the villages during the war: Valentina Ivanovna told me the story of her first trip away from the region of her birth.

> *Valentina Ivanovna:* My father died the twenty-ninth of June. He had been sick. . . . He had returned from the Finno-Russian war and was already

sick. . . . [He] had cancer and came back from the war sick. Mama was left with three children and I was the eldest. I was born in 1923, sister in 1926, and brother in 1929. There was nothing to eat or drink. And so they sent word. Father had been buried and I was sent there. They took us to the forest. In the forest, after the criminals had left, we lived there in barracks. After the criminals had been sent to the war, they called us there. We were all young girls. It was a peat bog. . . . We cry and cry. We hadn't been anywhere. Wail and wail.

I remember one time. There was this uncle Misha. A seller. He was at the peat bog, there. There had been criminals there, and there were already none there. And I want bread [lit: bread is wanted]. And so I went, I remember, with some girl but I forgot which one. "Uncle Misha, give us tomorrow's bread on a coupon. Or at least, let us eat some bread." We were only around seventeen years old. He looked at us and cut a loaf of bread in half. And says, "There, go and eat. Don't tell anyone." With tears, we left from there. And wept. There, well, we carried the bread to the barracks to the girls to share. How could we eat it alone? Eat it by ourselves and not give them anything? There, we understood, he made us understand that we could never come and ask again. It would be shameful to ask again.

The point here is that if, in most important ways, the crucial social categories in the village are local ones, the war necessarily extended those categories outward. People became intimate with strangers. As a little girl in an orphanage, Iuliia met children from several different countries, all of whom were alone, one way or another. From this she gained an early sense of an international community that could live in relative harmony, in line with the Soviet doctrines of her day.

The negative side of this pilgrimage to the reaches of the nation-svoi, was that the local community was devastated. As Valentina Ivanovna said, "They all died in the war. Everyone died in the war. . . . [A]ll that's left is trash." Over and over again, I heard this sentiment. The local community had been fractured by the war. There were no men left. How can the reproduction of a community be ensured without men? How can the gulianki continue? If that weren't enough, village resources were expropriated during the war.

Valentina Ivanovna: We worked very well. Worked honestly. There was a great work force. There, if the war hadn't happened, things would have worked out very well. Without the war. And the war happened, and everything was decided. They left and took the good horses. Took the bread. What was left for us but bad grain. They took everything from us. Even seeds. . . . There was nothing to sow with. There, that's how it was. The grain was hidden in the cupboard. Didn't think to lock it—so they broke it. Took the grain anyway.

The new categories of belonging brought on through the movements of the war were, as a secondary effect, accompanied by a weakening of the local categories of svoi. The new communities were no longer agrarian ones, but were military.

THE PLACE OF WORLD WAR II

"For those who take ancestors seriously," Verdery writes, "the politics of reburial engages the abiding sociality of relations between living and dead" (1999:106–107). Reburial is one way that the states of the post-Soviet space instrumentalize notions of territory, nation, and the emotion behind the death of the intimate "us." Yearly commemoration of the national dead is another.

World War II is called the Great Patriotic War by Russians for a reason. Although the Soviet Union shared with the Allies a German (known always in Russia as "fascist") enemy, there was no recognition that the moral battle that the war represented was shared as well. Official discourse surrounding the war put the moral high ground on the side of the Soviet state, and a generalized moral debasement on the side of the *bourgeois* powers.[43] During my time in Russia, I came to understand that the victory of the war was generally seen as a moral victory won by the Soviet Union. In that sense, the Soviet Union owned that war as its own moral capital, and used it as such in its nationalistic discourse.

There is certainly much to suggest that villagers live at great psychic distance from the power center of Moscow, that life goes on without much reference to national concerns—the most pressing concerns for villagers still being those of khoziaistvo. The state, as it has for centuries, interferes with local production in the village, but does not define local production. Over the centuries, it has squeezed farmers with taxes, and expropriated their foods, animals, seeds, and on and off their homes and

---

43. See Lyons (1976) for translations of Soviet textbooks that exemplify this view.

property. Over the centuries, villagers have reacted one way or another, sometimes through active and other times through passive resistance. One overall insight that I gleaned during my research in rural Russia was that while Solovyovo often made reference to the outside governmental powers, it saw those powers as essentially chuzhie (foreign).

The war, however, makes the nation an intimate category. In Chapter 4, I discussed the fact that the nation-khoziain comes to life only sporadically in the radiant past, and that the local rodina (mama rodina) becomes a nation-rodina (Mat' Rossiia) only in specific cases. World War II is, historically speaking, the most vibrant period in which the local svoi became national, and the most important khoziain became a national one (Stalin). The *fashisty* ("fascists," or Germans in this case) were a bona fide enemy; there was a moral cause to be won; there were brothers and fathers dying en masse, quite literally emptying villages of their livelihood. Stalin was the great khoziain of this nation-rodina, and villagers speak of his crucial role in winning that war.[44] As Smith[45] has noted, this positioning of Stalin as an epic-sized khoziain was all the easier because the way in which the rodina of Russia was invaded in the war by chuzhie Germans. A great national Soviet "we" formed in this battle. Today, veterans of this war prove to be active Soviet patriots, still sometimes honoring their first toasts, "To the Rodina, To Stalin!" On Victory Day, this nation-svoi is called into being through narratives of shared suffering, and songs and stories of achieving a victory over a morally degraded enemy. It is not surprising that part of this sense of nation-belongingness turns into nationalism.

VICTORY DAY AS DAY OF NATIONALISM

In Solovyovo, on May 9, 1995, we watched the Victory Day parade taking place in Moscow on television. Yeltsin sat, watching the goings-on and flanked by President William Clinton and Hillary Rodham Clinton. It was clear that the entire parade was carefully orchestrated. There was a replica of a huge medal saying "SSSR, Pobeda!" (USSR Victory!), and a picture of U.S. and Russian soldiers arm in arm in the style of war propaganda posters. Yeltsin finished the opening speech, and at the end, he

44. This is not, of course, the view of most historians.
45. Kathleen Smith, Georgetown University, Washington, D.C., personal communication, 2003.

yelled "Ura!" and there was a huge return of "Ura!" from the crowd of soldiers below. It sounded like a song.[46]

On the little television box that sits in the *krasnyi ugol* of the Belovs' home, the neatness of the soldiers, the crispness of their uniforms, the careful orchestration of their hurrahs, the large hulks of war machinery rolling past the benevolent, proud national leader, were all in such striking contrast to the local images of a tumble-down village, however beloved and kindred.

On one channel, the *ABC Evening News* broadcast the parade, with its coverage translated into Russian. Iuliia got quite offended at one point while watching: Peter Jennings had commented that "there were no surprises" in the artillery displayed in the parade. There is great pride in military machinery, and to make such an offhanded comment, implying that Russia was no longer a threat to be taken seriously on the world stage, was enough to tweak her rarely evidenced nationalist feelings. To make it worse, a Soviet broadcaster was, in contrast, saying that the weapons were being shown for the first time. Iuliia countered to the television that it must be spies who showed the Americans the weapons.

The reference, again by Jennings, that the Russians were responsible for developing the conflict in Chechnya also did not go over well. Russians, Iuliia said, were just keeping order, like Americans had done in Vietnam.

I would carefully watch such moments when, as if out of nowhere, nationalist sentiment would spring forth. When peaceful, hardworking, reasonable people begin to burn with nationalist fervor, proclaiming "Kill all the Chechens!" or some other such venom, it is worth paying attention to the context. Such feelings were masterfully ignited by the speeches of Vladimir Zhirinovsky, the ultranationalist presidential candidate of earlier post-Soviet elections. During my time in Solovyovo, when he spoke on television, his bellow would ring through the whole house and was recognizable even from the kitchen. I would watch people watch him. He would roar that the once-great world power was "on its knees!" The nationalist narrative says that it is the West, the Jews, and the "Southerners" who are causing this great shame, that only by uniting as a Rus-

---

46. For a most poignant discussion of the remembrance of World War II—the "choreographed ceremony" of official Soviet remembrance and the unadulterated stories of survival—see Merridale (2000).

sian people, can the pride owed to this great nation be re-gained. Such a narrative is and was, in other words, the standard fare of nationalism all over the world.

Tapping into that sort of nationalism is the business of manipulating feelings associated with svoi-formation, where the svoi has here become a nation-svoi. It is not so much for the love of Stalin, or the love of "freedom," or the love of the radiant future. The local community that is formed—the idealized moments of self-sacrifice at a local level—tends to be inherited by the svoi-formation at a national level. For these villagers, this loose cannon of a nation-svoi is formed through the shared experience of war-making and dying, a formation that is reiterated once a year on the grounds of the May timescape.[47]

Because the war included such varied acts of self-sacrifice, narratives about the war inspire the imagery of the radiant past, here transposing its warmth to a national scale. The war is a time when "we" were radiantly together as a nation, and not simply as a local community. Victory Day is thereby linked to some of the highest sentiments of what the world ought to be like, according to villagers' own constructs of their radiant world.

As well as being an issue of svoi-formation in a positive sense, nationalist instances in rural Russia are defined through the elaboration of a national chuzhoi. In the same way that the dogs are said to be fiercer and the husbands more brutal and the youths more prone to drink in the village of Guliaevo 12 kilometers away, this category of chuzhoi—as it extends to the nation-chuzhoi—continues along the analogous lines of an almost visceral suspicion. If, as I have argued, svoi formation bears a magical function of a positive nature, the chuzhoi category is the part of the landscape where dangers and risks accumulate. Svoi-formation is a defining action of the radiant past, that is, the construct that brings to life a social well-being marked by expansiveness and freedom. The chuzhoi, on the other hand, lingers in the darker corners of the mir chudesnogo. The chuzhoi is where one sickens by falling victim to the evil eye, or some weighty word from the wrong mouth. When the chuzhoi is a local one, there is a sometimes hostile social distance; there can be sickness and even death. When the chuzhoi is a national one, its construct teeters precariously, ever ready to fall into clamoring for war. This clamoring was pres-

---

47. The experience of shared war as a part of the formation of an imagined nation is treated in depth in Anderson (1983).

ent in the village, although it must be said that it was triggered rarely. Luckily, the village khoziaistvo and the local svoi take up far too much of the active mental landscape to allow villagers to be easily swept away.

Holidays such as Victory Day successfully grant a shared narrative of suffering; they re-kindle war memories of a svoi-formation where pilgrimages moved outward into a national arena; and they allow villagers to attach a sense of moral high ground at a national/Soviet level to the victory that their sufferings produced. But they also create a setting where nationalist sentiments are bound to be produced, which can be manipulated at the level of the state. As Verdery (1999:101) writes of the immense public funerals that occurred in the 1990s in Yugoslavia, "[S]uch mass events represented the state having 'collectivized' and nationalized the dead bodies hitherto mourned by families as their individual dead."

In this light, the actual celebration of Victory Day in Solovyovo, despite the nationalist pomp that surrounds it, is a profoundly sad day to honor the familial dead. If this commemoration creates a nation-svoi that can potentially be used by the state, it is also a manifestation of an activity that has always been a crucial part of agrarian spring rites. In other words, Victory Day creates, even today, a feeling of deep national belonging. Along the way, it is enacted with a mind to calling in the powers of the dead by forming another, no less potent sense of svoi. This svoi production has tremendous power in the village, and will be treated in more detail in the following section. For now, it can be said that the nation-svoi that is produced at the time of Victory Day is fed by the far deeper symbolic springs of the powers of the dead.

TROITSA AND REMEMBRANCE DAYS OF THE *RODINA*[48]

* * *

In keeping with the agrarian pattern that holidays are weather-changing days, Troitsa is a day on which rain should fall. In the spring of 1995, after twenty dry days of heavy heat, rain indeed fell onto the village of Solovyovo in the days before Troitsa. "Glory to Thee, Lord!" I heard exclaimed, as the first warm, fat raindrops fell.

But the relevance of Troitsa goes far beyond its role as a weather marker. Troitsa is a holiday filled with large and small meanings from a wide range of sources. Some of this meaning is among the loftiest that

---

48. An earlier version of this section was published in *The Anthropology of East Europe Review* (Paxson 1998).

outside orders (such as the Church) can offer, but is ignored in the village; some of it is cute and banal and also ignored there. At the same time, other sides of the holiday's relevance are, indeed, deeply wrought, and have endured in the village over the centuries in spite of the outside influences of the state and Church. The way that Troitsa is commemorated today offers a clear example of the way separate hegemonic orders can compete for dominance over the calendar, and the degree and kind of success and failure of the given orders.

In early June 1995, the celebration of Troitsa was newsworthy in Russia. Along with the regular pastiche of soap operas, game shows, war movies, and advertisements, there was an entire news program dedicated to the holiday. It had two parts. First, excerpts from a church service were featured. Standing in one of Moscow's glorious churches, Patriarch Alexei II was seen performing the service and explaining to the congregation some of the meaning of this sublime holiday. Candles were lit. There was solemn religious music. The second part of the program took us to an entirely different space. Here, the traditional "folk" expression of the holiday was featured, with a display of the brightly woven "traditional" clothes of the Russian farmers from hundreds of years ago, and the celebrations of the agrarian "festival of the birch tree," which was apparently linked to Troitsa in a way similar to how Easter is linked to spring equinox festivals. Indeed, on the news and other programs throughout the day, one could see somewhat mature maidens singing in idyllic nature scenes while men played balalaikas and sang along. The television presented two contrasting focal images: church solemnity (on the one hand) and idyllic nature (on the other) where this bifurcation roughly corresponds to the widely accepted view of Russian religion: that it is marked by *dvoeverie* or the "double-faithedness" that allows for a back and forth between sober religiosity and near-precious folk expression.

I spent two Troitsas in Solovyovo. I can say without hesitation that these television programs would not have prepared me for what I saw on this holiday. Not only was there a noticeable absence of singing maidens, birch twigs, and colorful clothing, almost no one went to church on that day. But the day was certainly celebrated. People came to Solovyovo from miles around, even hundreds of miles away, to honor this day. They came in 1995 and 1996 (when I was living there)—as they came all through the Soviet period—to their rodina and to their ancient graveyards. They came not to sing any particular song or light any particular candle, but to remember their dead, converse with their dead, drink and dance to them until they could drink and dance no more. In Solovyovo today, this is a holiday that matters.

Troitsa and the Problem of Memory and Hegemony

Troitsa is a holiday of particular interest for several reasons. First, and most importantly, it is one of a very few holidays that are observed collectively in the village every year. Furthermore, it has been observed without interruption (as is clear both from the literature and villagers' accounts) throughout the Soviet period and the pre-Soviet Christian period. My aim in this section on calendars is to demonstrate how Russian villagers have navigated through a range of hegemonic orders. The Troitsa festival is a holiday with roots in ancient Slavic religion, and has survived over the centuries by taking on various forms, including Orthodox and Soviet ones. It is a particularly vivid example of how calendrical milestones can become the locus of battling hegemonies.

Troitsa, or The Day of the Holy Trinity, is a holiday that has indeed shifted among several "owners." It takes its name from the Trinity, and in Russian Orthodoxy, it is the day that commemorates the very subtle Orthodox concept of "sophia" (wisdom), which represents the three aspects of God united in one sublime whole. Regardless of any calendrical overlap, the date for the celebration of Troitsa is defined most rigidly by the Orthodox calendar; it falls fifty days after Easter, usually in early June.

It is no surprise, however, that the holiday is linked to agrarian religion as well, the beginning of June being such a very good time to worry about how the newly planted crops will fare in the coming months—whether there will be enough rain or too much, whether the sun will hide or burn the soil. In the context of Solovyovo, where agricultural technology is still largely nonmechanized, planting and harvesting are marked by arduous labor and guesswork, where the stakes are extremely high. The tension that permeates the spring—"June tension" as it were—remains palpable.

There are disputes about the deeper meanings of many of the agrarian holidays in rural Russia. Propp (1974:402–403) generalized that Troitsa is tied to spring fertility rites that involve drawing land fertility from the force of dead ancestors. In its not-too-distant practice, Troitsa also involved certain fussing over the birch tree—on Trinity, girls from the village of Solovyovo would take birch branches from the forest and bring them into the village. According to literature on the subject, these branches were linked to the souls of the ancestors (Propp 1974:402–403;

see also Baranova et al. 2001). Today, Troitsa is a *graveyard* holiday, a holiday of the dead and of the newly fertile soil.

In the lifetime of the villagers of Solovyovo, the festival of the Holy Trinity was celebrated in two official ways and in several places. The physical placement of the holiday celebration has much to say about deeper calendrical habits.

The Church

The Day of the Holy Trinity is one of the "Twelve Great Feasts" of Orthodox Christianity. Unlike other Great Feasts such as Christmas, on December 25 (and lesser holidays such as Elijah's Day, on August 2), it is not a fixed day, but occurs sometime in late spring, with the date of Easter as its anchor. The concept that inspires this day—the unity of the Holy Trinity—is indeed one of great subtlety and far-reaching ontological power. As Clément writes in *L'Eglise Orthodoxe* (1961:57):

> For Orthodoxy, in effect, the Trinitarian revelation constitutes the foundation of all Christian anthropology, since man is "the image" of God and that the life of humanity ought to "imitate the divine nature." In the same way that there is a single God in Three Persons . . . since there are, divided by the fall but restored in its unity as the Body of Christ, a "single man" in a multitude of persons. The irreducible unity of the person, the ontological unity of humanity of which the visible cosmos constitutes the body, such are, by analogy with the Trinitarian reality, the two poles of the Orthodox anthropology (my translation).

The three-in-one God reflects the unity of the spiritual station of Jesus Christ; it extends unity to humanity and even outward to the whole of the cosmos. This Trinitarian unity has, in theological discourse, allowed for sociological metaphors to emerge that evoke the unity of the "collective." Metaphorically akin to this concept is the notion of *sobornost'*, or collective consciousness. As explained by Clément (1961:58),

> The personal consciousness is therefore not the consciousness of the self, but the consciousness of communion. Russian thought has often insisted on the "integral, superindividual, and community character" (S. Troubetskoï) of this consciousness. "The dogma of the Trinity is our social program," said Fedorov. . . . The Christian ought to struggle to introduce a ferment of communion into the whole of society. When the "encirclement of the planet" is

accomplished, the Orthodox sense of the Trinity as a concrete universal would be able to reveal itself as particularly fertile (my translation).

The "integral, superindividual and community" consciousness of the Orthodox collective is here linked to the oneness in the Trinity. From this philosophy flows a concept of society in which the collective conscience is the only individual conscience of import, one with the power to link the world as a whole with the holy Being and Body of Christ. Svoi-formation here expands to the broadest outlines of creation itself.

It is perhaps no coincidence that the radiant past of the villagers of Solovyovo—where they catalog a perfect society—revealed a notion of social unity that resonates with some of this notion of sobornost'. The centrality of the symbolism of the kollektiv (and the idea that the creation of a kollektiv, through the creation of a svoi-formation) is reminiscent, at some level, of the cosmic quality of the Orthodox sobornost'. And yet, the question remains whether this Orthodox-named holiday is being expressed and performed in Orthodox terms.

In the distant memories of childhood, many villagers in Solovyovo remember their parish church that stood on an island in the middle of Lake Tikhonskoe. In the winter they could walk to it over ice; in the summer the boat ride there would take ten minutes. Baptisms took place there, as did regular and holiday services. The church was a place that villagers would go to in order to turn toward higher powers in the hope of receiving protection or succor. The icons in the churches were particular conduits of grace, not only over the supplicant, but over the church grounds itself. Having churches and icons brought health. Whether or not villagers took sermons to heart, the church was treated by villagers as a special space—one where invocations could be made, and one that housed particular sorts of otherworldly figures: mediating saints and a universal khoziain-God.

The church on Lake Tikhonskoe was destroyed in 1934. Some of the people of Solovyovo witnessed this event, which was traumatic because of the way that it showed the sure and hard hand of the state working its way into even these backwoods. The destruction of churches, as described earlier, is understood to be an unpardonable crime against sacred space. So, even if Orthodoxy had failed to thoroughly insert its theology, it had not failed to invest its space (the church) with otherworldly powers. If the *izba* traditionally housed (as it still does) a domovoi (khoziain doma), and the forest housed a leshii (khoziain lesavoi), the church housed another kind of khoziain—one who could rage against you (and, indeed, the world and the cosmos itself) if you crossed Him. Crimes against churches—that is, destroying the church and its icons—cursed not only the perpetrator, but his descendants.

If villagers only very vaguely remember actual Church ritual, they do remember a place of power that was destroyed. The church, it can be said, is housed in the memory of these villagers as an opaque symbol. It is not filled with theological details, but is invested with otherworldly powers of a certain character. The physical church is gone, but the idea of church space remains. In any case, most villagers in Solovyovo have been to church only once or twice in their adult lives. They do not understand church language, and they cannot recall the details of church ritual. Now that going to church is once again possible, there is still a certain hesitation to re-enter the grounds of Orthodoxy. Andrei, who was in his mid-thirties, told me during my first full year in Solovyovo that he had recently become interested in religion and had been reading about Orthodoxy. Yet he still had never been to church, telling me that entering a church meant "crossing a great threshold," one that he did not take lightly.

Solovyovo did have one resident who had been a regular churchgoer. Weekly, Larisa Andreevna (who had lost her love in the war and remained throughout her entire life, "a suffering one") would climb onto a bus and ride for an hour and a half to Belozersk to get to the only active church in the region. Larisa Andreevna's relation to the church caused some friction in the village. She was constantly admonishing people for infractions of work taboos on holidays, or for celebrating the wild Sviatki when it was already Christmas, or for, in general, not being religious like she was. She had also been a communist. Villagers call her *bogomolka* ("one who prays to God") to annoy her. It worked; she had few friends in the village and would mostly stick to herself.

On Troitsa, she became one of the actors in an emerging argument over the day that Troitsa should be properly celebrated. Villagers had heard rumors of objections to going to the graveyard on the Sunday of Troitsa, that that day should be spent in church, remembering the dead there. Indeed, the church service on the day of Troitsa pays particular attention to honoring dead parents. On Saturday, a visit to the graveyard was acceptable and even encouraged, but on Sunday, the dead should be left to rest. To my knowledge, only Larisa Andreevna made it to church on Troitsa Sunday.

Deciding whether or not to go to church, as opposed to the graveyard, on Troitsa, marks a struggle over a calendrical day and, at another level, for power over collective memory. In spite of the rumors of church dissatisfaction, crowds gathered at the cemetery on Troitsa, along with families and distant relatives from distant towns and cities. No one had to be told what to do there. Clearly, the Church was making some move to overcome the dominance of this well-established graveyard practice. The Church is not only striving to reclaim the Russian soul for God, but to re-address other "pagan" practices, such as the healing/sorcery practice of *koldovstvo*. Efforts to control the practice of koldovstvo were discussed in Chapter 6. Father Osipov's book, *Do Not Participate in the Affairs of Darkness* (1992; my translation), was intended to frighten people away from "pagan" practices and bring them back into the domain of the church. Osipov, the charismatic leader of Belozersk's recently opened church, began carving an important place for himself in Belozersk, and even ventured into the affairs of local and national politics. This political adventuring was his downfall, eventually, and he was sent away from the city. There is little doubt, in general, that with its re-born political muscle, the Church will continue in its efforts to thwart activities that it sees as dangerous and devil-inspired.

The point is that despite efforts by the Church to control village practice, most villagers do not go to church on Troitsa. They do not, in short, enter that (hegemonic) space. The body can only be in one place at a time and on that June day, most village bodies make pilgrimages not to the houses of Orthodox authority, but again, to the soil that houses their dead.

Clubhouse (*Dom Kul'tury*)

Troitsa had a Soviet expression as well. Much more recent in the memory of villagers than Troitsa church services (if not more vivid in the recollections of villagers) were the "days of the birch tree," planned by kul'trabotniki and overseen by the regional "culture" administration. Villagers would be drawn in from their loose, unmonitored amusements outdoors and in each other's homes, into a space where they could be overseen and directed along ideologically acceptable lines by culture workers.

The Soviet "day of the birch tree" was described to me by Iuliia, who had worked as the kul'trabotnitsa for over thirty years. The birch tree, she explained, was a symbol of beauty. On the holiday that was once Troitsa, they would bring rows of *berezki* branches into the clubhouse and girls would dance under them. They would recite poems and sing songs in praise of the birch tree. "Birches are good for the *pochki* (kidneys) and can clean dirty air," she added. There was a program for children on this holiday (with events such as flower-naming contests), and in the later part of the evening adults would sing and dance.

Like the church, it was partly the job of the clubhouse literally to bring people in. Rein them in. To have them sit and listen and, once again, subject them to external judgments and authority. Intentional or not, it also served to mix symbolic space. It took activities (like dancing and singing) that had been traditionally performed in the open air (fields, forest, graveyard) and brought them inside, placing them in a sometimes tense administrative space. This could make for an odd and not altogether comfortable mix. Again, there were practical considerations to bringing these festivals inside: the clubhouse served to keep the violence of the gulianki under some control. It also could serve to bring in the norms of Soviet etiquette, where singing a dirty chastushki was a crime. The clubhouse was a place of relative sterility.

The celebration of the birch tree was also relatively sterile. It was supposed to be a cheery paean to the Russian folk, and it managed to take some of the right elements (girls, birch trees, songs), but literally decontextualized them. Like the Church before it, the Soviet state had rewritten the calendar and inserted its own holy days, using the calendar as one of its demonstrations of ideological muscle. Interestingly, where the Church had turned "pagan" holidays into religious ones, the Soviets subsequently took religious holidays and made them into "pagan lite." The overage maidens dancing on television were a symptom of this. The popular Soviet construction of village life can suffer from an awkward cutesification. The day of the birch tree could indeed be very cute, what with children reciting nature poems, but if, in fact, the agrarian part of this holiday was about fertility in June—just when the land is starting to feel the warmth of its powers—no play about the medicinal virtues of the birch tree would unleash this primal force. Any symbolic power that these elements in fact had seemed to have gotten lost in the translation. In the past several years, with no one to plan "the day of the birch tree," the holiday shriveled up along with trips to the church. On the other hand, trips to the graveyard on this day have never stopped.

The celebration in the clubhouse shared with the church celebration this aspect of pulling people into controlled space. The Church packed a symbolic power that the clubhouse did not seem to inherit, even while often physically standing on the same spot. The Church, while powerful, is gone. The clubhouse, while present, is boring, or, at least is not potent enough to bear the crucial function of Troitsa. This function emerges in looking at the agrarian expression of the holiday.

Troitsa in the Forest

The agrarian Troitsa fell in early June. It was the culmination of a week-long celebration known in the folk literature as Rusalka week. The birch tree was described in ethnographic literature as having been the focus of the festivities. "Birch branches or young birch trees," wrote Propp (1974), "were brought from the forest and distributed to the houses without any particular ritual acts." At the end of Rusalka week, birch branches were brought to church and blessed there. The branches were used in the year ahead for healing and other purposes (Propp 1974:379). Why the birch tree? Propp speculated that "the birch is the first and earliest tree to clothe itself in bright and festive green, while the other trees are only just putting forth buds. This gave rise to the idea [that] birch trees are endowed with a special power of growth" (Propp 1974:379). This appears to be reasonable, but may in fact be only speculation. Birch branches are clearly linked to healing in the village: Anyone who has been to a village bathhouse has been regaled with the benefits of being smacked with clumps of birch branches while steaming. They are also quite ethereal trees, with a white bark rarely seen in North America, and small, bright green leaves; standing in a grove of birch trees makes one feel light and airy, in a certain marked contrast to the other heavy browns of spring. If that were not enough, as if by happy coincidence, some of the best-loved mushrooms tend to sprout under them. Aside from this sort of speculation, it is clear that the tree is certainly symbolically marked in a positive way (linked, as it is, to healing), and certainly seen as beautiful.

Larisa Andreevna describes the holiday in much the same terms, here vividly remembering how she and her friends had decorated the village houses:

> *Larisa Andreevna:* What did we do? We were little, young teenagers. So we would carry birch . . . from the swamp, chop it up. In every little

window, all around the house we would place them. . . . On our shoulders, we tried to [carry] them. And the boys would chop it. The birch trees stood around everyone's house. Not everyone put them in the garden. . . . All three days they stand, the birch trees under the window. . . . Children in every house, all the children, one's own. In each [house] one's own children, one's own houses. They were [all] decorated with birch trees.

Q: Why did you use the birch trees?

Larisa Andreevna: It was the fashion, a former ancient one, that everyone decorates the whole house with birch trees. And three days pass, and these birch [branches] we drag [out]. They drag them, the guys, you have to take them back there in a pile . . . in the woods. They drag, and would force us to drag them, too. . . . "Drag them! Girls! Drag them!" . . . No strength. So there. And the birches we carry [there and back]. Once again, back to the swamp. . . . And the streets we sweep with the birch-twigs. We sweep up and pick up everything. Like velvet along the streets.

Anna Petrovna also remembers the birch trees:

Q: Before, you did something on Troitsa with birch trees, no?

Anna Petrovna: Birch [branches] under the window, chopped. Put them there. . . . Ran, ran the children. And now they don't run.

Q: Why with birch trees?

Anna Petrovna: So, there, it's Troitsa. It's all covered with birches.

The focus on the birch tree was evident not only in the act of "dragging" the trees from the forest, but also in the placement of the birch branches in the house. Here Aleksandra Ivanovna recalls placing the birch branches in the beautiful red corner:

Aleksandra Ivanovna: On Troitsa they break birch [branches] and place them in the house. I also bring them in. On Palm Sunday. I go and break off willow branches [*verba*]. They lay in my house, just like [on Troitsa], in the corner.

The corner is, as discussed earlier, one home of the ancestor/rod/khozi-ain; in keeping with Propp's view of the holiday of Troitsa, the birch branches are associated with the "guardian of the household" (Propp 1974:383). The birch branches appear to embody the powers of spring, but also the powers of household guardians. According to Propp's argument (Propp 1974:402), deduced through the work of scores of folklorists, this association with "household guardians" in fact brings us to the notion that the birch branches represent the "souls of deceased relatives." Dragging birches from the forest into the village, and then burning them and spreading their ashes over the fields was a way to access the life force of dead ancestors, and place that force where it could be used for agricultural production.

Rusalka week itself, about which I heard nothing in Solovyovo, was a purely agrarian (and non-Christian) festival where effigies of *rusalki* (mermaids) are burned. The rusalki, according to an analysis by D.K. Zelenin (1994 [1916]) represented the "unquiet dead." The ritual involved the participation of girls, in particular, and involves spreading the ashes of the rusalka effigy over fields. The imagery here is quite in keeping with that of gathering the force of the dead ancestors (Propp 1974:396–397).

If the birch tree rituals of the Rusalka week and Trinity, as interpreted by Propp and others, are no longer performed, they lead us directly to the part of the festival that has endured, that is, into the healing territory of the graveyard soil. The birch may no longer carry the magical function of bringing "vegetative power" to the soil, but that function is still fulfilled.

The Graveyard: Deep Memory

The family is a deep line, a *rod,* a root, a rod. In Chapter 5, the role of the dead ancestors who lie in the fields of the rodina was discussed at some length, with particular emphasis placed on the broadly healing powers that result from carefully maintaining bonds between the living and the dead. Ancestors must be taken care of for life to run smoothly. This means "remembering" them on their saint's name days and on other holidays designated for remembrance such as Troitsa. By remembering them, and by properly filling the requirements of khoziaistvo (the duties of farm- and house-keeping), the dead grant assistance to their family line and, collectively, to the fields of the rodina. The Orthodox calendar is filled with days on which the dead are remembered, but Troitsa is not simply one among many of these days. It is, as Propp argues (1995:29), the culmination of a series of remembrance days that begin around the dinner tables of individual families at Christmas and end in the large ceremony held in the parish graveyard known as Troitsa.

"Remembering" most often involves toasting the deceased and saying a few words to them. It also means, on Troitsa, taking care of the graves of the dead and not letting them get grown over with weeds. According to Orthodoxy, a person's soul should go "up to heaven" forty days after death (thereby exiting this human world and going into the "heavenly kingdom"). As discussed in Chapter 5, the common beliefs include, however, the idea that the dead stay rather close to their rodina. They are available for help, when necessary. They do not, in other words, fly off in any permanent way to the Orthodox heaven. They stay literally grounded and quite close. Troitsa is the day where the community as a whole goes to the lingering dead and speaks with them. In this way, they fill the calendrical function that this day offers.

On Troitsa, a small pilgrimage is made outwards from the village. The graveyard that houses Solovyovo's dead is outside of Kraskovo, another village on the shore of Lake Tikhonskoe, four kilometers away. There are still graves to Solovyovo's ancestors next to the battered parish church on Tikhonskoe's old church, and some villagers head there by boat on Troitsa as well. Kraskovo's graveyard contains the remains of villagers from Solovyovo, Vershina, Maksimovo, Kraskovo, and Iurino, roughly covering the territory of three former parishes.

In early June, there are already many relatives who have come to the village for the summer. That means that a few cars are available to give rides to the babushki—crowding eight people in a car meant for four, or riding on the back of huge pickup trucks. Many of these old people get out of the village very rarely, but this day is not to be missed. Indeed, I was shocked the first time I saw this festival. The graveyard was packed with people, many of whom I did not recognize. The gravesites of individual families are surrounded by iron fences, and jammed in with people. A snapshot of this sight would render a schema of the region's family tree: each branch a family plot, crowded with living members and, far below, family patriarchs and matriarchs.

On Troitsa, you go to the cemetery. You bring food and drink and materials to clean up the site of the graves of your relatives. The first year I went, the Belovs and I brought a fish pie, candies, some vodka, berry juice, and a sickle to cut the grass around the grave. Inside the iron gate that surrounds the graves, there are gravestones, a bench, and a makeshift table. Some of the graves are decorated with five-pointed stars, others with crosses. Some include a faded photo of the deceased. The individual families that gather sit at the bench and toast their deceased. They report the goings-on during the year, how well they worked, how family members were getting along. In short, they discuss the details of khoziaistvo and remark on any exceptional news, and any major failings of the year. We toasted Mikhail Alekseevich's father and mother, and Mikhail Alekseevich explained that things were going rather well this year. Food and drink are left at the gravesite for the deceased.

This part of the Troitsa ritual establishes bonds with the members of the familial line usually the paternal line. Such bonds bring force and protection to a given family line. They set things right for the coming agricultural cycle.

If the first order of the day is remembering and caring for one's own dead, the next task is to visit the graves of others and drink to the dead of other families. In this way, villagers wander from grave to grave, beckoned by families: "Come! Remember my husband! Come, remember my son!" Stories are told of life and death: "You never knew my babushka! She was a good woman!" Sometimes you cry at untimely deaths. Zinaida Grigorievna showed me the grave of her husband, who had just passed on. She herself has breast cancer, which I learned because I was sent to give her back massages by Iuliia, and I noticed that only rags filled one side of her bra. Along with his widow, I cried for Fedor Sergeevich, one of the dearest members of the community to me who had died while I was away from the village. He had lived through the war and Stalin's purges, and was a thoughtful, gentle man. His wife had lost a son not much earlier, all the more tragic because she had predicted it, based on the drinking crowd he was hanging out with in town. Marfa had lost her little granddaughter and her husband in the space of a year, and stood quietly with her daughter and more distant relatives. Anna Petrovna, as always, wanted to talk about her Stefan and what a fine *muzhik* he had been and how she had not been so bad, herself, when she was young.

At each gravesite, you toast the dead or accept some offering in their name. In these exchanges, you seal not only the svoi between the dead and the living, but between yourself and the familial line that you have visited. Here, in this phase of celebration, svoi incubates. It forms and re-forms, destined, at the end of the rite, to arch over the limits of the local community. The oldest people in Solovyovo have lived through revolutions, wars, famines, political upheaval, and the physical and psychic ills that followed in the wake of these events. Here, at the graveyard, the village can mourn its dead—but more than that, it can draw power from the dead. As the day wears on, and the graveyard resounds with drunken chatter, a threshold is crossed. People go home and continue their drinking, and some begin to sing and dance. What had been wailing becomes another *cri du coeur.* In short, this graveyard communion brings a state of effervescence. This is the same mournful, ecstatic effervescence described by Emile Durkheim, the coming to life of the social body in such a way that it feels like the very essence of religious reality.[49]

Near the end of the day in the graveyard, grain is scattered over the graves as it is thrown before a casket in a funeral procession. Some villagers said that this is "just a tradition," and others say that it is done so that the birds eating the grain would also remember the dead.

As it is faithfully practiced, Troitsa appears to serve two functions. First, it binds the living and the dead into a common sense of svoi (one's own). A community—some of the members of which have passed to another world and have access to its forces—re-establishes itself. After all, the first sense of rodina is not Mother Russia, but motherland—the place that gave birth to me and that houses the dead that are mine. Rodina is the place that extends to the edges of svoi; it is the earth that houses one's own people. Coming to the graveyard and remembering the familial and the village rod unifies the community and serves a second purpose as well. It allows the living to take advantage of the force that the dead—as a collective unit—have access to. Their force can help make the soil fertile, the sun shine, and the rain come in a timely way. And what could be more crucial to a farmer without an irrigation system, tractors, and combines, who must watch the weather every hour of every day to outguess its capriciousness to coax the land's bounty into reality?

Troitsa is the day on which this remembering reaches a crescendo, as it is, one would hope, the time when the fertility of the land is most firmly ensured for the coming year. This is the function of the day, and a great function it is. Even if no birch branches are dragged in from the forest, svoi is formed between members of families, between families and their own ancestors, between separate village members, and between the transindividual, local collective and the transindividual collective of the dead. This act of bonding allows for otherworldly powers to flow in. This is a magical function of no small consequence. With or without birch branches as an outward symbol, the agrarian function carries on.

49. In *The Elementary Forms of Religious Life* (1995 [1912]:402–405), Durkheim describes collective mourning in light of the effervescence that it imparts.

Is this function, then, connected to the sobornost' (collective consciousness) elaborated by philosophers of Orthodoxy in their musings on the meaning of the Troitsa in Russia? In the sense that the formation of community svoi has a magical function associated with it, yes. In the sense that, like the sobornost' that extends to the Cosmos and the body of humanity and of Christ Himself, that formation—known throughout this book as svoi-formation—has many analogs that include local, national, and otherworldly communities, yes, again. Does this very powerful part of symbolic space derive from Orthodoxy? Given that so many of the expressions of svoi-formation discussed in this work have gone on before or after or without regard to Orthodoxy, I would have to say no. Furthermore, it is crucial here, as it is in any other investigation into this very important matter of sociosymbolic organization in Russia, to respect the ethnographic details. There is a difference between saying that Russian villagers have a readily available idiom for the powers of svoi-formation, and saying that they are, essentially, group-minded (or naturally, natively "communal"). The unity of the Trinity is certainly a lofty concept, but the question of its direct relevance to the svoi-formation that happens in village graveyards in early June is another. Troitsa is given its date by Orthodoxy. It fulfills its function on its own.

To conclude, the deeply agrarian expression of Troitsa lasted because it continues to serve a meaningful function. It is fixed in social memory for a reason. Although not adorned with maidens' songs or church hymns, it has its own music, and its function is one that is crucial to the physical, social, and metaphysical operations of the agricultural community. Calendars, it can be said, are socially congealed memory; their commemorative days stand like milestones in a symbolic timescape. In this sense, the most basic agrarian expressions of this holiday form the most deeply cut pathways in the landscape of memory. It is not without a certain irony that with all of the outside force of the Soviet state and the Orthodox Church, this critical function is fulfilled at a fundamentally local level. Indeed, it is fulfilled at a brazenly local level, rendering, as it does at this level of memory's landscape, those great powers irrelevant.

Afterword

ON LIGHTNESS AND WEIGHT

> The weight of this sad time we must obey;
> Speak what we feel, not what we ought to say.
> The oldest hath borne most: we that are young
> Shall never see so much, nor live so long.
>
> —EDGAR, *KING LEAR*

> [I]s heaviness truly deplorable and lightness
> splendid?
>
> —MILAN KUNDERA,
>   *THE UNBEARABLE LIGHTNESS OF BEING* (1984:5)

* * *

In my very first visit to Solovyovo in summer 1994, I spent a night in a tiny house, which, it turned out later, was known to be haunted. I was with Svetlana Adon'eva, a folklorist who had graciously invited me to come with her students on a short expedition in the region, together with enough other people so that we found ourselves crowded on the floor, boiling hot, fighting mosquitoes, and tossing and turning all night. One woman awoke the next morning in a terrified state; she'd had bloody nightmares—a whole, seemingly endless adventure in the land of dark dreams.

Later, I heard the stories. Many years ago, a man had murdered his wife in the house (they were chuzhie who had come to Solovyovo for work, and not because their families were rooted in that rodina); and years after that, a drunken card game had ended there in a beating and death of a man who had no relatives in the village and whose murderer was never tried. That was my first exposure to the ghosts of Solovyovo: foreign, bloody, and dangerous.

It is true that the ghosts of Solovyovo, like its very past, can (to return to Marx) "weigh like a nightmare" on the minds of the living. How much lighter, how much easier would it be if the villagers of Solovyovo could simply be free of the seventy years of totalitarianism, and the hundreds of years of brutish exploitation that came before it? How much brighter and lighter would it be if the symbolic habits that grew up around exploitation could be simply forgotten, whisked away, and, like any sickness, be let to fly off in the wind?

Memory is a weight, indeed. And many stories in Solovyovo are hauntingly sad. But the fact of the weight of memory (combined with the sadness of the stories) does not mean that memory—social memory—is simply a dangerous and negative social force. Although something akin to social memory is used to speak of the throngs of veterans and the straggling poor who come to the streets with smiling photos of Stalin held above their heads, this is only one face of social memory. Depending on the rhetorical track that one chooses, social memory is not conservative (and stubborn and brutish), but a source of resistance to outside forces, including the force of the state and the call of "the nation." Is it right or wrong (or conservative or a mark of resistance?) for the villagers of Solovyovo to go to the graveyard on Troitsa, and not to church? Is it good or bad that they heal with whispered words when doctors' ministrations do not work? Or that their icons are loaded with potent symbolism that would be disapproved of by theologians? Or that money still feels dangerous and distasteful to them in important ways? Or that ghosts return to them sometimes haunting, sometimes terrifying, and sometimes as healers and friends?

Whether or not social memory marks "stubborn conservatism" or "noble resistance," the fact is that it is supported by repeated social actions that take place in some of the most meaningful (and meaning-generating and meaning-reproducing) spheres of life: language and metaphor, narrative, ritual, religion, commemoration. This is why, as I've aimed to show from the beginning, social memory is stronger and more resilient than it appears. So while it is true that memories can die with their bearers, photographs can be altered, streets can be renamed, and facts and faces and right rituals can fade away, it is also true that social memory, in its most meaningful sense, can't be wished away . . . by anyone. It also cannot be idealized away, or erased by the gulag, or even—

in the short term at least—by the market's invisible hand. I hope that this book has shown that remembering, in its important social sense, does not depend on any particular memory. And that desire, whether brutal or benevolent, is not enough to re-cast the actions that carry and reproduce memory. Whether conservative or resistant, social memory changes only when these actions come into their new forms and new iterative pathways.

At a crucial level, the questions that lie at the foundation of social memory are, we are reminded, not about the past, but about the present world, with its present exigencies of power and will: What is agency? What is a perfect society? What are the gestures of invocations to otherworldly powers? How does one become "one's own"? If social memory is a landscape, these questions make up its deep, tectonic principles: They do not depend on given symbols, nor do they depend on any one scrap of memory on its invisible piece of paper in the head. They do depend on a sea of individual choices (this pair of failing hands, that move to a town or city, these children coming to live not by the wind and the cloud, but by the clock) and long, insistent repeating of new ways, new words, new understandings of the power of other worlds, and the power of "us" and "we" and "mine" and "me." The present is cast into the future. The sad stories are told, in frail and failing voices, as are the stories of fealty and betrayal and awesome contacts with the "something" that is out there. There is much still to learn.

Heaviness is not truly deplorable, nor is lightness fully splendid. Ghosts do come at night, bone white, and with blood on their hands, but they also come quietly, with the perfumes of spring in the air, fussing about bees, caring about uprightness and familial peace, remembering the deeds wrought by hands and hearts, and urging bounties from the soil of which they have become a part. To forget that is to forget deep and important matters, in the long and winding walk from then to then.

Acknowledgments

* * *

In the summer of 2004, I was shown a tree that had been planted outside the clubhouse during my time in the village that I have called Solovyovo. The tree, transplanted from a nearby forest nine full years ago, was surprisingly small, reaching only just higher than my waist. Perhaps the roots—crowded by the roots of the other trees, or the weeds that grew up around the steadily crumbling clubhouse—could find no water or no room to breathe. I really had no idea of how this could have happened, nor did anyone else in the village. It didn't grow; it didn't die. It had been frozen for nine years in time. And yet, it was clear that that very summer, out of nowhere, the tree had begun to shoot up. A full foot of new bright green foliage was reaching up toward the sky. Perhaps, finding its place, the tree that had been called *derevo druzhby* ("the tree of friendship") was ready to survive in the thick rooted soil.

For nine years, this work also sought its space and its roots. The process was slow and hard, but I wouldn't have traded a moment of it.

This is perhaps because of the fact that from my first moments in Solovyovo, I was treated to the sort of kindness that can never be fully counted or recounted. The gifts—gifts of poor people enduring truly difficult lives—spanned far beyond the generosity with time and space and all that can be found around a table. I arrive now at the end of this journey deeply thankful and forever indebted. Therefore, I must thank first, and from the bottom of my heart, the family I have called the Belov family. Healers and teachers, I hope and pray that this work honors them. With the Belovs, I thank the villagers of Solovyovo, Vershina, Maksimovo, Iurino, Kraskovo, Guliaevo, and Gubino for their kindness, openness, and patience. The lessons they have all taught me have been as humbling and indelible as one could hope for in life.

Of course, the journey began before Solovyovo and ended long after my first long stay there. Three figures stand out for particular thanks for their support in the intellectual side of this research. Professor John Leavitt, my thesis advisor at l'Université de Montréal, has been a mentor to me since I first began to think about anthropology. His ability to reach out to the largest possible questions, and to find poetry in the particulars, has been a true inspiration. Many, many thanks to him for some of the best conversations about ideas I've ever been privileged to be a part of, and for his absolutely infectious curiosity and true guidance.

Professor Nancy Ries has been, in the past decade, one of the most tireless creators, definers, and shapers of the anthropology of the new Russia. Her own research has been consistently groundbreaking, and she has dedicated herself to the new work in the field with passion and intensity. She has supported my work from the beginning; she read many versions of this book, gave me careful edits, and pushed me at every step of the way. I am deeply indebted to her as both a colleague and a true friend.

Dr. Blair A. Ruble, director of the Kennan Institute, has been a man of distinct and brilliant vision in the field of Russian studies. While I was still writing my dissertation (and the beneficiary of a short-term grant at the Kennan Institute), he began to encourage me—a young anthropologist with a quirky subject and unusual research—to draw my work toward the broader questions in the field of Russian studies and to make my work relevant to the pressing questions in the world of foreign policy. In short, he encouraged me—as he has encouraged hundreds if not thousands of others like me—to make my work matter. For this, as well as for his moral support and his invaluable comments on this manuscript, I am truly grateful.

There are countless others to whom thanks are warranted. In Beloz-ersk, I thank especially my friend Tamara Golovkina for her warm hos-pitality, good talks, hard-hitting insights, and the use of her bathtub whenever I was in town. I also thank Tanya Groshnikova for her friend-ship (and her beautiful songs!), as well as the entire collective at the regional library.

In St. Petersburg I was offered home, hearth, haven, and so much more by Zina and Vitalii Kiriushchenko, Lidia Semenova and Sasha Borkov, Konstantin Bogdanov, Kseniia Pochtennaia and Alexander Mazhuga, and Nina and Andrei Lykov. In Moscow, Irina Makarova, Masha Lip-man, and Galina Ulianova were also exceedingly generous with their ideas, insights, and friendship. Svetlana Adon'eva must also be thanked for her exceptional intellectual and practical assistance; it is because of her that I came to live in the village of Solovyovo, and I am deeply grate-ful to her for her role in that turn of my life.

Lucian Perkins, photographer for the *Washington Post,* came to Solov-yovo several times and took stunning pictures of the village and its in-habitants. I so admire his clear and pure eye, and I thank him for believ-ing in the quiet beauty of the place (and, certainly, for his generosity in allowing his photographs to appear in this book). Lucian and his wife, Sarah Tanguay, have been real friends to me in Washington and I am grateful to both of them for their warmth. Kelly Doe has inspired me with her endless delight in beauty and her deeply inquisitive mind. I thank her for her friendship, of course, and for her lovely work in designing this book.

For their wisdom, for their guidance, for their generosity, their abid-ing friendship and more, I thank Deborah Brodey, Shiraz Felling, David Finkel, Alice O'Brien, Bob and Debbie Rosenfeld, Lidia Semenova, Ken and Carolyn Wilson, Alexei Yurchak, and James Fitta and Hrothgar. Among my friends, Chris Chulos, Willard Sunderland, Michael Thu-mann, Cindy Buckley, and Jeffrey Burds have been especially generous in sharing ideas. Special thanks to Jerome Rousseau, Paul Friedrich, Kevin Tuite, and Gilles Bibeau for being so important in shaping my thinking early on. Kelly Smith and Michele Rivkin-Fish gave me invaluable com-ments on the book manuscript in various forms, along with care, friend-ship, and moral support, for which, as well, I am exceedingly grateful. Marji Balzer—one of the true pioneers in the anthropology of the former Soviet Union (and whose work and edited volumes I have relied on heav-ily in this book)—has been very supportive of my research for years. I thank her for that support and for the exceptionally helpful comments she gave me on my manuscript in its final stages. I am certainly most indebted to Bruce Grant, who gave the manuscript two thorough and very thoughtful reads in earlier stages.

The Kennan Institute has played a crucial role in my development as a specialist on Russia. Having already been the grateful recipient of two grants (short-term and research scholar, both supported by the Title VIII program of the U.S. State Department), I began work at the Kennan Institute in autumn 2002. My time there has been a true learning experience. Every member of the staff has, in his or her own way, helped me in this process, including Summer Brown, Joe Dresen, Thecla Frazier, Edita Krunkaityte, Nancy Popson, Atiq Sarwari, Erin Trouth, and Megan Yasenchak. In particular, I wish to thank Jennifer Giglio for having done valuable readings for me as the project came to a close. As well, my intern, Anita Ackerman, was a pleasure to work with. At the Woodrow Wilson Center, I have had the pleasure of meeting many interesting people. In particular, I thank Lindsay Collins, Nida Gelazis, Lisa Hanley, Leslie Johnson, Michelle Kutler, George Liston Seay, Janet Spikes, Flip Strum, and Mike Van Dusen for the great conversations. Steve Lagerfeld, editor of the *Wilson Quarterly,* has been a wonderful person to talk about ideas with; he's helped me a great deal with my writing and has been a real friend. At the Wilson Center Press, it's been a great pleasure to work with Joe Brinley and Yamile Kahn.

Every member of my family has, in his or her own way, made this research and writing possible. They have given me the gift of curiosity, and taught me how to travel light. My mother, Florence Paxson, has read my work for years with a keen eye and terrific ear, and I have learned tremendously from her example. My father, Dana Paxson, launched me into the world of ideas and urged me toward the largest possible questions. I thank my sister Laura, brother Michael, niece and nephew Sammy and Michael, and my grandfather Sheldon and grandmother Dorothy for all of their love. Mark and Paula Siskind were generous with their home and their hearts. I am most grateful to them as well.

This project would have been impossible without generous financial support from the International Research and Exchanges Board, the Social Science Research Council, Faculté des Etudes Supériures de l'Université de Montréal, Département d'anthropologie de l'Université de Montréal, and from the Phi Delta Epsilon Memorial Scholarship from McGill University. Funding from the Kennan Institute supported the writing of my dissertation and the first draft of this book. In all, I have six times been the beneficiary of Title VIII-supported grants from the State Department. I owe my career to Title VIII, and I am profoundly grateful for that.

Portions of the manuscript are reworked versions of writing that appeared in my doctoral dissertation (1999); the *Washington Post Magazine* piece, "History's Harvest" (Paxson and Perkins 1997); the *Wilson Quarterly*, "Letter from a Russian Village" (Paxson 2002); and "The Festival of the Holy Trinity (*Troitsa*) in Rural Russia: A Case Study in the Topography of Memory," *Anthropology of East Europe Review* (Paxson 1998).

* * *

Lastly, and in memoriam, I thank 'Ali Akbar Furutan, for one conversation in a house in a garden on Mount Carmel, and for his promise to remember me.

Russian Terms and Phrases

NOTE: DEFINITIONS HERE REFLECT LOCAL USAGE

BABUSHKA (BABA, BABKA): grandmother, grandma;
form of address for any older woman

BARIN: landowner; master

BATIUSHKA (BAT'KA): father

CHASTUSHKA: humorous rhymed poem/song of four lines
(sometimes improvised)

CHUDO: wonder; chudesnoe: wonder, wondrous, miraculous

CHUZHOI: someone else's, another's, other's; strange, alien, foreign

DEVOCHKA: girl (child)

DEVUSHKA (DEVKA, DEVITSA): marriageable girl, young woman

DEDUSHKA (DED, DEDKA): grandfather, grandpa;
form of address to any older man; form of address to particular
otherworldly beings (e.g., dedushka lesovoi, grandfather forest)

DOBROM DOBRO: good through the agency of good

DOMOVOI (KHOZIAIN DOMA, KHOZIAIN DOMOVOI): house sprite;
host of the house

DUSHA: soul

DVOR: courtyard, yard, homestead

GULIANKA: fête; outdoor party (from guliat', to walk)

KHOZIAIN: host, male leader (worldly and otherworldly)

KHOZIAIKA: hostess, female leader (worldly and otherworldly)

KHOZIAISTVO: farm, household management

KILY: skin rupture caused by curses, evil eye, and so on

KOLDOVSTVO: the magic arts, practiced for purposes
of healing or harming

KOLDUN: (often derogatory) practitioner of the
healing/cursing/magical arts

KOLLEKTIV: collective

KOLKHOZ: collective farm (from kollektivnoe khoziastvo,
collective farming)

[CHELOVEK] KOTORYI ZNAET: "one who knows";
practitioner of magical arts

KULAK: "rich farmer" in the class analysis of Lenin.

KUL'TRABOTNIK (m.), KUL'TRABOTNITSA (f.): culture workers, feminine and masculine

LEGKOST': lightness; simplicity, easiness (related to: legkii, adj., light, slight, easy; legche, comp., lighter)

LESHII (KHOZIAIN LESOVOI, KHOZIAIN LESA, DEDUSHKA LESOVOI, DEDUSHKA, DED, DEDKA): forest host

MAT', MATUSHKA: mother

MUZHIK: village man; rugged man

NAROD: people, nation

OBKHOD: circumambulation

OGOVOR: excessive praise

OBRASHCHENIE: appeal, address

OBSHCHENIE: social interaction, communion

OBSHCHINA: pre-Revolutionary rural collective

PRIKHOD: parish

RAN'SHE: before

RASKULACHIVANIE: dekulakization; the effort to destroy the class of "rich farmers" in the 1930s

ROD: family line, kin, clan, birth, sort, kind

RODINA: motherland, homeland

RODNOI: own, native, dear

RODSTVENNIKI: relatives; extended family members

RUSSKAIA PECH': the large wood-burning stove typical of rural Russia

SEL'SOVET: village council; smallest unit of rural administration

SENOKOS: hay harvest

SILY: forces, powers

SGLAZIT': to curse with the eye; sglaz, the curse of the eye ("the evil eye")

SOVKHOZ: state farm

STAROSTA: elder; village leader

SVIATYE: saints, holy ones

SVOI (m.), SVOIA, (f.), SVOE (n.): one's own

SVOBODA: freedom, liberty

TIAZHEST': heaviness; related to tiazhelo (adv.), heavily; tiazhelyi (adj.): heavy, weighty, hard

UKRUPNENIE: program of village consolidation in Soviet Russia

Bibliography

Adon'eva, S.B., and Obchinnikova, O.A. 1993. *Traditsionnaia Russkaia magiia v zapisiakh kontsa XX veka*. St. Petersburg: Frendlikh-Taf.

Adon'eva, S.B., and Gerasimova, N.M. 1996. *Sovremennaia ballada u zhenskii romans*. St. Petersburg: Ivan Limbakh.

Afanasev, Aleksandr. 1966. *Russian Secret Tales*. New York: Brussel and Brussel.

Afanasev, Aleksandr. 1973 [1945]. *Russian Fairy Tales*. New York: Pantheon Books.

Afanasev, Aleksandr. 1982. *Narodnye russkie skazki*. Moscow: Pravda.

Aleksandrov, V.A. 1970. *Russkie: Istoriko-etnograficheskii atlas*. Moscow: Nauka.

Allina-Pisano, Jessica. 2002. "Reorganization and Its Discontents: A Case Study in Voronezh Oblast." In *Rural Reform in Post-Soviet Russia,* edited by David J. O'Brien and Stephen K. Wegren, 298–324. Washington, D.C.: Woodrow Wilson Center Press; Baltimore, Md.: Johns Hopkins University Press.

Althusser, Louis. 1974. *Philosophie et philosophie spontanée des savants*. Paris: Éditions Maspero.

Amelina, Maria. 2002. "What Turns the *Kolkhoz* into a Firm? Regional Policies and the Elasticity of Budget Constraint." In *Rural Reform in Post-Soviet Russia,* edited by David J. O'Brien and Stephen K. Wegren, 264–297. Washington,

D.C.: Woodrow Wilson Center Press; Baltimore, Md.: Johns Hopkins University Press.

Anderson, Benedict. 1983. *Imagined Communities: Reflections on the Origin and Spread of Nationalism*. London, New York: Verso.

Anisimov, V.I., and Aleksandrova, A.A., eds. 1992. *Russkaia pesennaia lirika*. Moscow: Sovetskaia Rossiia.

Asad, Talal. 1973. *Anthropology and the Colonial Encounter*. New York: Humanities Press.

Asad, Talal. 1983. "Anthropological Concepts of Religion: Reflections on Geertz." *Man*, n.s., 18: 237–259.

Ayer, A.J. 1952 [1946]. *Language, Truth and Logic*. New York: Dover Publications.

Bachelard, Gaston. 1940. *La philosophie du non*. Paris: Quadrige.

Bachelard, Gaston. 1964. *The Poetics of Space*. New York: Orion Press.

Bachelard, Gaston. 1969. *The Poetics of Revelry*. Boston: Beacon Press.

Bakhtin, Mikhail. 1984. *Problems of Dostoevsky's Poetics*. Minneapolis: University of Minnesota Press.

Bakhtin, Mikhail. 1986. *Speech Genres and Other Late Essays*. Trans. Vern W. McGee, and edited by Caryl Emerson and Michael Holquist. Austin: University of Texas Press.

Balzer, Marjorie Mandelstam, ed. 1992. *Russian Traditional Culture: Religion, Gender, and Customary Law*. Armonk, N.Y.: M.E. Sharpe.

Balzer, Marjorie Mandelstam. 1999. "Political Anthropology: Images of Leaders." *Anthropology and Archeology of Eurasia*, 38, no. 2: 4–6.

Baranova, O.G., et al. 2001. *Russkii prazdnik: Prazdniki i obriady narodnogo zemledel'cheskogo kalendaria: Illiustrirovannaia entsiklopediia*. St. Petersburg: Iskusstvo-SPB.

Barks, Coleman, trans. 1995. *The Essential Rumi*. San Francisco, Calif.: Harper Collins.

Barth, Frederick. 1969. *Ethnic Groups and Boundaries*. Boston: Little, Brown.

Barthes, Roland. 1957. *Mythologies*. Paris: Editions de Seuil.

Basso, Keith. 1996. *Wisdom Sits in Places: Landscape and Language among the Apache*. Albuquerque: University of New Mexico Press.

Belov, Vasilii. 1989. *Lad: Ocherki o narodnoi estetike*. Moscow: Molodnaia Gvardiia.

Benet, Sula. 1970. *The Village of Viriatino: An Ethnographic Study of a Russian Village from Before the Revolution to the Present*. Garden City, N.Y.: Doubleday.

Benveniste, Emile. 1964. *Les niveaux de l'analyse linguistique*. In Proceedings of the 9th International Congress of Linguistics, Cambridge, Mass., 1962.

Berdiaev, Nicholas. 1948. *The Russian Idea*. New York: Macmillan and Co.

Berdiaev, Nicholas. 1960 [1937]. *The Origin of Russian Communism*. Ann Arbor: University of Michigan Press.

Bernshtam, T.A. 1988. *Molodëzh' v obriadovoi zhizni russkoi obshchiny XIX-nachale XX v. Polovozrastnoi aspekt traditionnoi kul'tury*. Leningrad: Nauka.

Bernshtam, T.A. 1992. "Russian Folk Culture and Folk Religion." In *Russian*

Traditional Culture: Religion, Gender, and Customary Law, edited by Marjorie Mandelstam Balzer, 34–47. Armonk, N.Y.: M.E. Sharpe.

Berry, Loyd E., and Crummey, Robert O., eds. 1968. *Rude and Barbarous Kingdom: Russia in the Accounts of Sixteenth-Century English Voyagers.* Madison, Milwaukee, and London: University of Wisconsin Press.

Beznin, M. A., ed. 1993. *Belozer'e: Istoriko-literaturnyi al'manakh I.* Vologda: Rus'.

Beznin, M.A., ed. 1998. *Belozer'e: Krayevedcheskii al'manakh,* vol. 2. Vologda: Legiia.

Billington, James H. 1970. *The Icon and the Axe: An Interpretive History of Russian Culture.* New York: Vintage Books.

Bock, Philip K. 1980. *Continuities in Psychological Linguistics.* San Fransisco: W.H. Freeman and Company.

Bogdanov, K.A. 1995. *Dengi v fol'klore.* St. Petersburg: Rossiiskoi Academii Nauk.

Bourdieu, Pierre. 1977. *Outline of a Theory of Practice.* Trans. from the French by Richard Nice. Cambridge: Cambridge University Press.

Bourdieu, Pierre. 1984. *Distinction: A Social Critique of the Judgment of Taste.* Trans. Richard Nice. Cambridge, Mass.: Harvard University Press.

Bourdieu, Pierre. 1991. *Language and Symbolic Power.* Trans. M. Adamson and G. Raymond. Cambridge, Mass.: Harvard University Press.

Brodsky, Joseph. 1986. *Less Than One: Selected Essays.* New York: Russell and Russell.

Brown, Archie, et al., eds. 1982. *The Cambridge Encyclopedia of Russia and the Soviet Union.* Cambridge: Cambridge University Press.

Buckley, Cynthia. 2000. "Intergenerational Exchanges in Rural Russia." Paper presented at the First International Conference on Rural Aging, Charleston, W.V.

Burds, Jeffrey. 1998. *Peasant Dreams and Market Politics: Labor Migration and the Russian Village, 1861–1905.* Pittsburgh, Pa.: University of Pittsburgh Press.

Chadwick, H. Monroe, and Chadwick, N. Kershaw. 1936. *The Growth of Literature,* vol. 2. Cambridge: Cambridge University Press.

Chaianov, Aleksandr. 1925. *Organizatsiia krest'ianskogo khoziaistva.* Moscow: Cooperative Publishing House.

Cherepanova, O.A. 1996. *Mifologicheskie rasskayi u legendy russkogo severa.* St. Petersburg: St. Petersburg State University.

Cherniavsky, Michael. 1969. *Tsar and People: Studies in Russian Myths.* New York: Random House.

Chernikh, P. Ia. 1993. *Istoriko-etimologicheskii slovar' soremennogo russkogo iazyka,* vols. 1 and 2. Moscow: Russkii Iazyk.

Chew, Allen, F. 1970. *An Atlas of Russian History.* New Haven, Conn.: Yale University Press.

Chistova, K.V., and Bernshtam, T.A. 1978. *Russkii narodnyi svadebnyi obriad: Issledovaniia i materialy.* Leningrad: Nauka.

Chulos, Chris J. 1995. "Myths of the Pious or Pagan Peasant in Post-Emancipation Central Russia (Voronezh Province)." *Russian History,* 22, no. 2:181–216.

Chulos, Chris J. 1999. "A Place without Taverns: Space in the Peasant Afterlife." *Studia Historica,* 62: 191–199.

Chulos, Chris J. 2003. *Converging Worlds: Religion and Community in Peasant Russia 1861–1917.* Dekalb: Northern Illinois University Press.

Clément, Olivier. 1961. *L'Eglise Orthodoxe.* Paris: Presses Universitaires de France.

Clifford, James, and Marcus, George E. 1986. *Writing Culture: The Poetics and Politics of Ethnography.* Berkeley, Los Angeles, and London: University of California Press.

Cohn, Bernard S. 1987. *An Anthropologist among the Historians and Other Essays.* Oxford: Oxford University Press.

Coleman, James S. 1988. "Social Capital in the Creation of Human Capital." *American Journal of Sociology,* 94 (supplement): S95–S120.

Comaroff, John, and Comaroff, Jean, eds. 1993. *Modernity and Its Malcontents: Ritual and Power in Postcolonial Africa.* Chicago: University of Chicago Press.

Connerton, Paul. 1989. *How Societies Remember.* Cambridge: Cambridge University Press.

Conquest, Robert. 1986. *Harvest of Sorrow: Soviet Collectivization and the Terror-Famine.* New York: Oxford University Press.

Coustine, Marquis de. 1991. *Letters From Russia.* Trans. and edited by Robin Buss. London: Penguin.

Dal', V.I. 1911 [1863–1866]. *Tolkovyi slovar' zhivogo russkogo iazyka.* Moscow: Russkii Iazyk.

Daniel, E. Valentine. 1984. *Fluid Signs: Being a Person the Tamil Way.* Berkeley: University of California Press.

Daniel, E. Valentine. 1996. *Charred Lullabies: Chapters in an Anthropology of Violence.* Princeton, N.J.: Princeton University Press.

Dershem, Larry D. 2002. "How Much Does Informal Support Matter? The Effect of Personal Networks on Subjective Evaluation of Life." In *Rural Reform in Post-Soviet Russia,* edited by David J. O'Brien and Stephen K. Wegren, 385–401. Washington, D.C.: Woodrow Wilson Center Press; Baltimore, Md.: Johns Hopkins University Press.

Dillard, Annie. 1982. *Teaching a Stone to Talk: Expeditions and Encounters.* New York: Harper and Row.

Dostoevsky, Fedor. 1962. *The Possessed.* Trans. Andrew R. MacAndrew. New York: New American Library.

Downing, Charles. 1989 [1956]. *Russian Tales and Legends.* Oxford: Oxford University Press.

Dumont, Louis. 1972. *Homo Hierarchicus.* London: Paladin.

Dumont, Louis. 1986a. "Are Cultures Living Beings? German Identity in Interaction." *Man,* 21: 587–604.

Dumont, Louis. 1986b. "Collective Identities and Universalist Ideology: The Actual Interplay." *Theory, Culture, and Society,* 3: 25–33.

Dunn, Steven, and Dunn, Ethel. 1963. "The Great Russian Peasant: Culture Change or Cultural Development." *Ethnology,* 2, no. 3: 320–338.

Dunn, Steven, and Dunn, Ethel. 1967. *The Peasants of Central Russia.* New York: Hold, Rinehart, and Winston.

Durkheim, Emile. 1995 [1912]. *The Elementary Forms of Religious Life.* New York: Free Press.

Easthope, Anthony. 1983. *Poetry as Discourse.* London and New York: Methuen.

Etkind, Alexander. 1996. "Psychological Culture." In *Russian Culture at the Crossroads,* edited by Dmitri N. Shalin, 99–126. Boulder, Colo.: Westview Press.

Etkind, Alexander. 2003. "Whirling with the Other: Russian Populism and Religious Sects." *Russian Review,* 62, no. 4: 565–588.

Evans-Pritchard, E.E. 1969 [1940]. *The Nuer: A Description of the Modes of Livelihood and Political Institutions of a Nilotic People.* Oxford: Clarendon Press.

Evans-Pritchard, E.E. 1937. *Witchcraft, Oracles and Magic among the Azande.* Oxford: Clarendon Press.

Fabian, Johannes. 1983. *Time and the Other.* New York: Columbia University Press.

Fanger, Donald. 1968. "The Peasant in Literature." In *The Peasant in Nineteenth-Century Russia,* edited by Wayne S. Vucinich, 231–262. Stanford, Calif.: Stanford University Press.

Fedotov, G. 1948. *Treasury of Russian Spirituality.* New York: Sheed and Ward.

Fedotov, G.P. 1946. *The Russian Religious Mind,* vol. 1. Cambridge, Mass.: Harvard University Press.

Fedotov, G.P. 1966. *The Russian Religious Mind: The Middle Ages.* Cambridge, Mass.: Harvard University Press.

Feld, Steven, and Basso, Keith H., eds. 1996. *Senses of Place.* Santa Fe, N.Mex.: School of American Research Press.

Fentress, James, and Wickham, Chris. 1992. *Social Memory.* Oxford and Cambridge, Mass.: Blackwell.

Fernandez, James W. 1986. *Persuasions and Performances: The Play of Tropes in Culture.* Bloomington: Indiana University Press.

Fernandez, James W., ed. 1991. *Beyond Metaphor: The Theory of Tropes in Anthropology.* Stanford, Calif.: Stanford University Press.

Figes, Orlando. 1997. *A People's Tragedy: A History of the Russian Revolution.* New York: Viking.

Firsov, B.M., and Kiseleva, I.G., eds. 1993. *Byt velikorusskikh krest'ian-zemlepashtsev: Opisanie materialov etngraficheskogo biuro kniazia V. N. Tenisheva (na primere Vladimirskoi Gubernii).* St. Petersburg: Izdatel'stvo Evropeiskogo.

Fischer, Michael M.J. 1986. "Ethnicity and the Post Modern Arts of Memory." In *Writing Culture,* edited by James Clifford and George Marcus, 194–233. Berkeley, Los Angeles, London: University of California Press.

Fitzpatrick, Sheila. 1994. *Stalin's Peasants: Resistance and Survival in the Russian Village after Collectivization.* Oxford: Oxford University Press.

Fletcher, Giles. 1966 [1558]. *Of the Russe Commonwealth.* Cambridge, Mass.: Harvard University Press.

Forest, Jim. 1990. *Religion in the New Russia.* New York: Crossroad.

Foster, George M. 1965. "Peasant Society and the Image of Limited Good." *American Anthropologist,* 65, no. 2: 293–315.

Foucault, Michel. 1965. *Madness and Civilization.* New York: Vintage.

Foucault, Michel. 1969. *The Archaeology of Knowledge.* London: Tavistock Publications.

Foucault, Michel. 1971. *L'ordre du discours.* Paris: Gallimard.

Foucault, Michel. 1973. *The Order of Things.* New York: Vintage Books.

Foucault, Michel. 1986 [1978]. *The History of Sexuality: An Introduction.* Trans. from the French by Robert Hurley. New York: Vintage Books.

Freeze, Gregory L. 1996. "Subversive Piety: Religion and the Political Crisis in Late Imperial Russia."*Journal of Modern History,* 68, no. 2: 308–350.

Friedrich, Paul. 1979. "Structural Implications of Russian Prenominal Usage." In *Language, Context and the Imagination,* 63–168. Stanford, Calif.: Stanford University Press.

Friedrich, Paul. 1986. *The Language Parallax: Linguistic Relativism and Poetic Indeterminacy.* Austin: University of Texas Press.

Friedrich, Paul. 1992. "Interpretation and Vision: A Critique of Cryptopositivism." *Cultural Anthropology,* 7, no. 2: 211–231.

Frierson, Cathy A. 1993. *Peasant Icons: Representations of Rural People in Late Nineteenth-Century Russia.* New York: Cambridge University Press.

Froianov, I. Ia. et al. 1992. "The Introduction of Christianity in Russia and the Pagan Traditions." In *Russian Traditional Culture: Religion, Gender, and Customary Law,* edited by Marjorie Balzer. Armonk, N.Y.: M.E. Sharpe.

Gambold Miller, Liesl L. 2002. "Communal Coherence and Barriers to Reform." In *Rural Reform in Post-Soviet Russia,* edited by David J. O'Brien and Stephen K. Wegren, 221–242. Washington, D.C.: Woodrow Wilson Center Press; Baltimore, Md.: Johns Hopkins University Press.

Gambold Miller, Liesl L., and Heady, Patrick. 2004. "Cooperation, Power, and Community Economy and Ideology in the Russian Countryside." In *The Postsocialist Agrarian Question: Property Relations and the Rural Condition,* Halle Studies in the Anthropology of Eurasia, edited by Chris Hann and the "Property Relations" Group, 257–292. Munster: LIT.

Gatrell, Peter, and Harrison, Mark. 1993. "The Russian and Soviet Economies in Two World Wars: A Comparative View." *Economic History Review,* 46, no. 3: 425–452.

Geertz, Clifford. 1973. "Religion as a Cultural System." In *The Interpretation of Cultures: Selected Essays,* 87–125. New York: Basic Books.

Gellner, Ernest. 1983. *Nations and Nationalism.* Oxford: Blackwell.

Gellner, Ernest. 1988. *State and Society in Soviet Thought.* London: Basil Blackwell.

Gerhart, Genevra. 1974. *The Russian's World: Life and Language.* New York: Harcourt Brace Jovanovich, Inc.

Gessat-Anstett, Élisabeth. 2001. "Du collectif au communautaire: À propos des réseaux familiaux dans la Russie post-Sovietique." *L'homme,* 157: 115–136.

Goldmann, Lucien. 1976. *Cultural Creation in Modern Society.* St. Louis: Telos Press.

Gorboriau, Marc. 1970. "Structural Anthropology and History." In *Structuralism: A Reader,* edited by Michael Lane, 156–169. London: Jonathan Cape Ltd.

Gumperz, John. 1982. *Discourse Strategies.* Cambridge: Cambridge University Press.

Gibian, George. 1956. "Dostoevsky's Use of Russian Folklore." *Journal of American Folklore,* 69: 239–253.

Gilbert, Martin. 1993. *The Dent Atlas of Russian History, second edition.* London: J. M. Dent.

Ginzburg, Evgeniia Semenovna. 1967. *Journey into the Whirlwind.* New York: Harcourt Brace Jovanovich.

Ginzburg, Evgeniia. 1989. *Within the Whirlwind.* London: Collins Harvill.

Gorer, Geoffrey. 1962 [1949]. *The People of Great Russia.* New York: W.W. Norton.

Goricheva, Tatiana. 1989. *Cry of the Spirit: Witness to Faith in the Soviet Union.* New York: Crossroad.

Gromyko, M.M. 1986. *Traditsionye normy povedeniia i formy obshchiia Russkikh Krest'ian XIVV.* Moscow: Nauka.

Gromyko, M.M., Vlasova, I.V., and Listova, T.A. 1989. *Russkie—semenyi i obshchestvennyi Byt.* Moscow: Nauka.

Halbwachs, Maurice. 1992. *On Collective Memory.* Trans., edited, and with an introduction by Lewis A. Coser. Chicago: University of Chicago Press.

Halbwachs, Maurice. 1980. *The Collective Memory.* Trans. and edited by Frances J. Ditter, Jr., and Vida Yazdi. New York: Harper and Row.

Halbwachs, Maurice. 1925. *Les cadres sociaux de la memoire.* Paris: Presses Universitaires de France.

Handler, Richard. 1988. *Nationalism and the Politics of Culture in Quebec.* Madison: University of Wisconsin Press.

Hawkes, Terence. 1977. *Structuralism and Semiotics.* Berkeley and Los Angeles: University of California Press.

Hemschemayer, Judith, trans. 1992. *The Complete Poems of Anna Akhmatova.* Boston: Zephyr Press.

Herzfeld, Michael. 1982. *Folklore, Ideology and the Making of Modern Greece.* Austin: University of Texas Press.

Herzfeld, Michael. 1987. *Anthropology through the Looking Glass: Critical Ethnography in the Margins of Europe.* Cambridge: Cambridge University Press.

Hingley, Ronald. 1968. *The Tsars, 1533–1917.* New York: Macmillan.

Hingley, Ronald. 1977. *The Russian Mind.* New York: Charles Scribner's Sons.

Hivon, Myriam. 1995. "Ploughing through the Reforms: The Domestic Economy of Rural Households in Post-Soviet Russia." Ph.D. diss., University of Cambridge.

Hivon, Myriam. 1998. "Payer en liquide: L'utilisation de la vodka dans les échanges en Russie rurale." In Les cadeaux: à quel prix. Edited by Sophie Chevalier and Anne Monjaret. *Ethnologie Française,* 28, 4: 515–524.

Hobsbawm, E.J. 1990. *Nations and Nationalism since 1780: Programme, Myth, Reality.* Cambridge: Cambridge University Press.

Hobsbawm, E.J., and Ranger, Terrance, eds. 1983. *The Invention of Tradition:* Cambridge: Cambridge University Press.

Howe, Jovan E. 1991. *The Peasant Mode of Production.* Tampere, Finland: University of Finland.

Hubbs, Joanna. 1988. *Mother Russia: The Feminine Myth in Russian Culture.* Bloomington: Indiana University Press.

Humphrey, Caroline. 1983. *Karl Marx Collective: Economy, Society, and Religion in a Siberian Collective Farm.* Cambridge: Cambridge University Press.

Humphrey, Caroline. 2002. *The Unmaking of Soviet Life: Everyday Economies after Socialism.* Ithaca, N.Y.: Cornell University Press.

Huntington, Richard, and Metcalf, Peter. 1979. *Celebrations of Death: The Anthropology of Mortuary Ritual.* Cambridge: Cambridge University Press.

Hymes, Dell. 1964. "Introduction: Toward Ethnographies of Communication." In J.J. Gumperez and D. Hymes, *The Ethnography of Communication,* special issue of *The American Anthropologist* 66, part 2 (1964): 1–29.

Ivanits, Linda J. 1987. "Russian Folk Narratives about the Supernatural." *Soviet Anthropology and Archaeology,* 26, no. 2: 2–69.

Ivanits, Linda J. 1989. *Russian Folk Belief.* Armonk, N.Y.: M.E. Sharpe.

Ivanov, S.A. 1994. *Vizantiiskoe iurodsvo.* Moscow: Mezhdunarodnie Otnosheniia.

Ivanov, V.V., and Toporov, V.N. 1980. "Domovoi." In *Mify narodov mira,* vol. 1, edited by C.A. Tokarev, 391–392. Moscow: Sovetskaia entsiklopediia.

Ivanov, V.V., and Toporov, V.N. 1982a. "Leshii." In *Mify narodov mira,* vol. 2, edited by C.A. Tokarev, 52. Moscow: Sovetskaia entsiklopediia.

Ivanov, V.V., and Toporov, V.N. 1982b. "Slavianskaia mifologiia." In *Mify Narodov Mira,* vol. 2, edited by C.A. Tokarev, 450–456. Moscow: Sovetskaia entsiklopediia.

Jakobson, Roman. 1945. *Russian Epic Studies.* Philadelphia, Pa.: American Folklore Studies.

Jakobson, Roman. 1966a. *Slavic Epic Studies.* Vol. 4 of *Selected Writings.* The Hague, Paris: Mouton.

Jakobson, Roman. 1966b. "Slavic Mythology." In *Funk and Wagnalls Standard Dictionary of Folklore, Mythology, and Legend,* vol. 1, edited by M. Leach and J. Fried, 1025–1028. New York: Funk and Wagnalls.

Jakobson, Roman. 1969. *Essais de linguistic générale.* Paris: Les Editions de Minuit.

Kabat, Geoffrey C. 1978. *Ideology and the Imagination: The Image of Society in Dostoevsky.* New York: Columbia University Press.

Kerblay, Basile. 1971. "Chayanov and the Theory of Peasantry as a Specific Type of Economy." In *Peasants and Peasant Societies,* edited by Teodor Shanin, 150–160. Harmondsworth, Middlesex, England: Penguin.

Kerblay, Basile. 1983. *Modern Soviet Society.* New York: Pantheon Books.

Kingkade, Ward. 1997. *Population Trends: Russia.* Washington, D.C.: U.S. Department of Commerce, Economics and Statistics Administration, Bureau of the Census.

Kingston-Mann, Esther, and Mixter, Timothy, eds. 1991. *Peasant Economy, Culture, and Politics of European Russia (1800–1921)*. Princeton, N.J.: Princeton University Press.

Kolesnikov, P.A., and Korolev, I.M. 1982. *Krai nash Vologodskii*. Archangelsk: Severo-Zapodnoe Knizhnoe Izdatel'stvo.

Kroeber, Alfred L., et al. *Franz Boas: 1858–1942*. American Anthropological Association Memoir 61, 1943.

Kruglov, Iu. G. 1993. *Russkoe narodnoe poeticheskoe tvorchestvo: Khrestomatia*. Saint Petersburg: Otdelenie Izdatel'stva "Procveshchenie".

Kuhn, Thomas. 1962. *The Structure of Scientific Revolution*. Chicago: University of Chicago Press.

Kundera, Milan. 1984. *The Unbearable Lightness of Being*. Trans. from the Czech by Michael Henry Heim. New York: Harper Collins.

Lakeev, B., ed. 1988. *The Stalin Phenomenon*. Moscow: Novesti Press Agent.

Lakoff, George, and Johnson, Mark. 1980. *Metaphors We Live By*. Chicago: University of Chicago Press.

Lane, Michael, ed. 1970. *Structuralism: A Reader*. London: Jonathan Cape Ltd.

Leavitt, John. 1991. "The Shapes of Modernity: On the Philosophical Roots of Anthropological Doctrines." *Culture*, 11, nos. 1–2: 29–42.

Leavitt, John. 1992. "Cultural Holism in the Anthropology of South Asia: The Challenge of Regional Traditions." *Contributions to Indian Sociology*, n.s., 26: 3–49.

Leavitt, John. 1995. "Les travaux et les jours dans l'Himalaya central." In *L'anthropologie économique*, edited by Norman Clermont, 27–38. Montreal: Département d'anthropologie, Université de Montréal.

Lecourt, Dominique. 1975. *Marxism and Epistemology: Bachelard, Canguilhelm, Foucault*. Trans. Ben Brewster. London: New Left Books.

Ledeneva, Alena V. 1998. *Russia's Economy of Favors: Blat, Networking, and Informal Exchange*. Cambridge: Cambridge University Press.

Lee, Penny. 1996. *The Whorf Theory Complex*. Amsterdam: J. Benjamins.

Levin, Eve. 1993. "Dvoeverie and Popular Religion." In *Seeking God: The Recovery of Religious Identity in Orthodox Russia, Ukraine, and Georgia*. Edited by Stephen K. Batalden, 29—52. DeKalb: Northern Illinois University Press.

Lévi-Strauss, Claude. 1962a. *The Savage Mind*. Chicago: University of Chicago Press.

Lévi-Strauss, Claude. 1962b. *Totemism*. Trans. Rodney Needham. Boston: Beacon Press. (First published 1962 as *Le Totémisme aujourd'hui*. Paris: Plon.)

Lévi-Strauss, Claude. 1963. "The Sorcerer and His Magic." In Lévi-Strauss, *Structural Anthropology*, 167–185. New York: Basic Books.

Lenin, V. 1970. *Lenin on Culture and Cultural Revolution*. Moscow: Progress Publishers.

Likhachev, D.S., and Panchenko, A.M. 1976. *Smekhovnoi mir v drevnei Rusi*. Leningrad: Akademiia Nauk SSSR.

Lucy, John A. 1992. *Language, Diversity and Thought*. Cambridge: Cambridge University Press.

Lucy, John A., and Wertsch, J.V. 1987. "Vygotsky and Whorf: A Comparative Analysis." In *Social and Functional Approaches to Language and Thought,* edited by M. Hickman, 67–86. Orlando, Fla.: Academic Press.

Lutz, Catherine A., and Abu-Lughod, Lila, eds. 1990. *Language and the Politics of Emotion.* Cambridge: Cambridge University Press.

Lyons, Graham, ed. 1976. *The Russian Version of the Second World War.* London: Leo Cooper.

Macey, David A.J. 2002. "Contemporary Agrarian Reforms in a Russian Historical Context." In *Rural Reform in Post-Soviet Russia,* edited by David J. O'Brien and Stephen K. Wegren, 178–202. Washington, D.C.: Woodrow Wilson Center Press; Baltimore, Md.: Johns Hopkins University Press.

Maksimov, Sergei. 1989 [1903]. *Nechistaia, nevedomaia i krestnaia sila.* Moscow: Kniga.

Malinowski, Bronislaw. 1965. "The Role of Magic and Religion." In *Reader in Comparative Religion: An Anthropological Approach,* 2nd ed., edited by William A. Lessa and Evon Z. Vogt, 102–112. New York: Harper & Row.

Mamonova, Tatiana, ed. 1982. *Women and Russia.* Boston: Beacon Press.

Mandelstam, Nadezhda. 1970. *Hope Against Hope.* New York: Atheneum.

Marriott, McKim. 1966. "The Feast of Love." In *Krishna: Myths, Rites, and Attitudes,* edited by Milton Singer, 200–212. Chicago: University of Chicago Press.

Marriott, McKim. 1976. "Hindu Transactions: Diversity without Dualism." In *Transaction and Meaning: Directions in the Anthropology of Exchange and Symbolic Behavior,* edited by Bruce Kapferer, 109–142. Philadelphia: Institute for the Study of Human Issues.

Marriott, McKim. 1991. On "Constructing an Indian Ethnosociology" *Contributions to Indian Sociology,* 25: 295–308.

Marx, Karl. 1998 [1869]. *The 18th Brumaire of Louis Bonarparte.* New York: International Publishers.

Massie, Robert K. 1967. *Nicholas and Alexandra.* New York: Dell.

Massie, Robert K. 1985 [1980]. *Peter the Great: His Life and World.* New York: Ballantine.

Matossian, Mary. 1968. "The Peasant Way of Life." In *The Peasant in Nineteenth-Century Russia,* edited by Wayne S. Vucinich, 1–40. Stanford, Calif.: Stanford University Press.

Mauss, Marcel. 1990 [1950]. *The Gift: The Form and Reason for Exchange in Archaic Societies.* New York and London: W.W. Norton Press.

Mead, Margaret. 1951. *Soviet Attitudes Toward Authority.* New York: McGraw Hill.

Mead, Margaret, and Wolfenstein, Martha. 1963 [1955]. *Childhood in Contemporary Cultures.* Chicago: University of Chicago Press.

Medvedev, Zhores A. 1987. *Soviet Agriculture.* New York: W.W. Norton and Company.

Merleau-Ponty, Maurice. 1965. *Phenomenology of Perception.* London: Routledge and Paul.

Merridale, Catherine. 2000. *Night of Stone: Death and Memory in Twentieth-Century Russia.* New York: Viking.

Moskoff, William, ed. 1990. *Perestroika in the Countryside: Agricultural Reform in the Gorbachev Era.* London: M.E. Sharpe, Inc.

Murray, D. W. 1993. "What Is the Western Concept of the Self? On Forgetting David Hume." *Ethos,* 21: 3–23.

Myerhoff, Barbara G. 1974. *Peyote Hunt: The Sacred Journey of the Huichol Indians.* Ithaca, N.Y.: Cornell University Press.

Nagaev, Vladimir. 1991. *Russkii Kalendar'.* Moscow: El'f.

Nosova, G.A. 1975. *Yazychestvo v Pravoslavii.* Moscow: Nauka.

Novost Press Agency. 1990. *Stalin: For and Against. Soviet People on Stalinism and Its Consequences.* Moscow: Novost Press.

O'Brien, David J., and Wegren, Stephen K. 2002. "Where Do We Go from Here? Building Sustainable Rural Communities." In *Rural Reform in Post-Soviet Russia,* edited by David J. O'Brien and Stephen K. Wegren, 403–416. Washington, D.C.: Woodrow Wilson Center Press; Baltimore, Md.: Johns Hopkins University Press.

Oinas, Felix J. 1984. *Essays on Russian Folklore and Mythology.* Columbus, Ohio: Slavica Publishers.

Olgin, Moissaye J. 1917. *The Soul of the Russian Revolution.* New York: Henry Holt and Company.

Olick, Jeffrey K., and Robbins, Joyce. 1998. "Social Memory Studies: From 'Collective Memory' to the Historical Sociology of Mnemonic Practices." *Annual Review of Sociology,* 24: 105–140.

Ortner, Sherry. 1973. "On Key Symbols." *American Anthropologist,* 75: 1338–1346.

Ortner, Sherry B. 1984. "Theory in Anthropology since the Sixties." *Comparative Studies in Society and History,* 26, no. 1: 126–166.

Ortner, Sherry. 1995. "Resistance and the Problem of Ethnographic Refusal in Recapturing Anthropology." In *Working in the Present,* edited by Richard G. Fox, 163–190. Santa Fe, N.M.: School of American Research Press.

Osipov, Vitalii. 1992. *Ne uchastvuite v delakh t'my.* Belozersk: Vologodskaia Eparkhia.

Ouspensky, Leonid. 1978. *The Theology of the Icon.* Crestwood, N.Y.: St. Vladimir's Seminary Press.

Panchenko, A.A. 1998. *Narodnoe Pravoslavie.* St. Petersburg: Aleteiia.

Parthé, Kathleen. 1992. *Russian Village Prose: The Radiant Past.* Princeton, N.J.: Princeton University Press.

Patsiorkovskii, Valerii. 2002. "Rural Household Behavior, 1991–2001." In *Rural Reform in Post-Soviet Russia,* edited by David J. O'Brien and Stephen K. Wegren, 116–134. Washington, D.C.: Woodrow Wilson Center Press; Baltimore, Md.: Johns Hopkins University Press.

Patsiorkovskii, Valerii. 2003. *Sel'skaia Rossiia 1991–2001.* Moscow: Finansy i Statistika.

Pavlenko, G.V. 1995. *Vashi lyubimye pesni.* Smolensk: Rusich.

Paxson, Margaret. 1989. "The Notion of Science According to Hindu Scientists." Master's thesis, Université de Montréal.

Paxson, Margaret. 1997. "History's Harvest," *Washington Post Magazine,* January 7.

Paxson, Margaret. 1998. "The Festival of the Holy Trinity (Troitsa) in Rural Russia: A Case Study in the Topography of Memory." *Anthropology of East Europe Review,* 16, no. 2: 53–58.

Paxson, Margaret. 2001. "Letter from a Russian Village." *Wilson Quarterly,* 30–35.

Paxson, Margaret. 2002. "The Cultural Dimension: Social Organization and the Metaphysics of Exchange." In *Rural Reform in Post-Soviet Russia,* edited by David J. O'Brien and Stephen K. Wegren, 137–177. Washington, D.C.: Woodrow Wilson Center Press; Baltimore, Md.: Johns Hopkins University Press.

Paxson, Margaret. 2004. "Bearing Russia's Burdens." *Wilson Quarterly,* Summer, 21–26.

Perrie, Maureen. 1987. *The Image of Ivan the Terrible in Russian Folklore.* Cambridge: Cambridge University Press.

Pesmen, Dale. 1998. "We Lost Some Neatness: Mixed Imagery and Russian Incoherence." *Anthropology of East Europe Review,* 16, no. 2: 97–102.

Pesmen, Dale. 2000. *Russia and Soul: An Exploration.* Ithaca, N.Y.: Cornell University Press.

Petrovich, Michael B. 1968. "The Peasant in Nineteenth-Century Historiography." In *The Peasant in Nineteenth-Century Russia,* edited by Wayne S. Vucinich, 191–230. Stanford, Calif.: Stanford University Press.

Pipes, Richard. 1974. *Russia Under the Old Regime.* London: Weidenfeld and Nicholson.

Platz, Stephanie. 1996. "Pasts and Futures: Space and Armenian National Identity." 2 vols. Ph.D. diss., University of Chicago.

Pokrovskii, N.E. 2004. *Gorod i selo v sovremennoi Rossii: Perspektiva strukturnogo Bossoedineniia (nachalo issledovaniia).* Moscow: Soobshchestvo Professional'nykh Sotsiologov.

Poole, Ernest. 1919. *The Village: Russian Impressions.* New York: Macmillan.

Pope, R.W.F. 1980. "Fools and Folly in Old Russia." *Slavic Review,* 39, no. 3: 476–479.

Propp, Vladimir. 1958 [1928]. *Morphology of the Folktale.* Austin and London: University of Texas Press.

Propp, Vladimir. 1974. "The Historical Bases of Some Russian Religious Festivals." In *Introduction to Soviet Ethnography,* vol. 2, edited by Stephen P. Dunn and Ethel Dunn, 367–410. Berkeley, Calif.: Highgate Road Social Science Research Station.

Propp, Vladimir. 1987 [1963]. *Les fetes agraires Russes.* Paris: Editions Maisonneuve et Larose.

Propp, Vladimir Ia. 1995 [1963]. *Russkie agarnye prazdniki.* St. Petersburg: Izdatel'stvo "Azbuka."

Pulkhina, I., et al. 1979. *Russian: A Practical Grammar with Exercises.* Moscow: Russky Iazyk Publishers.

Radin, Paul. 1969. *The Trickster: A Study in American Indian Mythology.* New York: Greenwood Press.

Raeff, Marc, ed. 1966. *Russian Intellectual History: An Anthology.* New York: Harcourt, Brace and World.

Ralston, W.R.S. 1872. *The Songs of the Russian People as Illustrative of Slavonic Mythology and Russian Social Life.* London: Ellis and Green.

Ramanujan, A.K. 1989. "Is There an Indian Way of Thinking? An Informal Essay." *Contributions to Indian Sociology,* 23, no. 1: 41–58.

Ransel, David. 2000. *Village Mothers: Three Generations of Change in Russia and Tataria.* Bloomington: Indiana University Press.

Read, Christopher. 1979. *Religion, Revolution and the Russian Intelligentsia, 1900–1912.* New York: Barnes and Noble.

Redfield, Robert, and Singer, Milton. 1954. "City and Countryside: The Cultural Independence." In *Peasants and Peasant Societies,* edited by Teodor Shanin, 337–365. Harmondsworth, Middlesex, England: Penguin Education.

Redfield, Robert. 1955. *The Little Community.* Chicago: University of Chicago Press.

Riasanovsky, Nicholas V. 1968. "The Problem of the Peasant." In *The Peasant in Nineteenth-Century Russia,* edited by Wayne S. Vucinich, 263–284. Stanford, Calif.: Stanford University Press.

Ries, Nancy. 1997. *Russian Talk: Culture and Conversation During Perestroika.* Ithaca, N.Y.: Cornell University Press.

Riesman, David, Glazer, Nathan, and Denney, Reuel. 1950. *The Lonely Crowd.* New Haven, Conn.: Yale University Press.

Robinson, Geroid Tanquary. 1969 [1932]. *Rural Russia Under the Old Regime.* Berkeley and Los Angeles: University of California Press.

Rosenthal, Judy. 1998. *Possession, Ecstasy, and Law in Ewe Voodoo.* Charlottesville: University Press of Virginia.

Rosovietskii, S.K. 1984–1985. "Oral Prose of the 16th–17th Centuries about Ivan the Terrible as a Ruler." *Soviet Anthropology and Archaeology,* 23: 3–49.

Rossiiskii Statisticheskii Ezhegodnik. 2003. GosKomStat. Moscow.

Rousseau, Jérôme. 1978. "Classe et ethnicité." *Anthropologie et Société,* 2, no. 1: 61–69.

Royde-Smith, John Graham. 2002. "World Wars." In *The Encylopædia Britannica,* 15th ed., vol. 29, edited by Dale H. Hoiberg, et al. Chicago: Encyclopædia Britannica, Inc.

Ryle, Gilbert. 1949. *The Concept of Mind.* London: Penguin Books.

Sahlins, Marshall. 1976. *Culture and Practical Reason.* Chicago: University of Chicago Press.

Sahlins, Marshall. 1981. *Historical Metaphors and Mythical Realities: Structure in the Early History of the Sandwich Islands Kingdom.* Ann Arbor: University of Michigan Press.

Sahlins, Marshall. 1985. *Islands of History.* Chicago: University of Chicago Press.

Sandomirsky Dunham, Vera. 1960. "The Strong Woman Motif." In *The Transformation of Russian Society,* edited by Cyril E. Black, 459–482. Cambridge: Harvard University Press.

Sapir, Edward. 1949. *Culture, Language and Personality.* Berkeley and Los Angeles: University of California Press.

Sapir, Edward. 1970 [1921]. *Language: An Introduction to the Study of Speech.* London, Toronto, Sidney, New York: Granada Publishing Ltd.

Schama, Simon. 1995. *Landscape and Memory.* London: Harper Collins.

Schmemann, Alexander. 1963. *The Historical Road of Eastern Orthodoxy.* Chicago: Henry Regnery.

Schoeck, Helmut. 1993 [1955]. "The Evil Eye: Forms and Dynamics of a Universal Superstition." In *Magic, Witchcraft, and Religion: An Anthropological Study of the Supernatural,* 3rd ed., edited by Arthur C. Lehmann and James E. Myers, 226–230. Mountain View, Calif.: Mayfield Publishing.

Scott, James. 1985. *Weapons of the Weak: Everyday Forms of Peasant Resistance.* New Haven, Conn.: Yale University Press.

Scott, James. 1990. *Domination and the Art of Resistance: Hidden Transcripts.* New Haven, Conn.: Yale University Press.

Semyonova Tian-Shanskaia, Olga. 1993. *Village Life in Late Tsarist Russia,* edited by David L. Ransel. Bloomington: Indiana University Press.

Shanin, Teodor. 1971. "A Russian Peasant Household at the Turn of the Century." In *Peasants and Peasant Societies,* edited by Teodor Shanin, 30–36. Harmondsworth, Middlesex, England: Penguin.

Shanin, Teodor, ed. 1971. *Peasants and Peasant Societies.* Harmondsworth, Middlesex, England: Penguin.

Shanin, Teodor. 1986. *Russia, 1905–1907: Revolution as a Moment of Truth.* New Haven, Conn.: Yale University Press.

Shevzov, Vera. 1999. "Miracle-Working Icons, Laity, and Authority in the Russian Orthodox Church, 1861–1917." *Russian Review, Russian Review,* 58: 26–48.

Shinn, Jr., W.T. 1987. *The Decline of the Russian Peasant Household.* New York: Praeger Publishers.

Shipler, David K. 1983. *Russia: Broken Idols, Solemn Dreams.* New York: Times Books.

Shukman, Ann, ed. 1984. *The Semiotics of Russian Culture.* Ann Arbor: University of Michigan Press.

Shultz, Emily A. 1989. *Dialogue at the Margins: Whorf, Bakhtin and Linguistic Relativity.* Madison: University of Wisconsin Press.

Shvets, I.A. 1987. *Kommunist: Kalendar'-spravochnik.* Moscow: Politicheskaia Literatura.

Smith, Kathleen E. 1992. *Remembering Stalin's Victims: Popular Memory and the End of the USSR.* Ithaca, N.Y.: Cornell University Press.

Smith, Kathleen E. 1997. "An Old Cathedral for a New Russia: The Symbolic Politics of the Reconstituted Church of Christ the Saviour." *Religion, State & Society,* 25, no. 2: 163–175.

Smith, Kathleen E. 2002. *Mythmaking in the New Russia: Politics and Memory in the Yeltsin Era*. Ithaca, N.Y.: Cornell University Press.

Sökefeld, Martin. 1999. "Debating Self, Identity, and Culture in Anthropology." *Current Anthropology*, 40, no 4: 417–445.

Soloviev, Alexander. 1959. *Holy Russia: The History of a Religious-Social Idea*. Geneva: Mouton and Co.

Solzhenitsyn, Aleksandr. 1963. *One Day in the Life of Ivan Denisovich*. Trans. Ralph Parker. New York: Dutton.

Solzhenitsyn, Aleksandr. 1974. *The Gulag Archipelago, 1918–1956: An Experiment in Literary Investigation*, vols. 1 and 2. Trans. by Thomas P. Whitney. London: Collins Harvill.

Sperber, Dan. 1974. *Rethinking Symbolism*. Cambridge: Cambridge University Press.

Stites, Richard. 1989. *Revolutionary Dreams: Utopian Vision and Experimental Life in the Russian Revolution*. New York: Oxford University Press.

Stites, Richard. 1992. *Russian Popular Culture: Entertainment and Society since 1900*. Cambridge: Cambridge University Press.

Stocking, Jr., George W. 1968. "From Physics to Ethnology." In *Race, Culture, and Evolution: Essays in the History of Anthropology*, 133–160. New York: Free Press. (Reprinted in 1982 with a new preface.)

Sumner, B.H. 1962. *Peter the Great and the Emergence of Russia*. New York: Collier.

Taussig, Michael. 1987. *Shamanism, Colonialism, and the Wild Man: A Study in Terror and Healing*. Chicago: University of Chicago Press.

Thompson, Ewa M. 1987. *Understanding Russia: The Holy Fool in Russian Culture*. Lanham, Md.: University Press of America.

Timofeev, Lev. 1985. *Soviet Peasants (Or, The Peasants' Art of Starving)*. St. Louis: Telos Press.

Tishkov, Valery A. 1992. "The Crisis in Soviet Ethnography." *Current Anthropology*, 33, no. 4: 371–394.

Tishkov, Valery A. 1998. "U.S. and Russian Anthropology: Unequal Dialogue in a Time of Transition." *Current Anthropology*, 39, no. 1: 1–17.

Tolstoi, Nikita. 1988. "Paganism in the Slavic Cultural Heritage." In *Studies of the Slavic Peoples' Cultures*, 16–22. Moscow: Social Sciences Today Editorial Board.

Tonkin, Elizabeth. 1992. *Narrating Our Pasts: The Social Construction of Oral History*. Cambridge: Cambridge University Press.

Treadgold, Donald W. 1968. "The Peasant and Religion." In *The Peasant in Nineteenth-Century Russia*, edited by Wayne S. Vucinich, 72–107. Stanford, Calif.: Stanford University Press.

Tucker, Robert C. 1990. *Stalin in Power: Revolution from Above, 1928–1941*. New York and London: W.W. Norton.

Turner, Victor W. 1967. *The Forest of Symbols*. Ithaca, N.Y.: Cornell University Press.

Turner, Victor. 1974. *Dramas, Fields and Metaphors: Symbolic Action in Human Society*. Ithaca, N.Y.: Cornell University Press.

Turner, Victor. 1995 [1969]. *The Ritual Process.* Hawthorne, N.Y.: Aldine de Gruyter.

Tyler, Steven. 1986. "Post Modern Ethnography: From Document of the Occult to Occult Document." In *Writing Culture,* edited by James Clifford and George Marcus, 141–164. Berkeley, Los Angeles, London: University of California Press.

Tylor, Edward. 1965 [1873]. "Animism." In *Reader in Comparative Religion: An Anthropological Approach,* 2nd ed., edited by William A. Lessa and Evon Z. Vogt, 10–21. New York: Harper & Row.

von Geldern, James, and Stites, Richard, eds. 1995. *Mass Culture in Soviet Russia: Tales, Poems, Songs, Movies, Plays and Folklore 1917–1953.* Bloomington: Indiana University Press.

Vansina, Jan. 1985. *Oral Tradition as History.* Madison: University of Wisconsin Press.

Verdery, Katherine. 1999. *The Political Lives of Dead Bodies: Reburial and Postsocialist Change.* New York: Columbia University Press.

Vernadsky, George. 1969 [1929]. *A History of Russia.* New Haven, Conn.: Yale University Press.

Vernadsky, George. 1973 [1948]. *Kievan Russia.* New Haven, Conn.: Yale University Press.

Vlasov, V.G. 1992. "The Christianization of the Russian Peasants." In *Russian Traditional Culture,* edited by Marjorie Mandelstam Balzer, 16–33. Armonk, N.Y.: M.E.Sharpe.

Vlasto, A.P. 1970. *The Entry of the Slavs into Christendom: An Introduction to the Medieval History of the Slavs.* Cambridge: Cambridge University Press.

Vucinich, Wayne S., ed. 1968. *The Peasant in Nineteenth-Century Russia.* Stanford, Calif.: Stanford University Press.

Vygotsky, Lev Semenovich. 1962. *Thought and Language.* Edited and trans. by Eugenia Hanfmann and Gertrude Vakar. Cambridge, Mass.: M.I.T. Press.

Walicki, Andrzej, ed. 1979. *A History of Russian Thought.* Stanford, Calif.: Stanford University Press.

Wallace, Sir Donald Mackenzie. 1920. *Russia: Its History and Condition to 1877,* vols. 1 and 2. Norwood, Mass.: Plimpton Press.

Ware, Timothy. 1991 [1963]. *The Orthodox Church.* London: Penguin Books.

Watters, F.M. 1968. "The Peasant and the Village Commune." In *The Peasant in Nineteenth Century Russia,* edited by Wayne S. Vucinich, 133–157. Stanford, Calif.: Stanford University Press.

Wegren, Stephen K. 1995. "Rural Migration and Agrarian Reform in Russia: A Research Note." *Europe—Asia Studies,* 47, no. 5: 877–888.

Wegren, Stephen K. 1997. "Land Reform and the Land Market in Russia: Operation, Constraints and Prospects." *Europe—Asia Studies,* 49, no. 6: 959–987.

Wheeler, Marcus. 1992. *The Oxford Russian-English Dictionary.* Oxford: Clarendon Press.

Whorf, Benjamin Lee. 1939. "The Relation of Habitual Thought and Behavior to Language." In *B.L. Whorf, Language, Thought and Reality,* edited by J.B. Carroll, 134–159. Cambridge, Mass.: M.I.T. Press.

Willis, P. 1977. *Learning to Labour: How Working Class Kids Get Working Class Jobs*. Farnborough, U.K.: Saxon House, Teakfield.

Wilson, Colin. 1977. *Rasputin and the Fall of the Romanovs*. London: Granada Publishing.

Wolf, Eric. 1966. *Peasants*. Englewood Cliffs, N.J.: Prentice-Hall.

Wolf, Eric. 1969. *Peasant Wars of the Twentieth Century*. New York: Harper Torchbooks.

Wolf, Eric. 1982. *Europe and the People Without History*. Berkeley and Los Angeles: University of California Press.

Wolkonsky, Catherine A., and Poltoratzky, Marianna A. 1961. *Handbook of Russian Roots*. New York: Columbia University Press.

Worobec, Christine D. 1991. *Peasant Russia: Family and Community in the Post-Emancipation Period*. Princeton, N.J.: Princeton University Press.

Worobec, Christine D. 1994. "Death Ritual among Russian and Ukrainian Peasants: Linkages between the Living and the Dead." In *Cultures in Flux: Lower Class Values, Practices, and Resistance in Late Imperial Russia,* edited by Stephen P. Frank and Mark D. Steinberg, 11–33. Princeton, N.J.: Princeton University Press.

Yang, Mayfair Mei-Hui. 1994. *Gifts, Favors and Banquets: The Social Art of Relationships in China*. Ithaca, N.Y.: Cornell University Press.

Yates, Frances A. 1966. *The Art of Memory*. Chicago: University of Chicago Press.

Yurchak, Alexei. 1997a. "The Cynical Reason of Late Socialism: Power, Pretense, and the Anekdot." *Public Culture,* 9: 161–188.

Yurchak, Alexei. 1997b. "The Cynical Reason of Late Socialism: Language, Culture and Identity of the Last Soviet Generation." Ph.D. diss., Duke University.

Zabylnim, M., ed. 1990 [1880]. *Russkii Narod: Evo Obychai, Obriady, Predaniia, Suyevriia i Poeziia*. Moscow: Kniga Printshon.

Zelenin, D.K. 1991. *Vostochnoslavyanskaia etnografiia*. Moscow: Nauka.

Zelenin, D.K. 1994. *Izbrannye trudy: Statíl po Dukhovnoi kulíture 1901–1913*. Moscow: Indrik.

Zelnik, Reginald. 1968. "The Peasant and the Factory." In *The Peasant in Nineteenth-Century Russia,* edited by Wayne S. Vucinich, 158–190. Stanford, Calif.: Stanford University Press.

Zernov, Nicholas. 1973 [1942]. *Three Russian Prophets: Khomiakov, Dostoevsky, Soloviev*. Gulf Breeze, Fla.: Academic International Press.

Znayenko, Myroslava T. 1980. *The Gods of the Ancient Slavs*. Columbus, Ohio: Slavica.

Index

Adon'eva, Svetlana, 345
age groups: and *draki* (gang fights),
   298–300; formation of, 296–98
agrarian calendar. *See* calendars
agricultural reform, 83
agriculture practices and social
   organization, 61–62
Agrofirma Belozerska, 45–46
Alekseevich, Mikhail. *See* Belov,
   Mikhail Alekseevich
ancestors in icon corner, 254–60. *See
   also* red corner
Anderson, Benedict, 23
anthropology, 14–15, 157, 158*n*,
   160, 267–68
apparitions, 199–200, 244–45. *See
   also* dead and involvement with
   living; healing practices
arrests, 142–49, 238
Art of Memory, The (Yates), 21*n*
Asad, Talal, 160
autobiographical memory, 13

babushki (grandmothers), 90, 123
Bachelard, Gaston, 18–19, 251
bad forces, 166*n*

barin (feudal landlord), 75
batiushka (grandfather), 232
being "one's own" in Solovyovo. *See*
   social organization
Belov, Mikhail Alekseevich: agrarian
   history records of, 45*n*; biography
   of, 163; and calendar, 279; on
   calendars, 281–82; calf, birth of
   (rite of *naveshchenie*), 252–54;
   on clubhouses, 308; on coming
   of communists, 43*n*; on discipline
   and leadership, 101; exchange of
   goods and services, 70; on farming,
   6; on fear, 108; on fights, 298;
   as head of household, 56; and
   healing, 155, 163–66, 172–79,
   182–87, 197, 200, 209–10; and
   icons, 219*n*; and *Il'in Den'*,
   312–13; on *khoziain*, 236; on
   khoziain doma, 260–61; on loss
   of frameworks for social order,
   101–2; name of, 59; on political
   repression, 44*n*; on poverty and
   heightened morality, 95; on
   retribution, 248; role in study,
   46–47; and *senokos*, 310;